To Barbara —
From RoseMary

MW00779747

FROM PILGRIMAGE TO PROMISE

Civil War Heritage and the Landis Boys of Logansport, Indiana

The Landis Boys are our first cousins twice removed — Rose Mary + Alma Jean King

Lincoln Landis

HERITAGE BOOKS
2007

HERITAGE BOOKS

AN IMPRINT OF HERITAGE BOOKS, INC.

Books, CDs, and more—Worldwide

For our listing of thousands of titles see our website
at
www.HeritageBooks.com

Published 2007 by
HERITAGE BOOKS, INC.
Publishing Division
65 East Main Street
Westminster, Maryland 21157-5026

International Standard Book Number: 978-0-7884-3831-8

In memory of my grandmother,
Mary Kumler Landis,
mother of the Landis boys

Dr. Abraham H. Landis & Mary Kumler Landis
Our Great Uncle & Aunt
Rose & Alma King

Preface

The colorful careers of five brothers who grew up in a closely-knit Civil War family led me to investigate their lives from the latter half of the 19th century through the turn of the 20th century. After all, my uncles Walter, Charles, John, and Kenesaw Mountain, and my father Frederick Landis of Logansport, Indiana, had found national prominence in Cincinnati, Chicago, New York, Washington, D.C. and San Juan, Puerto Rico.

It was impressive that, from modest beginnings, they had become successful in a variety of pursuits including politics, diplomacy, medicine, law, the Federal Judiciary, literature, Broadway, and the executive authority over Major League Baseball.

A clue to their achievements appeared in the homespun optimism that I found in letters of the boys' father written during his regiment's "pilgrimage through the Confederacy."

The author

Acknowledgments

I am most grateful for many constructive exchanges with my wife Donna and son Tim, who offered good counsel and editing, and to my sons Jeffrey, Dean and Lincoln who provided support from longer distances. My sister Betsy Cullen Wright as well as sister-in-law Mary Sands Landis and Cousin Lorna Landis Walker helped with sound advice and excellent materials. Cousins Nancy Lucas, Jodie Garavanta, Susanne Newland, Keehn Landis, and Bill Phillips all offered moral support as well as recollections and photographs relating to their grandfather Kenesaw. Cousins Charles B. Landis, Pat Carson, Rose Mary and Alma Jean King, Bill King, Susanna Marion Baum, John Holden, Landis Wagar, and Deborah Landis were generous with ideas and memorabilia. Honorary cousin Hermann Scholl of Heppenheim, Germany, kindly confirmed details about the Landis ancestral household in that village.

Rose Mary King — Alma Jean King

Family genealogy compiled by my late brother Charles and his wife Mary was essential to my work. In addition, archival assistance was generously provided by Jill Costill of the Indiana State Library, Leigh Darbee of the Indiana Historical Society, and Archie Motley of the Chicago Historical Society. The Kumler file of the Butler County, Ohio Historical Society and the Landis file of the Logansport Public Library were most useful. Special attention must go to the many thoughtful contributions by curator Bryan Looker and his assistant John Henry of the Cass County Historical Society and valuable insights offered by historians Juanita Hunter of Logansport and Donald Proctor of Dearborn, Michigan. High school chum and accomplished writer David Petrie also provided keen insights about Logansport's earlier years.

*Love from your cousin
Linda Landis Line*

Contents

Illustrations follow pages 60, 82, 120, 130, 146, 242, and 274.

Introduction

Forebears -- The Landis boys' paternal and maternal ancestry of Landises and Kumlers reflect courage and spirituality of committed families that made their way from Europe to opportunity in the Pennsylvania province in 1749. They dealt with discord and uncertainties of the American Revolution and, as farmers, preachers, and physicians, prospered and sought further opportunity by moving west to Ohio in the early 1800's.

Pilgrimage through the Confederacy -- The families merged before the Civil War. In 1862, Abraham Landis, at 41, left his wife and five small children and served as a Union surgeon. While attending to the wounded, he chatted with Southerners, appraised their crops, and admired their countryside. After being wounded and imprisoned, he was discharged and taught his five sons about the "pilgrimage through the Confederacy."

Young Brothers -- The five brothers found small-town life to be a springboard for ambition and opportunity, leaving scars of the Civil War behind them. Determination and helping one another produced a friendly rivalry and the means to move beyond provincial ways and find prominence in public service of the rapidly-changing nation.

Journalism, Diplomacy, Politics -- Early professions in the 1890's were varied: editor-turned-Congressman; State Department aide; Postmaster of Puerto Rico; lawyer; and Cincinnati physician. Charles spoke of the healing of Blue and Gray, fighting for the same cause in the Spanish-American war. All five began to make their mark in a wider world, while building a fraternal bond to help advance one another.

Jurisprudence, Literature, Medicine -- Fields of endeavor grew in the 1900's and 1910's: Federal judge (Kenesaw), another US Congressman-turned-novelist (Frederick), and Health Officer of Cincinnati (John), while the Postmaster (Walter) continued his quasi-ambassadorial duties. Charles debated foreign policy and helped in military production for World War I. Frederick condemned corporate excesses and the lynching of Negroes and later joined Theodore Roosevelt's Progressive Party in 1912. Kenesaw challenged corporate power and defended "the little guy."

Commentary and Humor -- Frederick became an editor in New York, a public speaker, newspaper columnist, playwright, candidate for Governor, author, and successful candidate for Congress. He supported farmers and workers, fought for military readiness, foresaw the Japanese threat long before Pearl Harbor, challenged the Ku Klux Klan, assailed government corruption, and sought to clean up movies and the New York stage.

Baseball and Wartime -- Kenesaw assumed the role of executive authority over professional baseball after the Black Sox scandal of bribery in the 1919 World Series and remained vigilant to keep the game free of gambling. He continued through his late 70's to rule over Baseball and took on the added responsibility of monitoring the morale of all members of his extended-family who served in the Armed Forces during World War II.

The Landis Boys, heir to ancestral and colonial tradition, grew to appreciate their father's abolitionist stand and colorful experiences as a Civil War surgeon and, finding opportunity in a small-town setting, went on to achieve national prominence in the 20th century.

1. Forebears − 1600's to 1800's

. . . the Renaissance not yet finished . . . Religious war was why eight brothers Landis left Germany and settled in America. Dr. A. H. Landis, a descendant, left five sons, unusually bright and intellectual, quite successful men.

-- Savoyard, "The Brothers Landis," 1906 [1]

The children of Abraham H. and Mary Kumler Landis, two daughters and five sons, were solid Swiss. They were descendants of refugee families that left the Old World in the summer of 1749 to find freedom in the Pennsylvania province. Through a coincidence, these families linked up in a village near Cincinnati, 101 years later, with Abraham and Mary's marriage. It was through that union that "the Landis boys" emerged from modest circumstances to attain national prominence in the early 1900's. Were they perhaps reflecting a tested pattern of persevering generations of Landises and Kumlers?

The Landises

Here screened from the world, its enticements, enchantments, full meekly, devoutly, at worship they sat; But divided their number, the building abandoned, soon furnished a home for the owl and the bat.

-- Last Meeting House of Frederick Landis
and eight fellow-Mennonites in Pennsylvania,
in late 1700's [2]

In 1874, Abraham Landis traveled from his home in Seven Mile, Ohio to the site of his grandfather's house of worship and burial ground near Philadelphia. It was a time for the wounded Civil War veteran to reflect upon the eventful lives of colonial forebears and European ancestors. The village doctor had known about earlier travails of Anabaptist forebears, who were called "Swiss Brethren."

These 17th-century Believers also became known as "Mennonites" after Menno Symons, a Catholic priest who had become their chief leader. In Zurich canton in 1525, they had been pious folk who believed an early interpretation of our well-known public issue "the separation of church and state." In their terms, "no government had the right to determine the religion of its subjects." As a consequence, they faced persecution and death for their

"radical notion" of religious freedom: "believe and let believe:" [3]
To the Anabaptists the medieval church was "fallen" and apostate.[4]
Introducing "a fundamentally-different understanding of the Church
and Christian life" and rejecting images, an elaborate hierarchy, and
the Mass, these Anabaptists were in headlong conflict with core
religious doctrine. [5]

The oldest known Landis home, vintage 1488, still stands in
Hirzel, several miles south of Zurich. Research suggests that the
children of Abraham and Mary Landis were 8th-generation
descendants of martyr Hans Landis.[6] In the 16th century, Hans had
arrived in the Rhine River of Switzerland "to minister and preach to
those who were seeking after righteousness." He attracted wide
attention by preaching that baptism should be administered "only to
those who voluntarily asked for it following their declaration of
faith." [7]

Unfortunately, Hans' "transgressions" were noted at the
Council of Zurich, and, in 1614, he was sentenced to death. One
account tells of his response to the executioner at Walfstatt Prison
who, seeing tears in the eyes of Hans' children, prayed aloud before
the condemned man and said: "Oh God of mercy to thee be it
complained that you Hans have fallen into my hands. For God's
sake forgive me for what I must do to you." This account continues,
noting that Hans consoled the executioner, saying: "I have already
forgiven you, may God forgive you also so that nothing may hinder
you in this matter" . . . "Whereupon he was beheaded." [8] The
official charge, after Hans failed to recant, was simply
"disobedience to the authorities." [9]

History reveals that Mennonites suffered persecution not
only by authorities under the influence of Rome but by "reformed"
Protestant authorities as well. [10] One source observed: "Hans was
the last man beheaded for religious convictions in this locality,"
adding, however, that "persecution did not cease and his children
were shamefully treated and their property confiscated." [11] Although
executions for heresy seemed to be ended, harassment continued
during the Thirty-Years War 1618-1648 and into the last half of the
1600's. His son, also named Hans, followed suit as an outspoken
Mennonite preacher, resulting in his imprisonment in 1608 and loss
of property in 1633.

The latter half of the 17th-century fails to offer precise
information about Hans Landis' descendants because of the turmoil

of that period. During the Thirty-Years War, many Mennonites were forced to leave Switzerland, settling in the Kraichgau region of Germany and "the Palatinate" near Strassburg and Mannheim. They were welcomed to work the land for German nobles, who had lost many workers in the chaos of French-German warfare. [12] Landis ancestors frequently found work as weavers in cotton and woolen mills. [13] By 1660, most Mennonites appear to have left Switzerland.

New pressures were placed upon them by renewed warfare in 1674 and 1688-1689. King Louis XIV of France devastated Alsace by putting "a fine and fertile country, full of populous towns and villages, to fire and sword," [14] causing many to move northward along the Rhine river. In 1685 the first Mennonites chose to emigrate to America, thanks to the appearance of an English Quaker, who had plans to open a fertile colony in the New World.

Thus, William Penn, a statesman with religious views akin to Mennonite beliefs, visited the German Palatinate in 1677 with a message of hope. [15] He sought a commitment from the "Prince Elector Palatine of Heydelbergh" to assist in the resettlement of the pious folk, also called "Palatines," to America. Their skill as weavers could prove most useful in the southeast portion of his new colony. [16] The Elector's support to Penn's mission and the compassion of King Frederick William I of Prussia cheered the Mennonites, who soon learned that Penn's province in the New World would welcome them. Added impetus for their decision was a different kind of stimulus in 1685 -- when the French king vacated the Edict of Nantes that had given equality to Protestants. [17]

Frederick Landis, great-grandfather of the "Landis boys," was born March 4, 1739 in Heppenheim, the Palatinate countryside northwest of Heidelberg. The appearance of his given name Friedrich reflected an appreciation for kindness shown by the King of Prussia to Mennonites in the 17th-century. [18] Frederick, the youngest son of Henrich Landes, who died in Heppenheim in 1742, spent his childhood in that village in the vicinity of the old town of Alzey. [19] At this time, pressures were strong for Mennonites to join the German Reformed Church in Heppenheim, but Frederick's older brother Rudolph wrote of his adherence to the old beliefs through inspiration gained from friends in the nearby hamlet of Ober Floersheim. [20] Lacking a Mennonite church in Heppenheim, Henrich's family worshiped in the village's "reformed" church built in 1722, still standing as an active place of worship. [21]

3

The Landises' decision to move from Heppenheim to America may have resulted in part from the ruling authority's policy "to prevent the number of Mennonite families in the Palatinate to rise above 200." Rules would become more lenient during the reign of a Catholic Elector, "the enlightened Charles Theodore of the house of Pfalz-Sulzbach." [22]

In 1749, some five or possibly seven Landis brothers headed for Rotterdam, Holland, either down the Rhine river, or perhaps by wagon along its valley to make a perilous ocean voyage to the New World. They included eldest brother Henrich with his wife and two infants along with Rudolf, Christian, Frederick, Abraham, and perhaps Jacob and Samuel, departing May 3 and arriving at Philadelphia September 27th on the ship *Isaac*, which carried 206 "Palatines." One son is believed to have died and was buried at sea, and an older son may have preceded the family in the trip to America by ten years. [23] It is not known how many Mennonites perished on the *Isaac*, but average losses on such voyages often reached 30%. [24]

A few months after arriving in America, the Landis brothers moved to Bucks County north of Philadelphia, settling in Perkasie. [25] In the early 1760s, Rudolf, Abraham, Jacob, Samuel, and Frederick and their children started farming at Deep Run in Bedminster Township [26] and worshiping at the Deep Run Meetinghouse. Rudolph served as deacon there, and Abraham was a preacher for more than 30 years. [27] Like their ancestors, these Believers persisted in simplicity of worship and dress. They accepted "the life of Christ and His teachings as their only rule of conduct," and theirs was a credo of tolerance. [28]

In 1759, Frederick, the Landis boys' great-grandfather married Mary Kolb [29] who died the following year in giving birth to Henrich. Three years later, he married Elizabeth Hoch, and their first child was Philip, grandfather of the Logansport Landises, born 12 years before the Declaration of Independence. More than a hundred years later, the Landis boys' father Abraham visited the homestead near Paoli, west of Philadelphia. Here his grandfather Frederick, after moving from Bucks County with his wife and four children in 1774, purchased 160 acres from the family of soon-to-be Revolutionary War hero, General "Mad Anthony" Wayne. The Landises and Waynes were neighbors and were involved in

4

witnessing one another's official documents. [30] Frederick and Elizabeth's daughter Magdalene was born in 1776, and, a year later, Jacob, the last of six children, was born.

While the first half of the 18th-century meant great promise for Mennonite immigrants, the specter of colonial dissatisfaction with England grew especially following the Landises' arrival in 1749. Undercurrents of revolution soon led to the Declaration of Independence and the Revolutionary War. As "Franconia Conference" Mennonites, the Landises were facing a quandary: "Should they remain loyal to the British king or pledge allegiance to the new colonial government that was seeking independence?" [31] Since an English charter had assured the Mennonites a haven from persecution in the Pennsylvania province, great was "this conflict between matters of faith and responsibility." [32] Furthermore, many of their colonial neighbors displayed a sense of loyalty to the British Crown. [33]

A commitment to avoid warlike behavior was reflected in the appearance of the names of the Landis boys' great-uncles Abraham Landis, a preacher, and Rudolph Landis, a deacon of Deep Run, on the conspicuous list of "people who did not practice with the local Rebel militia" in 1775. [34] Yet, one would suppose that General Washington's victory over Hessian mercenaries the following year at Trenton, a few miles to the east, may have placed added pressure upon them to support the Revolution.

Indeed, one of Abraham and Rudolph's co-religionists invoked Biblical reasoning to declare for the Colonial cause. Thus, Christian Funk ascribed political legitimacy to the Revolution, noting "the Jews did not consider Caesar their legitimate ruler; yet Christ commanded them to pay taxes to Caesar . . . if Christ were here, He would say to give to Congress what belongs to Congress and to God what belongs to God." [35]

As for Frederick, who moved in 1774 to the pro-colonial region of General. Wayne's neighborhood, he exercised his legal option as a Mennonite to decline joining Revolution-minded colonists after hostilities began. In 1780, he was double-taxed and listed as "non-juror" in 1781 because he was opposed to war for religious reasons. His name appears next to his neighbor General Anthony Wayne's listing as "juror." [36]

Dr. Abraham H. Landis of Seven Mile, Ohio would have reflected upon his ancestors' dilemma. As a staunch partisan of the

Union cause during the Civil War, he might have believed with good reason that his grandfather Frederick, and father Philip as a teenager, were more than passive observers of the American Revolution -- perhaps they were its clandestine supporters! Because of Frederick's close ties to his Wayne neighbors, for example, might they have offered crops to the General's troops fighting nearby? [37]

Abraham was aware that, in December 1777, Frederick and Philip were close-up witnesses when the British tried to capture Gen. Wayne at his farm. How concerned they might have been upon learning that the Red Coats proceeded the same night to defeat Wayne a few hundred yards north at the Paoli Massacre! [38] Abraham could cherish the thought that family lore: Frederick and Philip could watch the comings and goings of Generals George Washington and Marquis de Lafayette a few hundred yards away near the Wayne home. Furthermore, he could easily imagine that these military leaders were updating battle plans during those visits.

Another historic tidbit in Abraham's mind during his visit was the fact that his father Philip often worked on the nearby farm of Robert Todd, grandfather-to-be of Mary Todd Lincoln. [39] (In another coincidence involving ancestors in Pennsylvania, Abraham recalled that Uncle Jacob Landis owned a farm near Lancaster, Pennsylvania alongside that of General Winfield Scott, hero of the War of 1812 and of the Mexican War, 1847-1848).

Several years after the Revolutionary War, correspondence flowed between the Rhineland village of Heppenheim/Alzey, which the Landis brothers had left in 1749, and their new residence in Bedminster Township of Bucks County, Pennsylvania. In 1786, cousin Jacob Rupp from Heppenheim replied to a letter from Rudolph and Abraham Landis of Bedminster that had made the transit two years earlier in the period of four months. Rupp reported that many families had moved to Mehro-Galicia in the former Kingdom of Poland and were provided with fifty acres of land, "cattle, implements, house utensils" free-of-charge. Rudolph Landis responded a year later, expressing the concerns of Mennonites in the American colonies as they faced the problem of mixed loyalties, whether to the King of England or to the revolutionary Colonials. [40]

Successes of the American Revolution began to take a toll on Old World practices of Mennonites. In 1795, during President George Washington's second term, the Landis boys'great-grandfather Frederick, with eight other believers, held to Mennonite traditions by buying land in Charlestown Township for "a place of worship and burial." Frederick and his diminishing band of faithful adhered to their faith until the end. Upon their deaths, these nine members of the "Society of Mennonists" were buried on the grounds of their meeting house in Chester County, where they had held services for over 50 years. [41]

Traditions gradually gave way under pressures of an expanding society in America, as each generation left behind memories of European persecution. With the erosion of religious practices, the descendants of Swiss martyrs gradually lost their buildings for worship. A memorial to the nine now stands near the site of their house of worship in a plot nearby. The gradual passing of the old ways was shown in a poem written before the building and old gravestones were removed for a changing society: [42]

> Close by on the hill top still sits an old building,
> Surrounded by poplars like sentinals grand,
> Whose ivy clad walls like the tombstones around it?
> Are crumbling to ruin neath times heavy hand.
> Where Mennonites, sore and deep scarred by
> oppression, Despised and reviled in their home over the
> deep,
> Found refuge from storm and erected their altar, Their
> turmoils now ended, in peace here they sleep.
> Here screened from the world, its enticements,
> enchantments, Full meekly, devoutly, at worship they sat,
> But divided their number, the building abandoned, Soon
> furnished a home for the owl and the bat.

Upon Frederick's death in 1803, the Landis boys' grandfather Philip acquired his father's farm at Paoli and sold it in 1816, when he and his nephew Jacob Landis moved to the southwestern corner of the new state of Ohio. There Philip bought a farm near Hamilton in Butler County. At the same time, members of the Wayne family moved from Paoli to the same region. [43]

Life was Spartan in the frontier country of the Ohio River valley in the early 1800's. Philip Landis' wife Catharine gave birth to a daughter while enduring the death of her two toddlers in less than a month. Their youngest child was Abraham Hoch Landis, born in 1821 and reared in Hickory Flats near Busenbark Station of the planned Cincinnati, Hamilton and Dayton Railroad. Abraham,

7

the Landis boys' father later recalled a visit to the area of his childhood: "I saw the old cabins where I went to school . . . an old fashioned round log cabin and if you could see it, about the last thing you would think was that it was once a school house." [44]

Abraham's visit enabled him to revisit the sycamore tree that he had planted as a youth. (At the turn of the 21st century it is finally showing signs of old age). He recalled that, as a youth of 16, his father died, leaving him responsibility for planting and harvesting crops and tending to the farm animals. This experience may have persuaded him to leave the farm life behind and become a physician, like the doctor of nearby Millville, Reverend Daniel C. Kumler. Upon completion of training, he not only set up practice in the same village but also married Dr. Kumler's eldest daughter Mary.

The Kumlers

> *Their religious platform was religion, pure and undefiled and fear of God, and keep his commandments . . . They didn't carry an Oxford Bible on Sunday and rob their neighbors the next six days of the week.*
> -- Description of the Kumler grandparent generation by cousin, Charles H. Kumler. [45]

Kumler ancestry bears a similarity to that of the Landises, beginning with their early years in Switzerland. [46] The Kumlers of Maisprach, Basel canton, like the Landises of Zurich canton, sought freedom from the Swiss government's pressure over their lives. The Kumler farm folk of the Swiss Reformed Church [47] were descendants of French Huguenots, who, as noted earlier, were exiled from France after its King vacated the Edict of Nantes that had granted equality to French Protestants. Beginning in the late 1600's, William Penn let it be widely known among such uprooted village people that they would find opportunity to work as weavers and farmers in the southeastern portion of the New World province chartered to him by the King of England.

It is likely that the Kumlers' village of Maisprach would have been a convenient stopping-off place for Rhineland-bound Landises from Hirzel, 50 miles to the southeast. Members of the two families in the 17th and 18th centuries might have intermingled here to commiserate about life around them and even shared ideas

8

on hopes to build a better life in America. In fact, such a connection between them could have led to the fact that the two families crossed the Atlantic within a few weeks of one another in the summer of 1749. Like the Heppenheim Landises, Maisprach's Kumlers would have faced similar concerns about cannibalism at sea and shipwrecks but must have concluded "that they could nowhere be worse off than at home." [48]

John Kumler, who had been born in Maisprach in 1709, brought his wife and three children John, John Jacob or Hans, and Anna-Maria to Pennsylvania. [49] John Jacob was seven years old upon arrival in America. Paternal great-grandfather of Mary Kumler, he married Elizabeth Young April 24, 1770 in Pennsylvania, and later served on active duty during the Revolutionary War in the Philadelphia area as a member of the Lancaster County militia under Captain Isaac Addams. [50]

John Jacob and Elizabeth had five children, including the Landis boys' great-grandfather Henry Kumler, born January 3, 1775 in Brecknock Township, Berks County. When Henry was six, Elizabeth died in a fall from a horse, and he grew up without the love and care of a mother. In 1797, Henry Kumler married Susannah Wengert in Dauphin County, and they had twelve children, including the Landis boys' maternal grandfather Daniel. Henry believed that tilling the soil and bringing up crops was "the natural means of gaining a living, and he reared his children to have a love for the soil." His religious devotion "was a powerful factor in church work, and he was an eloquent preacher." [51] This devotion became apparent in two of his sons, Henry Jr. and Mary Kumler's father, Daniel.

Henry Sr. began to preach in his mid-thirties as a layman with the German Reformed church. "He spoke with such simplicity, earnestness and much feeling, moving others profoundly, bringing into the church large numbers." He was ordained in the United Brethren in Christ, where he gained attention travelling a large circuit around Greencastle, Pennsylvania. In his second year, Henry became a delegate to the conference that "formulated the first discipline of the church." Through "his ability and eloquence" he joined the Virginia circuit, where he covered "370 miles every four weeks." The next year he became presiding elder, and such was the intensity of his work that he became exhausted and nearly died. [52]

9

In preaching, "Henry spoke as one man to another, simply and sincerely, using homely illustrations, well within their comprehension." Although his sermons were in German, such was his earnest manner that he converted many that did not understand his words, and "they followed the example of his upright, godly life." [53] His religious zeal led to a religious calling of his sons Henry, Jr. and Daniel. The clergy of the Landis boys' paternal and maternal lines were quite different in style. The simplicity of the former -- Mennonite preachers and deacons -- stood in contrast with the more formal United Brethren ministers and bishops.

In 1818, Henry moved his family to Butler County, Ohio, just two years after Philip Landis arrived there with his wife and children. Henry as a United Brethren pioneer carried the church's doctrine "west of the Allegheny Mountains" and remained an active bishop into his seventies. It is a coincidence that these Swiss families, who traveled to America within a few weeks of one another in 1749 and went separate ways during colonial years, came together, generations later, in Ohio's Butler County. The Swiss families merged there with the marriage of Abraham Landis and Mary Kumler, with Rev. Henry Kumler officiating.

Henry and Susannah's son, Daniel, the Logansport Landises' maternal grandfather, was born in 1807. Daniel became a medical doctor and minister and, in his late 40's, a missionary to Africa. Daniel and Catharine's first daughter Mary, the future bride of Abraham, was born in 1832 and grew up in Millville. At the age of 46, he left his wife and nine childrenon a missionary trip to Sierra Leone. He wrote a diary of the voyage and of his stay there. [54]

On the final day of the voyage, Rev. Kumler learned firsthand about two islands that were "rendevous of slavers." Several days later he visited Good Hope, saw "graves of the missionaries who have preceded us" and, after observing the dismal living conditions of the people, wrote: "O degraded Africa!" He learned about a secret society that inflicted unspeakable torture on people at will. [55] On his return, he lamented the plight of American slaves.

A final note on the Kumlers attests to their "strong religious feeling, honesty, industry, kindheartedness, and patriotism." At the same time, a Kumler cousin later noted that Aunt Hannah added diversity to Abraham's family ties by marrying a man who was not only a farmer and preacher but also a distiller. [56]

2. Pilgrimage through the Confederacy -- 1862 to 1864

Why don't you name him after that damned battle we've heard nothing else but since the war?. . . "Kenesaw Mountain" Landis.

-- Homespun advice to Dr. Landis
for naming his fourth son in 1866.[1]

Dr. Abraham Landis, father of "the Landis boys," joined the Union Army "for 3 years" on November 13, 1862 at the age of 41, leaving his wife, a growing family, and a medical practice in the village of Millville, Ohio. His unit, the 35th Ohio Volunteer Infantry, represented communities of the rural southwestern part of the state and was Butler County's first entire regiment to be formed. It "was composed mostly of young and intelligent men," and "its officers were citizens of standing." [2] It would make its mark in American history as a courageous unit that suffered its greatest losses on the field of Chickamauga. [3] The record of heavy fighting by the 35th would come to be known, in the words of its historian, as "a pilgrimage through the Confederacy."

Abraham enlisted because of a strong sense of patriotism and a belief that God was on the Northern side. His readiness to serve in the military contrasted with the dilemma faced in colonial days by his grandfather and great uncles, who, as devout Mennonites, were opposed to warfare. His decision was described in later years by a prominent, turn-of-the-20th-century journalist as a consequence of his outlook as "a radical abolitionist before the Republican Party was born" [4] Such an attitude would not have been surprising because of the likely influence of his father-in-law, who had penned a rejection of slavery in his diary, July 4, 1855, during a missionary voyage to Africa. [5]

While there would have been little doubt, given his background, that Abraham would sign on with the Union Army, still the complexity of his choice is illustrated by the strong sentiments of his cousin, Israel Landis. Believed to have been a Confederate officer, [6] Israel was arrested in Missouri, one of three "very active aiders in the Rebellion" during the early years of the Civil War. [7]

Dr. Landis left by train through Kentucky to join his unit in Tennessee. traveling a route followed by his regiment a year earlier. Officers of the regiment had earlier witnessed, in that divided state,

11

a strong animosity toward Yankee military units when orders came for them "to send their colored servants back to Ohio." [8] Abraham's abolitionist sentiments aligned him with attitudes expressed by the regimental historian who offered an assessment of the Union role in the conflict: "We were here under the commission of the nation to fight the slave power." [9]

While such a military objective may have served the cause of Union esprit, particularly after President Lincoln's Emancipation Proclamation September 1862, troops of the 35th Ohio were concerned about "latrine rumors" that the "Rebels" were contriving underhanded plans such as: "poisoning springs and other sources of water supply." [10]   Prior to Dr. Landis' arrival at his post in Tennessee, the 35th had been skirmishing with Confederates at Corinth, Mississippi and Perryville, Kentucky and worked to restore the rail route that retreating Southern forces had destroyed. [11]

Gallatin

> *This town and the surrounding country is said to be a sink of Rebellion, nearly all are Secessionists. They are paying dearly for their folly and wickedness.*
> -- Letter, A.H. Landis Gallatin, Tennessee to
> Rev. Daniel Kumler, December 3-4, 1862 [12]

Abraham Landis, newly assigned assistant surgeon of the 35th Ohio, soon widened his horizons at the military hospital in Gallatin, a few miles east of Nashville. Local residents who furnished provisions to the regiment proved to be skillful in hiding their Southern sympathies, according to the unit's historian: "The parties from whom we foraged threw up their hats a few days previous when Bragg's forces passed over the same country. They were Confederates to the backbone then, though they professed to be good Union men while Uncle Sam's boys were passing." [13]

Dr. Landis seemed to gain quickly a keen understanding of the attitudes of other local folk, when he described the confused loyalties and growing pessimism of Tennesseeans around Gallatin. Yet, one may wonder if Abraham might have read their deeper sentiments with undue optimism: "Everything indicates that the people were prosperous and happy before the Rebellion. I have talked with some of the citizens about our troubles and find they are

12

all sick and tired of the war, and willing to come back into the old Union upon almost any terms." [14]

Noting the war-weariness of local Tennesseeans, Abraham also worried about morale on his own home front back in Millville. In the first letter to his family, written as he undertook to support troops fighting south of Nashville at Stones River, he betrayed a concern for his wife's spirits. Addressing his father-in-law, Abraham hinted at his own need for word from home: "I want you & mother and all the rest to visit Mary as often as you can. Recollect she is lonesome, and a visit from her near-relations would be thrice welcome. The weather here is fine, clear days & frosty nights . . . I want you to write me a long letter when you get this." [15]

As a member of the regiment, Abraham learned that it was standard practice to gather food supplies wherever they could be found. [16] He witnessed this appropriation of private property and wrote home about the official Union policy, soon after his arrival in Tennessee: "When firewood is wanted, it is obtained from the nearest fence, and when horse feed is needed, it is obtained from the nearest cornfield. If the owner denies it, he gets a receipt, and if he can prove his loyalty he will be paid some time after the war." [17]

At the same time that the regiment was leaning on local communities for war necessities, it displayed a certain generosity toward the civilian populace. The regimental historian noted that this kindness to families of Southern soldiers at war with comrades in Blue, however, did not prove popular to its historian: "The wives and children of those in the secesh army were supplied with rations from Uncle Sam's commissary; this was simply an outrage." [18]

While at Gallatin, Dr. Landis would have learned about "the big picture" – that Confederate defeats in western Tennessee during February and April 1862 seemed to have taken a toll on citizen morale in the area: "The effect of the capture of Fort Henry on the people of the whole country, North and South, was electrical . . . the first great success won by Union arms within the limits of the Confederacy." [19]

Up to this point, the regiment claimed the distinction of having participated in "the first battle fought in the West and the first complete Union victory in the War . . . likewise the first genuine test as to what Union troops would do under fire." [20] An account of this early experience may have provided Abraham with insight about the work of fellow surgeons and the reaction of young

13

soldiers to the sight of casualties, as recalled by one of the unit's company commanders: "When a contest was going on, men would look on bodies horribly torn by shot and shell; but when the sound of battle had died out, then there were few that could muster courage to look at sights like those to be seen at a surgeon's tent near a field hospital." [21]

It is also likely that Dr. Landis learned about Southern chicanery experienced by the regiment in Kentucky just prior to the battle of Mill Springs . . . a bold attempt to smuggle arms to Confederate forces behind Union lines that succeeded. Thanks to a ruse, two coffins being escorted by "Rebels" wearing Union blue were allegedly those of Yankee soldiers. [22]

Abraham as a new member of the 35th would likely have shared an appreciation for the leadership qualities of his regimental commander, Colonel Ferdinand Van Derveer, who displayed great concern for his men during earlier actions in Kentucky. [23]

Dr. Landis would have been aware of the importance of the regiment's key mission of rail repair in the Tennessee campaign because the maintenance of Union supply routes into the South was critical to the administration of battlefield medicine. [24] In addition, one of a surgeon's main concerns was to arrange for the evacuation of dead and wounded to the Union rear area.

The principal assignment at Gallatin was to guard Cumberland River fords east of the city. For the moment, the natural beauty of its campsite on the north bank belied the ever-present threat posed by Confederate Colonel John Hunt Morgan's troops a few miles upstream. The 35th had to bide its time in this peaceful setting because action could come at any moment. Meanwhile, soldiers gathered around campfires to "spin yarns and crack jokes," while a few, grumbled, and were on ill terms with "all the world and the rest of mankind." [25] The men may also have discussed the charismatic Colonel Morgan, who developed his own techniques: using sawed-off rifles, employing telegraph, and leaving his horses to the side while his men fought as infantry in "a flexible, curved line." [26]

Gallatin's main facility was the general hospital of the Army of the Cumberland. Writing home, Dr. Landis paired the regiment's combat mission with a pastoral description of the area, reflecting his provincial background of Hickory Flats, Busenbark Station, and Millville, Ohio. Abraham, farmer and country doctor, was not yet wearied by the horrors of war and emphasized the positive nature of his surroundings and an upbeat evaluation of the regiment's medical condition:

> The Cumberland River here is about twice as large as the Miami. We guard a ford where Morgan and his bandittos have been crossing the River. We are encamped in a beautiful grove. We use River water and it is as palatable as any water I ever drank. The country about here is as fine as I ever saw. The land is well improved. There are turnpikes in all directions. The health of the boys is good; not more than ten (of nearly nine hundred) who are unfit for duty. [27]

Adding to the lighter side of camp life was an incident that stretched one's imagination about an imminent threat at Cunningham's Ford –"heifers and sheep" under command of a southern female. [28] The historian related that, after a failed attempt to conquer the old Rebel lady's sheep, officers of the 35th had another reason to question the efficacy of the regiment's combat mission. Instead of focusing on the threat posed by Colonel Morgan, the unit's operations seemed to zero in on a number of spirited fellow soldiers who were fraternizing with local lassies: "Our only duty seemed to be to patrol the surrounding country and pick up strolling parties that were out on enterprises not considered strictly legitimate, and deliver the chaps over to the kind hospitalities of the provo-marshal." [29]

During the regiment's stay at Gallatin, Abraham developed an acute skin affliction, erysipelas, on his head and face leaving his system in a very debilitated condition. [30] He was "furloughed for 20 days," returning to Millville to recuperate. [31]

As long as the 35th was guarding against Colonel Morgan's cavalry at Cunningham's Ford, the Confederates remained quiet in that area, but, toward the end of December, Morgan's men were in action again. The regiment kept watch on their movements, while Gen. Rosecrans engaged Gen. Bragg's Confederate Army at Stones River. [32] Here, at a crucial moment, Union General George H. Thomas, under whose senior command the 35th Regiment was fighting, affirmed his troops' resolve, declaring to Gen. Rosecrans: "This army does not retreat." [33]

After the regiment completed its assignment at Gallatin, it resumed the task of foraging -- acquiring and grinding "secesh wheat into good Union flour" to support the upcoming attack against Bragg's forces to the south. [34] With the foraging work finished, the 35th moved through Nashville to a location not far from Confederate forces defending Murfreesborough. [35]

In preparing for the next phase of the drive to the southern portion of Tennessee, the 35th Ohio obtained the improved Springfield rifle. [36] The regiment was now under command of General Brannan, who stressed discipline and successfully prepared his regiments for movement southward in the Army of the Cumberland. [37]

Because of heavy pressure from higher authority, General Rosecrans resumed his pursuit of General Bragg, who was occupying a defensive position along a river line. Troop movement on both sides was difficult because of incessant rain. As the 35th advanced, it came under fire from "a saucy Rebel battery," but managed to prevail, forcing the enemy to make a nighttime withdrawal. For a moment, enemy fire severely jostled Abraham's fellow surgeon: "Dr. Wright, had his horse killed under him; the action of the animal had the effect to toss the doctor into the air some distance coming to the ground somewhat like a flying squirrel." [38]

Again the enemy withdrew from his entrenchments, choosing to fall back across another river. It became necessary then to ford the swift and swollen river, but the inconvenience yielded to a final refreshing experience, a rare bath for the troops. [39] After repeated Confederate withdrawals to the south, fighting halted by July 4th. Weather had seriously slowed the movement of Union supplies, causing troops to do "substantial fasting." [40]

In a week's time, the 35th moved further to the south. Here Abraham, serving in the 3rd Brigade of the 3rd Division, managed to visit his brother Frederick in the 69th Ohio Infantry Regiment. [41] Abraham's regiment resumed movement in pursuit of General Bragg, who continued to fall back, and the historian wrote that the 35th "was in the front of the marching and fighting." [42]

The immediate task facing Gen. Rosecrans' forces was to cross the Tennessee River, while lacking suitable equipment to accomplish the task. [43] Another problem was the need to delay major movement south until the corn crop would ripen to feed the horses and mules. Yet the Army of the Cumberland continued to attract the attention of the High Command in Washington, that insisted upon early movement across the wide Tennessee, with little appreciation for the magnitude of the task of such a river crossing.

General Thomas ordered Gen. Brannan to make the initial crossing of the river on August 29th. It fell to Colonel VanDerveer's brigade and its 35th Ohio, to lead the way. Abraham's regiment made the first crossing and found no opposition by the Confederates on the south bank. [44]

Chickamauga

General Forrest told us to go ahead and attend to our wounded, and we should not be molested.
-- Guidance to Dr. Landis and fellow surgeons in captivity following the Chickamauga campaign. [45]

Not likely to have been prominent in Union plans, Chickamauga became an inadvertent road sign in the 35th Regiment's *pilgrimage through the Confederacy.* Chattanooga was the interim objective in a drive to bring the war to a favorable conclusion for the North.

With General Rosecrans' crossing of the Tennessee River, the Chickamauga campaign was under way. General Thomas' Fourteenth Corps, with the 35th Regiment and other units, then followed into Georgia past the northeast corner of Alabama into Georgia and took up a position on the western slope of Lookout Mountain. This movement forced General Bragg to evacuate Chattanooga in order to protect his communications to the south. During this time, the Corps Medical Director reported that the regiments "were all abundantly supplied with medicines and surgical instruments, previous to our march, thoroughly inspected and repaired by an expert."

This senior medical officer of the Fourteenth Corps reported that each Division would be issued "a train of 30 light two-horse ambulances," and each regiment would obtain one ambulance. In addition, his plan reflected the kinds of equipment that would be included in supplies issued to Abraham and his fellow regimental surgeons:

> A reserve supply consisting of hospital tents, blankets, sheets, hair pillows, shirts, drawers, bed-sacks, surgical instruments, bandages, lint, mess-chests (including cooking utensils), concentrated milk and beef, liquor,

chloroform, and such other medicines, surgical apparatus, and hospital stores as experience has taught to be most needed and useful in emergencies in the field. [46]

General Thomas' Fourteenth Corps entered Steven's Gap of Lookout Mountain, reached Missionary Ridge, and moved northward before Pigeon Mountain. With this maneuver, he was helping to trump Bragg's ambitious plan to attack the vulnerable Fourteenth Corps. [47] The Union troops faced dusty conditions and mountainous terrain, often with little water supply. [48]

In a timely letter to his wife Mary, Abraham understood but understated the peril facing the 35th Regiment and Union forces. His family would now gain a sophisticated and sobering picture of Dr. Landis' imminent brush with major hostilities, as he wrote from Pigeon Valley, Georgia on September 14:

> This morning early we were on the road expecting to march seven miles but we had hardly got started when the whole division was ordered back to camp. It was discovered that the Rebs are within four miles of us with a large force . . .We are between two ranges of mountains and the only way to advance is to pass through certain gaps held by the Rebs. [49]

Abraham was now far from the familiar territory of Ohio's Butler County, and his contact with family members was much on his mind. He had not heard from his brother Fred, of the 69th Regiment, since their meeting in July. Nor had he received mail for two months from his family although he knew mail service would be slowed because Union forces were on the move since June. [50] He sampled local attitudes, as was his habit, exploring local reaction to the fighting around them. This gave him a chance to reassure the homefolks, and he sounded a positive note in his letter: "I just had a talk with one of the citizens who says about half the inhabitants are Union . . . There are many Union people here, some who have been in the Rebel army, nearly every last one of whom is sick & tired of the war and anxious to return to the Union." [51]

Also, Abraham's appreciation of the Southern countryside showed a low-key response to the dangers of war. Sensing an early outbreak of hostilities, he tried to put his wife's mind at ease, not realizing that the regiment was maneuvering on the brink of a devastating battle along Chickamauga Creek:

Mary you must expect a change in the programme of affairs. We are now so far in the country of the enemy that Bragg may get behind us and cut off our communications for a time. Should such a thing happen there would be no mail but we could take care of ourselves, as our force would be ample, and there is plenty of provision in the country. I have seen as fine corn here in Georgia as I ever saw in Ohio, also potatoes, hogs, cattle, sheep etc. Should such a thing happen don't be uneasy as we can take care of ourselves. [52]

The following day, Abraham posted a final update of an ominous situation, seasoning the sobering facts with a touch of local color, as he had done in Tennessee. He had displayed a good sense of the enemy's intentions, and shortly the entire Union force under Generals Rosecrans and Thomas would be engaged: "This morning at seven o'clock we were on the way, and after going six miles we went into camp . . . it is necessary to move slowly when in the face of the enemy . . .We are encamped in a beautiful grove. We are pleasantly situated." [53]

In keeping with Abraham's opinion that Gen. Bragg might surprise the Fourteenth Corps, mentioned in his letter above, the 35th Regiment's historian noted that the current situation was one in which the top Union leadership had a much different outlook from that of their troops. The higher officers were now worried; the fighting men were relaxed. [54]

Records published after the war lend credence to chaotic conditions on the Confederate side which enabled the Union forces under Rosecrans to avert a serious splitting of their forces that could have led to an early Southern victory by mid-September. They have been commented upon in detail in the history of the 35th Regiment. [55] The unusual circumstances of this extended period of sorting out the location and intentions of the enemy, on both sides, were noted by the historian: "For twelve days the armies lay near each other, and neither commander knew the exact position of the other. This resulted from the fact that the country, practically, was a wilderness, and between the armies was a low range of mountains." [56]

No one could have foreseen the sudden outbreak of hostilities, which would start a few days after Abraham's late letter to Mary. The inauguration of warfare, which unfortunately would lead to heavy loss of life on both sides, may have, in a perverse sort of way, eased the worrisome mind of wondering when or where the fighting would start. As Abraham indicated in his September 15 letter from Pigeon Valley, his unit had just moved six miles "not directly toward the enemy, but off to the left." This was precisely the Union plan to move forces further north in order to keep Gen. Bragg from positioning his army between Rosecrans' troops and their base in Chattanooga. [57]

On September 18, three days after Abraham penned his letter, Union observations confirmed that Bragg's forces were moving to the north, which might enable him to attack the Union left and cut Rosecrans' supply line to Chattanooga. In response, during the night of September 18, the 35th Ohio Regiment of Col. Van Derveer's brigade accelerated the movement Abraham had described in order to reinforce the Union left. This tactic would enable the Union forces to meet Bragg's flanking attack. [58]

Col. Van Derveer's brigade, including the 35th Ohio, comprised the left flank of the Union position and conducted for several hours "a fair stand-up fight" that "beat back three attacks of the *elite* of the Rebel army." [59]Action of Abraham's regiment, on the right of the brigade, was described by its commander a few days after the battle: "The engagement soon became very fierce, but the accurate fire of the line soon broke the Rebel line. In this short fight our loss in thirty minutes was 60 killed and wounded. In a short time the Rebels rallied and made another desperate assault on the line, but were again repulsed." [60]

Abraham had the opportunity to render service in behalf of one particular casualty on this first day of fighting at Chickamauga, as described in a newspaper article published years later. It concerned a West Pointer, Colonel William G. Jones, 36th Ohio Regiment, to whom Abraham attended as he was dying. Before burying the colonel, Abraham removed his shoulder straps and two $1 gold pieces and safeguarded them until the end of the war and returned them to the colonel's brother. [61]

In view of the rapidly changing situation, orders came from the 3rd Division to implement a new plan for regimental and division surgeons. According to Dr. Landis' post-war report, "On Saturday, September 19th, soon after the commencement of the battle of Chickamauga, I was ordered by my division's medical director to move to the Division hospital. It was on Cloud's farm and at that time two miles north of the left wing of our army." [62] This location seemed for the time being to be relatively safe from Confederate cavalry attacks by Gen. Nathan Bedford Forrest, who was protecting Gen. Bragg's right flank. This site appeared to be a good choice because "a good spring, a church and several houses afforded comfort for the wounded." [63] It remained to be seen whether the fluid positioning of Union and Confederate forces would allow such calm to prevail for long.

This description, however, would belie the deplorable atmosphere resulting after the dead and wounded were brought in within hours of Dr. Landis' arrival there. On the battlefield, the 35th was embroiled in heavy fighting with Confederate forces that withdrew to the east, ending the day's combat. [64]

First-hand experience in Chickamauga hospitals on this first day of conflict evoked haunting memories of one veteran many years after the war: "All through the hours of that long night, by the light of blazing fires, the surgeons and assistants moved about among the hundreds that lay upon cots or upon the ground around the tents, stanching the wounds and administering food and cordials and water to the sufferers." Looking back some 30-odd years, the old soldier painfully recalled: "Often a pulseless, motionless form was borne away and laid in the fast lengthening row of those to whom death had come." [65]

The source of this testimony found the same hectic atmosphere at Dr. Landis' place of business when he concluded: "Conditions were no better six miles up the road at the Cloud church, where surgeons of Brannan's division had set up their field hospital in the sanctuary and in a nearby cooper's shop." [66] Activity at the 3rd Division hospital soon increased dramatically because the division hospital on the Union right flank was evacuated due to increasing enemy action. The dead and wounded were assembled here from many units, quickly overloading the limited staff and facility at the Cloud's farm location. One of Dr. Landis' fellow surgeons of the 3rd Brigade observed the action in this hospital: "All day countless ambulances arrived with wounded. At 11:00 p.m. those buildings were overfilled . . . we could see we must overcome supreme hardship in order to do a few of our duties correctly, if able to do any at all." [67]

With the onset of these great difficulties, Dr. Landis could begin to understand that his hasty move earlier in the morning had been most timely. It soon became very clear, however, that despite the best of plans, the battlefield situation was devastating the medical system of the Corps. Only a few days before, the staff and supplies available to all units had seemed adequate for all emergencies. Already on the first day of intense combat, the chances of minimal treatment for wounded men had become impossible. The Corps Medical Director described this situation: "The wounded from various divisions, including a large number of those of the enemy, were accumulating at this hospital, and before night the number reached near 1,000. Straw was brought for bedding, hot coffee and soup served, and fires built as near as practicable to the wounded, for their protection from the cold of the night air." [68]

The Corps Medical Director remained at the field hospital, helping Dr. Landis and his fellow surgeons tend to the most serious cases and returned to his headquarters the next morning, Sunday, September 20. There he learned of sporadic military activity in the vicinity of Cloud's farm and concluded with an air of finality that the tents and medical officers along with regimental supplies "fell into the hands of the enemy." [69]

Meanwhile, this second day of fighting, Sunday, September 20 had begun with the 35th Regiment occupying a position away from the left wing and toward the center of the Union line. This movement placed the troops nearly four miles from the Cloud's farm location of the 3rd Division hospital, where Dr. Landis and his fellow surgeons were operating. The 3rd Brigade with its 35th Ohio attacked the oncoming Confederate division of General Breckinridge, which succeeded in enveloping the Union left flank. The ensuing conflict "was severe and desperate, in the open field, and without any protection. Here was presented the uncommon spectacle of two armies charging each other at the same instant." [70] The 35th blunted and threw back these Confederate forces after surviving "murderous fire from artillery and musketry." [71] Then the Regiment had to withdraw, and this was done with great efficiency, "but not without heavy loss to the Regiment." [72]

General Bragg continued with his plan to envelop the Union Army through attacks at 9:30, 10:00; 11:00; and 11:30, proceeding from Rosecrans' left to the center and right. [73] During these early ground assaults, Dr. Landis' field hospital received "furious cannonading" which killed a wounded officer and injured several men. [74] By 11:00, following "shell and solid shot" which mostly passed over into Union front lines, Rebel skirmishers approached from the east in front of "a large force" of Gen. Nathan Bedford Forrest's cavalry. [75] They were part of General Frank Armstrong's division, of Forrest's Corps, which moved around the Union left flank, much as Breckinridge had done the day before. With this threat looming large, the hospital dispatched patients to Chattanooga using every ambulance and sent large numbers of walking wounded. Soon, Confederate cavalry appeared, and Dr. Landis pointedly recalled: "for the first time, we were in the hands of the enemy." [76]

Meanwhile, to the south, Bragg's last attack, using Longstreet's corps was highly successful in pinning back the Union right on Horse Shoe Ridge. General Brannan's 3rd Division was crucial to this new defense situation, and VanDerveer's 3rd Brigade with the 35th Ohio moved with dispatch to the right wing on Horse Shoe Ridge and held its position there heroically, repulsing two successive major assaults: "The fighting continued for nearly two hours, when our ammunition became exhausted. Nothing daunted, the regiment fixed bayonets and awaited the shock. Fortunately a load of ammunition arrived, and the firing was renewed with vigor . . ." Suddenly, a Confederate general appeared in the front lines and asked "whose troops we were" . . . "at the reply, 'Thirty-fifth Ohio,' he wheeled but received a volley from the Thirty-fifth which riddled him and his horse and raked the line of the Rebels . . . breaking their line, and sending all but three companies down the hill in confusion." [77]

General Granger, whose corps was in support of Rosecrans' Army from a position north of the Chickamauga battlefield, proceeded to move south to join besieged Union forces under Thomas on Horse Shoe Ridge. His greenhorn soldiers crossed through the field of wounded and dead Confederates following heavy fighting earlier in the morning. One touching account demonstrates the utter humanity shown by soldiers to one another across Blue-Gray lines. [78]

Dr. Landis' statement about having been captured, noted above, referred to the initial arrival of General Forrest in his role of protecting Gen. Bragg's right flank, when he happened upon the Cloud's farm hospital. There was no doubt that at that time, before midday, the medical facility at Cloud's Farm was indeed in "no man's land," [79] about three miles away from the 35th and unable to provide medical support to the 35th, already deployed on the right of Thomas' line on Horse Shoe Ridge.

In fact, Confederate cavalry had been "wreaking havoc on the Federal field hospital at the Cloud church . . . Since mid-morning, Forrest had held the church," and at about noon, as Union reserve troops under General Granger approached from the north, *Forrest withdrew*. Granger's troops found "long rows of dead Federals" at the hospital as they arrived after Forrest's troops departed.[80] A saga of the "now it's captured . . . now it's free" field hospital commenced when General Granger called off General Steedman's division, which had started to move infantry against Forrest and his troops as they fled to the east. Granger, saying: "they are nothing but rag-a-muffin cavalry," gave orders to bring up Colonel Dan McCook's brigade "to keep an eye on Forrest." [81]

Meanwhile Dr. Gross, the Corps Medical Director, reported unwelcome news with his impression of enemy activity on the Union left flank: "While attempting to reach the 3rd Division hospital, on the morning of the 20th, I received a slight wound in the neck by a musket ball, not disabling me, however, for duty." [82] From the vantage point of the hospital, the situation had vastly improved when Granger's troops chased Forrest away from the area of Cloud's farm. Unfortunately for the field hospitals of the 3rd Division, 14th Corps and 2nd Division, 20th Corps, the personal experience of Thomas' Medical Director contributed to their isolation on the battlefield with a fateful bit of reasoning: "On the morning of the 20th, I sent a messenger to Dr. Barrell (Corps Medical Purveyor), informing him that the 3rd Division hospital had fallen into the hands of the enemy, and directing him to take the Dry Valley road, which it appears he had already done." Building upon this unfortunate interpretation of the actual condition on the battlefield in the area of the hospital, the 14th Corps Medical Director foreclosed Dr. Landis' and his colleagues' opportunity to obtain needed military support, as the Medical Director later explained: "Being met by retreating troops and wagons, it was deemed prudent to halt this train of supplies, which was thus saved and subsequently taken to Chattanooga, where, by order of the medical director of the department, they were issued to the hospitals at this place and served a good purpose." [83]

This Medical Director's report, which presumed that the 3rd Division hospital was still occupied by Forrest after noontime,

24

created the impression that the facility could not be evacuated Sunday evening when Thomas withdrew from Horse Shoe Ridge to Rossville:

> The wounded continued to move to the rear nearly all night. On Monday morning, the 21st, ambulances were driven as far front as it was safe for them to go, and gathered up such wounded as had not been recovered in that vicinity during the night; a large number still at Rossville that morning were also sent to the rear. [84]

An official report noted the failure of the Army of the Cumberland to evacuate casualties from the battlefield: "Thomas fell back in the evening to Rossville, leaving the dead, and many of the wounded, in the hands of the enemy." [85] The report wrongly assumed that Dr Landis' hospital remained in Gen. Forrest's hands on Sunday, September 20th.

The fate of the 3rd Division hospital has been described in the history of the 35th Regiment but, ironically the Corps decision to separate the Cloud farm hospital from its own ambulances was not noted: "A large number of our wounded were left in hospitals near the field when Thomas withdrew the army from Chickamauga on Sunday night. This was a necessity, since ambulances and wagons had been swept back out of reach or control of Thomas during the break on the right." [86] Might not a fair commentary here be that historians record battles with emphasis upon combat elements, unfortunately leaving the circumstances affecting medical and support forces in a secondary light?

In summing up the casualties of Sunday, the second day of fighting, the regimental commander reflected the presumption that the Cloud farm hospital was in Confederate hands in the afternoon and evening when he wrote: "Dr. Charles O. Wright and Dr. A.H. Landis were left to take care of our wounded in the hands of the enemy." [87]

The notion that Gen. Forrest retained control of the hospital on Sunday remains gospel in the National Park Service data base, as reflected in reference to its "captive status as of September 20th" on the memorial plaque at the Chickamauga battlefield. [88] Abraham Landis would have disagreed with the date "September 20." In his own post-war report, he points out that the 3rd Division hospital was held for a short time on Sunday, September 20th by General Forrest's men, who then departed . . . only to return the next morning, September 21st to effect a capture of the facility. Landis wrote that, upon the arrival of General Granger's forces: "The Rebels fell back, and we saw no more of them until the following morning, when they took us into custody, and from that time on we were prisoners." [89] There is an indication that Abraham's feelings on this matter were deeply held, based on discussions with his family that he "was finally captured the next morning in some manner and at some time by the Confederates." [90]

In his last ditch action at Horse Shoe Ridge, Gen. Thomas became known as "the Rock of Chickamauga," when he enabled other elements of the Army of the Cumberland to withdraw from the battle area toward Chattanooga. Ironically, these "other elements" included senior officers Rosecrans, Crittenden, McCook, and Garfield with their troops along with "division commanders Sheridan, Jefferson C. Davis, Negley and Van Cleve. [91] These "other elements" did not include the medical personnel of the Corps hospitals. Thomas, having beaten off Confederate efforts to storm Horse Shoe Ridge, continued until evening and the next morning to evacuate the wounded from hospitals that had been disrupted by Longstreet's breakthrough earlier on Sunday morning. He apparently considered that the Cloud's farm hospital could not be reached safely for purposes of an orderly evacuation of the Hospital of the 3rd Division 14th Corps and 2nd Division 20th Corps staffs and patients. In fact, he would have known that the ambulances already assigned to the Cloud farm site were shifted for the use of other hospitals. [And Colonel Dan McCook, General Granger's brigade commander . . . "to keep an eye on Forrest" . . . Did he follow Granger's orders? If so, one must conclude that he failed to inform Granger or Thomas that Forrest had abandoned Cloud's farm hospital on Sunday.]

It is not known whether Abraham Landis or his fellow captive Dr. Charles Wright believed that Union forces should have tried to withdraw the field hospital Sunday afternoon, Sunday evening or Monday morning in order to prevent its capture. If the Division hospital had been protected from Forrest's return visit on September 21, the wounded and surgeons of the Second and 3rd Divisions could have been safely evacuated along with their tents and supplies. For the Second Division, that included four doctors and 30 non-transportable soldiers, and for the 3rd Division, three doctors including Dr. Landis and 60 non-transportable cases. [92]

Such an outcome would have meant that Gen. Thomas, in charge of the Union defense of Horse Shoe Ridge, would have learned from Granger's forces upon their arrival at his command Sunday afternoon that Forrest had not succeeded in taking the hospital on that day but had been "sent packing" to the east. Such information would have discredited completely the Corps Medical Officer earlier report that the hospital was already under Forrest's authority in the morning of Sunday. While Thomas' attention was clearly focused upon rebuffing Longstreet's furious attacks against Horse Shoe Ridge, perhaps he could have ordered the medical support wagons dedicated to the Cloud farm hospital to undertake to evacuate the patients, staff and equipment to Rossville on Sunday afternoon and evening as well as Monday morning.

Abraham would have been deeply saddened not only by the fate of the hospital but in a personal sense, by the loss in action of his young cousin George Kumler of the 93rd Ohio Infantry Regiment, [93] son of Dr. Landis' Uncle Jake. George's brother John had been killed at Stones River, when Abraham served at Gallatin. Painful memories of Chickamauga's veterans would later be rekindled at reunions of the 35th Ohio Volunteer Infantry Regiment, which Abraham Landis regularly attended.

Official word from one of the division surgeons in captivity seemed to indicate some hope for favorable treatment, stating "that all the medical officers with him have been paroled to report to the commandant of the post at Atlanta as soon as relieved from taking care of the United States sick and wounded prisoners." [94] This message did not indicate, however, that the surgeons would be incarcerated at Libby Prison.

Now, with guns silent on both sides, Abraham found himself not knowing the probable status of physicians in Confederate captivity. Dr. Landis may have faced a variety of difficult questions: Would surgeons be permitted to practice their craft on patients already in their care? Would they be allowed to find and treat wounded soldiers still lying in the brush or open fields along Chickamauga Creek? Would they have an opportunity to tend to the decomposing bodies of dead comrades whom they might find on the battlefield? Or would they face imprisonment? After all, Libby Prison and its sordid reputation was well known to Union soldiers, who did not relish the idea of paying it a visit. [95]

27

After the capture of the Division field hospital, one would hope that positive negotiations would take place between Union and Confederate headquarters on such matters. Whether the oft-times friendly exchanges between Billy Yank and Johnny Reb would suggest a measure of civility between Rosecrans and Bragg was not promising. Now clear, however, to prisoner Landis was that the good provisions he had written home about in Pigeon Valley in mid-September were now but a memory. Furthermore, the "uncertainties" he had experienced in Rebel territory on the eve of war soon gave way to the certainty of Confederate captivity.

As an early order of business, Dr. Landis and his colleagues apparently concluded that they had gained a positive, grassroots understanding with Confederate generals, who now had full authority over the former battlefield. Abraham wrote a painstaking report after the war, describing Confederate assurances that were not fulfilled:

> Generals Forrest, Cheatham, and Armstrong honored us with their presence. General Forrest told us to go ahead and attend to our wounded, and we should not be molested. He also told us that our wounded yet on the field should be removed to the hospitals and receive precisely the same treatment that their wounded received; also that parties had been detailed to bury the dead on both sides. In a conversation I had with Dr. Fluellan, medical director of Bragg's army, the following day at Cheatham's division hospital, he made the same promises. These promises may have been in good faith, but from observation I know – and every other medical officer who fell into their hands knows – they were not realized.

Dr. Landis' report goes on to cover the food situation for hospital staff following their capture on Monday, September 21:

> Our provisions ran out at our hospital two days after our capture, and then starvation stared us in the face. Finally, after two days' entreaties, we were furnished with fresh beef, hard bread, bacon, and corn meal. The bacon and hard bread were good in quality, but very deficient in quantity. The beef was of Pharaoh's lean kine, but we were glad to get it. Some of the corn meal was musty and scarcely fit for the swill barrel. [96]

It took considerably longer for an exchange agreement to be worked out at higher command levels, and arrangements were made to transfer Union patients, presumably those at Cloud's farm hospital where Dr. Landis and his fellow surgeons were caring for them during captivity. Dr. Landis wrote of the deteriorating situation:

> A week or so later an exchange of prisoners was effected, so as to get our wounded into our hands. A long line of ambulances was sent out to the field to bring the wounded to Chattanooga. At the Rebel picket lines the ambulances were taken charge of by Confederates, who proceeded to where the wounded were, and returned the trains with them to the lines where our men again took charge of the ambulances. The wounded men were in a pitiable condition. It was impossible that they could be properly cared for while in that wilderness away from railway facilities. The Confederates were not provided with the medical stores and other necessities needed for the wounded.[97]

Dr. Landis' report written after the war indicated his talent, under trying circumstances, for enduring optimism, which, a week after becoming captive, was apparent in a moment of limited celebration: "Monday, Sept. 28th, General Rosecrans sent us rations, and from that time, as long as we remained at Chickamauga, Uncle Sam was our commissary, and we fared sumptuously." [98]

The official casualties of the 35th Regiment at Chickamauga were stated as: 3 officers and 19 men killed; 7 officers and 132 men wounded; 1 officer and 26 men captured. [99] These figures are, of course, incomplete because two surgeons, whose comparable rank would have been captain or major, became Confederate prisoners: Charles Wright and Abraham Landis.

Another casualty of Chickamauga may have been the needless abandonment of the Corps hospital at Cloud's farm on September 20th, allowing the medical personnel, including Abraham and his fellow surgeons with their patients and equipment, to fall into Confederate captivity. Finally, there has been the casualty of incomplete and inaccurate historical treatment into the 21st century, of this miserable, isolated, and neglected corner of the Chickamauga battlefield.

From available evidence provided by Whitelaw Reid, *Ohio in the War*; *The Thirty-Fifth Ohio*; *History of Butler County*; *War of the Rebellion*, it seems beyond doubt that the decision "to write off" the Corps Hospital at Cloud's Farm rested solely upon the premature judgement of the Medical Director of the 14th Corps. He was the officer who received a nick in the neck from a minie ball Sunday morning, September 20 and then sent a cursory assessment that was quickly overtaken by events to Dr. Barrell, Corps Medical Purveyor. The prevailing situation proved to be that General Forrest hastily withdrew to the East under pressure from General Gordon Granger's forces heading "to the sound of the guns" to reinforce General Thomas on Horse Shoe Ridge. The impression that the hospital had "fallen in the hands of the enemy," proved to be misleading and fateful for the hospital, its patients and personnel. General Forrest did not reappear in the area until he regrouped and chose to pursue the Federals the following day, Monday, September 21. To his apparent surprise, the Cloud's farm Fourteenth Corps hospital with surgeons, patients and equipment was there for the taking.

The Medical Director's report is likely to have convinced General Thomas that his plans for withdrawal to Chattanooga by way of Rossville during the approaching evening of Sunday, September 20 should not consider an effort to evacuate the 3rd Division, 14th Corps and 2nd Division, 20th Corps medical staffs at Cloud's farm. In reality, the passage of General Granger through the hospital area meant that the hospital had been freed from Forrest's control but remained helplessly out of contact with Union command staff.

It is regrettable that official records have ignored this factual error of historical importance. The Medical Director's premature and disastrous report unfortunately later became gospel in Union Army documents, even to include Captain Keil's history of the 35th Ohio Regiment. Isn't it puzzling that General Granger's awareness that he had driven Forrest out of the area to the East may not have been conveyed to General Thomas Horse Shoe Ridge? Or was it so conveyed to General Thomas, "the Rock of Chickamauga," with the possibility that he chose to dismiss its relevance to his plan for withdrawal to Chattanooga? Finally, if a third possibility existed . . . accepting the fact that Forrest had withdrawn to the east, would not the evacuation of personnel, wounded men, and medical equipment, preventing their serious loss, have been tactically feasible? If so, an awareness that Forrest had withdrawn would have left the wagon train dedicated to the Cloud farm installation intact to serve the needs of that hospital including evacuation during the afternoon and evening of Sunday, September 20. [100] At least, it is ironic that the hospital proved to be available for capture through minimal "Rebel action" at one's leisure. As circumstances turned out to the Confederate advantage, the renowned cavalry general, who wanted to pursue Thomas to Chattanooga, had to settle for the booty of a mere, undefended Corps hospital, powerless to avert surrender. [101]

Libby Prison

The mere appearance of their faces told us starvation and exposure were closing the work of death. America will never know how many of her noble sons perished in the dens of Richmond.
-- A. H. Landis' observation of soldiers' fate
while he was held in Libby Prison, 1863. [102]

As if Chickamauga hadn't exhibited enough inhumanity to sunder the 35th Regiment's "pilgrimage through the Confederacy!" Shortly there would be the distressing sight of Butler County boys wasting away in a warehouse jail. Now, "in the hands of the enemy," it was time to be "paroled to authorities in Atlanta." Abraham was not one to court dismay as he traveled on Friday, October 2, under Confederate guard to Chickamauga Station. While this Union surgeon was faced with broken Confederate promises to allow him and his colleagues to care for wounded and dead on the battlefield, he could have drawn some measure of satisfaction from an apparent exchange of prisoners. Abraham was now bound for an unknown fate with six fellow surgeons and 73 soldiers. The reality of captivity was not long in coming. This Chickamauga-prisoner contingent found its barracks in Atlanta to be an open field enclosed by a 12-foot wooden fence. Abraham later recalled [103] life in the "barracks" provided by Confederate hosts: "while the privates and noncommissioned officers remained there, they were without blankets or overcoats, and spent the cold frosty nights with the earth for a bed and the sky for a blanket." [104]

After arriving in Atlanta, Dr. Landis noted that requests for assistance went largely unheeded by camp officials. At this phase of the war, early October 1863, there had been no penetration by Union troops into the deep South. That premise probably yielded little hope to Northern officers, aware of conditions at Andersonville and Libby Prison that, as prisoners, their troops might receive reasonable treatment. To that unpromising extent, they were not taken by surprise. They would soon learn that Federals were generally viewed as "invaders," not "friends from the North." Having witnessed the plight of Chickamauga's young men abandoned on the battlefield, despite assurances from high-ranking Confederate officers, they were left to worry that the worst lay ahead. And Abraham's assurance to Mary just before the fighting at Chickamauga "that we could take care of ourselves" had not proven to be "the last word."

One discouraging example at Atlanta was the failure of camp authorities to respond to requests for straw for patients lying on the ground. Another omen was the fate of a typhoid-fever patient from Tennessee, who wore a 50-pound ball and chain, day and night, until the day before he died. [105]

The heavy loss of medical personnel at Chickamauga was illustrated by the arrival of 40 additional surgeons captured there, accompanying several hundred soldiers. Two weeks after being captured, all surgeons except those left with sick soldiers departed Atlanta by rail, heading for Richmond. [106] Going in a northerly direction may have seemed encouraging to some, but few among them would have had much hope of gaining freedom.

Not long after leaving Atlanta, Abraham learned more unsavory details of Confederate captivity . . . In one case, a wounded Union soldier was proposed to be hospitalized instead of sending him with the contingent of prisoners to Richmond, and the commandant of the post "refused to receive him into the hospital, but told a lieutenant to knock him in the head." [107]

The journey continued through Hamburg, Branchville, and Columbia, South Carolina; and Salisbury, Raleigh, and Weldon, North Carolina. The prisoners arrived at Richmond, capital of the Confederacy, three weeks after the battle of Chickamauga. [108] Despite abysmal conditions so far, Abraham managed to find the opportunity to enjoy the the landscape and make a critical analysis of the state of Southern farming: "Of the cleared land we saw traveling from Chickamauga to Richmond, a distance of nine hundred miles, I do not think more than one acre in twenty was tilled this year." [109]

Upon arriving in Richmond, the prisoners were taken to a large warehouse on the banks of the James River, bearing the sign "Libby & Son, Ship Chandlers and Grocers." Taking good mental notes, Abraham determined that the brick building comprised three levels and a basement and was "150 feet long and 110 feet wide." He described the top two floors as being separated into "three rooms, and in these six rooms" would be housed more than 1,000 officer prisoners." [110] Recalling stark conditions, he described how his stay of a month and a half in Libby Prison had placed "the pilgrimage" on hold. He described the amenities available to Union officers: "Each room has a sink (toilet), immediately contiguous to it, and the stench coming therefrom is almost unendurable. The windows were all unglazed when we arrived, and at times we suffered terribly from cold." [111]

Conditions for ordinary soldiers were even worse as the officers held on the second floor were able to determine the situation below by communicating through a hole in the floor. The men, deprived of anything to eat for 24 hours, would ask the officers to share their food. Dr. Landis wrote that the officers obliged although they "had little to spare." In response, the commander of Libby Prison, one Captain Turner, "arrested three officers and reprimanded them severely, and ordered that the men should go forty-eight hours longer without food for the crime of talking to the officers." [112]

Abraham and his fellow officers on the second floor of Libby, continued to take note of the inhumane conditions of soldiers below, and the officers were forbidden to converse with them. In the cold of late fall and early winter, they observed that these prisoners often wore a minimum of clothing. On November 20th, Dr. Landis recalled seeing "twenty of our boys at work on the street, cleaning one of the gutters, and nine of them were barefooted." Conditions were so primitive among them, he noted, that "the mere appearance of their faces told us starvation and exposure were closing the work of death . . . America will never know how many of her noble sons perished in the dens of Richmond." [113]

Much as Abraham felt the pain of his less fortunate soldiers in the prison, he also had a capacity to view the monetary deprivations experienced by inmates such as himself who happened to have had currency in their possession upon capture: "The manner in which most of us were swindled out of our money at Richmond makes theft and highway robbery honorable . . . When we left, November 24th, they commenced paying us off in Confederate money." [114]

Toward the end of November, the results of a prisoner exchange brought welcome news for Dr. Landis and a number of his fellow inmates. This momentous news came, ironically, at about the same time that second-floor prisoners had learned that the jailers had taken a positive step for the inmates' benefit. Or could it have been a cynical going-away-present?: "Three days before our release, the officers in charge of Libby were so obliging as to furnish two stoves for each room, but strange to say, we were not furnished with a single stick of wood." [115]

Dr. Landis and a number of his colleagues found freedom on the eve of a historic assault by the 35th Ohio on Missionary Ridge to break the Confederate siege of Chattanooga. The freed prisoners were allowed to go to their homes, and Abraham headed for Millville. The relief he must have felt with the change of scene from Chickamauga and Libby to his hometown would, unfortunately, soon be met with sad news from the battlefield. *The History of Butler County* reports that two young Butler County soldiers of Company C, 35th Ohio, were killed in a heroic Union assault on Missionary Ridge, the day after Abraham's release from Libby Prison. One of the victims was Abraham's cousin. The description was terse: "Private Simon Kumler, 22, was shot through the abdomen and lived 24 hours." His comrade Sergeant Stokes, 21, was "shot through the head and lived but three hours." [116]

Finally, there is a consequence of the Chickamauga campaign that is deserving of special attention in order to bring certain battlefield truths to light, no matter how macabre they may prove to be. This matter was the discovery in mid-December 1863, three months after the bloody conflict, of bodies of Union soldiers, the evacuation of which General Forrest had promised Dr. Landis and his fellow captive-surgeons would be facilitated. Instead, it appears that Bragg's frustrated and ambitious generals were eager to get on with the pursuit of Union forces fleeing to Chattanooga and Forrest proceeded to Lookout Mountain, leaving the task of directing Union surgeons to the lesser authority of Dr. Fluellan, General Bragg's Medical Director. [117] The grisly facts were recorded by the Regiment's historian. [118]

After Abraham's furlough in Millville, he returned to duty in Chattanooga, where he managed to find the bodies of hometown heroes of Missionary Ridge, his cousin (Uncle Jake's son) Simon Kumler, as well as Sergeant Stokes of Butler County. In returning them to their families, Abraham wrote to his Uncle Jake, who had already lost two sons, John at Stones River, and George at Chickamauga:

> Chattanooga Jan 7th 1864
> Yesterday, we took up Simon and William Stokes. They will start home tomorrow morning. It was a sad sight to gaze upon the mangled bodies of the poor fellows, far, far from home & kindred. You have one glorious consolation in your troubles. Your boys bled and died for the best government, the light of Heaven ever shone upon. You need never blush when you acknowledge you are the father of George, John & Simon. [119]

Uncle Jake's fourth son would survive the Civil War.

Kenesaw Mountain

> *Dr. Landis sat propped up against the tree the rest of the night, protecting himself from his fellow doctors with his rifle.*
>
> -- a certain surgeon's vote against amputation after being struck by a cannon ball. [120]

Abraham's return to duty for the Atlanta campaign would be fraught with additional danger that would make him one of the few casualties of the Regiment at Kennesaw Mountain. (The mountain was spelled with two "n's"; the battle with one.) Fresh out of Libby Prison, he found himself taking the familiar route in the direction of Atlanta that he had taken under Confederate guard to his Richmond cell.

As a man whose interests went well beyond Butler County Ohio, Dr. Landis learned that Gen. Ulyssees S. Grant was now in overall command of Union forces and had named Gen. William Tecumseh Sherman to lead three field armies in the drive to Atlanta. It seems likely that tales about the new commander-in-chief after his arrival in the Chattanooga area would have been known to Abraham, because General Grant had acted wisely and swiftly to

35

relieve the sagging morale of Union forces after their defeat at Chickamauga. After all, Grant's leadership had brought relief to the remnants of General Thomas' forces that included such regiments as Abraham's old 35th Ohio.

General Grant, as later recalled in his Memoirs, brought a human touch to the battlefield that would have fitted Abraham's own feelings toward his men in the Regiment. One such personal recollection in Grant's Memoirs, describing his direct contact with a Confederate soldier when he was checking out the frontlines, might have stood out. [121] Grant later wrote that "the most friendly relations seemed to exist between the pickets of the two armies" and noted an occasion during his inspection of the forward positions near Lookout Mountain. The commander-in-chief rode up to a soldier who appeared to be wearing blue and asked "whose Corps he belonged to." The soldier "touched his hat to me" and responded that it was Confederate General Longstreet's. Then, Grant recalled, "I asked him a few questions -- but not with a view of gaining any particular information -- all of which he answered, and I rode off."

The 35th Ohio, its officers and men, took pride in their former commander, General Thomas' assignment to succeed General Rosecrans as head of the Army of the Cumberland. In their "pilgrimage through the Confederacy," they sensed that the Union cause was noteworthy and noble, but they could hardly have matched the brilliantly-worded perspective of their new commander-in-chief, General Grant, as he later wrote in his Memoirs. [122]

As early as February 1864, the 35th Ohio became engaged in fighting south of Chattanooga at Buzzard's Roost, a preliminary engagement for General Sherman's Atlanta Campaign. The commander would wait until May to launch his major drive into the heart of Dixie. This action would involve Dr. Landis' regiment at Tunnel Hill, Rocky Face, Resaca, Pine Mountain, and finally, in late June, Kennesaw Mountain. [123] As it happens, most of the small but important Union successes leading to Kennesaw can now only be discovered by visitors through skillful map reading and a healthy dose of imagination.

The Regiment enjoyed success as a part of Gen. Sherman's flanking maneuvers, pressing the Confederates to the south. As the 35th approached Resaca, a certain Union soldier of German descent, badly wounded at Chickamauga, became a regimental legend by turning up and fighting in hearty form. [124]

At Resaca, "the brigade was under fire of enemy guns, but Confederate forces withdrew apparently according to plan. General Sherman, using successful flanking movements, advanced against General Bragg's forces. The 35th as part of the 3rd Brigade pursued the enemy through Calhoun, Adairsville, and Kingston, occupying positions at Burnt Hickory and then Pumpkin Vine Creek. Following further Confederate withdrawals, the brigade became engaged in an exchange of fire at Pine Mountain and lost heavily. [125] Meanwhile, the 35th Ohio's surgeon Charles Wright resigned June 18, leaving Abraham the only surgeon on the Regiment's roster. [126]

After still another enemy withdrawal, the brigade shifted further south to Kennesaw Mountain June 19th. Subsequently, it "moved about one mile and took a position in front of Kennesaw and intrenched, where the brigade lay under a heavy fire of artillery and sharp skirmishing, which continued daily." [127] Now, it appeared that the enemy was changing tactics by making a stand in place rather than yielding more terrain in the Federal drive toward Atlanta.

The 35th Ohio was called upon to move "to the right" frequently, using the cover of darkness to avoid detection by well-fortified Confederates on top of Kennesaw Mountain. The Regimental historian used colorful detail to describe the developing situation on the ground, as major confrontation became inevitable: "We now occupied a position in front of the central knob of Kenesaw, and another line of works was being thrown up, the Thirty-fifth again held the front line; by morning all things were in readiness for whatever might happen." [128]

These repeated nocturnal shifts to the right brought an increase in hostile fire, but these maneuvers were a vital part of Gen. Sherman's frontal-assault plan for Kenesaw Mountain, as he switched from his earlier tactical style of a series of successful flanking attacks. The 3rd Brigade with the 35th Ohio soon made another shift to the right that would prove fateful for Abraham, who suffered a fractured leg from an enemy cannon ball. [129] The brigade commander described this latest maneuver: "On the night of the 22nd, the brigade moved about one-fourth of a mile to the right and occupied a similar position, but nearer the enemy and more exposed to his fire. . . While occupying this position the men of the brigade were closely confined to their intrenchments on account of the severe shelling of the enemy." [130]

The regimental historian provided his own description of this lateral movement, recording the date as *one-day earlier* than the brigade report. Records of the Union Army, documents now available at the battlefield, and Dr. Landis' personal report are in agreement that the maneuver, and Abraham's wounding occurred June 22. It is unusual that the regimental history failed to report the surgeon's wounding, particularly because the regimental roster lists him as the only officer of the 35th Ohio to be wounded at Kennesaw Mountain. The historian provides colorful detail in describing this action:

> The night of the 21st, we were sent to the right to replace troops withdrawn from the lines; the men carried arms reversed, so as not to "glisten" in the starlight. When near the place ordered, at a halt made, the men changed position of their arms, and in doing so the glint of the barrel, in the starlight, was observed by those on the mountain, and the batteries opened on us at once. [131]

One family account retold by Abraham's grandson, carries a humorous overtone -- what happened after Abraham . . . who knew full well the bloody process of amputation as he was operating on a soldier . . . saw and ignored the bouncing cannonball:

> Unfortunately, the ball hit a tree and glanced off and the next contact was with grandfather's knee. He had very little confidence in the medical profession, being an expert in it himself, and sat propped up against the tree the rest of the night, protecting himself from his fellow doctors with his rifle. [132]

Following the end of the war, an official version of Dr. Landis' wounding appeared in his regimental commander's testimony on the occasion of the surgeon's application for a disability pension: "Dr. Landis was at his tent. Standing at the end when a Cannon ball a round shot fired from a Rebel gun first struck a tree within the breastworks directly opposite Said Landis, and bounded from the tree at about a right angle and Struck the Said Landis on the left leg fracturing the Same." [133]

The Regiment's only assigned surgeon now found himself incapacitated and remained in the battlefield area during the bloody Union assault on Kenesaw Mountain June 27 and a week thereafter until the Brigade was moved on July 3 into camp about 10 miles south of Marietta. Then this unit undertook to garrison the town for a week and a half. [134] Meantime, Dr. Landis was moved to a prominent mansion, "Howell House," [135] in that town, where he would begin his recovery. Although his leg was slow to heal, he was ensconced in this elegant home probably until the 35th Ohio, as part of the 3rd Brigade, would end its garrison duties and leave on July 13.

Abraham's "pilgrimage" and that of his regiment were coming to an end. These words of the regimental historian would have had special meaning for Dr. Landis as he began recuperation in Marietta: "We had been on the move some eighty days; and were nearly all that time under fire, or where the bullets whistled about our ears. We were now not only away from the dull whirr of the shell, and the sharp whiz of the minie ball, but out of hearing and beyond the sound of the cannon's boom." [136]

Then the historian described the calm that set in for the 35th Ohio's young veterans during their own temporary rest and recuperation after an exhausting campaign, in the eerily peaceful atmosphere of Marietta: "Nothing now disturbed nature's quiet save the gentle rustle of leaves, as moved by the pleasant breeze; or perhaps -- a little songster that ventured out after the long and severe cannonading, while we besieged the vastness of Kenesaw Mountain, near by." [137] For Dr. Landis, this respite would have a special meaning too, although his leg wound kept him from enjoying the opulence suddenly available to his comrades-in-arms: "We remained here eight days . . . There was literally nothing for us to do, but to spread our shelter tents, and lounge in the refreshing breeze under the trees . . . We strolled through the fine flower gardens, along pleasant walks and made ourselves at home generally." [138] For the troops, this brief interlude of eight days in Marietta may indeed have reinforced the idea of a "regimental pilgrimage."

Dr. Landis remained in Marietta until he was evacuated to the Chattanooga area where he was mustered out with his regiment in the summer of 1864. He was "discovered" among the recuperating wounded soldiers by his father-in-law, Rev. Daniel C. Kumler, M.D., who, upon learning that Abraham had been wounded, engaged in a search for him. Although the family had not received definitive word for a period of time, during which heavy casualties were reported at Kennesaw Mountain, Rev. Kumler managed to locate Abraham "with maggots in his leg wound" and take him back home to Millville Ohio. [139] The minister-physician-father-in-law had persisted in the face of difficulties before he succeeded in passing through a war zone to accomplish his purpose. Union documents confirm that Rev. Kumler found a way to overcome a prohibition by Gen. Sherman. [140]

One can only speculate about Dr. Landis' thinking as he viewed the end of his own pilgrimage through the Confederacy. He had been one of the Regiment's few officers to fall into the hands of the enemy at Chickamauga and now was its only officer to be wounded at Kenesaw Mountain. In retrospect, he may have been grateful that his wound occurred on June 22nd, considering that, if his regiment had been in an assault role for the storming of Kenesaw instead of its reserve assignment five days later, [141] a large death toll would have faced the 35th. For Dr. Landis, the "pilgrimage" would not again become a reality until after the war, when he might be able to rebuild his life with family in the tranquility of Butler County, Ohio.

It may appear unusual to family members that Dr. Landis' fate at this battle was not mentioned in the official record of the Civil War, *The War of the Rebellion*, or in the acting brigade commander's after-action report written after the Battle of Kenesaw Mountain, or in the history of the regiments in *Ohio in the War*, or even in the history, *The Thirty-Fifth Ohio*. Yet it seems likely that, while unit surgeons and assistant surgeons were commissioned officers equivalent to that of major, they did not enjoy the military persona of troop commanders. In addition, theirs was an easily-forgettable, grisly role, as purveyors of a medical practice that resorted to amputation because the priority of combat crowded out the luxury of diagnosis and long-term care. It is likely that the very presence of knife- and saw-bearing doctors produced major anxiety among the wounded, officers and enlisted men alike. (One is reminded of the jocular explanation of the predicament of regimental surgeon Wright back in Tennessee, when the killing of his horse "had the effect to toss the doctor into the air some distance coming to the ground somewhat like a flying squirrel.")

The 35th Ohio's last combat action occurred shortly before the occupation of Atlanta. Nevertheless, Abraham Landis was mistakenly reported as "killed July 22, 1864 in the Georgia

Campaign" on the casualty sheet of the Military Division of Tennessee. After the war, his military records in the National Archives show that he was awarded a pension of $17 a month for "permanent total disability" based upon wounds received June 22, 1864 at Kennesaw Mountain. The wound had brought an end to Dr. Landis' active role as a regimental surgeon. He doubtless looked with great pride upon the accomplishments of his hometown soldiers, as acknowledged in *The History of Butler County*: "The Thirty-fifth was mustered out in August, 1864, at Chattanooga. In their term of three years of active service, the regiment never turned its back upon the enemy and was never driven from a field." [142] The 35th Regiment's own history, as already noted, added the novel idea that the unit's campaign was indeed "a pilgrimage through the Confederacy."

* * *

The war ended in the spring of 1865. Meanwhile, back in Millville, Abraham Landis and his family began the slow process of returning to a normal life. Mary had held the household together with the aid of elder sisters Katharine and Frances, now 13 and 11. Abraham had to try to rebuild his medical practice and to teach his growing sons Walter, 9; Charles, 6; and John, 4, and, the soon-to-be-born Kenesaw Mountain and, a few years later, Frederick, the techniques of raising pigs and planting crops.

The Civil War would become a constant family reminder of Gallatin, Chickamauga, Libby Prison, and Kenesaw Mountain after a name was selected for their first baby born, a year and a half after the conflict; Dr. Landis' grandson Reed recalled this process as related to him by his father:

> As the story goes, Grandmother wanted to give him a biblical name, and grandfather wanted to name him after Abraham Lincoln. There was an impasse that lasted for months, and according to old Uncle Charlie Kumler, who was grandmother Landis' brother, they called him 'baby' and 'dearie' for too long to satisfy him. He finally suggested: "Why don't you name him after that damned battle we've heard nothing else but since the war?" And that's how Dad became named "Kenesaw Mountain." [143]

3. Young Brothers -- 1870's and 1880's

The truth is, Squire, you are too young to think of
business yet . . . if you can make me a clod hopper of a
short hand writer I'll scratch around and send you
through college or bust my gizzard.
-- Letter to Kenesaw, age 16, from Charles,
college senior, 1883 [1]

America's fraternal strife brought the family closer together
with a zeal and shared sense of purpose to move beyond the cradle
of their universe – Millville, Seven Mile, and Logansport. Family
letters tell about the horse-and-buggy youth of the Landis boys,
reflecting close ties among father, mother, sisters, brothers, uncles,
aunts, and cousins. The Kumler connection lasted longer than the
Landis side because most descendants of great-grandfather
Frederick Landis remained in Pennsylvania in 1816 after his son
Philip Landis moved to "Kumler country" in Ohio. For example,
even after Abraham and Mary's later move to Indiana, ten Kumler
great-uncles and great-aunts continued to be in touch with the
Landis boys into adulthood. [2]

In reflecting upon the strict household regimen laid down
by Abraham and Mary Landis during the early years, a turn-of-the-
century writer reported an opinion apparently disclosed to him by
the older generation, possibly a proud and aging Mary Kumler
Landis: "every fellow round Dr. Landis' house had to work, and he
taught them to make it a pleasure and to take a pride in it. When
you have done that, your boy is educated in practical things. The
itch for work will keep the pot boiling." [3]

The young Landises had an opportunity to learn much of
village and small-town
upbringing from older sisters and brothers. The five boys grew up
under their father's guidance for farm chores to sustain the family at
Millville, Seven Mile and Logansport. An example of teenage
teamwork in Ohio recalled that Charles "prodded the oxen while
Walter held the plow handles." [4]

To the children, Abraham's letters from distant battlefields
reflected not only his personal manner but also the fighting-yet-
wholesome spirit of the 35th Ohio Volunteers. In the shadow of
bloody conflict, he wrote about a love of rural life, the honorable
service of young soldiers, esteem for President Abraham Lincoln,
and a strong sense of patriotism for the nation under God. What

43

may have puzzled them was the idea that his battle-hardened regiment could think of its military campaign as a mere "pilgrimage through the Confederacy." [5]

After Dr. Landis was mustered out with his unit in 1864, he slowly recuperated in Millville and fathered a fourth son, named after his last battle. From then on, little Kenesaw Mountain emerged as a daily reminder of positive things. Looking to the future, Abraham and Mary were prepared to nudge "the Landis boys" to make a solid mark in professional life. In February 1869, the Millville Landises moved to a larger brick house in Seven Mile, a small town that was home to a large number of Mary's kinfolk.

In Mary's mind were the thoughts that one of her sons might become a minister in the Kumler tradition of her grandfather Henry, her father Daniel, and her uncle Henry. For Abraham, it probably was premature to think of careers for Walter, a young teenager, Charles, John, and toddler Ken. It was a given that the elder daughters Kate and Frances, or Frank, in their upper teens, would remain close to the home front and help Mary in raising their brothers.

The 1870's

Abraham resumed his medical practice and in 1871 began making the rounds of population centers with plans to move westward in search of greater opportunity. As related by his grandson Reed Landis: "Grandfather (Abraham) believed that Ohio was pretty well filled up with people, and there wasn't much opportunity there for a pioneer with the spirit that he had. His itinerary included such cities as 'Cleveland, Detroit, Milwaukee, Chicago, St. Louis, Indianapolis, and Logansport,'" and he made a decision that Logansport had the best prospects "because it was at the confluence of the Eel and Wabash rivers, and river traffic, of course, would be the important future form of transportation." [6] A later account demonstrated that such lore could become ever more colorful with each telling. [7]

Upon visiting the new railroad town of Logansport, he wrote to his 17-year-old daughter, indicating that he had already decided to move there. Abraham also offered special thoughts for her and four-year-old Kenesaw: "I have been at work for several days building a wood shed, making fence etc. Tell Kenny I will get him a horn. I asked him when I left home what I should get him. He said I should get him a horn . . . I was glad to hear that you had started to school. You must be a good girl and learn all you can." [8]

In 1872, Abraham and Mary welcomed another child, their last, and named him Frederick after his great-grandfather. In this eventful year, the children's great-uncle Jake Kumler, father of war heroes, George, John and Simon, died. [9] The early 1870's illustrated the ambitions of the Landis girls, Kate attending Otterbein College and Frank teaching in Seven Mile High School while still a student there. Kate's attendance at Otterbein seemed notable because that institution was "the first to allow women to attend college 'without restriction, on the same terms as men.'" An opportunity for Frank or Walter to go to college seemed out of the question because of the family's modest financial resources: Abraham's Civil War pension of $17 per month and small income from his medical practice.

Abraham's visit to the homestead of his father and grandfather near Philadelphia in 1874 would have been of interest to his sons and daughters because he was able to turn back the clock to the Landis connection with General Wayne and the Revolution. [10] They would have been reminded of the Kumlers, who had filtered through the region in the mid-1700's and, in particular, his great-grandfather Jacob Kumler of Captain Addam's militia. [11]

While on this visit, he wrote a letter to Charles, age 15, praising his son for excellence in school and savoring a certain corn meal delicacy. Dr. Landis added perhaps a 19th-century version of today's "sexist remarks" or "man-to-man" comments about the antics of Seven Mile ladies, suggesting the comedic notion that "they ought to elect one of the women" to be mayor: "Charley . . . Your letter of Mar 13 came to hand yesterday. I was sorry you said anything about mush and milk. It made my mouth water. I wish I were at home to see the women go for the rumsellers. Tell them I bid them Godspeed." [12]

Abraham showed his Hickory Flats expertise, focusing on Charles' management of crops, now that Walter was tired of farm work and ready for a change of scene: "Our field has been too hard run to raise tobacco now. I want you to put the 7 acres in corn and I will give you the half. How many boxes of tobacco had you? Did you take care of the tobacco seed? I will write to the bee men tomorrow and order bee hives." [13] Walter, nearly 18, was ready to explore job opportunities, and his forward-looking sisters may have urged him to find a place in Logansport's professional world.

45

While visiting Pennsylvania in 1874, Abraham went to Washington, D.C. to attend the funeral of Massachusetts' anti-slavery senator Charles Sumner in the chamber of the US Senate. [14] His interest in the national political scene on this occasion was fed by the formality of the occasion as he made comparisons of the august building with his village church: "the galeries [sic] will hold at least five times as many as the U B (United Brethren) Church of Seven Mile. . . I was so lucky as to get in at the main entrance facing the Vice Pres, and had a splendid chance to hear and see the services from first to last." [15]

In moving to Logansport in 1875, the family undertook the trip of 150 miles from southwestern Ohio to north central Indiana, as described by Charles, who was 17 at the time. Kenesaw's son reported a few details of this event that happened when his father was eight years old:

> Uncle Charlie tells about the move that the tribe made from Seven Mile Ohio over to Logansport, Indiana . . . They hitched up the team to the farm wagon and loaded what personal property they were going to take and most of the family therein and then tied the buggy on the back of the farm wagon and loaded it. On top of all the load in the buggy, under the buggy cover, was put little Kenny and he held the rooster on his lap.
>
> From Ohio to Logansport, Indiana, of course, the doctor, as head of the family, rode horseback, as he did on all of his calls, carrying his pills, and his saws and his knives and his other medical equipment such as it was, in saddlebags, on Buckskin. [16]

The early days of getting established in the promising town named for Indian Chief Logan were described by Kenesaw to his son: "When the tribe did get to Logansport, they bought a piece of land outside of town on the Eel River as a farmsite and about a half block of city property. Dad's (Kenesaw's) stories about the many hours the whole gang put in out there trying to grow crops and barely getting a livelihood out of what turned out to just an oversized, poor garden was kind of pitiful." [17]

Work on the family farm fell increasingly to the younger boys, Kenny and Fred. Ken in particular recalled that Walter at 19 was no longer available for farm work when he became a reporter on the staff of the hometown *Journal* after graduation from

Logansport High School in 1876. Charles at 17 and John at 15 then carried the main burden on the family farm. Frank and Charles graduated from Logansport High School in 1878. It was apparently decided that Charles ought to go on to college with family funds that could be made available. Later on, financial support would be provided by the Broadway Presbyterian Church of Logansport.

Ken at the age of eight could see hard work on the Landis acres looming large in the future -- he would spend arduous time in dropping corn, weeding gardens, hunting eggs, and during the haying, riding out to the field and back on the load. [18] This prospect led him to engage in some long-term planning, as he would recall many years later: "When I was a youngster . . . scampering around barefoot . . . I had an ambition to become the head of something. I mean the man who was responsible to nothing except his own conscience." [19]

In Ken's desire to become independent, he had already entered the working world at the age of 10 by getting up at 3:30 in the morning, delivering the *Logansport Journal* astride the family horse Buckskin, covering five miles, and earning a dollar and a half each week on a route of 200 customers. He also was able to earn money as a clerk at the neighborhood grocery store. In later years, he recalls "how it taught him the proper value of a dollar." [20]

Charles at 21 entered Wabash College in 1879, and the "senior" farming duties fell to John, age 19. More labor was then picked up by 13-year-old Kenny, as he had foreseen, while Fred, 7, was too small to help much with hoeing, planting and harvesting crops. Ken's hard-working youth remained in his memory for many years: "I did my share -- and it was a substantial share -- in taking care of the 13 acres, including hoeing 8 acres of corn and digging that ditch as my father's colleague in the enterprise of draining the swamp created by construction of the railroad. I do not remember that I particularly liked to get up at 3:30 in the morning." [21]

The boys had ample opportunity to absorb lessons in life from their mother, who, like their father, was a product of rural Ohio's log cabin schools. While Mary struggled with spelling and syntax, she delighted in taking liberties with rules of the English language in signing off her letters. At the beginning of Charles' freshman year at college, she reminded him of the modest circumstances of the family and the importance that Charles, the first boy to go to college, should do well:

47

Now do you realise that you have entered college and that lots of hard study is in store for you but you will have a good time and not disapoint your mother and friends either . . . Charl get a little book and keep an account of your expenditures . . .I hope you can send your washing home . . . from your lovvin moder" [22]

Abraham spread a mixture of good feelings and light banter when, in his late fifties, he wrote letters to Charles at college. Proving that the effects of his war wound fifteen years earlier had not dampened his sense of humor, he wrote an effusive self-appraisal, presuming to elevate his social standing and his Civil War stature to a high level: "Charles . . . I am glad there are a few persons in the World who can appreciate real worth. I always told you I was one of nature's noblemen . . . I finished husking corn several weeks ago. You need have no fears of anything happening me on that hill at Camp Chase [a Logansport landmark]. Jeff Davis tried to dispatch me with a cannon ball and failed." Abraham then shifted to an uncompromising evaluation of the local court, expressing a view about suitable punishment for two murderers on trial in Logansport: "if they are not hanged our court ought to be abolished."

His tendency to glorify the output of the family farm differed sharply from young Ken's dismal assessment of its worth many years later: "Our apples are keeping splendidly, better than any we have ever had. I went after them alone, left home in the morning and had a wagon load picked by night. Could you have done that well?" Abraham couldn't resist twitting his politically-minded college son in the run-up to the Presidential race of 1880: "Do you really expect to make stump speeches next year? Don't let Sam Tilden know it or he will withdraw. I imagine I hear you letting off something like the following: 'Where the American Eagle shall stand with one foot on the South & the other on the North Pole and . . .'" Remaining on the topic of national affairs, he mentioned exciting news about a former US president that would surely put Logansport on the map: "Tomorrow Grant will pass through Logan. He will stop an hour and a half. I wish you could be here. I am going to take (seven-year old) Fred." Finally, Abraham offered a joshing, qualified compliment about the preaching of 30-year-old brother-in-law Reverend Lute Kumler: "Luther preached yesterday at the First Church. Acquitted himself very well. We were all agreeably disappointed." [23]

48

As the Christmas season approached, Mary enclosed her typical, wide-ranging letter to Charles, welcoming him home during college vacation: "Charlie . . . if you get out of clean clothes you better get a shirt or two washed twill be cheaper than to send them home Fred and Ken disputed the other day as to who should sleep with you when you come . . . I am real fat youd be surprised when you see me now take care of yourself and keep well. Ma" [24]

Now it was Kate's turn to save 2 cents postage by including her own breezy chit chat in the same envelope:

> Dear Karl: You old buzzard your letter came all hunky
> Sat night . . . I am making over a dress & consequently
> am in no religious frame of mind. Lord I wish I was
> rich, you bet - I would not make over any dresses . . .
> Why in thunder cant you come home Wednesday night
> before Christmas? Bye bye. Love to the boys [25]

Finally, Charlie's Uncle Lute added his own thoughts to encourage the family's only boy away from home. He spoke of good home cooking . . . "honey and apple butter and saurkraut" . . . and praised Charles for his growing reputation on the college campus. He added the good news from Logansport that Walter was planning "to dine with" President Grant. [26]

On a number of occasions, Kenesaw observed that his lame father was able to function well in everyday life, holding to his habit of extolling the Godly traditions of the Landis and Kumler clans. Recalling stories told to him by his father Kenesaw, Reed concluded that Abraham "was a very devoutly religious man. It was an old style religion . . . he believed that almost anything that was fun was a sin." One of his enjoyable diversions, however, that might not have set well with the United Brethren Church was his habit of following "a big prizefight anyplace in the country" and then taking an early-morning look at the newspaper to learn the results. [27]

Regarding the financial aspects of small-town, country doctors, Kenesaw later recalled that no cash was involved in his father's medical services: often the Landis household would suddenly benefit from "a turkey or a ham or some eggs" that had paid for Abraham's visit to patients in the countryside. Dr. Landis' records after his death revealed "an unpaid balance of accounts in excess of 25 thousand dollars," and his charges of "$2.50 for pre-natal care and delivery of a child" may have entailed a ride on old Buckskin "10 miles from town on a farm." Kenesaw's son Reed concluded that Logansport Landises "were a poor family as far as material things were concerned, but apparently there was a gorgeous relationship between Abraham and Mary . . . and the kids grew up together in a happy sort of way . . . in some strange manner they all got educated." [28]

There seems to be little doubt that Abraham Landis abstained from whiskey, but a staunch paternal stand around the fireside on one occasion inspired a young offspring to ask for clarification. Ken, accompanying his father to a reunion of the 35th Ohio Volunteers, proceeded to probe for possible limitations of his father's piety. When he "got old enough" to join his father in attending Army reunions, Ken observed a great deal of whisky drinking and asked his father about the sinfulness of it all. Since Abraham "always preached what a sin there was involved in the consumption of alcohol," the young lad asked his father to explain how these various viewpoints fit together." Abraham's response was: "an Army reunion would be kind of a poor thing if there wasn't a little bit of alcohol along with it to refresh the memory of those in attendance." [29]

The 1880's

While Abraham's sons were familiar with hard work, they also learned to relax and enjoy their father's sense of humor and their mother's playfully irreverent letters. One son was a romantic. At the age of 19, John, a Logansport High School graduate, embarked upon a business career with the local "Fine Hatter and Men's Furnisher" store, passing his farm chores to Ken at 13. John used the company letterhead in writing to Charles at college, sharing thoughts of the frivolous side of small-town life. In mentioning Charlie's chum Otto Gresham, John wrote at length about romantic notions, Logansport-style. He also spoke of one damsel with whom "he had 4 or 5 mighty good Waltzes" and noted: "She looked as pretty as a peach and I did not beat around the bush any to tell her so. She blushed and thanked me." John cautioned: "she is getting prettier every day and mashes every thing she comes across. She is a regular little flirt and will I fear have her self in a fix some fine day if she dont behave." Then his newsy up-date outlined a plan for romance with the intriguing young lady, mentioning "a whole lot of schemes laid" for "boat-riding some fine night" . . . "I'll make things lively on the Eel." In a practical moment, he wrote of his hope: "to get a good horse . . . blooded . . . for about $125." [30]

For his part, Charles corresponded with a young lady in his sophomore year, who responded by giving him a lesson in protocol. After noting her father's dismay that she had written a letter to Charles, "one that I knew so little about," she remarked: "you will not expect to hear from me again. And I close with many wishes for your success." [31]

In thoughts of a future career, Charles showed no interest in becoming a clergyman, as his mother had wished, but did find meaning in *New Testament* Scripture. [32] As a college sophomore, he had written of the need for man to acknowledge the influence of the Holy Spirit. For a man to reject that influence, he penned: "the heart becomes hardened, the desire for purity is obliterated, the germ of Christian love is enveloped in darkness," leading to "coldness, death and corruption." Whether this flight into such philosophy resulted from his rejection by the lady friend in the letter cited above is not known. Perhaps his thoughts were related to academic pressures or to the possibility that he would have insufficient funds to complete his study at Wabash College: "Today, anticipation of a collegiate education is probably blasted forever," concluding with a romantic notion in poetry: "I knew, I knew it could not last . . .Twas bright, twas heavenly but tis past." [33]

When Ken was 14, his mother took note of his hard work in a letter she wrote to Charles about her own ills and those of other family members (while overstating her age by a year). Mary focused mainly on advice to Charles about practicing thrift and avoiding the hazards of "tramping" from college to Indianapolis for recreation. Frances, or Frank, added a note to reinforce Ma's advice, cautioning that he should temper his expectations with a measure of restraint, adding a prescient thought: "Wait till your running for Congress." [34] Sister Frank again wrote to her college sophomore, suggesting that she was prepared to strike out into the world in a campaign of equal rights for women, mentioning plans for door-to-door salesmanship -- "canvassing," which sometimes yielded a few dollars that helped support Charles' stay at college. [35]

Mary, after failing to hear from Charles during his stay at an uncle's farm near Crawfordsville, dashed off a newsy letter with few capitalizations, commas or periods, and occasional misspellings, together with an update on recent Logansport events and a little gossip. Mother was pleased that Charles took family advice and abandoned his "tramping" plans. [36]

The Landis boys' pioneering, business-oriented sister Frank continued her correspondence with Charles, offering a few items about the Logansport household. She wrote of his friend Orpha Gresham and some ideas of little brother Fred, 8. Finally, she conveyed word that 14-year-old Ken, or "Squire" had set an academic example for brothers Walter, a newspaper reporter, and Charles, a college sophomore, by learning shorthand. [37]

Ken's diligence rubbed off on at least one boyhood chum, who, many years later, remarked how he had become motivated to pursue a career as court reporter: "The most outstanding and fortunate event in my life happened on the evening that I went to the Universalist church and saw Kenny taking down in shorthand the sermon by the minister, this occasion being an incentive to learn the art." [38]

Mary, who had hoped in vain for one of her sons to b
called to the ministry, was a devout member of the United Brethren faith. Accordingly, she would have been happy to read Charles' thoughts from personal philosophical notes citing Biblical verses that included a Psalm written by Moses . . . "Does it not behoove us as rational accountable human beings to improve the talents committed to our conduct so that our knowledge of Him may be enlarged? Teach us to number our days that we may apply our hearts to wisdom." [39]

As Charles was completing his sophomore year, his father wrote about newly-elected President Garfield's dispute, a few weeks before his assassination, with a Republican senator over the appointment of the collector of customs for the port of New York. Then he encouraged Charles with respect to his upcoming political debate. Meanwhile, Abraham continued to practice medicine although his leg remained quite painful, as he monitored work on the farm and kept all members of the family informed about the state of their crops. [40]

At this time, young Ken found work as an usher at the local opera house, "working for free" so he could see the famed minstrels George Primrose and Lew Dockstader. [41] Now 15, he found himself in a struggle with high school algebra and became the first of Abraham and Mary's children to question seriously the importance of a high school diploma. He expressed, however, an interest in gaining a special niche in a future career: an ambition "to become the head of something . . . the man who was responsible to nothing except his own conscience." [42]

Ken's goal of becoming independent began as a clerk with the Pennsylvania Railroad in Logansport. Soon he sought an upgrade of his duties, only to meet frustration from a decisive Superintendent, who informed Ken that his youth and small size wouldn't work in a big man's job: "Not only can't you have a job as brakeman on this railroad, but I'm going to see to it that you don't get a job as a brakeman on any other railroad." [43]

Kate, using a variant of Charles' nickname Gus, wrote to her brother, now a college junior, discussing their father's trip to visit Wabash College a day after his 61st birthday. If Abraham's physical condition proved a worry to the family under such circumstances, there seemed to be no concern about their mother's agility . . . Kate noted that she was sledding down a hill at the age of 49. The letter ended with a practical note: "If you have any dirty duds, you can send them home with your father. Dont send any collars or cuffs." [44]

While Ken continued to be in charge of farming chores, brother John at 21 was improving his status in the world by leaving his job at the men's clothing store to enjoy the greater prestige of working at the local post office. Writing with his new official letterhead and enclosing a photograph of himself, he offered Charles advice on an upcoming debate. Mark the envelope for return "if not called for in five days," and signing with his pen name "Hoof," John offered his older brother some confidential advice: "Keep your pants on when you make your speech. If you do not, you lay yourself liable to fine or imprisonment, or both, for indecent exposure," adding: "Don't strike out from the shoulder unless you stand a good show of killing the judge that intends voting for the other fellow." [45]

In April, Charles received welcome news from the Clerk of the Session of the Broadway Presbyterian Church in Logansport that "eight terms of his scholarship" were approved, effective January 1882, "to permit your fulfilling your collegiate course." [46]

Two months later, John wrote Charles again, rejoicing at a prospect of traveling to the distant western part of the nation. After offering an update on romantic opportunities in Logansport, he looked forward to the enchantment of the mountain atmosphere: "If every thing goes along as it should, I will in the course of three short months be breathing the air of the rockies, as comes from the dells and gorges, rendolent with perfume and loaded with polecat." [47]

Now in his senior year at college, Charles wrote to a hometown damsel who later recalled the happy days spent frivolously together in Logansport: [48] Charles responded with his own recollection: "I have been awfully embarrassed in my time, but once upon a time a pair of young ladies got up a picnic and invited myself and another modest young man and made us furnish the vehicles." [49]

Ken was growing weary of working on the family farm and of the burden of high school algebra. He hoped for more opportunity to ride his bike by letting Fred take over chores on the Landis acres. He would inherit Pa's horse Buckskin to lighten the load of early morning newspaper delivery and would be in a position to prepare for a career. Soon after his 16th birthday, he got in touch with Charles and sought advice on a serious job opportunity: "I just got a letter from a Mr. Miller of Richmond saying that he would give me an office position at Indianapolis at 40 dollars a month. Dont you think I had better accept it. Ask Pa what he thinks about it. You must talk it up big to him." [50]

Ken had dropped out of high school, but his new ambitions were not fully satisfying to his mother who reported to Charles that the family's teenage shorthand enthusiast was on his way to become a railroad clerk in the State Capital, 70 miles from home: "We are all well but feel very lonely this morning. Ken went to Indianapolis yesterday at 1.40. He is to work with Mr. Green. Train Master I think is his Office. I had a letter this morning but he did not tell me how to direct the little fellow. I am afraid he will be so homesick." Mary also offered a melange of local news and expressed joy about friends who were embracing religion. This permitted her again to raise the subject of the importance of having another preacher in the family. Showing steady improvement in sentence structure in her letter to Charles, who was nearing college graduation, she explained: "I should be so glad to hear of you and the Sen Class coming in to the church. You know I have wanted you to be a minister. It seems to me that the mantle of Uncl Henry Kumler and Father should fall on some of the grandsons." [51]

Walter, the oldest brother approaching 27, chose to broaden his experience by leaving his job as reporter for the *Logansport*

Journal in order to pursue unspecified opportunity in Mexico. He beckoned Charles to come home for a family reunion before his south-of-the-border expedition would get underway: "That will be my last Sunday in this part of the world vineyard for probably some time to come -- probably for years, and it is thought proper to get the gang together once more before I go." Walt closed out his letter with an item of possible mutual interest . . . "Was out to see the Black Crook stage show. Lots of leg, but the show dont amount to much." [52]

A few months later, Charles facing graduation, learned that Ken's position in Indianapolis did not work out. He then offered his ambitious young brother encouragement and a plan for higher education, despite Ken's rejection of a high school curriculum because it featured algebra. The older brother was persistent in offering Ken guidance on how best to prepare himself for a professional career, and his credibility was strong because he was also ambitious and committed to a four-year liberal arts education: "The truth of the business is, Squire, you are too young to think of business yet. If I can make any sort of a play and make enough money in the course of two years to give me hope for the succeeding years, I propose that you shall take a course here in Wabash . . . I'll scratch around and send you through college or bust my gizzard." [53]

Ken chose not to take Charles up on his generous offer and decided for the time being to seek work on his own initiative. With an eye for the future, Ken decided to take a job as night guard in the county jail and began to expand his horizons there. Kenesaw's son later reported: "While he was sitting there in the county jail, he began studying law and various other subjects. This created in him an extreme appetite for advancement that he really possessed from the beginning, and he decided to become a court reporter. Dad developed a shorthand almost of his own." [54]

Walter sent a letter to Charles from Chihuahua, Mexico,[55] telling about his expedition. He included comrades on his venture and planned to enter a part of the country which few Americans had visited: "The object of the expedition will be business, experience, pleasure and profit. Our direction will be southwest in Mexico's finest cattle and mineral country, where five Americans have penetrated." Walter showed he was not looking for a vacation by describing his preparation for the journey: "Before coming down here we bought a Winchester carbine (1000 yds), colt revolver 44 cal, and 500 rounds of ammunition, also saddles, bridles, spurs and blankets, so you see we are equipped for the expedition."

Walt was optimistic about the credentials of "a promising Mexican politico" he had chanced to meet: "He will probably be the next Governor of the State of Chihuahua and states, if he is, he would use his influence to get half the people of the United States down into Mexico. If he is elected, this will be peace for Americans during his administration." Walter spoke of conditions in the region and a bountiful yield of fruit trees: "In the evening the zephyrs are waffled in from the mountains and blankets are comfortable. Figs, apricots, and all the small fruits are ripe and peaches will soon be in the market."

The traveling Landis wrote seriously of his interest in visiting other foreign countries, particularly in the Latin World. At the same time, he also pointedly foresaw Charles' future success in national politics: "Spanish, French and Italian languages are very closely related, and if one is learned, the others are picked up almost immediately. When you go to Congress, I will rely on your political influence to secure me the Spanish mission." [a remarkable suggestion of events that would unfold at the end of the century.] Walter offered a fraternal assessment of the high quality of Chihuahua's damsels, suggesting that he was prepared to leave the Logansport social whirl behind in order to study in Mexico something more frivolous than business prospects: "There are some of the most beautiful women here I ever saw with tresses the color of the raven and eyes black as midnight. The complexion of most of them are beautiful but marred by the use of powder which is used to excess. The damsels of quality are mostly non-coinhabitable. They are not allowed to see the boys except in the presence of their mothers."

Finally, Walter wrote of Charles' impending graduation from college, expressing regret that he would be unable to be present. He offered his congratulations and expressed confidence in his younger brother's successful career: "I have no doubts nor fears for your future. I wish that mine was as fully assured as yours. There is too much room at the top of the ladder for you with your abilities to remain long on the lower rounds." Then, in closing this long and informative letter, Walter showed a good measure of confidence and respect in his younger brother's skills as he asked

Charles to help him take care of a social item back home: "Should Miss Freeman be present at the commencement hop, give her my love and dance a waltz with her for me."

Meanwhile, back in Indiana, Ken decided to accept Charles' invitation to come to the Wabash College campus where the senior collegiate pondered the wisdom of academics for his ambitious 16-year-old brother. The occasion did not lead Ken to accept Charles' generous offer, and he chose to go his own way as a court reporter. At least, Charles' support and ideas acquainted Ken with the possibility of pursuing additional education at some time in the future.

Mary wrote to Charles with an update on Logansport happenings, noting her concern about Walter's involvement in Mexico and also her husband's physical condition. In her letter, she displayed marked improvement in penmanship and articulation of thoughts: "Am so sorry Pa cant be present but he says he cant afford it and he is not a bit well He has had a pain in his side had to be blistered and is just able to be about again   He works too hard. I feel bad about it every day   He is 62 yrs old and ought not be obliged to work so hard" [56]

Kate, almost 32, weighed in with thoughts about Charles' upcoming graduation. She showed a preference in writing about social aspects of life rather than serious matters preferred by sister Fran, who spent many days going door-to-door to make money for Charles' incidental expenses at college. Kate spoke of her regret at not being able to celebrate with him on the occasion of graduation: "Am so busy that I can scarcely look up. I will not be present at your windup. Mom will go down Sunday morning and remain over until after the Ball. It is quite a disappointment, But you know its hard for Ma & me both to be away at once. Golly I would have enjoyed that dance." She ended the letter, with words about an elegant new garment she was making: "Aunt Lill (wife of "Uncle Lute," Mary's brother) and Doll (a relative) are both here helping me on my new green silk." [57]

Ken learned about two technologies that would enhance his life -- a contrivance to replace Buckskin as a means of delivering the local newspaper, and a device to speed up his stenographic skill. Mary was pleased for Ken's work prospects and forwarded the good news to Charles, who had finished college and moved to Jeffersonville, Indiana, for a summer job: "Ken is verry happy has a

Bycicle and Mr Watts is going to Chicago to get him a type writer so I suppose he will keep him." [58]

Frank at the age of 29 continued contact with Charles, citing Ken's new bicycle as a reminder of gender discrimination in Logansport and the wider world: "Thats another pleasure that I, being a woman, am debarred from. 'To ride, or not to ride' I wonder if that wouldn't be one of the questions for me to decide in case you men should suddenly decide she might have a say." Finally, Frank was looking forward to her teaching in Logansport High School when she mentioned: "I have been trying to get a focus on 'readin, writin -- & cipherin' to say nothing of the other ills I will have to contend with soon." [59]

Entering the picture of brother-to-brother communication was Fred, just turned 11, who sent a postcard to Charles: "Dear Gus Why dont you write to me . . . The street Cars are making money, they are going to run four cars   write soon   Yours   Fred" [60]

Mary wrote to Charles, again expressing concern about Walter's whereabouts in Mexico: "Walt I suppose is on another Wild Goose chase   how I do wish he was in a christian land, engaged in some righteous pursuit. ta ta   Ma" [61] Walter returned from his "expedition" without finding a future life there and moved from the *Logansport Journal* to become a reporter for a number of northern Indiana newspapers and a correspondent for the Cincinnati *Commercial Tribune*. Charles followed Walter into editing at the *Logansport Journal*, quickly became city editor and, after three more years, rose to editor-in-chief. In February 1887, Charles combined resources with a young journalist Victor Ricketts and obtained a loan to buy the *Delphi Journal* in neighboring Carroll county. In October, he married Cora Chaffin of Cincinnati, a young lady who had written him thoughtful letters.

Ken's self-taught shorthand skill and his use of the typewriter were important to his budding career in court reporting. Reed described the typewriter, with wooden parts, that was twice as large as modern typewriters and came in a large case. With this machine, Reed wrote, "Ken developed such a speed and such a line of gab that he talked himself into an assignment as a court reporter for the Circuit Court operating out of Indianapolis." [62]

It was in his later teenage years that Ken's introduction to a new sport would result in a small calamity. During a sandlot game of "shinny," he was umpiring behind the plate with responsibility for the infield:

> There apparently was somebody on base, first base, and
> at bat, and there was a hit, and Dad swung around to see
> the play at second base, and, as he did, his body turned
> but his foot didn't and he broke his hip. He was
> incarcerated in a plaster cast for a number of months. [63]

Kenesaw's work for the Circuit Court took him into cases in the countryside around Indianapolis. The circumstances of administering justice were strictly on wheels -- "the judge and his clerks and his bailiff and the lawyers . . . in wagons, carts, and buggies and on horseback." During his work with the Indianapolis Circuit Court, Ken had an opportunity to make the acquaintance of a federal judge for the Indiana district, Walter Q. Gresham, the father of Otto Gresham and close friend of Ken's brother Charles.

Reed recorded facts his father mentioned that conveyed an impression that judicial personnel were mediocre in their work. This led Ken to conclude that "if people of that caliber, character, and level of education could be professional in the law, he could too. So he went back to Indianapolis, quit his job, and went to Cincinnati where he entered Cincinnati Law School." [64]

In the meantime, John progressed through various positions in Logansport – from salesman in haberdashery and staff worker at the local Post Office to medical student in his father's tradition. Charles was editor of the *Delphi Journal* and a civic activist, calling for improvements in the town of 2,000 people, and supporting the building of waterworks and sidewalks. Fred, like Squire, dropped out of high school and, at 17, also cast his eye toward the field of law. Ken, after years as a court reporter, was studying to become the first attorney in the family after several generations of farmers, ministers, bishops, and physicians.

Abraham, seeking advice as to a legal career for Kenesaw, wrote to Judge Gresham, serving on the Chicago Circuit Court. The Judge, who, like Abraham, had served in different field armies during General Sherman's Atlanta Campaign, replied: [65]

> Chicago, June 14, 1888
>
> A. H. Landis Esq.
> My dear Sir:
> I am just in receipt of your kind letter of yesterday. . .
> Although I have not the pleasure of knowing you

personally, I know your sons, and, believing in the law of heredity, I think I know what manner of man you are. I need not say that I esteem the young men highly. Yours truly,

W.Q.Gresham [66]

Judge Gresham remembered Kenesaw from their former duties in Indianapolis and recalled his son Otto's friendship with Charles. In 1890, the Judge arranged for Kenesaw to switch for his second year from the Cincinnati School of Law to the Union College of Law in Chicago, later a part of Northwestern University. Here, Ken questioned the power wielded by social fraternities and decided to create a competitive group, "the barbarians." Such was the turmoil resulting from actions of "the barbarians" that scheduled classes were suspended: "For one week . . . they held a rump convention and refused to permit school to be conducted until they got full rights to participate in the election of class officers." The result was action by the faculty to reform the election process and, following these changes, Kenesaw's "barbarians" were successful in winning class offices. Kenesaw, Reed noted, was later named valedictorian and graduated with a Bachelor of Laws degree in 1891. [67]

Author visiting the 18th-century villages of the great-great grandfathers of
the Landis boys: Henrich Landes of Heppenheim/Alzey northwest of
Heidelberg, Germany and John Kumler of Maisprach near Basel,
Switzerland.　　　Photos by Donna B. Landis in 2001.

The Landes home in Heppenheim, the oldest house in the village, pictured
here in 2001, was owned by the Count of Shoenborn by legacy from the
family von Heppenheim of Saal/Danube river, in 1680. The Kumler home
in Maisprach was not identified.

Memorial marker for the Landis boys' great-grandfather Frederick Landis,
who died in 1803, and his fellow Mennonists. It is located at 109 Pikeland
Road, Charlestown Township, Chester County Pennsylvania.
Photo by Susanna Marion Baum.

Home and barn of the Landis boys' grandfather Philip Landis c.1816-1838
on Busenbark Road near Hamilton, Ohio in this photo c. 1950. A portion
of this boyhood home of Abraham H. Landis, who planted the still-
standing, sycamore tree at the left, remains on the property of Philip's
descendants, the William King family.

Dr. Abraham H. Landis   Mary Kumler Landis

Photos of Abraham and Mary Landis taken following their marriage in 1850 and the home and birthplace of their first six children in Millville near Hamilton, Ohio. The seventh, Frederick, was born in nearby Seven Mile. Recent photo by Donna B. Landis.

Dr. Abraham H. Landis, assistant surgeon of the 35th Ohio Volunteers, upon his enlistment at the age of 41 in 1862.

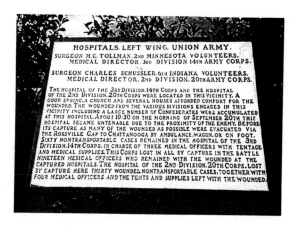

HOSPITALS. LEFT WING. UNION ARMY.
SURGEON M.C. TOLLMAN. 2ND MINNESOTA VOLUNTEERS.
MEDICAL DIRECTOR 3RD DIVISION 14TH ARMY CORPS.

SURGEON CHARLES SCHUSSLER. 61TH INDIANA VOLUNTEERS.
MEDICAL DIRECTOR. 2ND DIVISION. 20TH ARMY CORPS.

THE HOSPITAL OF THE 3RD DIVISION. 14TH CORPS AND THE HOSPITAL
OF THE 2ND DIVISION. 20TH CORPS WERE LOCATED IN THIS VICINITY. A
GOOD SPRING. A CHURCH AND SEVERAL HOUSES AFFORDED COMFORT FOR THE
WOUNDED. THE WOUNDED FROM THE VARIOUS DIVISIONS ENGAGED IN THIS
VICINITY INCLUDING A LARGE NUMBER OF CONFEDERATES WERE ACCUMULATED
AT THIS HOSPITAL. ABOUT 10:30 ON THE MORNING OF SEPTEMBER 20TH THIS
HOSPITAL BECAME UNTENABLE DUE TO THE PROXIMITY OF THE ENEMY. BEFORE
ITS CAPTURE AS MANY OF THE WOUNDED AS POSSIBLE WERE EVACUATED VIA
THE ROSSVILLE GAP TO CHATTANOOGA BY AMBULANCE. WAGON. OR ON FOOT.
SIXTY NONTRANSPORTABLE CASES REMAINED IN THE HOSPITAL OF THE 3RD
DIVISION. 14TH CORPS. IN CHARGE OF THREE MEDICAL OFFICERS WITH TENTAGE
AND MEDICAL SUPPLIES. THIS CORPS LOST IN ALL BY CAPTURE IN THE BATTLE
NINETEEN MEDICAL OFFICERS WHO REMAINED WITH THE WOUNDED AT THE
CAPTURED HOSPITALS. THE HOSPITAL OF THE 2ND DIVISION. 20TH CORPS. LOST
BY CAPTURE HERE THIRTY WOUNDED. NONTRANSPORTABLE CASES. TOGETHER WITH
FOUR MEDICAL OFFICERS AND THE TENTS AND SUPPLIES LEFT WITH THE WOUNDED.

Site of Union Field Hospital where Dr. A. H. Landis, fellow surgeons, and wounded men were captured at Chickamauga. Landis reported that Gen. Forrest's troops withdrew on September 20, 1863 and returned the next day to capture the hospital. The prisoners were taken to Libby Prison in Richmond. Photo by Donna B. Landis, June 1987.

Reunion of the 35th Ohio Volunteer Infantry Regiment in Hamilton, Ohio. Abraham H. Landis is 2nd reclining figure from the left. Photo circa 1890.

The Landis boys probably on the occasion of their grandfather Kumler's funeral November 8 1881. Left to right: Frederick, Kenesaw, John, Charles, and Walter.   Reprinted in *Logansport Journal* in 1902.

The Landis family probably on the occasion of Charles' wedding to Cora Chaffin in Logansport October 26, 1887. Left to right: front: Kenesaw, Frederick; Middle: Mary Kumler, Charles, Abraham; rear: Walter, Frank, John, and Kate.

4. Journalism, Diplomacy, Politics -- 1890's

It is seldom that five brothers attain eminence by reason of their own exertions and ability. Yet this is the record of the Landis boys.

-- *Washington Times*, 1902 [1]

The final decade of the 19th-century would prove to be one of expanding opportunity for the five brothers, leading them away from their hometown. The family was a congenial sort, with parental authority guiding the boys toward public careers. They in turn gained moral support from each other, father, mother, and sisters. Kate and Frank, while always seeking a measure of independence "in a man's world," generally helped family efforts from the fireside. Abraham and Mary would note that the five boys kept close track of one another's accomplishments in a friendly rivalry.

Abraham in his seventies and Mary in her sixties watched the professional paths of Walter, Charles, and John, in their 30's, and Kenesaw Mountain in his late-20's reach well beyond Logansport. Frederick, in his early 20's, followed a familiar pattern of getting his start in the working world of Logansport. Ken and Fred had chosen not to finish high school, but certainly not for lack of ambition.

Walter would proceed as a self-made man, a confirmed bachelor, who thrived on travel to faraway places. With no college education and no known connections, he moved on from small-town reporter to Indianapolis correspondent for the *Cincinnati Commercial Tribune*.

Like Walter, Charles was on the move in the newspaper business, a new and exciting pursuit for Landises and Kumlers. Walt had taken note of Charles' political promise in a letter from Mexico to his younger brother upon his graduation from Wabash College. Charles had already built upon his liberal arts education at college with a keen interest in journalism and a bent for politics. After working in his hometown for several years, he left the *Logansport Journal* to gain regional prominence as editor and publisher of the *Delphi Journal* for nine years. At the age of 33, Charles made a run for Congress in 1892, losing in the convention by a single vote, before going on to win in 1896 at the convention and the election.

61

The three younger brothers, including two high-school dropouts, would go on to benefit from a solid dose of academics -- John in Medicine, and Ken and Fred in Law at a time when a high school diploma was not required.

John hankered for the stability of a physician's practice and college-level teaching in a large city. He earned a degree at the Ohio Medical College in 1890 and started his practice in Cincinnati. He also broke new ground for the family by becoming a professor, with the specialty of pathology at the city's Presbyterian Memorial College.

Ken, the family's first lawyer, would also be first in getting acquainted with the nation's capital, which had enamored Abraham in his visit there for Senator Sumner's funeral in 1874. Ken was on an independent track moving "to become the head of something . . . responsible to nothing except his own conscience." [2] Abraham, an old-fashioned Republican, savored Ken's work under a "Greshamite Republican," albeit in the Cabinet of a Democratic President.

Fred followed Ken's interest in the legal profession by "reading law" in the office of Logansport attorneys, completing law school, and becoming the first Landis attorney to practice in the family's hometown. Fred wrote a philosophical piece about Logansport, going back to Indian days. With a natural gift for oratory and politics, he would soon be drawn to participate as Charles' aide, when he was elected in 1896.

Walter's work in journalism in Cincinnati, recalled years later by a colleague, reflected a talent for innovation and a strong will to compete with others of his profession in getting the story first. In one instance, Walter and a fellow journalist named "Gid" from another Cincinnati newspaper shared a nighttime office where a tip came in on the identity of a witness to a possible murder. Walt picked up the tip and quickly left the office. After Gid arrived and received the tip, he also left the office and succeeded in locating the prospective witness, a lady, who allegedly was well-informed with facts in the case. The account continued, noting that the lady would have nothing to say to him about the case because she had just been sworn to secrecy by Detective Kratz of Cincinnati, "who got her story and declared she must not breathe a word of it to another soul." When she mentioned that the detective was still in the vicinity, the account went on: "Gid demanded to be led to him. She complied, and there sat said Kratz, who proved to be none other than Landis!" It was said that, later on Walt shared his knowledge with friendly rival Gid, but the incident remained a part of journalistic lore in the offices, where from then on, "the fraternity knew him as 'Detective Kratz.'" [3]

Ken, noting that Walter and John had left Logansport for big cities, Indianapolis and Cincinnati, felt a similar urge and decided to hang out his shingle in Chicago. He and a college chum, a fellow "barbarian" from Northwestern Law School, Frank Lowden, opened their offices in Chicago in the Monadnock Building in September 1891, and, "to impress potential clients, they went out and together signed some notes and bought an old second-hand library." [4]

While Ken was establishing his law practice, Charles started was making waves in Indiana politics. From his influential perch as editor of the well-known *Delphi Journal*,[5] he threw his hat in the ring as a Republican contender for nomination to the US Congress in 1892 at the age of 34 and lost by one vote.

At the same time, Ken, got started in the practice of law, but, after a year and a half, left his fledgling office to accept an unusual opportunity . . . he would become private secretary to President Grover Cleveland's Secretary of State. His employer, Judge Walter Q. Gresham of the Circuit Court in Chicago remembered Ken from his early years as a court reporter and later from appearances in the Judge's courtroom and, finally, as the father of Charles' boyhood chum, Otto. This prominent turn in Kenesaw's career followed Abraham Landis' first contact with Judge Gresham the year before Squire entered law school.

For nearly a hundred years, references have asserted that a wartime bond existed between the Judge and Dr. Landis, citing General Gresham's position as "Landis' commanding officer in the Civil War" in General William T. Sherman's Army. Such a personal relationship had allegedly influenced Gresham in naming Kenesaw as his private secretary in 1893. The proposition, however, is fiction.

Gresham entered the Union Army from his native state of Indiana, while Landis joined a unit of Ohio. Gresham never was a commander of Dr. Landis' unit, the 35th Ohio Volunteer Infantry Regiment. Information in Steele's *American Campaigns* [6] confirms that they were assigned to separate field armies under General Sherman in the Atlanta Campaign, which began May 5, 1864.

Official War Department documents reflect Gresham's assignment to 17th Corps, Army of the Tennessee while Landis' 35th Ohio Regiment belonged to 14th Corps, Army of the Cumberland. It would be extraordinary indeed for Gresham, a general officer in one field army (24,465 men) to be closely associated during a major military campaign with an assistant regimental surgeon in another field army (60,773 men). [7] Confirmation that Gen. Gresham and Dr. Landis had never met also appeared in correspondence between them long after the war. [8] Ties between their respective children proved to be the only connective tissue between Abraham Landis and Walter Gresham.

Although Kenesaw at 26 had been a lawyer less than two years, it was sufficient time for him to demonstrate his legal skills to Judge Gresham. Kenesaw's son Reed noted that: "in the early days of Father's legal career, his practice before Judge Gresham made quite an impression upon the old man." [9] One journalist quoted the Judge's assessment of Kenesaw: "I have met lawyers of all ages. Any man who has been a judge for a number of years necessarily comes in contact with them. Landis is the brightest and soundest lawyer for his years and the quickest lawyer for his years and a man who has the most common sense for his years that I have ever known.[10]

Kenesaw's appointment in March 1893 provided a salary of "two thousand dollars per annum."[11] News of his new position in Washington traveled fast to the folks in Logansport, to Walter in Indianapolis, Charles in Delphi, John in Cincinnati, and Fred at the University of Michigan.   Words of advice came to Ken from another farm boy of southwestern Ohio, a young Republican who would soon become Senator Albert J. Beveridge of Indiana: "Keep your eye open old man . . . With your mind, your temperament & your opportunity, you are on the threshold of a great career. Don't for one instant give up, get blue etc." [12]

Abraham, although enfeebled at 72, had the opportunity to savor Kenesaw's early success. And Mary would have been pleased that her fourth son, still in his twenties, was undertaking such important work. Yet, perhaps in the hope that he would not let the prestige of Washington "go to his head," she kept him informed about the family, Logansport crime, and local gossip while offering homemakers' advice to President Cleveland's wife:

My dear Ken

. . . I am so glad you remember to write me . . . the only bit of news that I know is that two thugs held up the Broadway M. E. preacher last night but did not get much . . . one landed in jail . . . the other had a gun and by shooting got away . . . We are expecting aunt Lizie the last of this week she comes to Elkart to preside at a missionary meeting . . . I must tell you a bit of gossip and mums the word tis said that Clintie Stevens who was bereaved last sumer is paying His court to Miss Hattie Coleman now did you ever . . . you said if I wanted anything just to let you know . . . there is just one thing I wish to have done . . . I would like to have my pension increased . . . Pa is as usual . . . we are glad he is as well as he is . . . Write us every week deare for we are allways glad to hear from you   How are the Cleavelands . . . now love to you and all the Cabinet . . . tell Mrs. Cleaveland that this is a good time to air Her blankets and sun the feather beds . . . set the early chervil.

M. K. Landis [13]

A week later, Mary wrote again, teasing about Otto, the Judge's son and poking fun at President Cleveland. She offered a mother's advice on how to save the Government's money, implying an early suspicion of corruption in the nation's capital: "Ken keep a tight hold of the pucker string of that little sack of gold that is still in the treasury don't let those thiefs get there cloven fingers on it or it will all be gobbled up." Finally, she complimented Ken and added an important development: "I am saving a hen to cook when you come home." [14] Kate joined in with a chatty note, and Mary offered homespun advice for the President: "Tell Grover that we think you need a week anyhow. One day wont be a circumstance." [15]

Mary wrote again after learning that Ken had traveled to New York. She teased about the President, talked about the pressing of pants, and discussed local happenings: "we had a gass explosion last night . . . we felt the shock very plainly it blew out two sides of a two story house burn 4 peopl pretty badly . . . now Ta Ta your Mothr" [16]

Kate took advantage of the same mailing and slipped in her own note, tweaking Ken on his failure to visit Logansport. She spoke of their father's regimental reunion, which deteriorating

65

health kept him from attending it. Finally, Kate prescribed medicine that would help President Cleaveland after "bumping his head." [17]

Mary's artful irreverence toward the President and First Lady, echoed by Kate, reflected Abraham's habit of poking holes in pretense and hypocrisy. Ken followed suit in jesting about the narrowly-focused bureaucrats in the Nation's capital.

John, who had been Charles' pen-pal in earlier years, now kept in touch with him at nearby Delphi. He also reported hometown events to Ken, recalling his questionable standing with a former Sunday School teacher. His postscript took note of John's keen appreciation for Logansport's pulchritude. [18]

In 1893, Frederick was on track to follow Ken into the legal profession, and in his spare time published a treatise on Logansport: "It was with a graceful gesture that the Creator wrought the Wabash Valley, fitting it for the maintenance, comfort and happiness of the thousands later to thrive upon its hillsides and in its meadows." With regard to the considerable merits of the city, the principal city of Cass County, Frederick mentioned: "Agriculture and manufacturing, the two mammoth pillars of prosperity, are here happily blended and promote the welfare of 18,000 residents." [19]

In the decade of the 1890's, it had become quite clear that none of the Landis boys would gratify their mother's hope of carrying on the clerical tradition of her father as minister and her uncle and grandfather as bishops of the United Brethren Church. By now, Walter had cut his teeth in journalism beyond the environs of Logansport. Charles also displayed an interest in journalism in Delphi, seasoned with political ambition. John was pursuing the medical field in the pattern of his father. Kenesaw kept his eyes on the future, seeking responsibility and independent action. Frederick possessed a literary interest as well as a taste for politics. All found commitment in fields distinct from the clergy; all reflected an independent streak; Mary's hope for a preacher to emerge was destined to wither away.

As for Kenesaw's first days on the job in Washington, the fledgling diplomat attracted attention in Washington because of his "lack of convention . . . outspoken manner . . . new ways . . . original style of address . . . and wit." His appearance and actions may have raised the question: "Was this hayseed-appearing young fellow from Indiana a joker or a young man of great depth?" [20] One writer, Alfred Lewis, described how the Hoosier farm boy brought contrived mischief to bear against the tradition of the nation's bureaucrats. It was as if Mr. Lewis was hiding behind the curtains of Foggy Bottom when he detailed his narrative about Ken's antics. [21] He knote that the bureaucrats, intent on keeping their jobs, were unable to "pierce the Landisian mask, and discover the humor it concealed." They felt that "dire were his attributes" and so . . . "dreadful might be his deeds."

The writer, who was Washington correspondent for the *Chicago Times*, described the teamwork in which Kenesaw enlisted Secretary Gresham to break down the crustiness of State Department staffers. The two conspired, he noted, to apply humor of the outlands to the culture of the Capital with telling results and added: "Secretary Gresham loved Landis and trusted him as a father loves and trusts a favorite son. Also, the latter was wholly at home with his chief."

Kenesaw became deeply involved in the case of an American passenger ship seized by Spain in the early 1890's. During Judge Gresham's final illness, Ken intervened when Acting Secretary of State Uhl signed a message to pressure the Spanish government to apologize for its action, which occurred outside Cuban territorial waters. Kenesaw showed the telegram to Judge Gresham in order to gain his signature instead of Uhl's, and Gresham complied. As a result, Gresham gained widespread credit, which angered President Cleveland. At first, Kenesaw's position seemed to be endangered, but the President softened his attitude and offered Gresham's young aide the post of Minister to Venezuela. [22]

In his mid-twenties, Kenesaw staked out a knack for getting into hot water, when some charged him with releasing information to newspapers without authority. When the President again appeared ready to fire Kenesaw, he changed his mind upon learning that Judge Gresham would resign "if Landis was ousted." [23]

Many aspects of Kenesaw's unique assignment were reported in colorful detail by his son, who took detailed notes of his father's recollections. On one occasion, a revolution in Central America resulted in unsuccessful insurgents taking refuge on a British ship. The established government claimed an infringement of its sovereignty, and Ken, upon receiving the coded message after midnight, recognized the problem as a violation of the Monroe Doctrine. He wakened Secretary Gresham, who dressed and rode in Ken's carriage to the British Embassy. Upon being informed "with the utmost courtesy but firmness" that the Ambassador, Lord Pauncefote, was in bed, Judge Gresham responded to the footman: "I understand that the Ambassador was asleep -- will you please go up and tell him that the Secretary of State is awake and in his drawing room." After Lord Pauncefote arrived in bathrobe and slippers, Judge Gresham told him about the report and that he believed it to be untrue, saying: "I know and you know that Great Britain would not violate the Monroe Doctrine" and added: "Mr. Ambassador, I must be able to tell the President and the Cabinet at 10 o'clock this morning that it is not true. Good evening, Mr. Ambassador." Judge Gresham and Ken went home while the British ambassador telegraphed the ship with instructions to return the revolutionists to shore. When this was accomplished, Lord Pauncefote visited Judge Gresham and reported: "of course, these people were on shore and were not on the cruiser." International incident averted! [24]

Secretary Gresham's condition soon worsened, and Kenesaw later noted that President Cleveland chose to invite Gresham's private secretary, instead of the Assistant Secretary of State, to sit in Cabinet meetings in place of Gresham. On one such occasion recalled by Kenesaw and told by Reed, domestic politics became a factor involving the President with a railroad strike, and President Cleveland asked Kenesaw to bring him a copy of an important message during the Pullman railroad strike in Chicago. Kenesaw observed that the President, in summer garb, was "very heavy and grossly fat and . . . hanging over the sides of his chair." Kenesaw remembered that the President, who was conversing with the commanding general stationed with the Army District in Chicago via a telegraph operator, threatened to fire the General if he did not protect US Mail deliveries there. President Cleveland took this action because the General, who was a possible candidate for President against Mr. Cleveland, had failed to use military force against the strikers who were interrupting the mail. [25]

Kenesaw's impressions of Walter Gresham seemed to have made a lasting reminder about his philosophy of the "open-door policy," as Landis would recall some years later: "The thing that most impressed me about Mr. Gresham was that when he went to the office of Secretary of State he made the doorman sit over in the far corner, threw open the doors to the public and ran a democratic, open house." [26]

Ken's work in Washington had not been the only source of satisfaction shared by Abraham and Mary Landis because Charles, over at the *Delphi Journal*, was making political waves. Having lost by one vote in 1892, Charles made another try for the Republican nomination to the House of Representatives in 1894. After barely losing two years earlier, Charles learned first-hand about political games that were played in those years: his opponent's friends took the train cars designated to carry Charles' supporters to the district nominating convention, the forerunner of today's primary system. Because of the "train-stealing" episode, "a historical event in Indiana political history," the convention was beset with confusion, and a second convention was called. Meanwhile, Charles withdrew, showing that he was, at the age of 35, a "good Republican" by placing the good of the party above his own political interests. [27]

John continued his young career as a physician in Cincinnati. Now came the occasion for a second Landis boy to take a bride as John married Daisy Graham in his adopted city in 1894. For the time being, Ken remained an eligible bachelor in the nation's capital, in the words of his future son Reed: "This young, dashing lawyer had a team of very fine horses, a very lovely carriage, and he dressed of course in the height of style, including a black opera cape with a white satin lining, carried an ebony stick with a gold head and wore a top hat whenever the occasion permitted." In the social whirl, the private secretary of the Secretary of State enjoyed "exalted stature," as did his bride, whose sister was wife of the Comptroller of the Currency. [28]

The year 1895 brought the passing of Ken's mentor and friend, Judge Gresham, bringing to an end Kenesaw's assignment in Washington. During this year Ken courted and wed young debutante Winifred Reed of Ottawa, Illinois on July 25th. The newlyweds settled in Chicago, and Ken reestablished his law practice, barely begun before his assignment in Washington.

On a number of occasions, Ken would be asked about his politics. "You are a democrat, are you not?" Ken replied: "No, since I severed connections with the Cleveland administration, I've been a life-long republican." [29] Ken's son Reed recalled his father's account of getting his practice of law underway again by getting to be known in the social arena. For example, he finagled an election

69

into the most select club in Chicago in those days, the Calumet Club, and borrowed enough money to pay his initiation fee. [30]

Meanwhile, Frederick followed the course taken by his brother in Chicago, setting his sights on the legal profession. After "reading law" in the Logansport offices of McConnell and Jenkins, he proceeded to graduate from the University of Michigan Law School and, in 1895 to establish a law practice in his hometown.

As for Dr. John, here was the young man, who had sent humor-laden notes to his older brother Charles in college, turning his entertainment skills to younger brother Kenesaw. John wrote that Ken, the Chicago lawyer, had reason to be envious of one Cincinnati physician who "evinced a measure of cultural superiority" in this letter: "My Dear Squire . . . You can prepare to take on a pea green hue. I have realized your great ambition and that too without wishing for it - or trying to 'cultivate' it. I have a slight attack of gout, and feel that my claim to respectability and gentle birth are receiving powerful backing." Assuming a serious mood, John congratulated his younger brother for being named to serve as assistant US District Attorney for the Beef Trust case, adding: "We were all very much pleased to learn of the appointment and if you get as much glory out of it as we anticipate, you will be wearing a crown in a few months." [31]

In 1896, Charles resumed his political ambitions from his vantage point as editor of the *Delphi Journal*, and again entered the race for Congress. On his third try, the family's first politician gained the nomination in the Republican Convention of the new Ninth District at Crawfordsville, Indiana. Charles was praised even by a Democratic newspaper from his congressional district as "about as good a man as the enemy could have picked out." [32]

A Crawfordsville newspaper's editorialist with Democratic party leanings rambled in considering Charles' qualifications and finally concluded with a favorable slant: "C. B. Landis is of that republican school who believe that democracy (Democratic party) represents treason, riot and Rebellion . . . Friends he has by the score in all parties. No one who knows him fails to respect him and to esteem him highly." [33] Yet another newspaper editor rejoiced in Charles' nomination, while expressing an overriding caveat: "As a member of the craft desiring to see a fellow-member successful and honored, the *Crescent* extends to Mr. Chas. B. Landis its congratulations and best wishes, but as an exponent of democracy fighting republicanism, it can offer the brilliant Delphian nothing but the marble heart. [34]

The momentous nature of this small-town convention was assured by the presence of its chairman, the distinguished soldier, statesman, diplomat, politician and novelist General Lew Wallace. His remarks stirred the delegates, as he delivered partisan criticism of Grover Cleveland's current administration (1893-1897); praised that of Cleveland's predecessor, Benjamin Harrison (1889-1893); and then declared support for the Republican candidate for President in 1896, William McKinley.

At last, with his first political victory, Charles could begin to bask in editorial commentary spawned by grassroots press coverage: "Men stood up on their seats and whooped lustily swinging their hats and canes. It was with difficulty that order was restored . . . There were then loud calls from all over the hall for Mr. Landis and he came forward amid wild cheers and applause. When the tumult had subsided, Gen. Wallace introduced Mr. Landis." [35]

With his nomination, Charles now could enjoy the early fruits of his college ambitions. He could rejoice at the fulfillment of Walter's prediction at the time of Charles'graduation that the younger brother would become a Congressman. Favorable, fiercely-partisan treatment began to appear in the local newspaper: "Charles B. Landis is one of the most brilliant young men who ever went out as a graduate of Wabash College. It is predicted by his friends, and he has hosts of them, that he will yet make his mark in the field of statesmanship. He is young, industrious, well posed, finely equipped, has an engaging presence, of commanding talents, and an eloquent public speaker." This newspaper, exhibiting collegial respect and affection for Charles, fellow journalist and friend from Delphi, endorsed his acceptance speech and commended him in forceful terms:

> He should not have said less. He ought not to have said more. It
> could not have been better . . . In him the people – the laboring
> man, the old soldier, the merchant, the mechanic, the
> manufacturer, the high, the low, the rich, the poor, everybody –
> will have a friend. Charles B. Landis is the man of the hour. [36]

At this time in Chicago, Squire took a step forward in his legal career by being elected to the city's Bar Association for the admission fee of ten dollars. [37] After getting settled in law practice in Chicago, he received a letter from his friend Albert J. Beveridge,

71

who chastised him with "Why in the blazes have you not let me know," and regretted not finding "pleasure to have spent an hour or two lying about old times." Beveridge noted that Ken's brother Charles was needlessly worried about his recent political campaign and praised Charles by quoting "Polonius' advice to Laertes in Shakespeare's Hamlet:" "What friends thou hast, and their adoption tried, Grapple them to thy soul with hooks of steel." [38]

Meanwhile, in Cincinnati, John received an appointment to serve in the Cincinnati Health Department. He was living up to the opinion of Ken that, among the Landis boys, John soon carried an honor as "the most useful one in the family because he heals the sick." [39]

John wrote to Ken from Cincinnati during Charles' campaign, offering an assessment of the presidential campaign climate in his locale: "Things down here are red hot politically. Unless all signs fail Ohio will go 250,000 for McKinley." Ken, at this time, seemed to be distressed, perhaps because his cousin Willie Kumler died in the summer of 1896. In addition, the boys' father was in his final illness in November. John wrote to Ken with a helpful suggestion: "Can't you make an excuse for a trip down here and give me a better chance to size you up than can be done by mail. If you have, what I think you have from your description (and which by the way is a good one) you can be relieved but I want to look you over before I suggest a line of treatment for some Chicago doctor to carry out." [40]

Abraham's death came November 9, 1896, and family members assembled at Logansport for the funeral of their patriarch. Dr. Landis had become aware of the positive directions his sons were taking in the current decade. Walter had advanced his journalistic career to Indianapolis and Cincinnati. Charles' achieved editorial and political success. Abraham knew of John's promising medical practice in Cincinnati and of Ken's return from Washington to the practice of law in Chicago. He was aware of Frederick's law degree and early legal career in Logansport. Finally, he appreciated that daughters Kate and Frank had not only been looking after the boys' interests but were also making strides in trying to succeed in "a man's world."

Charles as an energetic and forceful congressman quickly became known as a leader of his Party. He wasted no time in attracting public attention as the United States faced major problems of change, foreign and domestic. With oratorical skills, he spoke of politics and patriotism, and newspapers echoed his sentiments with eloquence and style. His prescriptions carried a dash of optimism, drawing upon his interest in the stature of the United States in the modern world.

A few weeks after Abraham's death, Kenesaw's uncle, the preacher who had served at his recent marriage, also became concerned about Ken's health and wrote: "My Dear Nephew I have wanted to write you ever since Aunt Susie saw you at your Father's funeral . . . Rather than be a wreck physically the balance of your life, turn yourself out to pasture, kick up your heels like a colt and canter around at your pleasure." [41]

Whatever ailed Kenesaw apparently subsided as the months passed, when he consolidated his legal work in Chicago. He became a corporate lawyer and, in the words of his son . . . "a general counsel for the Northwestern Railroad, the Grand Trunk Railroad, and the Chicago and Eastern Illinois Railroad and also had an interesting number of other clients and quite a few personal injury suits." [42]

In 1897 Fred went to Washington, D.C. and became private secretary to brother Charles in the House of Representatives and, at the same time, did newspaper work and became a correspondent for several journals. After a few years, he returned to his Logansport law practice. When Charles asked him: "When will you return to Washington?" Fred replied: "not until I come back as a member of Congress." [43]

Charles' bent for reform stemmed from his conviction that party politics provided the impetus for efficient democracy. Two Indiana newspapers covered Representative Landis' maiden speech, which he delivered only a few weeks after the convening of the 55th Congress. In them, Charles proceeded to expose Democrats who, he asserted, only pretended to reform Civil Service in recent years. He sought with success to make his case by charging that political excesses in the past threatened the basis of our two-party system. Charles strongly defended party workers: "I believe in political parties . . . the standing armies of peace in a republican form of government." [44] He was challenged by Representative Johnson, a fellow Indiana Republican, to state precisely what corrective actions he envisioned should be taken. The query evoked Charles' strong support of Civil Service employees' freedom to express an active interest in politics and would require their participation in the voting process to show their "good faith." Republicans under Cleveland, Charles argued, had been fraudulently discharged, although they should have been protected: "Continue to discredit party politics, continue to sneer at men who take an interest in party organization, and the time will come when congressional elections will be but rich men's reunions, and both branches of our national Congress nothing less than bankers' clubs." His style was clearly partisan as he declared: "A patriot . . . it was he who carried a gun in time of war and took an active interest in party politics in time of peace." [45]

Newspapers in small towns reflected partisan support for Charles, following his maiden speech: "Mr.Landis is not opposed to the civil service law, but in the manner in which it has been enforced and its subjection to abuse." [46] Another Indiana newspaper drew a comparison between two Hoosier congressmen, Charles Landis and Henry Johnson, both Republicans, who were on opposite ends of the Civil Service debate. Johnson's response that Charles' questioning was "like a pigmy's challenge to a giant" enlivened the exchange on the House floor., [47]

In the aftermath of Charles' first speech, one of the leading Indiana newspapers offered a sampling of editorial opinion from a variety of newspapers and press organs. [48] The *Indianapolis Journal* prefaced its listing by being impressed: "Just think of it! An Indianan makes a hit in Washington that holds the whole flock of statesmen spellbound, and that too, without Hoosier dialect!" The article proceeded with the *Chicago Record* that noted: "It contained more fun and fervor than any that has been heard in the house since the Hon. Robert G. Cousins of Iowa burst his bonds two years ago and made a reputation in fifteen minutes." The *Chicago Post* declared: ". . . no new member has made such an impression upon the House since William Jennings Bryan's initial appearance five years ago . . . Landis was a complete surprise." The *Washington Post* reported: "In two minutes he was being listened to with attention, in ten minutes he had a throng around him, in half an hour he had captured the House and for the rest of the hour and a half he was on the floor, he carried everything before him." The *Associated Press* dispatch noted, with regard to the debate between the two Indiana Republicans: "Mr. Johnson became involved in a controversy with his colleague, Mr. Landis, and during the crossfiring the galleries became so boisterous in their approval of the latter that the Chair was obliged to suspend the debate and admonish the spectators that such demonstrations must cease."

Chicago's leading newspaper took careful note of Representative Landis' first speech on the floor of the House. From Charles' neighboring state of Illinois, this editorial gave a glowing interpretation of his first performance in Washington: "When interrupted by questions, Mr. Landis did not rant, tear his hair, and decline to be interrupted but gave a respectful hearing to each query and in reply never raised his voice above the tone which marked his utterances throughout his speech." [49]

Charles gained wide attention of House members by citing specific, colorful examples of overzealous actions in discharging Republican employees during the administration of the previous president, Grover Cleveland. His maiden speech during the first session of his freshman term in the House in 1898 attracted the attention of colleagues on both sides of the aisle and of the leadership of the body itself: "Speaker Reed, who had surrendered the chair to Mr. Hopkins of Illinois, lingered a moment to see how the Indiana man began his maiden effort. He stayed five minutes and then he leaned his huge bulk against the clerk's desk and remained there an hour and three-quarters. His face throughout wore an expression of cherubic pleasure and satisfaction." [50] While another paper from the same city, the *Dayton Press*, heralded Charles' description of a party worker as "a patriot" in contrast with "the Mugwump . . . political nondescript," the Washington correspondent for the St. Louis *Globe Democrat* found Charles' maiden performance as rich in political meaning: "On Wednesday he obtained the floor and delivered a speech which made him one of the famous members of the Fifty-fifth Congress." [51]

Charles spoke in partisan political terms, bringing into question not only activities of President Grover Cleveland's Democratic Administration during 1893 to 1897 but also the supervisory functions exercised by members of the House Committee on Civil Service, present at this session: "Take the gentlemen who are responsible for the perversion and prostitution of the principle of civil service reform. They have played the political guerrilla in every campaign since 1880, and you know it just as well as I." [52]

According to the press, Charles displayed a fiery independence and staunch partisanship. His arguments in the House of Representatives were free of guile, brooking no middle ground. Members easily chose to agree or disagree, but even those in opposition often took note of his oratorical skills and genial manner. A month after Charles' first speech, a leading Philadelphia paper, declaring its reliance on "Gossip from Washington," took issue with his position, while acknowledging that Charles "is a man of the people in a higher sense than is implied in long hair or an absence of socks . . . His manner is frank and earnest, and a naturally impetuous energy is held in check by a disposition to think and reason and to be right." [53]

At a time when pressure groups were not remotely a part of the political scene, Landis carried his partisan banner during election years from town to town, Chautauqua-style, lauding Republicans on a variety of topics familiar to voters. His welcome was warm, according to many news accounts, suggesting a high level of grassroots interest in Washington affairs.

A few weeks after his first appearance on the floor of Congress, Charles delivered a speech in Boston on the occasion of Abraham Lincoln's birthday. The partisan flavor of his remarks on the Chautauqua circuit was unmistakable. He wasted no time in using his oratorical skills to criticize colleagues as a part of what we would call today, "the Washington establishment." In contrast with today's reticence to invoke Biblical passages on the House floor, the *Washington Post* reported that Charles did it with some effect: "The House of Representatives . . . would have been a great place for Jeremiah to distribute his lamentations. Never since the flood has there assembled in so small a space so many Pharisees and false prophets." In this *Washington Post* article, Charles spoke of economic problems such as workers' strikes resulting from sharp competition between cotton mills of New England and of the South. He offered a critique of the South's concentration on the cotton crop and other limitations of Southern agriculture in contrast with diversified farming in the North and in such states as Indiana. Southern congressmen, he charged, failed to find a vision for a "New South" featuring diversity and industry. He added sharp criticism of the "free silver" sentiments of Senate Democrats, focusing upon the Resolution of "Weeping Willow" Teller. This gentleman, according to Charles, led Senate and House Democratic members to disregard the prevailing sentiment of the electorate, which had decisively voted in the last election for "sound-money" Republicans.[54]

On the campaign trail, Charles' renomination for a second term seemed to be a given as he was greeted by supporters as "man of the hour" in Kokomo, where the District Convention was held in March, 1898. [55] Back on the floor of Congress a few months later, Charles turned in the direction of waste and privileges enjoyed by Executive agencies and Congress. According to the *Washington Post*, he took to task numerous officials of the Administration who enjoyed at taxpayer expense the privilege of having horse-drawn carriages at their disposal. His amendment to limit this convenience prevailed in the House vote following his description of how existing rules were abused: "This is the way it has been done by the heads of other departments for years – laborers have been suddenly metamorphosed into coachmen, have been equipped with silk hats and with boots, and have been placed up on the box where they have done service in approved fashion for subordinate officials." [56]

With the conclusion of the Spanish-American War in the late summer of 1898, President McKinley appointed Walter to establish the Postal Service in the newly-acquired territory of Puerto Rico and to become the first U. S. Postmaster there. Charles' early prominence in House Republican politics would seem to have played a role in opening this assignment to the candidacy of one Cincinnati journalist, who happened to be his older brother.

Mary, now a widow, kept in touch with Ken and Fred, who were carrying forward their father's tradition by attending the late surgeon's regimental reunion in Butler County Ohio in 1898: "My Dear Sonbeams . . . I write to send greeting to the 35th . . . wish I could be there but tis to hot . . . remember me to all the old friends . . . Walt expects to sail Oct 2d (to Puerto Rico on his new assignment) we will expect you soon to spend a vacation love to all" [57]

Typical of Chautauqua meetings like the earlier one in Boston was Charles' appearance in a town in Indiana in 1898, where he faced a friendly, partisan audience. Charles reviewed the growth of prosperity under President McKinley, called for annexation of territories after the war with Spain, and praised the heroism of "the Blue and Gray . . . now camping in the same tent." The local newspaper wrote of Charles' speech: "there seemed to be

77

no end to his eloquence, and toward the end, when he would fain have stopped, voices on all sides urged him to continue." [58]

During this period, Walter kept Kenesaw well posted about his experience during the first few weeks of America's occupation of territory gained after the war with Spain. There he made an early, optimistic appraisal of entreprenurial prospects on the island and reported meeting a solid acquaintance of his younger brother: "This is a great country and I think a few dollars planted here will turn itself over a good many times. The first American I ran across here was your friend Major Stewart and we have become fast friends. He evidently thinks you are a great man and has promised to see that I don't get the worst of it at any turn of the road." [59]

As he neared the end of his first term in Congress, Charles was already his party's chief spokesman on important legislation. A country editor "turned-statesman," Charles prospered in both vocations, showing no concern that press reports might offend some constituency. A small-town newspaper noted that, in his first term in Washington, he was "the most talked-about, wrote about and heard about man in Congress." [60]

Meanwhile, Kenesaw was about to become a regular part of his adopted city by joining the Chicago Club as a Resident Member for the sum of $226.67. [61]

The genesis of America's overseas commitment of military forces had emerged in 1898 with "the Spanish war." Its consequences led to freedom for Cuba and territorial status for Puerto Rico and the Philippines. Charles quickly became an earnest and influential spokesman for Presidents McKinley and Roosevelt's position favoring an expanded US role in the world. Meanwhile, US Army troops stationed in the Philippine Islands became a major point of party controversy in Congress.

Charles' active support of such a role highlighted the policy division between the political parties, with most Republicans favoring American involvement in foreign lands and the majority of Democrats opposing it. Charles' presentations in Congress at the start of his second term, drew widespread coverage in newspapers of the era, when, to the dismay and delight of many, he sharply challenged his veteran Republican colleague, Representative Johnson from Indiana, with whom he had recently jousted over the matter of Civil Service reform. (Imagine "such discourtesy" being shown by Members today!)

Charles sharply contrasted Mr. Johnson's "pessimism" with the positive contributions of such famous Hoosiers as Henry S. Lane and Oliver P. Morton, former governors and senators; and Schuyler Colfax, vice president under President US Grant: "I want it known in this hall, throughout the country and by Indiana's sons and daughters everywhere that, in this day and hour in this crisis, the voice of that magnificent commonwealth is not the voice of pessimism and detraction, but [applause], as in the days of Lane and Morton, and Colfax . . . the voice of inspiring hope and stalwart patriotism." [Applause]   In the following excerpts of the same article, he continued his critique, charging that Johnson preferred to spend time on the New Jersey seashore instead of staying in touch with his constituents. Charles' continuing personal criticism of his colleague, a practice that would be likely to be rejected today as undignified, seemed to find favor among many Members, both Republican and Democratic.   He also argued with these words that the United States should remain in the Philippines and oppose guerrilla leader Aguinaldo: "Liberty does not speak through the voice of Aguinaldo any more than the people of Indiana speak through the voice of the distinguished gentleman (Representative Johnson) from the Sixth district of that State." [Renewed applause on the Republican side] [62]

The above article and others to follow described the personality and character of Charles B. Landis -- a sense of humor, a love of speechmaking, a marked ability to gain and hold his audience, a commitment to causes, and a fighting instinct to settle scores with protagonists like the controversial Johnson.   In reviewing such newspapers, a reader today may choose to agree or disagree with Landis, support or reject his positions, and find his style congenial or perhaps "inappropriate."   However, one conclusion seems clear: his message was consistent, and Republicans and Democrats alike believed that the congressman from Delphi, Indiana enlivened the proceedings of the House with humor, patriotic appeals, and candor.

Press reports kept the issue of "American troops overseas" on the front pages for several years, and a few editors began to hint that Charles' prospects for higher office were on the rise. One such editorial stated: "He is the man for the emergency and generally equal to it. He is the coming man.   Many names have been mentioned in connection with the next Governorship, but none that would be more popular or give more general satisfaction that Charles B. Landis . . ." [63] Another editorial stated: "Mr. Landis eloquently and vigorously repelled the innuendoes and slanderous vituperation hurled against the President by the gentleman from the Sixth district." [64] Still another reported: "We hold that Mr. Landis represents the people of Indiana, and that Mr. Johnson does not." [65] This newspaper acknowledged that one of the reasons "for giving so much space to this episode" was that it "makes what the newspaper man calls 'good stuff.'"

The combat between two Republican congressmen Johnson and Landis became a spectacle for the enjoyment of both sides of the House of Representatives and the regional newspapers. As reported by one Indiana editorial: "Representative C. B. Landis removed some more of Henry U. Johnson's cuticle this afternoon. The operation was of brief duration, but interesting while it lasted. It brought members running in from the cloak rooms and filled the galleries as by magic." [66]

In a manner much more personal and combative than recent Congressional debates, the Landis-Johnson contest, between two Indiana Republicans, continued to dominate affairs of the House of Representatives. With their last blood-letting over Civil Service reform less than a month old, the strife erupted again on precisely the same topic -- Representative Johnson sharply criticized President McKinley on the issue of American troops in the Philippines, and Congressman Landis responded with increasing fervor to defend the President. Members, far from showing concern for a possible blow to the dignity of the House, seemed to relish the fray, and journalists were alert to this renewed opportunity to inform the public with specific details: "I deny that the distinguished gentleman from Indiana (Mr. Johnson) is the personification of the people of the district which he pretends to represent. But I do sanction the statement that it is not possible to hold him responsible for anything he says while he fills the office of representative on this floor." [Laughter] [67]

The scene shifts to Puerto Rico where Walter, after a few months on the job, wrote Kenesaw, expressing enthusiasm about his assignment: "I am getting along first class. Have good health and am saving some money. If the government appreciates my services and insists on keeping me here I shall probably stay several years, taking time occasionally to get home to visit." [68]

As the American economy grew during President McKinley's first administration (1897-1900), the issue of controlling business conglomerates intensified as a keen national issue. Charles, in his second term in Congress, delivered speeches in his home state on the growing problem of trusts and their negative effect upon small businesses: "There must be some remedy adopted and at once, for the people are becoming alarmed, and I am being told the trusts are being discussed in all parts of the country." [69] Several articles dealt with Landis' analysis of the problem, bringing it down to the local level . . . "These vast combinations are throwing men out of work and are closing factories. The wire nail factory at Crawfordsville has been closed up and dismantled . . ." and he expressed the conviction that the Republican Party would pursue a more prudent course in controlling trusts: "I am confident that the Republican party will deal with this great issue to the satisfaction of the people . . . I have been thinking of a graduated tax on products . . . Then restrictions might be put on capital stock." [70]

Charles made a dire prediction about the economic consequences of the uncontrolled power of corporations. An editorial appearing in the same newspaper, however, with an obvious concern for the national interest that rises above politics, looked into the future with an uncanny appraisal that would seem to foretell the disastrous stock market crash of 1929, three decades later: "It is imperative that something be done not only because [trusts] are injurious to trade and to the people generally at present, but because the damage will be infinitely worse when the crash that is almost sure to follow the top-heavy institutions . . . There will be a reckoning – a great, grand reckoning." [71]

Walter underscored his enthusiasm for the Puerto Rican assignment and introduced Ken to high-quality cigars, a pleasure that would last him a lifetime. The fraternal tie between these brothers was reaching a new level: "A few days ago I sent you a box of Porto Rican cigars. If they don't taste good at first, lay them aside for a time to dry out, and let me know how you like them. This is a cigar that costs three cents apiece." [72]

In his first term, Charles had emphasized the importance of correcting abuses in the Civil Service system, with many illustrations of the Cleveland Administration's disregard for the idea of merit. His prominence had led to speculation that he might be a candidate for governor of Indiana. The following account raised a question as to consequences of the position he had taken on that matter. It argued, with a view toward the 1900 elections, that Charles as governor of Indiana would be a spoilsman, subverting the issue of merit in Civil Service:

> Mr. Landis may win in spite of his position on this question; but we are inclined to think that he will find that he has seriously mistaken the public sentiment prevailing in Indiana. It is not difficult to make "brilliant" assaults in Congress on the merit system. But the last word is with the people. [73]

As circumstances unfolded, Charles was not a candidate for governor in 1900, suggesting that the case made in the above editorial may have been decisive in his decision not to enter the state-wide campaign.

Back in Logansport, as the century came to a close, youngest brother Frederick was becoming known in Logansport for his literary talents, as noted in the local press, which acknowledged an editorial he had just published regarding the recent national election: "His writings are vivid, his eloquence blended with sense, his metaphors striking, his diction pure and clear. There is a freshness about his writing that partakes of the bee upon the clover, the sunshine on the lattice, the dew upon the daisy." [74]

As Christmas 1899 approached, Ken's mother again wrote to her young Chicago attorney son, asking about the health of her grandson: "Your letter came duly to hand it was a sweet letter and I was so glad to hear from you I have wondered about Reed hope he is better let us hear come down soon wish the children could come with you." [75] Walter corresponded with Kenesaw again, this time with word about presents for Ken and Winifred's children, Susanne and Reed. He confirmed his unbounded admiration for getting a good deal on high-caliber cigars: "I send by this mail a cigar box containing a fan of the bull fight variety for the girl & a cap for the boy. I am not much of a hand for selecting Christmas presents but hang these on the tree & let them throw sticks at them. It is quiet here except that we are having one h--l of a time getting the Christmas mail off." [76]

The Landis boys at the time of their father's funeral in November 1896. From left to right: Frederick, Kenesaw, John, Charles, and Walter.

Home of Dr. Abraham H. Landis and his family in Logansport; built in 1875 and razed in 1952.

Reaction to Charles' speech on the floor of the House of Representatives during his first term 1897-1898. [Marconi a few years earlier devised a practical method of signaling as a forerunner of radio.]

Syndicated cartoon by John T. McCutcheon.

Charles running for reelection c. 1900: his campaign pin [TFL file] and his
presence on the train (at left) with President McKinley (center).

Unidentified newspaper print.

A GROUP OF BROTHERS.

5. Jurisprudence, Literature, Medicine -- 1900's and 1910's

The 1900's

> *"The Landis boys" have gained a reputation in this State as good politicians and fine fellows, and it would not be surprising if one of the name should one day be in the Governor's chair.*
>
> -- "A Group of Brothers," *Indianapolis News*, 1900. [1]

In the early 1900's, America under the leadership of William McKinley and Theodore Roosevelt was sensing its own destiny through industrial growth and a deepening involvement abroad. Meanwhile, Mary Kumler Landis, with daughters Kate and Frank, offered moral support as the "Landis boys of Logansport" found success well beyond their hometown.

After the turn of the century, Abraham and Mary's five sons attained national prominence. Walter continued to serve as US Postmaster of Puerto Rico . . . Charles was an advocate of government reform and a military presence in the Philippines . . . John became a pioneering Health Officer of Cincinnati . . . Ken, a successful corporation attorney in Chicago, served as a dynamic Federal judge . . . and Frederick, alongside Charles in Congress, became an author and joined Theodore Roosevelt's Progressive "Bull Moose" Movement. So much for the Landis boys of Millville, Seven Mile, and Logansport.

Charles and Kenesaw preserved their collegial ties long after Ken's teenage queries for career advice from his older brother at college. Their continuing dialogue appeared in now-Congressman Charles' letter to the up-and-coming Chicago lawyer. On this occasion, Charles expressed his support for Ken and inferred his own possible candidacy for a higher position: "You have certainly had remarkable success in your work . . . Cannot you cut down that office expense? . . . Should I ever become governor of Indiana we may, by reason of that prominence, be able to attract enough attention that would be advantageous to us." [2]

Charles' first-term effort to uphold high governmental standards through Civil Service reform surfaced again in his second term when he opposed the seating of a polygamist, Brigham Roberts of Utah. This forerunner of today's concerns about "separation of church and state" drew wide attention in 1900 because of its moral and constitutional dimensions. Charles was the chief Republican spokesman to deny admission to this congressman-elect with several wives. At the outset of the Session, Charles found "a layman's argument" to make his case against "the backbone of the Mormon contention" that the Utah enabling act did not apply to polygamous marriages like Roberts' that occurred before its enactment. Charles turned to the dictionary definition of marriage as *a condition* rather than *a mere ceremony*, averting complicated legal judgements: "I am not a lawyer, but in the light of the debate on the Utah enabling act, it is clear to me that the purpose of Congress was to eradicate the practice of polygamy in the State and put the ban of the law on the further continuance of polygamous conditions." [3]

While most members of the House agreed with Charles in his debate with Representative Charles E. Littlefield of Maine, one New York newspaper editorial favored the seating of Mr. Roberts. It noted that Charles "got a whirlwind of applause" but argued that *The Constitution* would suffer from Charles' appeal to popular sentiments. Speaking of Mr. Littlefield and a like-minded colleague, the editorial stated: "They fear that the imposition of unconstitutional requirements in the case of a polygamist may open the way to obstruct the admission of some Representative-elect to whom there is no more valid objection than that the majority in Congress do not like him." [4]

Press coverage of the Roberts hearings expressed positive and negative views of Charles' arguments, including this balanced assessment from Detroit: "Littlefield did not believe the House ought to exclude Roberts; he argued his right to a seat on presentation of proper credentials . . . He spoke as a lawyer. Landis responded . . . The rebuke, said he, is not to any one man; it is to Utah, the state he charged with entering the Union by stealth, by conspiracy, with a lie on her lips. She had guaranteed that polygamy did not exist; and Roberts had proved how false was the claim . . . Landis spoke to the hearts of his hearers; Littlefield has spoken to their intellect." [5]

A St. Louis newspaper defended Charles against criticism that he had used false information in his case against polygamy, noting that the Indiana congressman's main source was the 1890 manifesto of Mormon Church President Woodruff. It also cited a political lesson to be learned if Roberts would be seated and then expelled: "That would have shown to the people of Utah that . . . there would not have been five votes against his expulsion except by Representatives of adjoining states who are looking to the Mormon vote in future elections." [6] Charles' speech against polygamy was celebrated by a city's religious newspaper that provided copies free of charge. A prominent Christian newspaper stated: "Landis' speech is worthy of world-wide circulation." [7]

Meanwhile, back in Logansport, Frederick was building a legal practice, proving to be "very effective before a jury, and as a political debater having few equals in the State." Although not yet a political candidate, he took part in Republican "love feasts," and "was in great demand . . . his speeches, bristling with epigrams, were a hit at every meeting." [8]

As Congress addressed the question of whether corporations should be controlled, Charles took a prominent position. An Indiana newspaper criticized his statements, asserting that Republicans had sided with "the trusts" in 1896: "The people are at last becoming aroused and are in special earnest against all sorts of trusts and monopolies. They cannot be fooled all the time, although Congressman Landis evidently thinks so." [9]

In response, Charles delivered a Chautauqua speech on Washington's birthday in Noblesville, Indiana, drawing a vivid picture of progress made by the McKinley Administration in the wake of Grover Cleveland's last term. He noted that the Democratic platform of 1892 had promised to prosecute trusts to the extent of the law and added: "On that platform the Democrats elected a president and both branches of Congress, and I defy any man to point to a single attempt either to enforce the law or to add to the effectiveness of the law." [10]

This question was but a sample of the rivalry between parties at the turn of the last century and was an issue in the national campaign for the reelection of President McKinley and was important in Charles' race in Indiana. After he was renominated for a 3rd term in 1900, Charles argued that Republican rule under President McKinley had brought the country out of the depression of the Grover Cleveland era, 1893-1896. He illustrated this point by comparing the Republican and Democratic platforms, noting that progress lay in the change from Democratic free trade to Republican protectionism.

Having touted economic recovery in this speech, Charles sketched party differences in foreign policy relating to the recent victory over Spain, and the prospect of American assistance in the development of newly-independent Cuba, Puerto Rico and the Philippines. Democrats had charged Republicans with "imperialism" as Charles argued for a new US presence overseas. He supported Republican action to establish the gold standard in place of the Democrats' "free silver." He also touted President McKinley's plan to strengthen America's position by building a canal joining the Atlantic and Pacific Oceans.

Charles summed up the difference between the two parties in terms of patriotism and national destiny with regard to the international orientation of the United States since the turn of the century. Charles concluded that "a divine purpose runs" through the appearance on the American scene of Washington, Lincoln, Grant, and McKinley.

In his first few years in Congress, Charles had taken the lead on topics that still have a familiar ring: governmental reform, congressional ethics, free trade versus protectionism, the US role in world affairs, and maintaining American troops overseas. Cartoons covered his debates with venerable legislators like Champ Clark of Missouri and John Sharp Williams of Mississippi. The *Washington Post* took note of the "editor from Delphi, Indiana" serving in his second term in Congress: "To be sure, most members of the House do not grow at all . . . eclipsed and obscured by brighter men . . . A few stand out as leaders after long years of service, and just behind them one always finds a number of men, conspicuous for ability and of promising futures, if the voters are only willing to keep them in Congress. Of such material is Charles Landis." [11]

Frederick phased out his service as aide to Charles in Washington, becoming active on the Chautauqua lecture circuit and making political speeches. He took issue with the foreign policy position of William Jennings Bryan, the Democratic Party's candidate for president in 1900. After Mr. Bryan asserted that the US military presence in the Philippines was "imperialism," Frederick went on the attack against President McKinley's opponent. In an early campaign speech in Anderson, Indiana, he criticized Bryan for being inconsistent in his positions and declared him to be "an arch-imperialist," citing his recent stance: "He it was who leaped from his horse, grabbed the 'limited mail' for

Washington, rushed breathlessly among Democratic senators, snorting party mandates and compelling them to support the Paris treaty, which placed our soldiers, our mission and our flag in the distant East to stay." [12]

Meanwhile, Ken's stature was growing as a corporation attorney in Chicago, catching the attention of one of his relatives in the practice of law in Ohio who chose to share thoughts about a "promising" commercial venture. There is no indication that Ken paid attention to this offer, but it posed for him the issue of whether financial proposals by family members belonging to the United Brethren Church were in keeping with Godliness. [13]

Mary, a widow of 68 at the turn of the century, was busy keeping track of Charles' exploits on the House floor and in Chautauqua appearances. Yet, she did not neglect her corporate lawyer in Chicago, providing Ken with a voluminous account of current events from the Logansport perspective. While improving her self-taught grammar and punctuation, Mary continued to show some disdain for precision: "My Dear Squire tis so long since we have heard something from you this story of you jumping in the lake to save a drowning boy has gone the rounds here and I have said I was afraid you ruined a suit of clothes and twould be to bad if you did let us know if there is anything in it . . . now love to all especialy your own dear self Write Me a letter and tell me if you did jump in the lake my dear sonbeam" [14]

Charles wrote a feature article for a new national magazine, choosing a subject of his personal experience: "The Evolution of a Country Editor." Upon reflection, he placed heavy emphasis upon the press of small-town America, suggesting that this institution is decisive in shaping public opinion: "The country newspapermen of today really mold the sentiment of the republic and have done so for the last fifty years." He continued his evaluation by reining in the alleged importance of the well-known press of the nation's big cities: "The metropolitan papers cannot successfully champion any proposition that meets with the united opposition of the country press." [15]

With regard to Landis lawyers . . . Kenesaw presented his independent style as a step in the direction of exposing hypocrisy, using tactics that often challenged traditional practices. As a lawyer representing corporations, he emphasized detailed knowledge of the issue at hand. Operating from a position of sentiment for the underdog, he could display humorous antics even in the presence of distinguished members of the profession, such as casually using their first names: "When the federal judges in Chicago were Christian C. Kohlsaat, Peter S. Grosscup and James L. Jenkins, Judge Kohlsaat once said sternly to lawyer Landis: 'I understand that you have been referring to me as Chris Kohlsaat' . . . 'I'll bet I know who told you that,' exclaimed Landis, 'It was either Pete Grosscup or Jim Jenkins.'" [16]

John, the sole surviving medical advisor to the Landis family, would in turn call upon Ken for advice in the realm of legal matters. In one instance, he sought to collect an outstanding debt, querying: ". . . can these bastardized S of Bs proceed to beat me out of nearly $500 on the contention that their father died without leaving an estate?" On reflection, John, showing his familiarity with Squire's often-colorful manner of speech, added: "I may desire to submit your opinion to an attorney here, so eliminate the profanity not absolutely necessary to a clear statement." [17]

Frederick in his law practice in Logansport turned to writing on topics of current interest to include sensitive subjects of society. One such topic was race relations in light of whether President Lincoln's Emancipation Proclamation proved successful in freeing Negroes from their low standing in American society. On one occasion, he managed to pair the race topic with another item that became a matter of controversy -- whether Confederate flags captured during the Civil War ought to be returned to the Southern states. He dealt directly with one subject, then the other, in a manner that left the reader of a Hoosier literary weekly utterly aware that no "fence-straddling" had taken place. [18]

Down in Puerto Rico, Walter, while savoring his task of administering the US Postal Service, stepped into the legal world with thoughts of a lucrative career opportunity. Squire could not, however, readily be distracted from his chosen profession. This was another case of brother trying to help brother: "I believe there is a great chance here for a good attorney in the matter of the collection of claims against the Government for duties unlawfully collected through the custom houses of the Island on imports from the United States." Walt went on to season his letter with an observation of climatic differences between the Nation and its territorial attachments in the Caribbean: "Our Porto Rican soldiers went up to attend the inauguration, and I would not be surprised to hear that they have had the balls frozen off of them." He returned to family thoughts, speculating that Charles, likely to be facing "an extra session of Congress," would not be able to come south for a visit. In closing, he returned to his proposition that Ken consider leaving his law practice in Chicago and sail to Puerto Rico in order to work on uncollected state revenues, thus "combining business with pleasure." [19]

Mary continued to keep her sons informed of major happenings in the family. At the turn of the century, she passed the exciting word that the head of this small-town homestead was planning to travel with her son Charles, who was on vacation from congressional duties, to see Niagara Falls and New York. On this occasion, Mary wrote to Ken some local gossip, including distressing news that one of the well-known citizens "Henry Wiler rec a letter last sat telling him to put 500 out in a basket at the fair ground or his 13 year old boy would be kidnaped." She then grew concerned about her grandchildren in Chicago, saying: "so look out for Reed and Susanne the dear little darlings" Finally, Mary signed off to her "darling Ken." [20] Kate enclosed a note chastising Kenesaw for not writing, suggesting that Walt did a better job of communicating: "Why all the silence? You would do better if you were in Porto Rico." Adding that her mother and Charles would visit Niagara Falls, Kate wrote: "Soon as they return you must come home. A year ago I was with you. Wasn't it fine? I tell you I enjoyed it . . .You ought to see how aristocratic Frank looks with her spectacles. Ma & I to go this morning to be fitted with them."

Charles' speeches on the Chautauqua circuit and his addresses on national holidays tended to differ from his appearances on the floor of the House of Representatives in one important aspect: On the road, he left critical remarks to the side and sounded a note of strong optimism, flavored, to be sure, with partisan commentary. As with Charles' appearance on the floor of Congress or in visits to cities and towns, the press was always on hand to provide detailed reporting and editorial comments. Before the years of radio and TV . . . newspapers and Chautauqua were the sole media for stirring the political consciousness of citizens, and Charles made the most of his oratorical opportunities.

While media coverage in later years has drifted to topics of an unhappy nature . . . violence and crime, "the Charles Landis menu" was largely positive: the affairs of state were on track and, under Republican stewardship, promised to get even better: "Charles spoke of a reunited North and South . . . of the extinction of the "death's-head" of slavery and a final riddance of prejudices left by "the Cuban war." [21] He carried his positive theme westward, recalling the common purpose in the Philippines following the war with Spain and noting: "A higher standard of morals is required of politicians." [22]

Describing Charles as "one of the most prominent and conspicuous figures in Congress," a local newspaper in Iowa approved of his Chautauqua lecture in Columbus Junction. There he sought to justify the Republican shift away from protective tariffs to resemble the traditional Democratic position by referring to the abandonment of block houses used to protect against Indian attack. Charles concluded: "We had to tear them down as the country developed . . . So it is with the tariff. It must be revised as the country develops." The editorial went on to describe Charles' "necktie trouble" that persisted in bothering him during his lecture by slipping around in the direction of his ear. When it repeated this movement several times, Charles remarked, to the partisan crowd's delight: "Our democratic friends would have us run away from the Philippine question just as this necktie of mine does." [23]

Following the assassination of President McKinley in Buffalo in September 1901, Charles addressed Chicago's Marquette Club, dubbed as "one of the largest and most influential political organizations in America." The occasion was the annual remembrance of the disastrous Chicago fire of 1871 and was "an elaborate affair." Speaking on the subject of the untimely death of the President, he shared the platform with editor William Allen White, Professor Booker T. Washington, and Civil War hero General Arthur MacArthur, military governor of the Philippines. Charles recalled utterances President McKinley had made in his fateful Buffalo appearance: "We must build more ships, and they must be under the American flag . . .We must build the Isthmian canal . . . The construction of a Pacific cable cannot be longer postponed." [24]

Charles also addressed a Republican meeting in Zanesville, Ohio, where he spoke of the unification of North and South as their soldiers fought and died together in the war against Spain. He referred to timely portions of McKinley's last speech stating that we not only dominated our own markets but were about to capture the world markets. [25]

For his part, Frederick continued to gain public notice through his speechmaking in behalf of Republican causes. He had begun to appear prominently at Indiana "love feasts," attracting wide attention toward the end of 1901. One of his appearances in Indianapolis was entitled "A Glowing Tribute Paid to Republican Idols," and Frederick offered a toast to the recently martyred President: "We drink to the great McKinley. He came in obscurity . . . but ere he fell he was the Ben Hur in the race of nations." [26]

In Kokomo, where Charles sought re-nomination for a fourth term at the Ninth Congressional District Convention, there was a colorful account circulating in the hall that "an enthusiastic Landis man punched a delegate from Tipton County for applauding Hamilton County, but the police say it was a Kokomo man who took a poke at him." [27]

The newspaper of one of the more prominent towns of the Ninth District wrote that Charles' re-nomination for a fourth term would be "a foregone conclusion." Going a step further, the editorial predicted a promising future for Charles, apparently beginning with the 1904 election year, when Theodore Roosevelt would be a likely candidate to succeed himself as President: "We hear possibilities and probabilities mentioned in connection with the United States senatorship, the gubernatorial nomination, and the vice-presidency." [28] Charles won re-nomination to Congress and was elected for a fourth term in 1902.

It had been said that, when Frederick left Charles' staff to go back to Indiana, Charles asked his youngest brother: "When will you return to Washington?" and Fred replied: "not until I am elected to Congress." [29] It did not take long for the youngest of the five brothers to make good on his plan. Frederick, practicing law in Logansport at 29 sought the nomination in 1902. His first campaign speech was in the small Cass County town of Lucerne. [30]

Frederick shared the platform with well-known speakers as the campaign of 1902 got underway. Encouraged by his success in helping other candidates, Frederick had developed a serious interest in becoming a contender to represent the 11th district. Delegates at the Wabash convention in 1900 had tried to adopt the primary system to replace the party convention for the campaign of 1902, [31] but the convention system remained in place.

Logansport and Cass County provided an enthusiastic backdrop for Frederick's political foray, including plans for a special train to carry his supporters to the congressional convention. The local press took notice: "It is expected that a thousand County people will go to Wabash next Wednesday to shout for Frederick Landis." [32] On the last day of the campaign, someone hollered at the youthful candidate: "Hey, boy! Does your mother know you're out?" "Yes," replied Frederick, "and when the votes are counted tonight she'll know I'm in." [33]

Frederick attracted a large number of supporters in his bid to unseat a solid Republican, Major George Steele of Marion, Grant County, who had held the post of district congressman for many years. The stage was set in the city of Wabash for a battle among other aspirants from nearby counties, who also chose to challenge Major Steele. The enthusiasm and loyalty of Frederick's 22 delegates, many years older than the candidate, would prove decisive in determining the outcome of the convention.

Logansport's newspaper found interesting details to report. It described a 2 o'clock-in- the-morning conference of Frederick's advisers "at which Landis appeared garbed solely in pajamas." One of Landis' opponents seeking to strengthen delegates in a move to unseat the venerable Major Steele, adopted an imaginative scheme as "his badges in most cases adorn the breasts of fair women instead of the lapels of the active participants." The Logansport paper estimated that the "Landis Special" train to Wabash would be served by "the Odd Fellows' and Elks' bands, and the drum Corps will form the escort." One observer noted that "while perspiring delegates are being hustled from one headquarters to another," and "candidates are twisting themselves into hard knots trying to clasp each extended hand," the hotel proprietor "stands behind his register and smiles and smiles and is a villain still." This selfish individual "doubleth up his rates and taxeth the late comer seven simoleons for a chance to sleep on the piano if some other fellow doesn't retire first." The newspaper account also observed that Frederick's "lieutenants got busy as June bugs." [34]

Frederick's name was placed in nomination by Stewart T. McConnell, who spoke of the virtues in selecting the youngest candidate at 29 years of age. He noted that "older employers of all great business enterprises, judges and preachers are rapidly retiring and their places are being filled with young men . . . this trend 'we are told is the voice of God.'" He referred to Frederick as possessing "all the qualifications of a great Congressman . . . original, eloquent, learned and logical." Mr. McConnell then added that Landis had traveled during the campaign with Senator Mark Hanna and Colonel Theodore Roosevelt. McConnell noted that in 1901, in response to Frederick's "matchless eloquence and inimitable powers," President Roosevelt linked Frederick with distinguished American orators and patriots:

> It was one of those fascinating and peculiar efforts, that reminded one of Rufus Choate, coupled with the angularity of Abraham Lincoln, and the miraculous humor and comparisons of Tom Corwin in the flights of electric eloquence unsurpassed by Robert G. Ingersoll in his brightest days. [35]

Throughout the long day and night of balloting, delegates of the various candidates remained loyal, and by 2:30 in the morning, the race had still not allowed a likely winner to emerge . . . The deadlock after 12 hours of balloting would have to be addressed the next morning at eleven o'clock. [36] The next day, Frederick defeated the long-time incumbent after one thousand and twelve ballots: "When the result was announced there was a great demonstration. When order was restored, Major Steele took the platform and moved to make the nomination of Frederick Landis unanimous." [37] "The most thrilling convention that has been held in Indiana for half a century" brought forth Frederick as the nominee, following a record-breaking number of ballots. His success came after the Cass County delegation of 22 members adamantly remained solid through the many hours of the convention. [38]

Frederick's return to Cass County was met with great celebration as "every man, woman and child in Logansport seemed anxious to do honor to 'Buckskin.'" Frederick addressed the assembled crowd, declaring: "This reception means all the more to me because no political spirit is manifested -- Democrats, Republicans, Populists and Prohibitionists have joined in this magnificent meeting." [39]

Frederick went on to express his pride in being named to represent the 11th Indiana district, declaring his belief that "a happy home with an honest American father and a glorious American mother and a band of unparalleled American children is grander architecture than Egypt, Greece or Babylon ever knew." [40]

Commentary by the hometown newspaper summed up the sentiments of Frederick's loyal delegation that led to its extraordinary endurance and success: "They were there to nominate a young man who had good words instead of evil ones for every man." [41] The newspaper noted that the victorious candidate would receive "loyal support" from not only Republicans "but also among the Democrats with whom he is deservedly popular." [42] The *Logansport Journal* summed up the competition that existed in the campaign: "It was the determined attempt of a man grown gray in the honorable service of his district to maintain himself in office against the claims of other men who had aspirations for the same office." [43] Frederick's acceptance of the nomination stirred him to pay homage to Republican Party national platforms: "I am proud to belong to a party whose platforms never were and never will be battle cries for the enemies of my country." [44]

Newspapers of the Eleventh district and the upper Wabash Valley were supportive of the party nominee. In one instance, the editor recalled favorable impressions of Frederick on a previous visit to the town of Warsaw: "The people had come to Warsaw to see and hear Mark Hanna in the last Presidential campaign, and it was no easy matter to secure and hold the attention of the thousands of people who filled the public square; but Mr. Landis did it, and not a complaint was heard over the delay, either!" [45]

Now came coverage by a Wabash newspaper that had favored one of Frederick's opponents, which approved of the winner and, after a strong endorsement, summoned the reader to unite against "the common foe:" "The *Plain Dealer* made a sturdy fight for Cary Cowgill. It earnestly desired his nomination, but since it was impossible for him to win, the honor has gone to an opponent who shall have its unremitting endeavors in the campaign soon to begin. And it is not promising too much that Fred Landis, 'Buckskin,' will have the full party majority of good old Wabash county at the counting of the votes on the night of November 4." [46]

"After action" journalistic analysis began to focus on the youngest of the Landis boys in the local newspaper. One editorial, "The Crime of Being Young," centered upon statewide commentary to the effect that Fred's youth was considered by opponents as representing insufficient experience to become a candidate for national office: "The young man of today does not take life in a flippant manner. In these days of intense living the rising generation is brought face to face with the problems of life earlier than formerly, and it is better equipped at twenty than the former one was at thirty." [47]

The local newspaper also chose to quote a Chicago daily that described the qualities of "the Landis boys" on the occasion of Frederick's victory: "Frederick Landis is one of five brothers, all of whom have achieved prominence in one way or another at an unusually youthful age. As if the family had been selected as a conspicuous example of what pluck and spirit can do, all the brothers began life in poor circumstances, and all of them have risen to the top with the buoyancy of a cork in water." [48] The Logansport newspaper continued to print editorials about Frederick, including some old-fashioned advice: "There is no necessity for him to embalm all the unkind remarks in his memory, any more than there is for him to take seriously all the nice things that are said about him." [49]

Shortly after Frederick received his Congressional victory, Walter gained national attention by his role in connection with a natural disaster of widespread proportions. In the short span of two weeks, Walter, while serving in Puerto Rico, was called to important service during a natural catastrophe. He was one of the first US officials to inspect the still-erupting volcano on the island of Martinique in the Caribbean, which killed about 30,000 people. The eruption of Mt. Pelee destroyed the city of San Pierre. Walter hurried to San Pierre with the first band of observers aboard the ship *Potomac* for the purpose of rescuing members of the American Consulate or recovering their bodies. [50]

After his party returned the bodies of the US Consul, his family and the attaches, "all of whom were buried in the sea of lava," Walter wrote widely-circulated newspaper accounts of the tragedy. In one article, he observed the horror left in the streets of San Pierre after the first eruption: "The bodies of the dead lay as thick as sheaves in a wheatfield newly harvested . . . Had the Rue de Victor Hugo been a running stream, and dead bodies stepping stones we could have traversed it for blocks dry shod." Walter described the situation that continued to threaten greater casualties: "My investigation got no further, for at that instant a low rumble like a distant train smote our ears . . . One glance in the direction of Mt. Pelee revealed a situation that to us seemed fraught with deadly peril, for the volcano was in full eruption." [51]

In a few weeks, public attention turned to Charles in the House of Representatives, who argued "the Army question" in favor of a continuing American military presence in the Philippines, as he had done against fellow Hoosier Republican, Representative Johnson in 1899. With Johnson no longer in Congress, Charles' opposition now came from Democrats such as Champ Clark of Missouri. In the House, "Mr. Clark unlimbered his ponderous voice and shouted that the Democrats had dragged the Republicans into the war 'by the scruff of the neck,'" and Charles responded: "when the war came, with its problems, consequences and responsibilities . . . you Democrats turned your backs and ran away . . . they not only turned their backs and ran away, but they are running yet." Charles then distributed his fire to Congressman Gaines of Tennessee, pointing to his sponsorship of out-dated legislation concerning Spanish war taxes. [52]

Coverage in another major newspaper also emphasized a verbal bout with Congressmen Gaines when Charles quoted the plea of a dying veteran: "We soldiers who served in the Philippines do not want to have it said in the years to come 'we followed a retreating flag.'" Charles continued: "We gave the people of Cuba ultimate freedom and independence and have been sacrificing millions for the people of the Philippine Islands" and added that Democrats had accomplished nothing. [53]

In this same article, Charles broadened his endorsement of the Republican position on keeping US troops in the Philippines by recounting the Democratic Party's "errors" during the presidency of Grover Cleveland. He went on to link Representative Clark, soon-to-be Speaker of the House, to his past and predicted his future political support of Mr. Cleveland. Clark proceeded to acknowledge, "amid much laughter,": "That is one of the things that I expect to pray Almighty God to give me absolution for in the day of judgment." As if to rub salt into the wounds of the Congressman from Missouri, Charles alleged that Clark had led a march of the Cleveland delegation in 1892, singing: "Grover, Grover, Four years more of Grover, Then we'll be in clover."

A sub-title of this same *Washington Post* article described Charles' appeal to patriotism in terms of his religious belief and conviction that God's hand has guided America as a land of destiny. Perhaps, the heavy immigration from Europe of several decades helped to bring him to the conclusion that this nation was a model for mankind.

One of the leading newspapers in Indiana covered the same address on the Philippine question in the House under a range of title and sub-titles: "LANDIS STIRS HOUSE . . . Vigorously Defends the Administration's Policy and Excoriates the Democratic Party . . . Flays Missouri's Clark . . . And Silences Another Democrat With a Single Shot." [54] An example of strong partisanship by a major city newspaper, more direct and less subtle than examples of today's media coverage, is evident in the following summary account of Charles' House speech on the Philippines issue: "We greatly admire the way in which 'Charley' Landis, of Indiana, used up the blovating and demagogic Champ Clark of Missouri yesterday . . . It was a body blow and doubled up Champ Clark like a knife." [55]

Another large-city newspaper showed its political colors with no apology as it offered a resounding theme of support for Charles' position on the Philippines, stating that he "gave the Democrats in Congress precisely what they deserved yesterday afternoon . . . Eager for the war before it began, the Democrats have cravenly avoided responsibility for its consequences." [56]

An editorial by a renowned public-affairs writer of the turn-of-the-century compared the principals in the Philippine debate, Charles and Representative John S. Williams of Mississippi, and offered a colorful, bipartisan analysis of Charles' record since his arrival on the Washington scene: "one was the heavy artillery of the Democratic side and the other the light cavalry of the Republican forces . . . Williams reminded of the magnificence of Solomon's temple; Landis suggested the utility of a Chicago skyscraper." [57]

In contrast with the overt partisanship of many large-city newspapers was a local account that underscored Charles' strong support of US troops in the Philippines, and added his concluding statement: "the Anglo-Saxon race was destined ultimately to rule and triumph throughout the length and breadth of the world." [58]

While Charles was visiting New York City, he spoke with friends in the Waldorf Astoria hotel about his private ambitions: "I believe I am a farmer, pure and simple . . . The ambition of my life would be satisfied if I were able to own 1,000 acres of bottom land on the Wabash and till it." He was called up short by one of his friends who doubted the Congressman's zeal for physical labor, saying: "You mean and see it tilled." [59]

Back in Logansport, a major event in local history was the arrival of President Theodore Roosevelt. He delivered a "27-minute speech" before a crowd of some 5,000 citizens during his Midwest swing of late September 1902, and Charles and Frederick were fortunate in occupying the platform with the President. It was a memorable occasion because the President appeared to have a problem with his leg. After his departure from Logansport and arrival in Indianapolis, it was found that his infected leg required surgery. A matter of national concern, his medical condition was corrected, and the rest of his trip was cancelled. [60]

In the conduct of Frederick's fall campaign for election to Congress, he made numerous appearances in good weather and bad, attempting to speak to as many voters as possible in the waning weeks before the election. The interest of his audience of about 2,000 citizens in North Manchester was severely tested, according to the Logansport paper: "The rain was coming down in torrents most of the time, but the people stood in the mud on the race track and listened. Repeatedly they cheered, and when it was over most of them went to the platform and shook hands with Landis." [61]

One of Frederick's last campaign stops before the election was a visit to the village Roann where "almost a hundred voters" was considered a large turnout. He spoke for nearly an hour, explaining party differences on "political issues of the day." The local press reported that he finished with "a deserved compliment to teachers and our great school system." [62] Frederick made an additional speech at Peru, near Logansport, finding a record turn-out in the County Court House. The local *Republican* described the crowd as "enraptured by his oratory," and an editorial observed that the speaker "puts things in a startling way that strikes people with great force." [63]

Frederick concluded his campaign with a hometown appearance at the local rink, where Ken as a teenager had operated his rolling skate enterprise. The budding politician made it clear that he was "in the Teddy Roosevelt camp," supporting our troops in the Philippines and favoring a policy that would place limits on corporations. Frederick pointed out that political parties were not a factor in the experience of the Founding Fathers who counted on the ability of citizens to select "from the body of the people, those men whose eminent ability commanded their devotion and confidence." This was the basis for establishing an Electoral College. As for political parties, Frederick explained that they came about later because of a need for one party "to transact business" and for another "to watch that party to see that it does transact business." [64]

The strong victory over Major Steele in the nominating convention was impressive, but the fact that Frederick won handily over his Democratic opponent in the Election came as a surprise. The numbers showed a heavy cross-over vote in his favor, having gained "almost 800 Democratic votes in his home county." [65] His appeal to Democrats would continue as a feature of his later campaigns as well. Meanwhile, Charles scored a win for his fourth term over in the Ninth District. Charles' support consisted mainly of Republican voters.

Frederick as congressman-elect attended his swearing-in at the opening of the First Session of the 58th Congress, scheduled in those years onr the first Monday in December 1902. This was an opportunity for him to participate in the coming weeks as a part of the Republican caucus for the purpose of selecting the Speaker of the House. In the meantime, Representative Joseph G. Cannon of Illinois acknowledged Kenesaw's support for this post. [66] Frederick offered his views about Representative Cannon to the local newspaper . . . "venerable, intense, candid, absolutely and everlastingly honest, filled with information, endowed with keenest wit yet possessing the kindliest and most companionable of natures, cool when apparently otherwise, and ever ready for an opponent's thrust." At the same time, Frederick expressed a concern that "Uncle Joe" at 66 might have been too advanced in years to be able to serve as Speaker. [67] While in Washington on this occasion, Frederick called on President Roosevelt and was able to visit with Walter who had come from his post in Puerto Rico to celebrate his brothers' victories. [68]

Frederick's recent election boosted his credentials for Chautauqua events, and he was invited to speak in Boston at the Middlesex Club on the occasion of Abraham Lincoln's birthday. (Charles had been the featured speaker at the club six years earlier.) Frederick returned to Indianapolis, where he briefed political friends on matters of political interest and looked forward to the main political occurrence in Washington, the election of the Speaker of the House. [69]

Frederick continued to be active with speechmaking during 1903 as a diversion from his duties as a freshman seated alongside brother Charles in the House of Representatives. [70] He spoke at Decoration Day services (later known as Memorial Day) at Denver, Indiana, population about 500, where farm folk had assembled from surrounding villages of Miami County. The local paper reported that: "although very much bothered in his speech by a sore throat from outdoor speaking, his speech was the finest effort of its kind on the subject that it has ever been our pleasure to listen to, and everybody seemed delighted and glad that they had come." [71] A Kentucky journalist recalled his presence in Logansport on Decoration Day that led him to note Frederick's address honoring veterans who had given their lives. He concluded that Indiana would include among "eminent men of our Union" this "splendid, talented, magnetic and eloquent young statesman from the banks of the Wabash." [72]

Shortly after Independence Day, Frederick accepted an invitation to honor veterans in Peru, where the annual assembly of Indiana Sons of Veterans featured a program including the Congressman-elect with the Governor and Lieutenant Governor. [73] Frederick found it necessary to revise his planned text because of an outbreak of racial tension in the nation and the southern part of the state. The cause was the burning at the stake of a Negro in the South. This led to a lynch mob in Evansville that had to be contained the previous evening by local militia and companies from Terre Haute, Vincennes, and Indianapolis. [74] In addition, in a highly-charged atmosphere reaching to a nearby city, it was reported that "a bitter feeling existed between blacks and whites." [75]

Frederick started with a patriotic introduction: "The Glorious never die. The heroes of the human race enjoy eternal youth. We celebrate again the valor and victories of an army of boys whose average age was under 20 years, but whose holy cause was as old as Mother Earth." The young congressman then sharpened his remarks. [76] The editorial noted that Frederick declared that it was time for people to treat the Negro with respect and to bring an end to the race issue: "Liberty and opportunity for man, woman, and child . . . Slavery is dead, but its child survives to vex us, and the name of this child is 'The Race Problem'." He

100

spoke of his mother's strong faith and religious ancestry and his grandfather's anti-slavery sentiments shaped by a missionary trip to Africa in 1855. Frederick paid tribute to Abraham Lincoln's Emancipation Proclamation. He referred to his father Abraham's abolitionist commitment and noted: "In the south we can understand this prejudice; in the north we cannot . . . As a result, Indiana stands today in shame and in tears."

Then he posed the question: "'We have not a race war,' you say? . . . Perhaps not, but shots are fired, men fall, women and children are terrorized, and unoffending colored men are driven from different counties in this State." One of the few in public life who chose to discuss this topic in the early years of this century offered an allegory: "There was a time called 'yesterday,' and this serpent was then the whip of a slave driver!"

He concluded: "The colored man is here to stay." He offered a prescription to treat all people the same without regard to race or belief. Frederick appealed to the Sons of Veterans: "Let us leave this theatre determined to liberate the mind of our beloved State from . . . this un-American wrath against fellow beings." Uttering a challenge with which his late father and elderly mother would agree, Frederick said: "Lynching must cease . . . mark my word the night will come when the bells will ring!" And he invoked the names of distinguished Negroes who contributed to the American culture: "Paul Dunbar the poet . . . Booker T. Washington the philosopher." Frederick cited the case of military accomplishments of Negro soldiers: "The colored man never betrayed a Union soldier and though tortured, never disclosed the secret of the prisoner fleeing from Andersonville or Libby Prisons." Finally, he closed with a tone of optimism that race problems will be eliminated.

Quoting from the *Warsaw Northern Indianian*, another small town newspaper in Frederick's congressional district had comments to make about the controversy of recent political campaigns concerning the youth of candidates like Frederick:

"Most public men that we have ever heard of were young, gawky, green and awkward, at the earlier period of their lives; but even young as he is, Fred Landis has been freer of such blemishes than even many older men when they first began to show up in Congress [77]

101

Walter and John watched politics from the sidelines, leaving the others to be bitten by "the bug." Kenesaw while practicing law, chose not to take the plunge himself but instead to serve as campaign manager for his friend Frank Lowden, a candidate for Governor of Illinois. His son Reed described this unsuccessful venture during 1903-04: "The whole campaign terminated in a drawn-out convention in Springfield." [78]

Charles engaged in efforts, supported by the President, to cut waste in the Government Printing Office. His prominence in reform legislation led a Minnesota congressman to recommend Charles as a possible candidate to pair up with Theodore Roosevelt in the national election of 1904. [79]

Looking ahead to the national campaign of 1904, Senator Mark Hanna of Ohio confirmed Charles' value by requesting his assistance in bringing out Republican voters in the Buckeye state. [80] Meanwhile, Charles' had his own preferences to address in the House of Representatives during the end of the First Session of the 58th Congress in late 1903. One writer wrote an editorial describing Charles' unusual enterprise in striking a successful blow against drinking alcoholic beverages in Congress. It appeared that his pursuit of such a goal would place his popularity with other members to a severe test, but the scheming Congressman proceeded to challenge the old maxim: "Liquor has been sold at the United States Capitol since the memory of the oldest inhabitant runneth not to the contrary." The writer went on to note that in the end, however, legislators quickly managed to bypass their own toothless anti-saloon law. [81]

Upon the conclusion of the First Session of the 58th Congress, an Extra Session of that body was convened November 9, 1903. On that occasion, Frederick took his seat next to Charles, and the *Indianapolis Star* wrote in its editorial: "The Landis brothers attracted much comment among visitors. When the House convened they took seats side by side. Occasionally, their eyes wandered to the gallery, where sat their aged mother, whose cup of happiness was complete." [82]

Again on a Chautauqua schedule at the middle of his fourth term in the House, Charles was enthusiastic about the rapid growth of the nation in the new century. His positive view of the country's future found good response in a New England village as well as in a thriving small city in Illinois. One editorial from Vermont

102

expressed the notion that citizens situated away from the activities of the Nation's capital were uninformed. At the same time, they wanted to understand politics and to be a part of the process. Accordingly, Charles did his best to plant the seed that the Government, that happened to be in Republican hands at the moment, was serving its constituents well: "He struck the note of national greatness, and the heart swelled with pride in the grandeur of the young Republic, where all men have an equal chance, and whose presidents, risen from the ranks of the common people, oftentimes control the policy of monarchs descended from a long line of kings." [83]

Charles appeared in Rockford, Illinois to feature the life and politics of US Grant but succeeded in changing his topic to the broad subject of "Optimism." The Chautauqua agreement, according to one newspaper, was made to accommodate the speaker who felt a positive message was fitting to the special occasion of a temperature of 13 below zero "when a good share of the winter was inside of the opera house." [84] Another local paper noted Charles' success: "Even then the address warmed the hearers up so that the cold was well nigh forgotten." [85]

Just after Christmas 1903, Mary wrote to Ken about his young brother's decision to seek election to a second term in Congress: "Fred will go to Indianapolis Wed of this week to be there for the love feast . . . well now in a few days he will announce . . .write me sweet heart." [86] At the end of the year, this conclave for party unity brought Fred and Charles together with leading politicos of the State, including Frederick's old-time opponent, Major George Steele of Marion.

Charles took the political offensive in January 1904 against the Democratic Party, charging that election boards in the South slighted Republican representation. House Minority Leader John S. Williams of Mississippi, Charles' old foe in debating the question of "US troops in the Philippines," again defended the Democratic Party position. The *Washington Post* published commentary on Charles' alleged "conversion" in the matter of upper-level politics with the line: "Twitted of the fact that he had not always been an admirer of President Roosevelt," Charles provided an explanation that, during the Administration of William McKinley, "he had said some harsh things about the future President" . . . Now, however, he found reasons to adopt a different view and, according to the editorial, "the tribute he paid the President was about the most eulogistic Mr. Roosevelt has ever received on the floor of either House." [87]

With regard to Charles' claim of unfair treatment of Republicans in staffing election boards in the South, an Indiana newspaper commented: "At times the exchanges between the Indiana man and his critics on the Democratic side were charged with humor, but on two or three occasions some bitterness was manifested, especially when Landis referred to the 'shotgun' practices followed in Mississippi and other Southern States." Charles found himself again in the position of explaining his shift from opposing Theodore Roosevelt to enthusiastic support of the President by citing Colonel Roosevelt's personal courage in fighting Spanish forces and in his performance in the White House following the death of William McKinley. The article concluded by quoting Charles . . . "Passion and greed were facing each other, and Theodore Roosevelt said: 'Come, brethren, let us reason together.' A coward in the White House would not have spoken. A brave man was in the White House, and he spoke . . ." [88]

Theodore Roosevelt's first candidacy for President occurred in 1904. The same year, Charles' campaigned for a fifth term, focusing on his prominent role in speaking for Republican legislation. Frederick, as a freshman congressman, was learning about the processes of the House of Representatives, but his public appeal came largely from Chautauqua appearances. In his race for a second term, he was again opposed by Major Steele in the Eleventh District convention.

Partisan items from regional newspapers appeared in *Fair Play Journal*, a publication strongly supportive of Frederick's candidacy. From Major Steele's hometown came a report of "noise in opposition of Fred Landis," based on criticism of the incumbent's decision not to hire a private secretary at the start of his first term. An irony lay in the fact that the editorialist, who was opposed to Landis' candidacy two years earlier, proceeded then to seek employment as the Congressman's private secretary. The critic's use of the pejorative expression "of wordy wind" seemed to be based upon Frederick's refusal to hire him. [89] The *Peru Journal* countered Major Steele's bid for constituent support as a soldier with honorable service by citing the patriotic example of Frederick's father in the Civil War. [90]

The *Hartford City Gazette*, in discussing the two candidates, argued that veterans "are under no deeper obligation to the living soldier (Major Steele) than to a soldier's widow and orphans." [91] In rejecting the alleged support of Steele's candidacy by the Speaker of the House of Representatives, Joe Cannon, the journal *Fair Play* supported Frederick by citing the *Indianapolis Star* that described the Speaker as indignant at the allegation and quoted Mr. Cannon as saying the supposed interview "does him as well as Fred Landis a great injustice." [92]

Fair Play praised the candidacy of Frederick, remarking that the young congressman "has gone through the rough side of life and emerged as bright as a dollar and fit for any kind of battle," adding: "Landis is not campaigning in kid gloves and the commonest citizen is greeted as heartily as the man in broadcloth." [93] The journal also touched upon a likely rift among Republicans between traditional party men identified closely with President McKinley and "progressive" Republicans as embodied in the presidency of Theodore Roosevelt, whose view was that corporate wealth should be controlled. Frederick, in his speeches was clearly "an open and avowed supporter of Roosevelt." [94]

A regional newspaper entered public discourse, noting that "Opposition to Hon. Fred Landis is largely based upon the fact that he is a young man." The editorial goes on to argue: "Young men fought the battles of the Civil War, of Cuba, and the Philippines and make up the standing Army and the Navy . . . They are protectors of the Republic on land and sea, and why may they not be just as valiant in the legislative halls of the Capitol as upon the tented fields?" [95]

One of the "Political Points" made by *Fair Play Journal* was: "Outside of Grant County, where Steele support is bound, bucked and gagged and led to the voting booth by political highwaymen, Fred Landis would carry the majority of Republicans in every county in a vote between himself and George Steele." [96]

President Roosevelt's personal interest in getting Frederick re-nominated was reported in connection with an incident involving support of Major Steele's candidacy by Captain Ira Myers, US Consul in New Brunswick, Nova Scotia. A native of Peru, Indiana, Captain Myers, who had affirmed that he was at home because of an ailment of the eyes, came to Frederick's attention as a person absent from his post without official authorization. Frederick communicated this idea to President Roosevelt and added: "Captain Myers' eyes might be affected, but he could easily distinguish his friends from his enemies." As a result, the President "ordered the US Consul back to New Brunswick." [97]

Not all coverage of the campaign was political; for example, one newspaper account discussed the culinary tastes of certain delegates: "An early, demonstrated fondness for pie on the part of the Republicans in attendance devastated the lunch counters. At 7 o'clock, it was stated, not even a quarter-section of pie remained within hailing distance of a Peru lunch counter." [98] In another item, Frederick's sister Frances, or Frank, a veteran of previous political campaigns, was helpful in greeting "most of the population of Miami County" . . . and "has done her part in making Landis' headquarters attractive." One reporter stated that when Frederick arrived in Peru, site of the convention, he received a grassroots welcome: "From the driver of the local bus to the bankers and heavyweight merchants along the path, Landis was universally hailed," and "his faculty for remembering names and faces was put to the severest test." [99]

With a well-organized campaign behind him, Frederick was optimistic of his chances of defeating Major Steele for the second time in a row, stating at 2 o'clock in the morning of Election Day: "We have seventy-eight delegates -- loyal, devoted Republicans who will not be swayed from the position they took and on which they were elected as delegates to this convention. The convention will nominate me by acclamation." [100] One account stated that, shortly before the convention was to begin, Major Steele had met with Frederick and offered "not to be a candidate" in return for unknown considerations that "Landis saw fit not to grant." [101]

E. B. McConnell of Logansport placed Frederick's name before the convention as a candidate, recognizing the intense competition that marked Steele's second attempt to defeat the "boy orator of the Wabash." Mr. McConnell stated: "A youth? Aye, a youth, but booted and spurred and ready for the battle. Young in years but old in wisdom. Young in years but ancient in integrity and honor; manly, clean, fearless and loyal." After his decisive victory, Frederick accepted the nomination, stating: "We need two parties in this country. We need the Republican Party to transact business and we need the Democratic Party to prepare us for future calamities." He recognized the presence of his mother, and the newspaper noted: "When the crowd called for Mrs. Landis, her son, taking her by the arm, stepped to the front and introduced her as follows: 'This is my philosopher and financial manager, Mrs. Landis.'" [102]

Charles showed his political colors in 1904 by supporting his fellow Hoosier, Senator Charles W. Fairbanks, for the presidency, when Theodore Roosevelt, the incumbent, was expected to be unopposed in the convention. Editorial comment on Charles' speech nominating Fairbanks noted: "The audience wanted a speech, and they wanted it to ring. It did. It was surcharged with the "vim, vigor, and victory" idea. It was electric . . ." [103]

After Roosevelt's expected nomination, Charles campaigned for his election, sounding the call for protectionism, criticizing the Democratic Party's "free trade" policy. The same newspaper displayed its Republican leaning, as it quoted Charles' speech three years previously: "The Republican Party has changed leaders, not principles . . . that means that every Republican ought to vote." Then he added a curiously frank comment, unlikely to encourage citizens to cast their ballots: "At times I think the gnat-brained fellow is the only fellow suited for public life." [104]

Several months later, Charles reflected the same despairing tone about his profession. Politics had been fun for Charles, but it would not last much longer. In fewer than ten years, his talent for public service, once fired with optimism and promise, began to succumb to the myriad demands of statecraft. His zest for public service gradually yielded to thoughts of early retirement, when he made the following comment in private correspondence to his teen-age daughter in school in France: "Sometimes I feel that no one but an intrigant can get along in politics." He longed for the pastoral scene of his large brick house and farm near Delphi: "Do you know that sometimes I get sick of this political work, and feel as though I wanted to get out in the country and remain there all the time? . . . But somebody has to support the burdens for the public weal." [105]

Just as Charles was enjoying the prospect of retiring to the country, Ken displayed a knack for finding diversion from the demanding work of a Chicago lawyer by relaxing as a fisherman. Going on fishing trips was his key to get away from official business and enjoy the great out-of-doors. Kenesaw's son recalled such occasions . . . heading for northern Wisconsin: "While up there, game and fish rules just didn't exist . . . a string of fish that included 40 or 50 for a day's catch. Just as rapidly as the concept of conservation became popular, Father grasped immediately the importance of it and was a very strict observer of all the rules and regulations." [106]

In 1905, Kenesaw was on the brink of receiving an appointment to the Federal Judiciary. Charles' prominence in the Republican Party was likely to have played a role in bringing his brother's name to the attention of President Roosevelt when an important vacancy appeared in Chicago. In later years, Charles' daughter affirmed as much in a letter to her niece: "Uncle K. got his judgeship through father's friendship with Roosevelt." [107] Charles claimed, however, that Mr. Roosevelt simply followed a recommendation by Congressman Lowden and a Senator Hopkins, and this version seemed to be confirmed by thoughts conveyed to Charles by Vice President Charles Fairbanks. [108]

On this subject, Charles related an anecdote that took place when the President invited two Congressmen named Landis to the White House in 1905 and in "a very dignified and serious" manner stated he was considering a Federal judicial appointment in Illinois. He told them the crux of the matter: "There is one Kenesaw Mountain Landis, I believe his name is, who has been very highly recommended. I did not feel that I should make the appointment, however, until I consulted with you. What do you think of it?" [109] Charles' and Frederick's responses can well be imagined, and the question became clear – other explanations to the contrary, a troika in the Oval Office produced Kenesaw's appointment.

As a Federal judge, Kenesaw, like Walter, was now a Presidential appointee. The other brothers were doing well in friendly competition with one another . . . Charles serving on the Committee on Foreign Affairs of the US House of Representatives . . . John gaining stature as a pioneering physician in Cincinnati . . . and Frederick, also in the House, preparing to shake up the insurance industry with proposed legislation that would meet with Theodore Roosevelt's enthusiastic support. Again, so much for the Landis boys of Logansport!

The news traveled fast to Logansport about the appointment of 38-year-old Kenesaw to the US District Court for Northern Illinois. Sister Kate wrote: "My goodness, Squire, isn't that appointment great? I find myself rejoicing in my sleep. When may we see the new Judge?" [110] His selection gave rise to a cogent question among those of the political and legal communities: "Why would a 'trust-busting' President Roosevelt select a well-known *corporation lawyer* for a key post in the Judiciary?" Even the appointee, in a rhetorical way, appeared to discount his suitability for the position . . . he stated that the job of representing corporations: "steers a man's mind into certain grooves, and does not admit him to the facts that make up the bulk of the cases coming before the Federal Court." [111] One answer to the question would be that the President believed Kenesaw to be qualified for the Federal court precisely because he was a farm boy who graduated from the "college of hard knocks" -- from teenage years as a railroad clerk and court reporter -- and would be able to look fairly at both sides of any given case before him.

Skeptics continued to wonder why the President picked a corporation lawyer in view of Ken's personal relationship with Illinois's pro-corporate Congressman Frank Lowden . . . wouldn't this judicial appointee reflect the point of view of "such men who look upon trust-busting as an extremely low form of amusement, somewhat less spectacular than bull-fighting and somewhat more vulgar?" [112] An editorial view reinforced this thesis by noting the clout of Ken's corporate clients . . . Chicago and Eastern Illinois . . . Calumet Electric Railway Company . . . Grand Trunk railroad. It seemed clear: "What he was not counsel for did not amount to much in Chicago." [113]

Yet, from another angle, Ken's son Reed offered one explanation that might appear specious to some . . . that the President favored a corporation lawyer because he "would know all of the problems on both sides because of personal participation in them" and thus would be a "free-thinking" and "forward-looking" individual. Indeed, Ken's maverick style -- like Frederick's, the Republican who got a lot of Democratic votes -- may have reassured the President that Squire would not disappoint him in ferreting out the essential facts involved in judicial matters.

Frederick's first appearance on the floor of the House of Representatives in the First Session of the 59th Congress "made a hit" when he supported Mr. Roosevelt's plan for a "two-battleship navy." He challenged his opponent Congressman Burke Cochran of New York who, as a Representative "from a seaport town," declared that "his constituents felt able to protect themselves." Frederick retorted: "Is it not true that during the Spanish-American war, your constituents pleaded that the whole navy be sent to New York harbor in order that their slumbers might not be disturbed?" [114]

As summertime approached, John from his home in Cincinnati proposed a family get-together with Ken. What an opportunity to celebrate Ken's appointment by breaking out some of Walter's Puerto Rican cigars! [115] Perhaps, they would enjoy the concern expressed by their mother, who was worried about the perils of Ken's newly-found recreation of sailing. They might take note also of her hometown report that "a big storm two weeks ago blew down one of our big maples." [116]

In December 1905, Frederick's maiden speech at the end of the First Session of the 59th Congress invoked a populist view against large corporations. Thus, he aligned himself with Teddy Roosevelt's trust-busting propensities and distanced himself from brother Charles' party orthodoxy. As family pioneer in pursuing corporate transgressors, he introduced legislation targeting the three major insurance companies: New York Life, Metropolitan, and Equitable. In the days before his presentation on the floor of the House of Representatives, Frederick had paid a visit to the Oval Office in order to sound out President Theodore Roosevelt on his legislative initiative. The President described Frederick's proposal to restrain insurance conglomerates as "a good bill and ought to receive consideration by Congress." [117]

Frederick's speech proposed that the insurance industry be placed under supervision of the Federal Government for interstate commerce activities. This bill emphasized the need for public confidence in curbing abuses involving the sale of insurance policies amounting to "five times greater than all the money in circulation in the United States." Expressing concern about wealthy firms that make deals with insurance companies, he added: "I want to take away from the death bed of the policy holder the ugly faces of Harriman; Kuhn, Loeb & Co . . . and Pierpont Morgan, the international kleptomaniac." [Applause and laughter.] [118]

The New York Times noted that it was the kind of legislation Theodore Roosevelt fully supported. The editorial cited Frederick's argument: "Subject these corporations to national supervision, and the eagle will keep the vulture from plucking the bodies of the dead." He declared that this legislation would compel insurance companies to function only in the realm of their own business -- not add-ons like "the saloon business, the hotel business, the banking

110

business, the trust business." [119] A Massachusetts newspaper observed as well that the conglomerates would receive telling blows under the legislation: "Representative from Indiana Makes Maiden Speech Full of Timely Hits." [120]

A newspaper in Michigan headlined: "Landis Flays Big Companies" noting Frederick's proposal would require insurance companies to make annual reports to the Department of Commerce and, in the speaker's words, "will direct attention to an amazing field of fraud" and "disturb the touch of kin that makes the whole company a Christmas tree." [121]

It so happened that cases soon to arrive on Kenesaw's docket in Chicago would bear a similar judicial pattern, addressing possible interstate commerce infractions by large firms like the Union Station Company of Illinois and the Standard Oil Company. As will be noted in later pages, big companies would again be the subject of close scrutiny – suggesting that, thanks to Fred and Ken in the Teddy Roosevelt mould, corporations were receiving a "double whammy" because of their interstate commerce involvements.

Mary Landis at 73 seemed to take Ken's judicial appointment in stride, so she did not seem to be distracted by Frederick's stirring proposal to rein in wealthy corporations. Instead, she reported strictly on family matters and the upcoming Christmas season. [122]

Soon after the first of the year, a relative from Ohio who had earlier asked Kenesaw for pro bono advice, again wrote, erring by spelling Ken's name with an extra "n," making a simple request with no entangling conditions. A perusal of Kenesaw's correspondence suggested that the letter's blunt style [123] was not welcome and probably found its way to Ken's "pismire file," his favorite euphemism for a waste basket.

Brother-to-brother letters like one from John were certain to receive a favorable response: "My Dear Judge," asking Ken for a smaller favor -- would he agree to be listed as a career reference for John's Cincinnati acquaintance who had been "in hard luck" . . . and wouldn't it be well to plan for a summer family get-together in Michigan again this year? [124]

Syndicated columnist Savoyard, who had traced the ancestry of the Landis boys from 17th-century Europe, now chose to discuss Congressmen Charles and Frederick. He concluded that the

111

pair were . . . "both young and eloquent, fine debaters, fluent, ready, capable, Indiana is to be congratulated, and the Republican party is the stronger for them by more than the two votes they possess." Of interest also was the writer's similarly generous opinion of Major George Steele, whom Frederick had beaten twice in Republican conventions: "I sometimes think Steele is the most wonderful man I ever came across." [125]

In Frederick's 1906 campaign for renomination, he visited "Major Steele country," whose Civil War veteran was no longer a candidate. This part of the State was important to Frederick even though he was running unopposed this year. Party officials of such locales as Hartford City and outlying villages of Montpelier, Mill Grove and even little Dundee in Blackford County were not known to be staunch supporters of the young man from Logansport. His presence there for several days suggested his belief in the need to touch base with this southeastern, mostly rural, portion of his district. The *Indianapolis News* found it worthwhile to send its columnist to Frederick's hometown to ride the train with the candidate to this part of the state and to cover his itinerary there. The correspondent wrote colorful accounts, reported epigrams, and produced cartoons to depict events. One early impression he gained was: "It was a handshaking fest from Logansport to Hartford City, and Landis enjoyed it all." [126]

The following day the excursion began with Frederick's trip to the village of Dundee, not even on the published map of the County, for a "heart-to-heart talk" with the people. The writer painted the scene: "when it was heralded from the post office to the blacksmith shop that Mr. Landis was in town . . . everyone was in great glee . . . the crowd came rushing on." Frederick let the folks know in pure populist tactics that their vote counted in the process of government. With this direct approach, however, he was trampling on the prerogatives of the County's foremost figures, going over the heads of party leaders to connect with the common man – *and enjoying it*. Such a style revealed the essence of this candidate as he went across party lines at village level to seek support from Republicans and Democrats alike. One of Frederick's epigrams was: "I loathe the brutality of money in politics. No man should be bought and no man should be rented." After his speech, a fair maiden, "the pride of Dundee," complimented Frederick on his "pretty hair," causing the bachelor candidate to wonder whether the country damsel may have been "kidding him." [127]

In the smaller town of Montpelier, Frederick found enthusiasm in the crowd for his support of President Roosevelt and his plans for legislation: "He said he wanted to remain in Congress long enough to see a bill passed that would rightly reward all the veterans of the Civil War for their sacrifices in that conflict." [128]

The Indianapolis correspondent also covered the Montpelier event, noting one epigram that reinforced Frederick's call for honesty in government: "Does a man have to be rich in order to represent you in Congress? If so, send a detective with him to Washington, for he will sell you out." The reporter added an observation of his own illustrating this problem at the local level when he wrote about the race for State Senate now underway between hopefuls from Montpelier, Hartford City and Bluffton, to be resolved in a convention in nearby Marion: "The price offered for votes around here was $10. There was a lovely gang of political 'moochers' in town, and some of them went over to Marion last night, so as to be at the convention this morning." [129] Frederick continued his campaign with one more speech, in Hartford City, county seat of Blackford County, where the local newspaper wrote favorably about the young Republican: "Graceful, fluent, dramatic, oratorical and logical, he will gain a national reputation." [130]

Further correspondence addressing Kenesaw's job performance within his first year on the Federal Bench was forwarded by Charles with the words: "two letters in which I take more pride than any letters I have received relative to myself." [131] They also added credence to Charles' likely role in having helped Ken win the President's attention prior to making an appointment to the judgeship. Interstate commerce was the theme as in Frederick's performance three months earlier when he cracked down on "Big Insurance:"

The Attorney General
Washington
March 3, 1906

My dear Landis:

I have just received a copy of Judge Landis' opinion in the case of the Interstate Commerce Commission v. Raichmann rendered on February 27th. Get a copy of it and read it. Apart from the decision in the case on the merits of the question discussed in the opinion, it is a long time since I have seen an opinion where the reasoning was stronger or more lucidly expressed. Evidently we made no mistake in his appointment as judge.

Sincerely yours,

W. W. Moody

The White House
Washington
March 3, 1906

My dear Mr. Landis:
Just a line to say how glad I am at the admirable reports I hear of your brother's work as judge. It is delightful to have been instrumental in getting him on the bench.

Faithfully yours,

Theodore Roosevelt

In closing, Charles wrote to Kenesaw: "Can you imagine anything handsomer than this? I presume I ought to give these letters to you but I am so devilishly selfish that I feel that I ought to retain them at least for the present. By George! Old boy, I am proud of you!" And Charles now might have begun to acknowledge that younger brothers Fred and Ken were gaining prominence after trumping Charles' traditional, party-line philosophy.

In another matter involving Interstate Commerce, Kenesaw's son in later years spelled out the Union Station Company case. A train wreck occurred when an operator of a railroad control tower had been weary because of his 12-hour tour of duty. Reed recalled: "Father decided that the railroad was liable, that the fact that these employees controlled the movement of railroad trains obviously engaged in interstate commerce, making these people part of the interstate commerce problem, and it is well known as the 'burden theory'." [132]

Frederick's campaign for re-nomination to Congress in 1906 included a speech in Rochester well attended by Republicans. The local newspaper took note: "It is difficult for the rank and file at least to see why he should not be nominated" and then added a positive tone of: "We are in favor of returning him and of course that settles it." [133] For the 3rd time, Frederick was nominated for

114

Congress, this time unopposed in the convention held in the city of Wabash. [134]

Soon a presidential letter to Kenesaw indicated that Theodore Roosevelt tended to favor "the Landis Court over the Humphrey Court" in a recent case gone awry:

> The White House
> Washington
> Personal
>
> April 16, 1906
>
> My dear Judge Landis:
> I heartily appreciate your telegram.
> Perhaps you will pardon my being so indiscreet as to say that it would indeed have been a fortunate thing for the decent elements of the country if that beef-packing case had been brought before you and not before Judge Humphrey.
>
> Sincerely yours,
>
> Theodore Roosevelt [135]

Frederick continued his regular appearances at Decoration Day services at Mount Hope Cemetery in Logansport: "a most eloquent speech to an immense throng" of about 6,000 people, "the largest in the history of the burying ground." [136]

Mary wrote to Ken, displaying her own brand of humor: "I see by Chicago papers that you are very busy   I saw that some white-livered sneak was treated to do you up   he better not if he wants to sojourn on this terestrial ball any longer . . . you speak of my two smart boys   I have always thought that after myself you had the brains of the family." [137] As a follow-up, she expressed an interest in selling the family farm while noting: "The last month Pa lived he advised me to hold it as it would be valuable some day." [138] John, writing from Cincinnati, again showed his admiration for his younger brother, addressing him "My Dear Judge," and renewing a call for a mini-family reunion in Michigan. He closed with humorous intent, playing upon Ken's tendency to find occasional discomfort in the Scriptural sphere: 'have you forgotten your early training in biblical lore?" [139]

During the course of Fred's promising campaign, several District newspapers reported favorably on his candidacy. One commentary noted the view that Frederick was in demand as a speaker: "The governor of New Jersey has invited him to speak at Newark on July 4 . . . Congressman Littlefield of Maine and several others have tried to secure him for campaign work this fall." [140] This was the same Littlefield who came in second-best in 1900 to Charles in the debate over seating a polygamist from Utah. A visiting congressman from Saginaw, Michigan remarked that Frederick "is one of the bright members of the House and when he arises to make an address commands the respect and closest attention of the members of both parties." [141] The same newspaper cited the *Lincoln League* journal, that observed Frederick's manner in Congress to be different from that of Charles . . . "a quietly-working member of the House of Representatives, industriously seeking and securing the mastery of the intricacies of legislation, rather than posing as a spellbinder." [142]

A leading paper in the state provided an assessment of a growing opposition movement within the Republican Party to defeat Frederick in his campaign for reelection. A well-known correspondent characterized such a challenge as "a few frogs doin' a lot of hollerin'." He offered a favorable assessment of Frederick's prospects by noting: "a prediction that winter will follow summer is not a safer venture into the realm of prophecy than that his plurality will run up into several thousands of votes." [143]

This writer also provided quotes from Frederick's speeches. With respect to the Democratic politico William Jennings Bryan of "Cross of Gold" fame, Frederick referred to him as "the colonel": Bryan, the unsuccessful Democratic candidate for President in 1896 and 1900, was planning to run again in 1908. "Nothing should mar the coming of this great patriot, whose heart beats for the American people at the rate of $500 dollars an hour. Long live the colonel!" Continuing on the theme of the present campaign, Frederick remarked: "This is the most quiet campaign we have ever had . . . The people are too busy to attend political meetings. It is different from 1896, when every lamppost was an opera house and every man a constitutional lawyer." [144]

In the last week before the election, Frederick planned to accompany Vice President Charles Fairbanks to neighboring Peru, "a distinguished honor for the young candidate." Frederick spoke at the Peru Opera House before traveling to Cincinnati to speak in support of the election of Congressman Nicholas Longworth, son-in-law of President Theodore Roosevelt. Representative Longworth

116

agreed to "return the compliment" by speaking at Marion, Grant County, Indiana. [145] Frederick's appearance in Cincinnati augured well in the closing days of his campaign, according to one local paper. [146] The main newspaper in Cincinnati, however, published a partisan photograph of the five Landis brothers, portraying them as elitists from Indiana: "Opponents to the re-election of Congressmen Frederick and Charles Landis have seized upon the sobriquet 'The Royal Family' applied to the Landises as a means toward their defeat." [147]

Meanwhile, another threat to Frederick's re-election originated in the press of Grant County, home of his former opponent Major Steele, during the last week of the campaign. This was an "Anti-Landis Club" that consisted of Republicans who sought Frederick's defeat, citing serious charges by "the Club" that Frederick had "departed from the principles of the Republican party." The signers urged support of Frederick's Democratic opponent . . . they "respectfully request that every Republican believing in and desiring honesty in politics, cast their ballots for Hon. George W. Rauch at the coming election and solicit their friends to do likewise." [148]

Meanwhile, Frederick planned a speech at Wabash, expected "to be the big one for this city this year, the meetings addressed by Congressman Landis always being well attended," according to the local newspaper. It added: "there will be plenty of music and much enthusiasm from the start," and the Ladies Quartet of Huntington, from a nearby town on the Wabash River, which had just sung for Frederick and Nicholas Longworth at Marion, was scheduled to perform. [149]

On October 31, Frederick's last campaign appearance in Wabash at the crowded Eagles theater showed his "Theodore Roosevelt colors" when he described the President's policies that transcended political parties: "The matchless leadership of our President in his great fight for civic reform, in his great struggle against the trusts, and his great warfare upon intrenched privileges has won for him the admiration of almost the entire world." The timing of this observation was important in terms of the impending Election Day, when Frederick's popularity with both Republicans and Democrats meshed with his statement that "there never has been a time in the history of the republic when party lines have been so nearly obliterated as they are today. [150] Such thinking was apparently anathema to the higher-ups of the Republican Party structure.

As the end of Frederick's campaign approached, he spoke to his hometown crowd about the deficiencies of the Democratic Party, "which for the first time in twenty-five years has advanced no reason why it should be placed in public power." He then responded to "Anti-Landis club" criticism from within his own party as to this campaign being all about *education*, saying: "This is not a campaign of education, for we have all been educated . . . we all took a four-year course in the University of Starvation under Professor Cleveland . . ." While probably still confident in spite of the revolt by Republican Party leaders close to Major Steele, Frederick fondly described the reply once made by William McKinley after defeat as a congressional candidate. He felt that: "it was full of the patience of Lincoln . . . and of the sublime courage of Ulysses S. Grant" in the following words: "My friends, it is only for a moment. The people have made a mistake. They will correct it at the first opportunity." [151]

Grant County Republicans, long supportive of George Steele against Frederick's candidacy, were the driving force behind the "Anti-Landis" movement. Following this last-minute revolt on the eve of the election to turn Labor Democrats away from voting for Landis, a Grant County newspaper wrote of an effort made on the eve of the election to enable Democratic Labor to support Frederick. This *Marion Chronicle* newspaper, taking a position in favor of Frederick's candidacy, thus printed on its front page "Last Hour Attempt of Dozen Non-Republicans to Commit Organized Labor to Democracy (read Democratic Party) Proves Failure." The article's lead-in stated further: "Highest Federation of Labor Official in Indiana Characterizes Effort to Drag Trades Unions Into the Campaign as Unprecedented, Unwise and Unauthorized. - Democratic Leaders Condemned for Attempting to Prostitute Labor's Cause to Partisan and Political Ends." The newspaper article went on to note that some labor member claimed "that there is a life-sized 'nigger in the wood-pile.'" [152]

The Trade Union campaign was stated as partially responsible for an unexpected and decisive defeat for Frederick on November 6, as another Marion newspaper the *News Tribune* wrote: "In a most unexpected and remarkable landslide, the voters of the Eleventh congressional district cut down the big majorities of

Congressman Fred Landis in every county yesterday." [153] The *Marion Chronicle* reported: "Eleventh District Swept by a Political Cyclone. - Every County is Democratic." [154] Another regional newspaper, supportive of Frederick, hinted at a possible cause of his sudden, surprising defeat: "Mr. Landis, whose record in congress is an excellent one, had to combat the usual off-year influences, coupled with the disagreeable consequences that always follow the naming of postmasters and pension boards. [155] Finally, a District newspaper of a larger city made a strong suggestion that his opponents had finally settled an old score and offered speculation about Frederick's likely future. [156]

Later on, a Chicago newspaper concluded that Frederick's congressional career was interrupted after his second term when he was defeated for re-election in 1906 because of 'factional strife in his party." [157] Was not this "factional strife" a result of opposition by traditional Republican Party leaders to Frederick's pro-Teddy Roosevelt stand on issues and his candor in criticizing big business in the halls of Congress? And were, perhaps, his bold statements on sensitive racial matters not also considered too controversial for regional leaders of the Republican Party?

This explanation of intra-party strife is supported by the philosophical split in the Republican Party caused by President Teddy Roosevelt's "trustbusting" policies, with which Frederick was linked by his recent actions in the House of Representatives. In December 1905 he had shown his own strong sentiments against corporate interests when he presented legislation, as already noted, charging large insurance companies with unfair profiteering in interstate commerce at the expense of ordinary policy holders. In his stand against "big business," Frederick was moving away from the traditional Republican Party position of former President McKinley that had been shared by brother Charles. Kenesaw's position would soon also display his affinity for Theodore Roosevelt's "trust-busting," but by then, he would have been in a federal "lifetime" federal post quite beyond the reach of partisan Republican retribution that had ensnared his "little brother."

On the heels of Frederick's defeat for reelection to Congress, Mary Landis, appearing to be in denial about his setback, chatted about other Logansport matters in a letter to Kenesaw and reported that visiting journalists came to interview and photograph her as "the mother of the brothers Landis:" "O yes the photographer

came up yes and I sat for a picture he photographed the house and
Kate and Fred nearly broke up the meeting at me sitting in state here
looking at the camera Fred said I looked like Napolean and made
all of his fool speeches. [158] Quickly following up on her recent
letter, Mary wrote again to Ken, continuing to avoid mention of
Frederick's defeat, and speaking mainly of Thanksgiving plans. [159]

Frederick's unexpected loss in the 1906 election was a
major disappointment for the entire Landis clan, and Mary
continued to avoid mentioning it in her letters. Leaving politics
aside after his defeat, Frederick returned to Indiana to employ his
Chautauqua skills and to emerge as the family's first novelist.

Kenesaw's second year on the job as federal judge in 1906
brought satisfaction from juridical work and a major diversion
through regular attendance at Wrigley Field to watch the Chicago
Cubs in action. Adding to his pleasure was the opportunity now to
expose his son to the sport he had himself enjoyed from teenage
years. Focusing on the 1906 World Series, Reed later recalled his
impressions as a 10-year-old: "Father had a box, and it was of
course on the Cubs' side and right at a point where the ball players
on their way to bat would go by from the bench." Reed
remembered meeting up with Tinker-to-Evers-to-Chance . . .
Mordecai Brown." [160]

The year 1907 brought Kenesaw along in Frederick's
footsteps to challenge large companies for interstate commerce
abuses. The younger brother's "progressive politics" in the House
of Representatives was about to be echoed by Kenesaw's
"progressive judgements" in the courtroom, and his rulings against
large corporations would gain widespread attention. Meanwhile,
Fred and Ken were finding decisive distance from the traditional
political stance of their boyhood mentor, Charles.

Kenesaw's son recalled that at age 11 he was an eye-witness
to his father's court proceedings starting March 4, 1907 in a case
that concerned the Standard Oil Company and its possible violation
of Interstate Commerce provisions. Reed recalled his father's
explanation that railroads had been paying rebates to the oil
conglomerate, an illegal procedure in commerce across state lines.
[161] The trial finished April 13, with the jury rendering a verdict
against the defendant after deliberating two hours. The Standard Oil
Company sought a new trial in Chicago, while Kenesaw began to

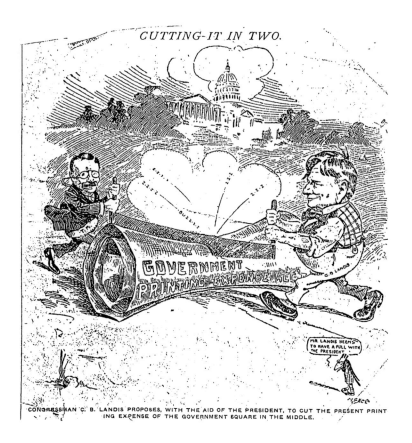

CUTTING-IT IN TWO.

CONGRESSMAN C. B. LANDIS PROPOSES, WITH THE AID OF THE PRESIDENT, TO CUT THE PRESENT PRINTING EXPENSE OF THE GOVERNMENT SQUARE IN THE MIDDLE.

President Theodore Roosevelt and Congressman Charles Landis working together in the early 1900's.   Unidentified newspaper.

REPUBLICANS OF HIGH AND LOW DEGREE
GATHERED YESTERDAY FOR THE LOVE FEAST

CONGRESSMAN JAMES E. WATSON.   UNION B. HUNT.   MAJ. GEORGE W. STEELE.   W. L. TAYLOR.
               G. A. H. SHIDELER.   CONGRESSMAN CHARLES B. LANDIS.   —Sketched at the Denison by a Star artist.

Charles puffing cigars with the man Frederick recently defeated, Major Steele -- truly a time to try to bring Republicans together for a national campaign to be waged in 1904. *Indianapolis Star*, December 31, 1903.

FREDERICK LANDIS.   **KENESAW M. LANDIS.**   **JOHN H. LANDIS.**   **CHARLES B. LANDIS.**   **WALTER K. LANDIS.**

LOGANSPORT, Ind., May 24.—The nomination of Frederick Landis for Congress by the Republicans of this district adds one more triumph to the long list already achieved by the remarkable family of which the nominee is a member. Frederick Landis is one of five brothers, all of whom have achieved prominence in one way or another at an unusually youthful age. As if the family were selected as a conspicuous example of what pluck and spirit can do, the Landis boys began life in poor circumstances, and all of them have risen to the top with the buoyancy of a cork in water. Frederick Landis is 29. As a boy he used to sell newspapers in Logansport. But he studied, graduated in law and became a campaign orator, doted upon by the Republican crowds in election times. One of his brothers, Charles B. Landis, is already a congressman, representing the ninth district. He lives at Delphi, and began his career as a newspaper man. He is now serving his third term. "Kenesaw M." Landis is another brother of the family. He has lived in Chicago for the past twelve years, and served as private secretary to Walter Q. Gresham when that noted jurist was Secretary of State. John H. Landis, a fourth brother, elected to devote himself to medicine, and is now one of the leading surgeons in Cincinnati. The fifth brother, Walter K. Landis, is postmaster in Porto Rico. It is quite probable that a record like this can be shown by very few families in any or any other country. Abraham H. Landis, the father of these remarkable young men, was a prominent figure in the great antislavery movement, which preceded the civil war. He was an Ohio surgeon. Out of patriotism and principle, and when the war came he entered the union army as a surgeon. During the battle of Kenesaw Mountain, while he was looking after the wounded, he was struck by a spent cannon ball, which so severely injured one of his legs that he never thoroughly recovered. He was confined in Libby prison for six months and otherwise earned a capital record for courage and suffering on the fields of the South. He passed away in 1896. The Landis family are of German-Swiss origin, and have been settled in America for five generations. They were pioneers of the Ohio River, and have always been noted for their steadfastness of purpose and for their patriotism to their country.

Article following Frederick's first nomination to Congress in May 1902.   Landis Wagar file.

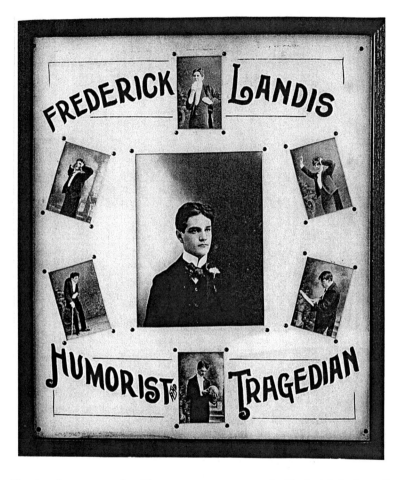

Theater sign announcing Chautauqua appearances by Frederick in the early 1900's.

Frederick, at 29, (center) and 22 delegates who delivered his nomination to Congress in 1902 on the 1,012th ballot in Wabash. [Kenesaw is an observer at left end of the 2nd row.]

INDIANA OFFERS A REMEDY

Indianapolis
NEWS DEC. 13-1905 54

FINE LAD

FRED LANDIS

INSURANCE REGULATION BILL.

J. DOWERS

A WASHINGTON DISPATCH SAYS CONGRESSMAN FRED LANDIS, WHO CALLED AT THE WHITE HOUSE, SPOKE TO THE PRESIDENT ABOUT HIS INSURANCE REGULATION BILL AND THE PRESIDENT SAID THAT IT WAS "A GOOD BILL AND OUGHT TO RECEIVE CONSIDERATION BY CONGRESS."

Preside ... Congressman Frederick Landis working together in 1905 to curtail the corporate power of the insurance industry through legislation.

"The only brothers in Congress" c. 1906: Frederick driving Stanley Steamer with Charles seated in rear. Rock Ridge Park in Washington, DC. TFL file.

John in front of Landis' horse-drawn carriage. Left to right: sister Kate; mother Mary; John's wife Daisy; their daughter Mary; Frederick, sister Frank c.1906. Landis Wagar file.

"THE ROYAL FAMILY" OF INDIANA.

October 26, 1906 Cincinnati Enquirer

From left to right: United States Judge Kenesaw M. Landis, Chicago; Representative Chas. B. Landis, Representative Frederick K. Landis; Walter K. Landis, Postmaster San Juan, P. R.; Dr. John Landis, of Cincinnati. For several days Congressman F. K. Landis has been "stumping" Hamilton County.

SPECIAL DISPATCH TO THE ENQUIRER.

Logansport, Ind., October 25.—Opponents to the re-election of Congressmen Frederick and Charles Landis have seized upon the sobriquet "The Royal Family," allied to the Landises, as a means toward their defeat. All but one of five brothers admittedly hold Federal office, but the Landis brothers consider it no stigma to be styled "The Royal Family." Saturday, October 27, Congressman Nicholas Longworth and his bride, formerly Alice Roosevelt, will visit Congressman Frederick Landis's district in return for several days' speechmaking Frederick Landis did in Longworth's district. On his return from Panama President Roosevelt will be the guest of Walter Landis at San Juan, P. R., for 24 hours from the evening of November 22. Both Landises in Congress are candidates for re-election this year, and both have hard fights, which impartial observers of politics declare will be won by the "Royal Family."

Ploy in the Republican hierarchy's revolt in 1906 against Frederick's election for a third term after a solid victory in his renomination -- a reason for Republican leaders' unusual opposition apparently tied to Frederick's strong appeal to Democratic voters! It worked.

VICE-PRESIDENT FAIRBANKS COMING TO PERU.

VICE-PRESIDENT C. W. FAIRBANKS.   CONGRESSMAN FREDERICK LANDIS.

Frederick's campaign pin [TFL file], shown with press coverage of high-level support for his candidacy for a third term in 1906. Republican district leaders, in the final days of the election, turned against him by asking the Party to support the Democratic candidate.

ONLY ONE OF THE "LANDIS BOYS" NOT IN THE PUBLIC SERVICE

DR. JOHN LANDIS.

Dr. John Landis, who is a practicing physician at Cincinnati, is the only one of the five well-known Landis brothers of Indiana who is not a Government office-holder. Regarding the brothers, the New York World said recently:

"Charles Beary Landis represents the Ninth Indiana district in the House of Representatives. Frederick Landis represents the Eleventh Indiana district. President Roosevelt has appointed Kenesaw Mountain Landis a United States judge for the Northern district of Illinois. A fourth brother is postmaster at San Juan, Porto Rico. But there is still another who is unprovided for. He is a physician, and the least Mr. Roosevelt can decently do is to make him surgeon-general of the regular army."

John Landis would join public service as Health Officer of that city.
Unidentified newspaper c.1906.

inquire about the relationship between Standard Oil of New Jersey and Standard Oil of Indiana in order to assess an appropriate fine.

Meanwhile, hometown news, gossip, and advice arrived from Ken's mother: "The old town is gossiping along as usual I was out to a Lunch Wed with a lot of Ladies at Mrs. John Tiptons the great topic of interest is the divorce of Dr Stewart and Mame McGee." Mary was becoming the target of photographers and the press. At the same time she began to realize that her son's judicial actions were making news in both the national and international press. Mary questioned the wisdom of Kenesaw and Winifred's decision to try out living in a hotel instead of a house: "Now I hope you are getting on fine dont work to hard in the standard oil let it go and you take your rest how are the children will they like the hotel life." [162] Shortly another letter came from his mother: "I sent you last Sat a week ago a small basket of grape fruit and a coupple of glasses of Jell the grape fruit Walter sent me from San Juan I hope you rec it all OK." [163]

Back in the courtroom, Kenesaw ordered subpeonas in order to dig into the background of the Standard Oil case by compelling the appearance of its responsible officials. For the Judge, this meant tediously going from the bottom to the top of the oil conglomerate and of the Union Tank Line railroad. In the words of Reed, his father proceeded, "gradually working up in ranks from the basic bookkeepers to the accountants and comptrollers, into the treasury department and the traffic department and the vice presidents of the company, and finally, when nobody else had been able to tell him anything about this, he issued a subpeona for Mr. John D. Rockefeller, president of the company."

Reed noted that the prestigious oil magnate displayed ingenuity and resourcefulness, "artful dodging," in efforts to avoid becoming a witness in Ken's courtroom. As Reed noted, "Mr. Rockefeller left New Jersey and went to his home in Rhode Island. The subpoena was then issued returnable in Rhode Island, and he went to some other area." Reed's father, weary of a game of cat and mouse, "issued the next subpoena returnable in all United States Marshals offices, and Mr. Rockefeller came to court." Reed continued with the Judge's description of the courtroom response by this distinguished industrialist, whose presence on the witness stand could no longer be deferred by his lawyers: "All of their motions were overruled, and Mr. Rockefeller went on the stand and, like his subordinates, stated that he knew nothing about this money that was coming in from the railroads or why they had gotten it." Judge Landis asked the corporate head of Standard Oil a series of nineteen questions but received only generalities in return, with the venerable witness claiming that he had been away from his office for years. [164] On the eve of the announcement of Ken's decision as to an appropriate penalty, one writer who had followed the case from its beginning made a prediction that would prove to stand the test of time: "Should he assess the maximum fines, there is no doubt that his name would belong to history from that moment." [165]

Reed finally summed up the Judge's decision, as related to him many years earlier:

> The net of the whole case was that the Standard Oil Company was found guilty of accepting these rebates, and they had done so, the Government proved, in several thousand instances. Each of those instances was a violation of the regulations, or of the law, and Father applied a fine against each violation. . [166]

It didn't take long after Kenesaw's noteworthy feat in bringing Mr. Rockefeller into court to testify as a witness and in assessing a penalty for wrongdoing for speculation to suggest Kenesaw as a candidate for the White House in the upcoming 1908 election. One small city newspaper in Ohio believed that, in view of his recent performance as Federal Judge, he should be considered as a Republican candidate to succeed Theodore Roosevelt. Its headline noted: "Intrepid Chicago Man, Friend of the Masses and Believer in Rooseveltian Policies, is Put forth as the Logical Candidate." The text continued to paint the picture of a confusing situation as to Theodore Roosevelt's hoped-for successor. Teddy's success as President indicated that the new candidate should be a "trust-buster." Who else to elect than the man who had just bested a monarch of the corporate world! Reminding the reader that Abe Lincoln from Illinois had proved to be a great Chief Executive, the editorial continued: "Illinois is the home of a judge who believes that the law should be upheld by all classes of citizens, be they rich as Croesus or as 'poor as Job's turkey.' If Judge Kenesaw Mountain Landis presided over the nation, it is confidently believed that everybody would get a square deal." [167]

The large-city press also reacted quickly to the Judge's procedure in questioning of Mr. Rockefeller. One prominent newspaper headed a story with a photograph of Kenesaw and the following caption: "When Judge Kenesaw M. Landis brought to bay the richest man in the world and his fellows of the oil trust, the light, thus suddenly turned on Judge Landis, revealed him as one of the strongest and most interesting men before the American people today." [168] To add to the wide publicity of the case, a month later Judge Landis announced the amount of the fine, a record-setting amount for such cases. Reed recalled that his father's calculations in determining the fine were rounded off by one reporter who used his own math . . . "3,003 counts in the indictment times whatever the fine amounted to per count and came up with a 29 million-dollar fine" but "the correct figure was $27,240,000." [169]

In a humorous comparison, public attention was drawn to an earlier occasion, when Kenesaw "haggled with a loan shark over a few pennies of interest due from a poor man." This process finally came to an end with the Judge paying the loan shark out of his private purse and telling him to be gone out of his sight before he forgot himself and gave him a thrashing." [170] The 29-million-dollar fine assessed against Standard Oil proved to be an aftershock following the earlier decision to find the company guilty of accepting illegal rebates in restraint of trade. Logansport's newspaper noted that public attention about the fine "was almost equal to the interest manifested when John D. Rockefeller appeared in court." [171]

A Chicago newspaper displayed a cartoon showing alleged reactions by President Theodore Roosevelt and other prominent figures to Kenesaw's Standard Oil Decision and the famous fine. This publicity left no doubt as to the President's thoughts on the matter. The Vice President of Standard Oil issued a statement to a New York newspaper suggesting that President Roosevelt himself was responsible for the "attacks upon us that occurred so frequently as to rob them of even an appearance of being accidental." [172] This account went on to print an article: "The Remarkable Landis Family," featuring accomplishments of the five "Landis boys."

A Logansport newspaper reported that Standard Oil had dispatched three individuals to the Judge's hometown to follow him in order to find derogatory information, presumably to discredit his judicial decision: "The spotters have been with Landis ever since Aug. 5 -- two days after Landis' ruling attracted the attention of the entire world." [173]

123

Standard Oil Company published a collection of editorial critiques in a pamphlet that challenged "the prosecutions lately instituted against it in the Federal Courts" in the face of "the Company's absolute innocence of wrongdoing." [174]

The Judge's presence in Logansport proved to be a precedent-setting continuation of his formal judicial duties there, an action causing excitement in the city and full local press coverage. In this setting, Kenesaw ruled in favor of a local man who purchased bills of lading by Chicago banks later found to be fraudulent, stirring editorial comment: "Judge Landis did not care to have the matter become public, fearing that it would precipitate upon him a bunch of other Federal matters that he ran away from Chicago to avoid during the vacation season." [175] The next day *The New York Times* attested to this latest hometown example of his innovative skills: "Career of Kenesaw Mountain Landis, Tamer of Standard Oil Octopus, is Not Lacking in Originality." [176]

A Chicago newspaper summed up Kenesaw's judicial career after reviewing his first two years on the Bench: "Judge Landis has looked upon the question of deciding the issue whether corporations shall control government or government shall control corporations with the one view of getting at the net result." The article cited Kenesaw's reaction upon hearing the opinion of a man-on-the-street who expressed support for his ruling in the Standard Oil case. This experience touched the Judge's feelings about the responsibility of those engaged in public service: "I tell you that the greatest position that a man can achieve is the one upon which his fellow man looks with approval. The meanest man in the world is the man who destroys the faith of any human being in anything." The editorial then quoted Kenesaw's statement that such an occurrence meant more to him . . . "than to have all the money in the world." Regarding speculation about his possible quest for high political office, the article noted that the Judge was adamantly opposed to such a notion. [177] To a local interviewer who asked Kenesaw about his interest in "presidential honors," the Judge responded: "Presidential candidate! Me? Ha-ha-ha-ha-ha-ha-ha-ha." [178]

The wide reputation Kenesaw gained from his landmark ruling led to Chicago newsprint about the Landis boys and their aging mother: "29,240,000 Fine Brings The Landis Family Again Into Limelight." [179] "Rivalry" within the family was seen as one of the most positive and friendly sort: "the five Landis brothers are devoted each to the others. When one of them takes a step forward and upward, each of the others shakes hands with himself." [180]

After opening the fall session of County Court in an Illinois town, Kenesaw told a story about Abraham Lincoln that he had heard from men who knew Abe as a young politician. The women of the town had taken up a collection and were hoping to use it to boost the morale of young soldiers who had left home for the Civil War . . . An old gentleman attempted to get high-level approval to serve as a conduit to Union soldiers fighting in the Confederacy. Failing in his efforts to gain access through a congressman to Secretary of War Stanton, the old fellow managed to go over Stanton's head and obtain an audience with President Lincoln. The President cautioned that he did not wish to overrule Secretary Stanton and would not do so but decided that he needed "a special commissioner to go among the rank and file of the army to find out what the soldiers of this country think of the government of the United States in its greatest crisis." The gentleman emissary had won the opportunity to oblige the local women by delivering their generous contributions. [181]

One editorial observed that, in view of Kenesaw's role as corporation lawyer for the Chicago and Eastern Illinois, Calumet Electric, and Grand Trunk Railroads; "something better might have been expected of him" than to render tough judgements against large firms. This writer found examples showing Kenesaw paid no heed to his previous connections: "He is not hostile to corporations any more than he is friendly to them. If the law had been in favor of Standard Oil it would have been acquitted. The law happened to be against it and it was convicted . . . He is a judge." [182]

Musician George H. Littlefield chose the occasion of Kenesaw's Standard Oil decision to compose "A Topical Song" entitled: *Can't You See the Coming Day,* featuring Marguerite Lambert, "the charming vocalist," and published by New York's North American Music Co. Among the five verses and chorus were such lines as: "The 'crush a feller' crowd got hit, Right in the standard a blow . . . They corralled them in Chicago, Judge Landis was on the bench, And he let a piece of law go, That gave the Standard a wrench . . . Say can't you see the dawn of day when, Right holds sway O'er the hearts of all mankind." [183]

125

Amid controversy over some of his decisions, especially the Standard Oil case, and facing speculation about his "political prospects," Ken succeeded in finding diversion by attending the 43rd annual reunion of his father's 35th Ohio Volunteer Infantry Regiment. As was usually the case, the Judge addressed the group. It was held at Camden, Ohio on the anniversary of heavy fighting at Chickamauga, September 19th, 1863, the day before Dr. Abraham Landis' hospital was overrun by Gen. Nathan Bedford Forrest's troops. Kenesaw met Private Jeremiah Boatman of Company I, "who carried his father from the field" after being wounded by a cannon ball at the Battle of Kenesaw Mountain. Charles and John were present on this occasion to hear Kenesaw deliver the main address on the responsibility of public servants: "Find out what ought to be done and then do it. All this talk about the great courage that is required of the man in office today is what Sherman called poppycock. A man in a position of trust owes 100 percent loyalty." [184] Another newspaper noted a treasured lesson Kenesaw learned from his elderly mother who, instead of offering him congratulations for his judicial record, provided simple but powerful advice: "Always be a just judge." [185]

The Judge's visit to his father's regimental reunion gave him the opportunity to attend a game between the Chicago Cubs and the Cincinnati Reds. An avowed Cubs fan, he cheered for Cincinnati because the Cubs already had enough games in the "Win column," and he felt the Reds needed another game. Then he left for the scenes of his childhood. A Dayton Ohio newspaper suggested Ken's nostalgia: "He will walk over the fields where he turned up the sod with the help of a team of mules . . . also in the fields in which he used to cradle wheat, and where he used to go barefooted among the briars and drive up the cows." [186]

The following month a prominent journalist noted that Kenesaw's new prominence came along after public successes by his four brothers: "There are other Landis boys; collected they make a distinguished group and look as much like one another as a handful of bullets, being one and all run in the same mold." He wrote that the nomination of Kenesaw to the Federal Bench showed Theodore Roosevelt to be "that wizard at sterling selection!" He described in favorable terms Kenesaw's knack at making anti-trust rulings: "Like Mark Twain, he tries to treat a rich man with all the deference and respect he does a poor man " The writer told of an exchange between Kenesaw as a Federal Judge and an admiring friend: "Strange, what a genius you Landis boys have for office! Let me see; four of you are officeholders;" and Kenesaw responded: "That's not correctly stated . . . My brothers are office holders; I am a public servant." [187]

Charles, as Chairman of the House Committee on Printing reported "great irregularity" in "expenditures for furniture in the Printing Office and for the purchase of supplies" as well as serious deficiencies in "the present audit system of the Printing Bureau." President Theodore Roosevelt wrote a letter in reply, asking Charles to look into the matter and assuring him of his own interest and support. [188]

Subsequently, the President enclosed his reply to Charles in correspondence with one William Rossiter of the Census Bureau, stating "in accordance therewith you will assume immediate charge of the Government Printing Office." He instructed Rossiter to "place yourself in communication with Congressman Landis and afford him every facility for obtaining the information his Committee desires in their investigation." [189] President Roosevelt also requested inclusion in an appropriation bill of "a thousand dollars" to recompense the head of the Census Bureau for his investigation of the Government Printing Office, noting that this project "was really suggested by Chairman Landis of the House Committee on Printing." [190]

One newspaper account in 1908 recalled that "corporations began to whistle softly as they thought of Judge Landis" because his pattern of rulings were costly to such firms as the Chicago and Alton Railroad, a large meat-packing company, a furniture trust, and Allis-Chalmers Company that imported contract workers. It summed up his public performance in terms of parental influence: "He has improved well the inheritance bequeathed by a union of paternal strength of character and maternal loftiness of aim." [191]

Reed added a sequel to his father's record-setting fine against Standard Oil: the Appellate Court proceeded to nullify the fine on the grounds that Kenesaw had exceeded his judicial powers by compelling Mr. Rockefeller to appear as a witness. This ruling occurred a year after the Judge's landmark decision. A Logansport news story on the item attracted much less public attention than the original report of Ken's fine. Its title of the article on the Appellate Court's reversal of Kenesaw's record-breaking fine was "Fiercest

'Roast' Ever Given a High Jurist." The article included an observation that the wording of the judicial action was extraordinary, not without personal overtones, relating to the person of Appellate Judge Grosscup, mentioned earlier in this chapter . . . (It was noted earlier that Ken, as a junior lawyer in Chicago, had not always seen fit to refer to senior judges such as Mr. Grosscup in the traditional manner.) The local newspaper alleged that relations had long been strained between Kenesaw and this judge as a result of Ken's criticism of ethical missteps by certain justices. [192]

Concerning the reversal of Kenesaw's Standard Oil case ruling, an unsigned, undated, and sharply critical note from the Judge's file apparently had been mailed to him several months after the Appeals Court action in July 1908, remarking: "In legal attainments you are a Jackass, in disposition a Jackal." [193] The fact that Kenesaw kept this clipping in his file suggests that he found some appreciation of the item in later years, although there is no indication that the writer later identified himself as he had promised in the letter.

As noted by Reed, a subsequent legal ruling in later years brought about the break-up of Standard Oil because of its activities "in restraint of trade." [194] Such judicial action broke the Standard Oil cartel, tending in an indirect way to vindicate Kenesaw's tough ruling against the company. In addition, Reed's personal account that, after ten years, John D. Rockefeller acknowledged to him the correctness of Kenesaw's ruling and its ultimate benefit to the head of Standard Oil comes to the point. After Reed returned to the United States from his assignment as a fighter pilot in the World War I, he was invited for a session with Mr. Rockefeller, during which the oil mogul made the following assertion: "When you get back to Chicago, young man, please tell your father that the decision of his was the best thing that ever happened to the Standard Oil Company. It woke us up, and we have made more money since by using modern methods of sales and business than we ever made before." [195] Years later, in 1929, one of the Judge's cousins informed Kenesaw that a senior official of Standard Oil of New Jersey acknowledged his own involvement in the activities charged in the case and affirmed the guilty verdict as fully justified. [196]

In the category of folksy information from Logansport, Mary wrote to Ken to update him on the family: "your dear sister Frank is in Dayton . . . CB is campaigning . . . Fred is getting a good many letters asking him to make speech . . . Walt will start home the 14th of Oct on the *Philadelphia* . . ." [197] Mary wrote again at Christmas time with more news and gossip ". . . we see by morning paper that Booth Tarkington fell from the watter waggon . . . what a shame for a man who has succeeded in a litterary way to so forget his manhood but so it goes . . ." [198]

A major Western newspaper chose, in response to "a dozen letters," to reprint a "character sketch" of Kenesaw . . . "some picture physical, moral, mental of Judge Landis" in light of his fine of Standard Oil. The article noted that "an honorable curiosity lives on" about "the soul that could so far triumph over a native knee-bending snobbery as to pile up a fine against Standard Oil, as though it had been your ordinary pick-purse." [199]

Kenesaw revealed his personal philosophy about the role of a Supreme Being in a newspaper interview, a topic that he rarely addressed in discussions with journalists: "The older I get the more I am impressed with the profound belief that God rules the world. There is more mystery in the growth of a tree than any human mind can grasp." Kenesaw was firm, according to the interviewer, on the equality of man: "He is elementally a commoner and an exponent of the thought that when the Declaration of Independence said that all men were created equal, that sentence was not intended as a governmental joke." On raising children, Ken continued: "If I can do it, I am going to have a farm, and I am going to bring my boy up in the clean atmosphere of the farm, where men come up in equal ranks and where there is little sham and deceit." [200]

In 1909, the year Theodore Roosevelt turned the presidency over to William Howard Taft, Charles was defeated in the race for a seventh term in the House of Representatives. Growing dissension within the Republican Party that had brought about Frederick's defeat in 1906 contributed to Charles' failure to be reelected, and he returned to his home in Delphi, Indiana. Charles continued to participate in the Chautauqua system with an appearance at La Crosse, Wisconsin. A brochure for this occasion re-stated the goal of Chautauqua as "The Best of Everything" and "Nothing Too Good for our Patrons," recalling a write-up from the *Washington Morning Star* about Charles' performance in Congress. The prominent occasion was his debate with Representative Littleton on the question of admitting a Mormon to the House of Representatives, Mr. Roberts. The newspaper called Charles' action in Congress

129

"the best speech of all" and described its effect upon Representative Cox of Tennessee: "With tears streaming down his face he crossed over from the Democratic side to shake hands with and thank the eloquent young Hoosier Republican." [201]

The year 1909 was important for John who was named to membership on the Cincinnati Board of Health, when the Board was taken from control of the Director of Public Service and reorganized. In the same year, Mary wrote to Kenesaw "My Dear boy" about Frederick's efforts to obtain a publisher for his book manuscripts, including *The Glory of His Country* and *The Angel of Lonesome Hill*: "Ken . . . Fred has not heard a word from Bobbs Merell and co . . . he is so anxious . . . tis terrible the suspence and I feel the result if turned down he gets nearly frantic . . ." [202]

On August 12, 1909, Frederick married Bess Baker of Leases Corner, teacher in a one-room school outside of Logansport, and his brother-in-law Dr. Arthur Baker chauffered the bride and groom to their honeymoon destination, brother Charlie's country estate "Peaceful Valley" near Delphi. The vehicle was Dr. Baker's luxurious, 1906 Stanley Steamer with leather seats, a precursor of the gasoline-driven automobile.

HERE IS A TABLEAU THAT WILL LIVE IN HISTORY

This photograph was taken in the United States District Court yesterday during the personal examination of John D. Rockefeller by Judge Kenesaw M. Landis. The oil king is seated in the witness chair and the court is plying him with questions.

Kenesaw wa[...] [...] court to testify in
the Standard [...] *Chicago Examiner*, July 7, 1907.

The aftermath of Kenesaw's strong judicial treatment of oil and railroad conglomerates reflected numerous cartoons that made this Chicago judge known across the nation and in foreign countries as well.

One Chicago daily newspaper, not identified, presented the above as one of
"Some Interviews on Judge Landis' Decision" shortly after Kenesaw's
ruling on the Standard Oil Case in 1907.

The Literary Digest

PUBLIC OPINION (New York) combined with THE LITERARY DIGEST

(Title Reg. U S. Pat. Off.)

Vol. XXXV., No. 8. Whole No. 905.   NEW YORK, AUGUST 24, 1907.   Price Per Copy, 10c

CONTENTS

FUNK & WAGNALLS PUBLISHERS, NEW YORK and LONDON

Kenesaw's fame followed his Standard Oil decision to the literary community. TFL file.

THE
TELESCOPE

DAYTON, OHIO, JANUARY 29, 1908.

EX CONGRESSMAN FREDERICK LANDIS
JUDGE KENESAW MOUNTAIN LANDIS
CONGRESSMAN CHARLES B. LANDIS
POSTMASTER WALTER KUMLER LANDIS
DOCTOR JOHN HOWARD LANDIS

A QUINTETTE OF MASTER MINDS

Feature cover of a journal from Dayton, Ohio, January 29, 1908.
RoseMary King file.

PART FIVE
The Chicago
Sunday Tribune.
FEBRUARY 9, 1908.

W
For th

in These Eyes They F

By

Mrs Mary K. Landis
Mother of Judge Kenesaw Mountain Landis

Mrs Junius Spencer Morgan
Mother of John Pierpont Morg

Abraham would have been pleased by the sudden fame of his wife as mother of the Landis boys indicated above and, particularly, by her placement beside Mrs. Morgan. For it had been just two years since Frederick, while discussing his proposed legislation to curtail corporate excesses, chose to describe Pierpont Morgan, the banking executive, on the Floor of the US House of Representatives as "the international kleptomaniac."

The 1910's

There will be a minimum wage law for women and for girls when women vote.
And the mills and mines and factories will stop child slavery when women vote.
They will lift the children of the poor in their sympathetic arms and stop this Republic's blackest infamy! (Applause)

-- Frederick Landis addressing the 1912
Indiana Progressive Party Convention [203]

In this new decade, Walter would lose his position as Postmaster of Puerto Rico because of his youngest brother's support of Teddy Roosevelt in 1912. Charles would become an executive of DuPont Powder Company providing war materiel in support of US forces in World War I. John would become recognized nationally for his work in controlling epidemics in Cincinnati as the city's Health Officer by requiring the pasteurization of all milk entering the city. Kenesaw would fulfill his childhood goal of "being in charge" and "responsible only to his conscience," serving as an independent and dynamic Federal Judge. Meanwhile, Fred would put into practice his instincts as an independent "Teddy Roosevelt Republican," and, in the field of the arts, he wrote several plays and advanced one of his novels to the stature of "a Broadway hit."

The year 1910 made Frederick's new career as a published author a reality. [204] The March issue of *Scribner's Magazine* that featured Theodore Roosevelt's article "African Game Trails" included an extended article on Frederick's forthcoming novel about Mr. Roosevelt "The Angel of Lonesome Hill," illustrated by N. C. Wyeth. [205] Scribners Sons published this book in 1910 as well as Frederick's Civil War novel *The Glory of His Country* that featured a Northern traitor -- a "copperhead" -- who, in a suspenseful ending, turned out to be a Union hero. Using a subtle idea, Frederick employed ancestral given names of Philip and Daniel in the book and went on to fictionalize the "backroom politics" that had defeated him for re-election to Congress in 1906. He dedicated the book to his aged mother, portraying her in a delightful role as "the Lady of the Portico" and showed a devotion to his hometown of Logansport, called "Happyville."

131

Theodore Roosevelt generously acknowledged Frederick's rendition of him in *The Angel of Lonesome Hill*:

> The Outlook
> 287 Fourth Avenue
> New York
>
> June 28, 1910
>
> The Hon. Frederick Landis
> Logansport, Ind.
>
> Dear Landis:
> Of all the compliments that could be paid to me,
> nothing could touch my heart more than to have me
> appear just as you make me appear in your stories. I
> especially valued the volume because it came from you.
> If you are to be in the East this Summer, will you not
> give me a chance to see you?
>
> Sincerely yours,
>
> Theodore Roosevelt [206]

For Kenesaw, 1910 proved to be a productive year on the Bench, with his ruling in the "Beef Trust case" that brought a welcome note of appreciation from the same President-turned-elder statesman:

> The Outlook
> 287 Fourth Avenue
> New York
>
> July 22, 1910
>
> My dear Judge:
> Of course, I have read your charge to the Grand Jury
> with the greatest interest. I wish I could see you. I
> particularly like the fact that in your charge you quoted
> that admirable paragraph of Lincoln's. How I wish
> that some of those who pay him lip service today
> would apply his principles to present conditions!
>
> Faithfully yours,
>
> Theodore Roosevelt [207]

After five and a half years on the Bench, Kenesaw appeared as a prospect for the US Supreme Court in the view of "friends and admirers in Chicago and the west." According to an Indiana newspaper, sentiment was growing because Kenesaw had "demonstrated his worth and his liberal, progressive attitude on the Bench." [208] The game of politics, however, would place a damper on such a possibility because his Rooseveltian actions against large corporations were not a priority to Teddy's successor, President William Howard Taft. Mr. Taft's lack of interest in elevating Kenesaw was indicated earlier in an editorial that focused on the Judge's judicial activism in the ruling against Standard Oil, when President Taft referred to Kenesaw at a news conference as "an obscure demagogue of a judge." It should be noted, however, that a handwritten note attached to a copy of this editorial suggested that, a few years earlier, Secretary of War William Howard Taft indicated his favorable opinion of Kenesaw's action in the Standard Oil case. [209]

Changing the scene from Chicago to Cincinnati, a local newspaper noted that Dr. John Landis advanced in position in medical affairs of the city through his appointment as Health Officer in 1910. His work in that capacity drew national attention because of his success in containing the spread of tuberculosis by requiring pasteurization of all milk supplies. He was also considered a pioneer in requiring "the inspection of dairies, markets, groceries and restaurants." John was accorded praise for competence "on all health problems" and the managerial skill of developing subordinates who were imbued with his energy and enthusiasm." [210]

Mary, now in her 79th year, was eager to show off Fred and Bessie's firstborn . . . her 8-month-old grandson Kenesaw II to his namesake . . . "you will have to come soon or you wont know the babe, he is so fine and good has 8 teeth he is so fond of his buggy." [211] Kate added a sisterly note: "come home to see your mother eat soup & soft victuals." Mary wrote to Ken again a month later, adding family news and urging him to pay a visit at the same time that John would arrive from Cincinnati. [212]

Following up on his publication of historical novels about the Civil War and Theodore Roosevelt, Frederick undertook the writing of plays, beginning with "The People Are Coming" in collaboration with author Bayard Vellier. Plans were noted in an entry of June 5, 1912 in a history of Logansport, that called for the two to work together in Logansport the following month. [213]

When Teddy Roosevelt became a Progressive (Bull Moose) candidate for President in 1912, Charles' McKinley-era, party-line instincts led him to be at odds politically with Frederick and Kenesaw, whose "trust-busting" ways meshed with those of Roosevelt. In later years, Charles' daughter suggested that fraternal ties exercised in the background by her father had paid off handsomely in the case of two timely Presidential appointments. First, she believed it was Walter to Puerto Rico by William McKinley . . . then Ken to the federal judiciary by Theodore Roosevelt. [214] Her reasoning suggested that Kenesaw's obligation to TR for his judgeship would not have matched his obligation to Charles for bringing Ken's skills to the President's attention in 1905. Ken's ambition and partiality to Theodore Roosevelt's philosophy were more likely to be at play in 1912 than to yield to Charles' preferences who had been out of politics for several years and had no plans to return. Also Frederick's urge to get back in stride with a political career and his strong admiration for TR would likely have overridden any concern for Charles' feelings who now was retired from politics. Finally, the anti-trust sentiments "in the gut" of both Ken and Fred placed them squarely in TR's camp, coincidentally, at a time when Charles had become a part of the corporate world at DuPont Powder Company.

After taking his turn at writing books, Frederick's political bug brought him to join Theodore Roosevelt's Bull Moose movement as candidate for Lieutenant Governor of Indiana. He was also temporary chairman of the Indiana Progressive Party Convention at Indianapolis in August where he delivered a speech citing the Progressive Party as "the marvel of American politics," and closing with these remarks:

> We, the Progressives of Indiana, bid both of the old
> parties farewell. [Applause] We follow the funeral
> procession of dead issues no more. [Applause] We chant
> the empty nonsense of party prejudice no more.
> [Applause] We march with living issues and we fight the
> people's fight! [Applause] [215]

Frederick described Republican Party bosses in uncomplimentary terms, much to the pleasure of delegates in the convention hall. His style reflected the experience of a young congressman who had moved beyond a boyish-looking persona into the wider world of tough politics. He had not forgotten the last-minute tactics of the party apparatus in the election of 1906 that defeated him after he had won the party nomination unopposed. Frederick had apparently incurred the displeasure of party leaders during his campaign in the eastern part of the State when he went directly to the villagers of Blackford County without their entourage. In addition, as already noted, he may have been particularly "suspect" because he attracted a sizable number of Democratic votes. At the Progressive Convention in 1912, he "proved himself master of sarcasm, biting wit, ridicule, denunciation, epigram and eloquence . . . He referred to officials of the Republican Party as 'bandits,' and repeatedly the delegates and the galleries voiced approval of his charges of fraud made against the Republican Party bosses." [216]

The Bull Moose Party in Indiana issued "a pocket memorandum to keep with you" providing "Thirty-Three Notable Achievements of the Roosevelt Administration," which included a reminder of John D. Rockefeller's day in Kenesaw's courtroom:

> #25 Directed prosecution of railroads and other corporations for violations of Sherman Anti-Trust Law (the Harriman, Tobacco and Standard Oil suits.) [217]

This small document included several ambitious goals to achieve upon victory for the Progressive Party, including:

> #6 Equal suffrage for Women.
> #7 Nomination of candidates for President and Vice-President by preferential
>   primaries.
> #8 Efficient child labor laws, national and state, and the rigid enforcement
>   thereof.
> #9 A national income tax, and a state inheritance tax.
> #10 Liberal pensions to soldiers.
> #18 We favor the organization of the workers, men and women, as a means of protecting their interests and of promoting their progress.

Frederick was delegate-at-large to the 1912 Progressive National Convention in Chicago.

With the Roosevelt-Taft rivalry reaching serious proportions, all of the Landis boys except Dr. John of Cincinnati became involved in one way or another. Walter's service as postmaster of Puerto Rico, continuous since 1898, quickly gained the spotlight in Washington, D.C. because of Frederick's Bull Moose activities. This prompted President Taft, who was contending with both Theodore Roosevelt and Woodrow Wilson for reelection to the presidency, to remove Walter from office. A letter from Walter to Kenesaw presented the evolving situation as reflected in enclosed correspondence between Washington, D.C. and Puerto Rico. [218] Walter received his dismissal as expected under the political circumstances. After leaving his position at the San Juan Post Office, Walter engaged in fruit-growing in Puerto Rico with property in the Barios of Bayamon, Begabega, Algaroba and Manati [219] and spent summers with his sisters in Logansport.

Frederick's credentials as a "Progressive" were of long standing, dating from Theodore Roosevelt's first and second terms in the White House. One local newspaper testified as to Frederick's qualifications in the race for Lieutenant Governor in the three-sided national and state campaigns of 1912, writing about "those early days of progressivism . . . he stood by Roosevelt consistently on behalf of the Roosevelt policies." The article offered this explanation for Frederick's departure from Congress after serving just two terms: "In 1906, at a time of Republican reverses, the standpat organization in Indiana marked Landis down for retirement, and his defeat was brought about by a combination of local agencies directed chiefly from Indianapolis and the same machine headquarters which now controls the Taft standpat campaign." [220]

Kenesaw's invitation to be Teddy Roosevelt's running mate on the Bull Moose ticket was described by Reed, who was 16 at the time. He garnered impressions from his father about the essentials of the Bull Moose campaign including the attempt on candidate Roosevelt's life while in Milwaukee for a campaign speech. On that occasion, Reed went with his father to the hospital in Chicago to visit the recuperating leader of the Progressive Party and recalled TR's pessimistic outlook on his presidential bid. Mr. Roosevelt referred to the attitudes of the average citizen, remarking: "Yes, they turn out and they yell for me, but they aren't going to vote for me." [221] Election results were in fact disappointing for him and for the

Progressive movement when Woodrow Wilson, the Democratic candidate, was victorious. The Bull Moose Party came in a respectable second, and Mr. Taft, the Republican Party standard bearer, came in third.

Mary Landis died November 1, 1912 at the age of 80 . . . Walter, in Puerto Rico, was unable to attend the funeral. Charles arrived from Wilmington, Deleware; John came from Richmond, Indiana, where he had been planning to hear Frederick's campaign speech; Kenesaw traveled from Chicago; and Frederick left the campaign trail at Muncie to come home. "Always an adviser to her famous sons," a local newspaper observed, adding an opinion expressed by Frederick at Lincoln School: "All great men had great mothers . . . Of the great mothers, one was Mrs. Landis, brave in trial, resourceful in time of want; with wise words of counsel for her children." [222]

Kenesaw resumed his judicial innnovation of holding court in one's hometown as a means of keeping the docket on schedule, as he had done five years earlier after his well-publicized verdict and maximum fine against Standard Oil. In the present case, Logansport continued to enjoy its role in the history-setting precedent the Judge had established. Thus, on the evening of his mother's funeral, he convened lawyers in the offices of McConnell, Jenkins, Jenkins and Stuart for an urgent hearing on the McEvoy bankruptcy case. [223]

The year 1913 was a busy one for Frederick who wrote several plays . . . "The Water Wagon," "Montana" and "The People are Coming." [224] For his part, Charles had settled into his executive position with the DuPont Powder Company in Wilmington, Delaware. War clouds in Europe were setting the stage for that company's role in providing munitions for American military forces, and Charles was active in that effort. Union City High School held graduation exercises in 1913 with Frederick as principal guest speaker on "the most American of all immortals, Abraham Lincoln." The town newspaper described the occasion as "the most successful commencement in the life of our schools," stating that his address was "simple, eloquent, beautiful," telling "the simple story of a great American in a way that a child could understand it." [225]

In the following year, Kenesaw became newsworthy in sports publications when he was named to rule in a lawsuit brought by the Philadelphia Phillies against the leaders of an upstart Federal

137

League. One writer discussed the occasion as a "baseball war" in terms of "breach of contract or agreement or moral obligation" through the Federals' effort to break the primacy of the American and National Leagues. The choice of Judge Landis to hear the case meant that he would get into details, reflecting his own experience as a dedicated fan . . ."he is likely to stump some of the lawyers by asking them about batting and fielding average, the number of stolen bases allowed by Killifer per game and the number of bases on balls Brennan gave." [226]

Kenesaw's keen interest in watching the Chicago Cubs had made him a no-nonsense partisan of the Game as an American institution. When the suit charging that Baseball was a monopoly operating outside the law was filed in the Judge's court, *The Sporting Life*, a journal "devoted to Base Ball and Trap Shooting," reported its significance in a nutshell: "Greatest Danger that ever Menaced the System . . . An Adverse Decision and Judicial Order of Dissolution Would Imperil the Capital Involved, End Feasible Control of Players and Nullify the Labors of 43 Years . . ." [227]

The Sporting Life kept its readers up-to-date by reporting on the judicial proceedings of the Judge's court: "The Issues in the Suit Brought By the Federal League Against the Two Major Leagues of Organized Ball Well Threshed Out Before Judge K. M. Landis, Who Reserves His Decision." [228] The journal concluded that, in the event Kenesaw would dismiss the charges, the Federal League would not likely appeal the case because of the attitude of "baseball men," who "have come to realize that the public does not take very kindly to the prolonged legal and political features of baseball . . . What they want is the Game itself, and the less the public knows of the inside workings of the organizations the better they like it." [229]

Silence from the Judge lasted several weeks, and one editorial showed foresight by speculating that his ruling could be either quick or might not occur for several years: "There'll probably be a whirl of action when Judge Landis has something to say - which may be tomorrow or September 14, 1918." [230] After a few months, *The Sporting Life* spoke out, declaring "The learned judge states that the long delay will doubtless benefit the Game." [231] Still later, one newspaper at mid-season observed a crack in the Federal League's resolve to hold onto some cameo players . . . "a shattering of those idols proudly displayed by the Feds when they were hot on the trail for recognition and star players." [232] Kenesaw chose not to rule on the case for a period of almost a year, at which time the Federal League decided to drop the suit. Years later, a sportswriter analyzed the Judge's strategy: "On the Federals' case, Landis deliberated slowly, so slowly in fact that events rendered the case moot." [233] Another sports journalist concluded that the Federal League case would prove important in the annals of baseball because of Kenesaw's position that baseball was "a national institution." [234]

In the years approaching the United States' entry into World War I, Kenesaw was on hand to introduce President Woodrow Wilson during his visit to the Auditorium Theater in Chicago, as recalled by his son. Reed recognized that, although the President and his father differed in matters of politics, they remained personal friends. The occasion was a sensitive one for Mr. Wilson because he was abandoning his campaign slogan of "keeping us out of war" and was preparing the Nation, after the sinking of the *Lusitania,* to move to a war footing. Kenesaw's introduction of the President was frank, direct and strongly supportive: "Ladies and Gentlemen, while the next guest of honor was not my candidate, he is my President." [235]

Frederick, after his ill-fated candidacy in the Progressive Party in 1912 went down to defeat under its leader Theodore Roosevelt, decided to rejoin the Republicans and notified Will H. Hayes, State Chairman of the Party, on January 10, 1916 that he was to be entered accordingly in the poll book. [236] During the year's Presidential race, Charles from his position in military sales for the Du Pont Powder Company, kept the family political pot boiling with an insightful letter to Kenesaw concerning impromptu remarks of Republican Vice Presidential candidate Charles Fairbanks. [237] The issue seems to have been whether the United States was doing the right thing by President Wilson's decision to enter World War I. [238]

Back in the Federal courtoom, Kenesaw considered a little-heralded case in which two women, one wealthy and one poor, filed claims to take custody of a one-year old baby. Judge Landis made his ruling in favor of the poor woman because, unlike the woman of means, she was prepared to testify in court that the baby belonged to her. [239] After his foray into the baseball world the previous year, Kenesaw headed in a new direction in 1916 that would involve the administration of the city of Chicago and its ability to enforce laws respecting the banking industry. [240]

When he was interviewed by a major city newspaper reporter on the occasion of his 50th birthday, he recalled as a barefoot boy his thoughts about a future in the wider world outside of Logansport, as already noted . . . "when I was a youngster I had an ambition to become the head of something. I mean the man who was responsible to nothing except his own conscience." [241]

he advent of America's entry into World War I was a time of growing concern by the populace of the United States, and one newspaper took note of Frederick's appearance on the West Coast, describing him as "more than a humorist" and adding: "He is a philosopher. He contributes to the joy of living in this over-serious world. Long may he thrive!" [242] A few months later, the *Chicago Tribune* featured a photograph of Kenesaw with retired statesman, Theodore Roosevelt . . . "Militant Citizen and Militant Judge Talk Over Old Times." In its summation of Kenesaw's career in Chicago, it described him as "A Just Judge" who emphasized love for one's country in the rearing of young Reed: "He is raising his son to discharge his duties as a patriot, and the son is in a training camp." [243]

With the United States entering World War I, and his son preparing to be a military pilot, Kenesaw decided to explore the possibility that a 50-year-old Federal Judge might do likewise and made an inquiry at the highest level of government. Reed told of his father's efforts to accomplish that goal on a trip to the Nation's capital. After obtaining a waiver on age and passing the physical examination for air cadet training, Kenesaw visited President Woodrow Wilson in order to resign his Federal judgeship. The President's response was sure and swift: "You go on back to Chicago and keep on judging. You can do far more good for the people of this country in that job than you ever could as a pilot in the Air Service. Now, go on back to Chicago." [244]

Soon thereafter, Kenesaw received the following formal note from President Wilson:

The White House
Washington

The President deeply appreciates your very generous and patriotic proffer of your services, and he wishes in this informal way to express his grateful thanks. [245]

140

Frederick's Chautauqua appearance before the Illinois Bar Association was considered a financial bargain by the Secretary of that organization: "I still hear echoes of praise of your address before our State Convention. I have never issued a voucher when I felt that we received more for our money than in this instance." [246]

With the nation's entry into the World War, Frederick made patriotic speeches including one in which he sketched the course of American military power from colonial days. Speaking of George Washington's colonial troops called to secure our interests, Frederick said: "We sent them out in 1776, and, after keeping every crowned head in the world awake since that time, they have wandered home because they had no place else to go. And they will stay home and this world will have no peace until the infernal Kaiser and the Imperial German Government is in hell to stay . . . President Wilson has done wonders in the 90 days in which he has had something with which to fight . . . And we're all with him now. I didn't vote for him but I'll stick with him now until he makes the world safe for democracy if it takes all the rest of my life." [247]

Walter Kumler Landis, eldest of the Landis boys, "had been ill some time from complications" and died November 5, 1917. Reed offered his father's recollection of the cause of Walter's death, believing that it was a hookworm infection acquired in Puerto Rico and diagnosed too late to save him. [248] In his will, Walter specified that his Puerto Rican properties in the Barios of Bayamon, Begabega, Algaroba and Manati be sold and the proceeds to be divided equally between his two sisters, Kate and Frank. Brother Charles was Executor of his will. [249]

Broadway's popular play *The Copperhead*, based on Frederick's Civil War novel, *The Glory of His Country*, was a timely production in view of America's participation in World War I. The play opened at Parson's Theatre in New Haven January 16, 1918 and appeared at the Shubert Theater in New York February 18, the only appearance of Augustus Thomas' work at the Shubert. After 120 performances, with leading roles played by Lionel Barrymore and Doris Rankin, *The Copperhead* went on tour. One account noted that the playwright "triumphed over almost insuperable difficulties in order to produce the effect he desired." [250] In the words of one New York critic, "Mr Landis' graphically

141

truthful story as a footnote to the Civil War has been so delicately elaborated and judiciously condensed by Augustus Thomas that the literary simplicity and achievement alone present an event of import to the stage. It is the best thing that Thomas has ever done." [251] Another New York critic noted the popularity of the Civil War theme, observing that the play "was greeted so vociferously that it seemed likely that the spirit of '61 will rage on Broadway for some months to come. . . The audience responded to the patriotic appeal with a fervor born of the times we are living through rather than the reminiscences of the past." [252]

Throughout 1918 and the Armistice of November 11, *The Copperhead* remained on tour with Barrymore "'storming the cities' . . . On December 2 a first-night audience in Chicago 'stamped, whistled, and yelled for ten minutes until the star reappeared' . . . Critics the next day out-hyperboled themselves over the sensational triumph at the Garrick." [253] Mr. Barrymore continued with the show, even to include a rare matinee performance in Logansport. According to a family biographer, the actor, whom sister Ethel considered as a rival for family accolades, "would knock Broadway (as he would say) for a row of Chinese pagodas" by his performance in *The Copperhead*. [254]

In a climate of some uncertainty about the idea of donating money in support of a War Chest and the Liberty Loan campaign, Frederick was featured speaker on a program with the Great Lakes Marine Band, appealing to a large crowd in Logansport for generous contributions. The local press observed that Frederick "launched into a patriotic and fiery tirade, dropping his metaphorical bombs into the audience with regularity and precision and much to the delight of the vast assemblage." He also noted the reluctance of some clergy in Cass County who had "religious objections" to the War Chest, declaring: "This is no time to talk about Catholics, Jews or Protestants . . . God have mercy on the miserable, microscopic soul that mentions Catholic, Jew or Protestant, until this war is ended." [255]

Kenesaw and Winifred had reason for a sense of pride in young Reed's achievements on the field of battle as a pilot with British and American forces in Europe. Their nephew West Pointer, Captain John F. Landis, Charles' son, hoped for an assignment in the war zone but found himself limited to training troops in the United States. With an eye on military progress of the war from his unwelcome stateside perch, he noted Reed's impressive service as a pilot flying in a British aviation unit. Captain John also offered advice to his Uncle Ken regarding the Judge's recent judicial proceedings against the socialist International Workers of the World: "I see by the papers you are trying the I.W.W. Be careful don't give any of that gang a chance to take a pot shot at your illustrious corporosity." [256]

Reed wrote of his recent experiences in a letter passed on by the censor: "Yesterday - we spent the day down south and eight of us got chased home by 23 Hun scouts -- we then climbed up and chased them twelve miles over the lines to their aerodrome." [257] The following week, another letter from Reed stated: "Last night I chased a high Hun two-seater for 35 minutes . . . I shot 700 rounds at him but only managed to chase him home." [258]

John Howard Landis, 3rd oldest of the brothers died unexpectedly August 23, 1918. He had served as Health Officer of Cincinnati since 1910 and "was largely responsible for placing Cincinnati's department in the front rank among America's cities." [259] He served as director of the Visiting Nurse Association of the Council of Social Agencies and was a member of the Commission on National Milk Standards of the American Medical Association. In his last year, he was President of the Cincinnati Academy of Medicine. [260] In the last month of his life, John, unlike Walter who had died in 1917, was able to savor baby brother Frederick's Broadway prominence as the footlights continued to shine on *The Copperhead*, [261] with Barrymore in the actor's favorite role of Colonel Milt Shanks. [262]

As the Armistice approached with the winding down of the World War toward the end of 1918, good news arrived for the Landis family through word of an award to Reed of the Distinguished Flying Cross by the Commander, Royal Air Force in the Field [263] It had been forwarded as a confidential message, in advance of public notification by the Secretary of War. [264] In addition, Reed was promoted from captain to major. The following month, just after the Armistice, Kenesaw received a telegram of an international news agency that Reed "is one of the leading American aces having downed twelve Huns." [265] Shortly before Christmas, with the war concluded, Kenesaw received a letter from Reed, who claimed to be in a state of boredom now that the fighting was over, adding: "I don't believe it would be awfully hard for me to find something to do, and I have gotten jammed full of pep and ambish of civilian prospects." [266] Kenesaw also received a lengthy letter from his cousin Captain Preston Kumler, who arrived to serve in Europe a week after hostilities ceased and offered detailed glimpses of the US Army's difficult situation in its initial occupation of Germany. [267]

Praise for the American military achievement in the World War was a natural topic for Frederick. Local press commentary followed his Chautauqua address to the Victory Dinner of the Toledo Chamber of Commerce. [268] Kenesaw, upon being invited to speak before a group of wounded soldiers recently returned from France to the Fort Sheridan hospital in Chicago, took the opportunity to sound them out on personal grievances. As a result, he "did not name the officers responsible but assured the men 'the gentlemen in charge of this camp will straighten it out.'" [269] The caption of a published photo of Reed and his parents after the "fighter ace" returned from the war read: "Captain Landis was with the American Aviation Service in France, and during his stay over there downed twelve German flyers." [270]

A reminder of nephew John's recent warning, Kenesaw was the intended recipient of a bomb several months after the end of World War I. It was presumably sent by socialist elements because of the Judge's sentencing of Bolshevists and members of the Industrial Workers of the World for espionage activities. [271] His response to a report that Chief Inspector Stuart of the Post Office had examined the mechanism of the bomb and was saving it for the Judge's return to Chicago was reported to be: "That's very decent of Stuart. It's my bomb. He hasn't any business monkeying with my bomb." [272]

After the successful run of Frederick's play in 1918, *The Copperhead* hit the press again during a strike against the anti-union Actors Fidelity Association in the summer of 1919 with a benefit performance staged by Actors Equity at the Lexington Opera House in New York. Barrymore was again the star . . . In the climax of the production, it was reported that "Lionel came back again and blew everyone away with the Lincoln scene from *The Copperhead*." [273]

Kenesaw tried to remain in contact with his elderly Uncle Jake Kumler back in Seven Mile, Ohio. Reunions of the 35th Ohio Regiment were opportunities for family get-togethers with the Kumlers who remained in Butler County after Abraham Landis' branch "went West," and Uncle Jake kept track of such events and frequently invited Kenesaw to come back home. [274]

Over the years, Reed had found time to observe his father in action in the courtroom, and his conclusion was that Kenesaw's innovative style in handling witnesses "resulted in the dispensing of justice in a way that might have been a little unusual, but it was all mighty effective, and it produced honest answers for the benefit of the public." [275]

The year 1919 produced Frederick's illustrated book *Days Gone Dry* in recognition of the ratification of the 18th Amendment to the Constitution, the Prohibition Amendment. Although it forebad the manufacturing and sale of alcoholic beverages effective January 16 1920, *Days Gone Dry* anticipated likely effects of Prohibition on the nation's culture. It featured color illustrations by *Chicago Tribune* cartoonist Gaar Williams. It displayed a fat-bellied gentleman atop a State Capitol building dome, trying unsuccessfully to open it with a gigantic corkscrew, and with the accompanying text: "The Corkscrew Has Not the Pull It Used to Have -- And America is Doomed!" [276]

Teddy Roosevelt's "Bull Moose" Party would outdraw Taft Republicans in 1912. Left to right: Albert J. Beveridge, for Governor and Frederick for Lieutenant Governor of Indiana. *Indianapolis Star*, August 2, 1912.

Scenes from Augustus Thomas' 1918 Broadway play, *The Copperhead*, based on Frederick's Civil War spy novel *The Glory of His Country*, Scribners, 1910. Lionel Barrymore and his actress-wife Doris Rankin in leading roles above.

JUDGE KENESAW MOUNTAIN LANDIS *His Son* CAPTAIN REED LANDIS
And MRS. LANDIS. © I.F.S

Photo of Reed Landis with his parents Kenesaw and Winifred, upon his return from World War I, where he earned the honor of War Ace by downing 12 German flyers. He was soon promoted to the rank of major.
                                        New York Herald, February 15, 1919.

Portrayal of Kenesaw's court by cartoonist J. T. McCutcheon.
Chicago Tribune, November 9, 1920.

6. Commentary, Humor -- 1920's and 1930's

The 1920's

> *The amount of valuable time that is being lost in discussing whether man sprang from monkey would seem to indicate that if he did so, he had a round-trip ticket.*
> -- Frederick Landis, "Hoosiergrams," July 11, 1923 [1]

> *In view of the fact that less than half of us participate in presidential elections, we suggest that our archaeological diggers let antiquity sleep for the time and join shovels to dig up American voters for November.*
> -- Frederick Landis, "Reason," August 18, 1928 [2]

From the 1920's on, Frederick wrote wide-ranging commentaries about our national culture and re-entered politics as a candidate for Governor of Indiana in 1928 and 1932, both without success. Finally, he was again elected to Congress in 1934 but died before he could assume office.

His commentaries appeared as "Hoosiergrams" in the *Indianapolis Star*; "Americanisms" and editorials in the *New York American*; "Reason" in the *Logansport Pharos-Tribune*; and "Here at Home" in the *Logansport Press*. He criticized the Democratic Party and tried to liberalize the Republican Party. The Ku Klux Klan was his frequent target, and he spoke for justice and equality. American women were a favored topic after they gained the right to vote in 1920. A regular commentator in the early days of radio, he also gained success in theater productions. Upon returning to politics, he had moved on from the Bull Moose Movement to become a "regular Republican" again, although his attractiveness to Democratic voters would continue to cause suspicion among upper-level Republicans. The unexpected deaths of sister Kate in 1921 and brother Charles in 1922 left Kenesaw as the last of the brothers, and Frank was their only surviving sister.

1920 to 1922

With the beginning of the decade, Frederick's play *The Copperhead* became a Hollywood item in a Paramount Production entitled "Artcraft Special for Famous Players," with screenplay by Charles Maigne. Like the Broadway play, the silent film with subtitles featured Lionel Barrymore and Doris Rankin in leading roles. Frederick continued in Chautauqua, speaking before "the most noted clubs and the greatest banquets in the country," in the words of promotional literature. On one occasion, a brochure noted that Theodore Roosevelt had introduced Frederick in New York, remarking that his novel, *The Angel of Lonesome Hill*, "is the picture of me as President by which I wish my family to remember me." Frederick discussed "The Real Lincoln," "Our Dawning Civilization," and "James Whitcomb Riley" with appearances in New York, Chicago, Toledo, Cincinnati, Cleveland, Des Moines, and Rockford Illinois. [3] One newspaper compared Frederick with well-known orators, Rufus Choate and Tom Corwin, and even saw in him "the angularity of Abraham Lincoln." [4] After another appearance in New York, the Speaker of the US House of Representatives noted: "there was not a sentence that was not striking – either witty or epigrammatic eloquent or entertaining," [5] and, in Chicago, the US Secretary of State commented that Frederick was "as good an after-dinner speaker as I ever heard."

Frederick joined Kenesaw and other gentlemen of the public realm at a meeting of the Indiana Society of Chicago, a good-natured spoof of the American system of government represented in "the Hoosier Republic." [7] Frederick delivered the Society's Inaugural Address that included a light-hearted religious interpretation. [8] For the largely-Republican audience, he poked fun at the Nation's number one Democrat, President Woodrow Wilson, whose stature had nose-dived with Congress' rejection of his pet formulation, the League of Nations. Frederick quoted from a mythical letter sent to him by President Wilson, stating: "Once I was gratified to be acclaimed as a 'Second Moses,' but now I feel that the distinction runs the other way. Any man can start in the bulrushes -- but it requires a very high degree of intellectual horseradish to finish in the bulrushes."

In one Chautauqua appearance in a small Indiana town, Frederick argued against mandatory college education for practicing attorneys, noting: "such requirements would have barred both

148

Abraham Lincoln and John Marshall," the renowned American jurist. [9]

1923

Frederick began to write short editorials for the *Indianapolis Star* several times each week during May to September, 1923. These "Hoosiergrams" addressed a range of topics presented below.

The Nation

With the celebration of Flag Day, June 14, Frederick wrote: "Liberty is in it and pioneer loneliness . . . The inheritance of opportunity and fair play. [10] On Independence Day, he reminded readers of the death on July 4, 1826 of both John Adams and Thomas Jefferson. It had been just 50 years since the adoption of the Declaration of Independence -- "Jefferson's immortal paper, defended by the eloquent Adams . . . they were high priests at an altar when a people wedded independence -- they asked to see the golden wedding" and succeeded. [11]

While the American tradition of equal opportunity is enshrined in *The Constitution*, Frederick rejected the notions "that this government was organized for the purpose of making somebody rich . . . that Washington crossed the Delaware in order to incorporate in New Jersey."

Pride in the historical foundation of our country continued strong among many citizens in the 1920's, but a "new look" at the traditions and policies of the United States seemed to be undergoing ill-advised scrutiny. For example, what might be the cause of a tendency among American officials to utter criticism of US policies while visiting England? "There has always been a peculiar microbe in a London fog which inoculates Americans with an irresistible desire to take a shot at their own country."

Fuel supply had from time to time become a problem in the United States following the first World War, and it was not clear whether the coal industry or the labor union was responsible for the shortage. In either case, the matter appeared to be moot: "For this land to fear a coal famine is as if Canaan should have feared a famine of milk and honey."

The decline of marriage was being reflected in a novel manner, as in the case of a lady of some social standing in one of our major cities . . . "A Chicago woman has just issued cards,

149

announcing her divorce. . . Once a scandal, divorce has become one of our honored institutions." [12]

Politics

The Administration of President Warren G. Harding and Vice-President Calvin Coolidge was coming to a close, and, as is frequently the case in Washington, DC, officials began to leave government positions before the end of their term of service. This produced either the temporary existence of vacancies or the selection of "short-timers" to complete the term of officials in the Federal bureaucracy. What was the likely result? "According to the spring appointments that have been made at Washington, 'lame ducks' are going to cost us even more than turkeys."

The sudden death of President Harding resulted in a spectacle of the seamy side of the political process. There soon occurred "the rush of politicians to Washington to file claims upon President Coolidge," an event "that has not been equaled since the Cherokee Strip was opened for the filing of claims by settlers." [13]

Political considerations may follow different paths, but a contention that the Nation would be better off if the White House were to be occupied by a Southern candidate was difficult to support: "We have but to keep on splitting the United States into geographical, religious and occupational fragments; we have but to continue squirting 'the spirit of '76' through an atomizer, and some of these days we will have a perfectly wonderful country!"

New York Governor Alfred E. Smith's run for the highest office in the Land exposed a dubious campaign strategy resulting from his opposition to the Prohibition Amendment that proscribed the manufacture and sale of alcoholic beverages: "For a Tammany Governor to sign a wet bill is as great a shock as if the presiding elder of Mecca should declare for Mahomet . . . It is only a few hours through wet territory from Albany to Washington, but Governor Smith must go through every dry state in the Union before he can get to the White House." [14]

Henry Ford of the Motor Company, expressed an interest in the presidency of the United States and then denied it. This was understandable because the new industrialist had his hands full turning out Model Ts, affectionately known as "flivvers." Some reflection suggests, however, that his intentions are otherwise: "All of the signs point to his candidacy" for four reasons: "First, he denied it. Second, he publicly endorsed the Bible. 3rd, he tells how he loves the simple life. Fourth, he has been feeding the squirrels but withdrew this as a campaign document because his opponent fed them first."

Switching to the foreign field, Frederick was optimistic about prospects for democratic rule in Ireland: "The Irish care nothing for self-government, their recent election being very disappointing. There were riots and hair was pulled, but nobody was killed. A few more campaigns and they will become as indifferent as we are!"

Religion

Modernized versions of *The Holy Bible* have appeared in print through the years, seeking to clarify Scripture or perhaps to bring certain passages to support the position of various denominations . . . "How much better it would have been if the Lord had called these experts up on Mount Sinai in the first place."

To some, religious sentiments may be found in expressions of simplicity and beauty, and actions taken to ignore such opportunities are not to be welcomed: "We wish the Presbyterian Church had taken some action to put the church bell back in the steeple. It was the most eloquent voice, that faith ever knew; it was the most religious thing the church had." [15] Some may find it a stretch of logic to believe that varying interpretations of Scripture may assist in understanding the effectiveness of our judicial system: "Women are much stronger on coeducational juries than the men. All of which goes to prove that when God made Eve, he took Adam's backbone out of him, instead of his rib."

Drawing upon Scripture to understand the international political realm, Frederick wrote of efforts being made in the 1920's to institute peaceful relations between countries because of the dreadful costs suffered in Europe on both sides by the first World War. The pessimistic side of such hopes for international amity also needs to be taken into account: "There is no doubt of a more brotherly feeling among the nations of the world, but it is almost entirely of a Cain and Abel variety."

While not a man to wear religion on his sleeve, Frederick took a stand for the Almighty that was never in doubt and found many opportunities to express his sentiments on the subject. His approach to Christianity was not far from sentiments expressed by

151

martyr Hans Landis [16] and the Mennonite creed -- *Believe and let believe*: "Another divine hurries to the rescue to inform us that the King James version of the Bible was not inspired. The bandit who holds up the midnight train and takes only money and jewelry is a public benefactor alongside the highbrow highwayman, who to make a fine point, would rob the plain man of his faith." [17] Christianity and other faiths are diverse indeed, and these differences are illustrated by the simple connection Frederick made between air flight and religion: "It seems strange that two airplanes should ever run into each other, until we reflect that two religions have never been able to occupy the sky at the same time without having a collision."

National Defense

The issue of selecting high officials with unquestionable qualifications may ultimately yield to a practice of political patronage, wherein military considerations are minimized in the process. It is appropriate to argue that only reputable persons should be charged with the august responsibility of assuring a high state of readiness for our nation: "The head of the American Lawn Tennis Association has been appointed assistant secretary of war. This should scare the daylights out of any nation that thought of attacking us."

Europe

A report stating that Italy was embracing the incorporation of American canoes to embellish its favorite river sport suggested a very attractive opportunity in terms of our ties with the Old World . . . the possibility that "our government could well afford to supply such craft to every nation in Europe, in the hope that they might learn to paddle them for themselves." Speaking of one such country, Germany, that was reluctant to pay for reparations levied by the Treaty of Versailles, Frederick raised the question of what that nation's stance would be if the conditions were turned around, and the vanquished had become the victors in World War I . . . "If she had won the war, the rest of the World would have had no rest until it had paid the last cent -- and it would have been the last cent . . . For a musical nation, Germany has a strange aversion toward paying the fiddler."

One current aspect of international relations was the question of the proper relationship between the United States and the communist government of Russia. There was no doubt that in the early 1920's, Vladimir Lenin had given the United States cause for serious concern about the direction of the Bolshevist government. On the one hand, there appeared to be a shallow state of communication between that government and American representatives, lacking in matters of substance: "The American Relief Expedition gave a 6 o'clock party in Moscow the other evening in honor of Soviet officials, and a pleasant time was had by all. There was a full attendance of Russians, it having been announced that refreshments would be served." On the other hand, the diplomatic question facing the United States since the October Revolution of 1917 was whether "to recognize" the new government. After all, we had been generous in helping to solve its agricultural problems through shipments of food. Frederick suggested it might be an appropriate time for pragmatism to rule over principle: "The average man begins to feel that if we are going to continue indefinitely to feed this bunch, we might as well recognize them." [18]

Frederick found contemptible the practice of an English nobleman to express himself in our midst with utter frankness about our government: "We are fully capable of criticizing our Presidents; we need no Lord Birkenhead to come from his Albion to tell us who Woodrow Wilson is. We were against him, but we don't want any bloomin' lord coming to the United States to talk about him; we fight, but it's all in the family."

1924

Frederick completed his "Hoosiergrams" series with the *Indianapolis Star* in order to write syndicated editorials for Hearst newspapers from his new home base of *The New York American*. [19] After moving from Logansport to Great Neck, Long Island, he became a commentator on New York radio station WEAF. Selected excerpts of his "Americanisms" and titled editorials during 1924 and 1925 appear in the following pages.

The Nation

Following the lead of the American Legion, Frederick issued rules for showing respect for our flag including the caution that we should not find ourselves leading a parade that draws the line on participation by "any man, woman or child!"

Frederick was consistent in efforts to persuade Washington to improve the livelihood of the American farmer. With respect to government assistance in the agricultural sector, he believed that the farmers should get a reasonable price each year instead of a high price in a particular year when nature has delivered a very poor crop of wheat. [20]

The breadth of Frederick's commentary knew few bounds. While he would have supported any proposal, for example, that might achieve considerate treatment of barnyard animals, he questioned the usefulness of a position of some activists involved in such an effort. Judging that Americans are "tender-hearted," Frederick noted that the law caught up with a vanful of chickens to be processed for our dinner table because the vehicle was not properly ventilated.

In the words of the *New York Journal* editor, Frederick delivered an indictment of pretense in American society when he penned an "order of march" for his notion of "a national parade." The newspaper introduced his editorial with the heading: "One Fine Procession--and Washington Ought to See It" and went on to state: "What we print here is from yesterday morning's *New York American* -- not any TOO good naturedly about eighty per cent of the commercial, industrial and financial hypocrisy of this country." Frederick's editorial ridiculed as alleged "defendants of the United States" the following "marchers:" "Coal Barons; Trusts; Bar Associations; Bootleggers; Eminent lawyers; Indicted lobbyists; Insanity lawyers; and Rats of perjury." [21]

Frederick was frequently prepared to reach into the international arena to apply his analysis of the underlying cause of a certain domestic problem of special concern to him and perhaps his fellow man. Referring to the execution of Chinese pirates that attracted spectators, he found a tie-in between "the brutalizing effects of such public executions" and "the wanton cruelty which Chinese laundrymen inflict upon helpless shirtfronts."

Women

Frederick took up the plight of the young, particularly those who have had little opportunity to grow up under reasonable conditions. He pursued the same thought, while taking an occasional swing at those who flaunt their social status. He cited the case of the plan of a society lady in the United States to go lion-hunting in Africa, and he had a better idea of how she could occupy her time, that is, to "go to some orphanage, adopt a child and give it a chance in life."

Many of Frederick's published viewpoints dealt with weighty issues facing our government. One of the exceptions happened to relate to women's fashions. He noted that the Rumanian Queen Marie had come out against short skirts, not thinking that, "on windy days," they are the cause of more traffic accidents.

Children's welfare

In a more serious vein, Frederick's passion to alleviate labor conditions in the United States was illustrated by his condemnation of the use of children in factories as American industry proceeded to expand in the early 1920's. In one case, he expressed his concern about the stakes involved in congressional consideration of the Child Labor Amendment. Frederick criticized a deficiency that tended to favor Evil over Good in the functioning of government: "Civilization must win thirty-six States to ratify this amendment, while Greed need win only thirteen to defeat it -- an unlucky number for the pale, emaciated prey of this economic beast." Frederick also took issue with efforts of the National Grange that assumed a position opposed to the constitutional amendment prohibiting child labor, saying: "Child labor helped the children." Frederick, known to favor strongly the interests of farmers, felt differently about their lobbying organization and mocked their political stance by appearing to praise the Grange for "coming to the rescue of these helpless children!"

Upon learning of an imaginative solution to the problem of neglected children offered by a member of the clergy, Frederick supported the idea with his own estimate of its end result. He noted the case of a preacher in Chicago who believed that parents were responsible for the behavior of their children and consequently, should be spanked. Frederick felt this would be certain to "reach the seat of the trouble."

Politics

The possible candidacy of automobile-maker Henry Ford, who switched to the Republican Party, gained notice in newspapers with regard to a second race for the United States Senate. Frederick took note of Ford's flexible ways that seemed to be supported by the industrialist's design of the thrifty Model T automobile. He recalled that Ford ran for the Senate on the Democratic ticket and that Republicans and Democrats are so similar that Henry can switch parties on "a spoonful of gas."

Frederick believed in the importance of honesty and sincerity in public service and found that politicians frequently succeed because of personality traits that mask unworthy intentions. The aspirations of devious candidates happened to be served, unfortunately, by a prevalence of citizen apathy. He cautioned voters to beware of "the Good Fellow," who devastates the general welfare and continues to be charming because we keep on electing him to office.

When Frederick believed that our mechanism of government had strayed from its intended purposes, he bluntly spoke his views. In particular, he criticized officials who failed in positions of law and leadership. He noted the saying "money talks," but that it is likely never to be able to talk as effectively as in the halls of justice in the United States. His attention to the performance of judges and leaders in public institutions was unrelenting. He wondered why we credit political leaders with good behavior even though they don't measure up -- noting that we keep them on a pedestal, but "they jump off."

Frederick was committed to flexibility in Party matters that often challenged political orthodoxy and critiqued Republicans and Democrats by reaching into antiquity. He observed a unique aspect of *The New York Evening Journal* feature of Ramses' avenue of rams in Egypt. He likened it to "a political convention" that is "awaiting instructions from the boss." No doubt, Frederick had in mind the Republican Party's apparent long memory concerning his own "lack of party loyalty" by participating in Teddy Roosevelt's Bull Moose movement of 1912.

Judicial system

The Ku Klux Klan seemed to appear in print often enough for Frederick to make not only comical references to their peculiar uniform but also to remind readers of the seriousness of the Klan's pattern of intimidation and intolerance. He noted that a Kentucky judge showed a good deal of courage by denying the Ku Klux Klan the honor of jury duty. Frederick also observed, however, that there was a case across the river in Indiana, when the murderer of a black man felt reassured because he learned that "there were four Klansmen on the jury."

Religion

Frederick shifted gears, offering commentary on the state of clergy relations in the nation. In his writings, he invited "clergymen seeking to improve on the Christian religion to consider Benjamin Franklin's reply to the president of Yale College, who had asked Mr. Franklin's views on a religious discussion then raging." Frederick, expressing disdain at religious rivalry among denominations in America, concluded: "If Franklin, the wisest American that ever lived, could speak, he would tell both sides among the quarreling clergymen to quit fighting each other and help humanity." [22]

The international sphere was also not immune from religious rivalries, where differences lay in faiths other than Christianity. Frederick read that, in India, Moslems no longer keep Hindus from "playing music near mosques" and in response, Moslems can "slaughter cows." His conclusion was that since the beginning of time, the world stage has been featuring "the religious vaudeville of the human race."

Regarding a penurious aspect of Protestantism in America, Frederick showed sympathy for the financial plight of clergymen and commended a private effort to create a fund for those who reach retirement age. He recognized the challenge of pastors "to accumulate anything but their sermons."

Frederick's faith in "The Almighty" guided his thought processes to appreciate the rare gesture by members of one denomination to assist members of another denomination. He welcomed any sign, for example, when fraternal feelings prevailed among religious organizations. To Frederick, such actions were fully congenial with patriotism. He had praise for Gouverneur, N.Y. when the town's Masonic Lodge overcame religious differences by deciding to allocate the sum of "$100 toward the erection of a Catholic church."

Frederick called to account the top level of one Protestant denomination that displayed a sharply-revisionist view of Christianity. He charged its stance could unravel the Faith in a manner not unlike the idiocy of honoring America's most prominent atheist. Frederick suggested further ridiculous action by the New York Presbytery, that is, by providing a memorial window for Robert G. Ingersoll . . . he had noted that the Presbytery hired a preacher who denied "the Virgin Birth of Christ."

National Defense

In one of his early editorials, Frederick focused upon international naval power and criticized negotiations of our Department of State that related to our national defense. Just a few years after the United States and Britain fought on the same side in World War I, he warned against cozying up to England and to Europe, believing a future conflict might be in the making. Characterizing the United States as "a bear in battle," he also judged America to be "a lamb in diplomacy," concluding that the Washington Naval Treaty enabled England to gain a significant edge over us through a superiority in small ships and naval bases. [23]

Reflecting upon a potential enemy in terms of its emphasis upon naval preparedness, Frederick perceived the growing danger to the United States from Japan when he commented upon the recent death of a dauntless American explorer. He noted the death of the last living member of the Perry expedition that brought free access and new stature to Japan and wondered if the late voyager might have concluded that "the expedition had been a bad idea."

Military readiness was a serious consideration for Frederick who became an early advocate of greater American capabilities for air warfare a year before Billy Mitchell was court-martialed. It is likely that the achievement of his nephew Reed, a highly-decorated pilot in the first World War, urged him in this direction. When President Coolidge spoke of the need for disarmament even in the air, Frederick objected and declared the importance of air power in our defense establishment. He discounted the prospect that arms control could be achieved in the air and came up with a more practical solution. Instead of trying to rely upon arms control now, he argued by predicting that commercial aircraft "will soon be as common as blackbirds." In view of that situation, all that would be needed, he felt, was the arming of these commercial planes in the future, when our "hot air" would give way to air superiority, and we could, with thousands of planes, tell an enemy "to keep off the clouds!"

1925

Frederick continued to write "Americanisms" and Editorials for *The New York American,* and rounding out his professional life in New York were his continuing weekly broadcasts on radio station WEAF. He was gratified to be in a position to report from a high-profile perch in New York City, while perhaps also longing to get back to his hometown in Indiana. Speaking from personal experience, he wrote about public servants in Washington who frequently are retired by the voters. Frederick commented upon the usual practice of Congressional families to follow along to the Nation's capital to taste the niceties of society there, and he sympathized with their heartbreak when the statesman is defeated -- they would do better to stay in their hometown. [24]

The Nation

Monticello, the home of Thomas Jefferson, became a national shrine after it was purchased by a group of his admirers. Frederick had been an advocate of that philanthropic gesture in his editorial "Jefferson's Home Should Be a Shrine" a year earlier. He described Jefferson as "an apostle of freedom and justice," who stood for the welfare of people in all countries of the world. [25]

Frederick's friendship with Will Hays, president of the Motion Pictures Producers and Distributors of America, probably attracted Landis to take note of statistics that established a preeminent position for the United States in Mr. Hayes' particular industry. Frederick noted that Hollywood provided the vast majority of films enjoyed in England and the British Commonwealth. For this outstanding achievement, he praised "the quality, originality, and irresistible appeal of this great American art. [26]

In reflecting upon the importance of the corner drug store, Frederick chose to elaborate upon the fact that druggists and pharmacists perform essential functions that the average American could not do without. He wrote about these kinds of productive citizens, reflecting with enthusiasm his affection for an institution that plays a unique role in our lives by providing everything "that could not be found anywhere." [27]

In one after another matter calling for reform, Frederick took hold and spoke his piece, that, along with efforts of others, have brought about positive change to benefit our everyday life. So it was in the problem of unsafe railroad crossing that was proving to be deadly in the early years of the automobile age. Frederick wrote with little patience for the idea that there could be some question as to "the wisdom of saving human life" through stronger efforts to prevent train accidents. [28]

While Frederick placed himself on the side of the workingman, he also was alert to excesses gained by labor in a series of past strike negotiations. In particular, he had little sympathy for corrupt union leaders who held the threat of denying people the means of heating their houses in exchange for union benefits. Frederick was suspicious of those union actions in which a strike leads to negotiations and then to "the bleeding of our dear old public" for much more than the strikers were able to gain. [29]

Frederick shifted his attention to developments in his temporary hometown, New York City. Expansion of the subway system was a matter of excitement for residents and business interests. In his column, Frederick called attention to a wrinkle in the form of political influence by those who were involved in building the transportation system. He likened the affection of railway officials and their media organs for the man-on-the-street to the sweetness that "cannibals have for a missionary." [30]

Values

As editorial writer of the *New York American*, he reflected his progressive philosophy in writing an overline above the front-page mast on Decoration Day, May 30, 1925, later known as Memorial Day: "Let Prejudice Stand Without the Gate This Day as We Go in with Flowers for All Who Fought and Fell for Us. For They Are Not Protestants, Catholics, Jews Nor Gentiles NOW -- Nor Whites Nor Blacks -- Only Old Glory's Silent Brotherhood."

One of the national leaders most respected by Frederick was the commanding general of American Expeditionary Forces in the recent World War. The notion that this popular hero would enter the controversial world of politics was not congenial to Frederick, who explained why it was a bad idea. He believed that the

American people had a right to feel that General Pershing "belongs to all of us," and, consequently he should be allowed to "remain upon the pedestal" he richly deserves. [32]

Frederick was concerned about the state of morals in America's theater. As a playwright with stage experience himself as writer and performer in Chautauqua, Frederick observed a particular trend that seemed to be taking hold on Broadway. He delivered harsh criticism of the immorality appearing in theatrical performances, recommending that they "be fumigated" or "quick-limed and buried." He believed that many plays were a detriment not only to the general public but to the actors and others associated with the stage as well. [33]

Religion

Recognizing the chaotic scene between religious denominations, Frederick observed a disconnect among "believers," who happen to be permanently estranged from one another in the volatile Middle East region. He suggested that plans of Turkey and the Kurdish folks "to kill each other wholesale" over a dispute about installing a religious man as supreme military leader should remind us that, in the realm of religion, "this world is largely an open-air lunatic asylum."

Frederick lamented the rivalries also evident in Christendom in the 1920's and, in his own direct style, placed the futility of such practices before his readers. He found a curious distinction in the activities of missionaries and New York preachers. The former attempt to bring religion to others, and the latter "attack one another." He felt that a glance at city newspapers would likely shift the heathen "back into cannibalism."

Frederick wrote not only about missionaries and cannibals but also about women's contemporary fashions. He suggested that that missionaries should bid cannibals farewell and return home in order to "persuade the ladies to put on something -- not much, of course -- but something."

Teapot Dome Trial

Oil executives Harry Sinclair and Edward Doheny were charged with corrupting the Secretary of the Interior Albert B. Fall and fraudulently grabbing oil leases of the American Navy. Involved was Mr. Sinclair's $25,000 loan to Mr. Fall under a "suspicious circumstance," and the defendants refused to testify on the ground that it might incriminate them. During the Teapot Dome case, Frederick noted that key witnesses chose either to fail to testify because of the possibility of self-incrimination or to leave the country. Frederick developed an analogy to make his point about the recently-concluded trial. He made an observation about the end of the Teapot Dome case, rejoicing at the prospect that oil witnesses who fled overseas would come back. He likened the event to the work of Mother Nature, noting that "as black birds stay with us" until winter, "one cold glance from a Grand Jury" would send "a flock of oil witnesses" to warmer climes. [34]

Scopes "Monkey" Trial

Frederick enjoyed poking fun at the deep-thinking related to the theme of the "Scopes Monkey Trial" -- creationism versus evolutionary theory. Leaving Teapot Dome to the side, he developed a simple, straightforward solution for this dispute that had captured national attention. His solution was straightforward and simple. He lamented the lack of "a telescope and a sense of humor" among those arguing the case for Evolution, who placed stock in "insect-man's" ability to grasp the origins of the world. Frederick continued, offering a novel interpretation about the lawsuit's central focus. He saw the triviality of the entire legal skirmish, concluding that the Scopes "monkey trial" would lead to nothing but the notoriety of various courtroom participants sharing the limelight, referring to the production as a "hootchy-kootchy performance." [35] Frederick's conclusion was that an Anti-Evolution Amendment to the Constitution was a fruitless undertaking because of the inability of the average citizen to exercise reasoned judgement at election time. He faulted the apathy that allows unwanted policies to take root, and when citizens begin to criticize them, "it is too late." [36]

Ku Klux Klan

On the occasion of a parade in the Nation's Capital by the Ku Klux Klan, Frederick criticized those congressmen who remained quiet about their connections with the KKK. In an example of Frederick's urge to get the truth out into the daylight, he noted his interest in the Klan's parade in the nation's capital. He believed that the public would also be interested if the KKK's members in Congress "should march down Pennsylvania avenue!"

National Defense

The topic of military readiness appeared regularly in Frederick's editorials underscoring the point that there was not enough of it. He pointed to fuzzy brainpower at high levels in the defense establishment, criticizing a position taken by the Assistant Secretary of the Navy, who had joked about the importance of air warfare as a matter requiring "a sense of humor." Frederick then cited a scenario involving a possible bombing of our nation's major cities, concluding that we should apparently "hold ourselves in readiness to roar with laughter."

Frederick showed foresight about reform of our military establishment . . . it would take more than twenty years and World War II to confirm the necessity for a Department of Defense. In 1925 he wrote that the military forces of the United States should be organized in a single department that would consist of "the army, the navy, and the air!" [38] Frederick was also adamant in the need to build up the American Merchant Marine [39] and to rid it of the practice of giving special rates to celebrities. [40]

Expressing his dissent to policies that tend to denigrate the nation's military readiness, Frederick wrote a critique of an "aircraft fiasco" in his *New York American* editorial. He targeted the Manufacturers' Association that allegedly had a monopoly in the aircraft industry. He criticized this association for spending huge amounts of the taxpayers' money while "failing to send one single fighting plane to France" during the first World War. [41] Finally, he concluded that the nation's weak air power made us "defenseless on land and sea against air attack from every quarter," leading to his conclusion that President Coolidge's Secretary of War should resign. At the same time, Frederick had praise for General Billy Mitchell for his warning about the nation's weakness in the air and believed that this military leader "might well be recognized by a Congressional vote of thanks." [42]

Frederick foresaw serious military confrontation between Japan and the United States long before Pearl Harbor, 1941. He wrote a critique in 1925 questioning the competence of our national military strategists, concluding that a concern for Japan's warlike posture may in the future correct "the paralysis of our national defenders" in the nation's capital. Long before our rivalry with Japan became a fighting matter, Frederick had a comment on that nation's diplomatic methods which, World War II historians say, were precisely at work sixteen years later at the moment Japan was conducting its attack at Pearl Harbor. He accepted with tongue-in-cheek the denial by Japan's top diplomat of secret ties with Russia, and he concluded by affirming that an Ambassador from Tokyo would never "deceive you." He added the warm thought that such an individual evinces "a childlike innocence that is one of the sweetest things in all this world."

Frederick issued another early warning about possible warfare with Japan because of a lack of resolve in the Coolidge Administration that made it possible for future foreign foes to gain intelligence information with little effort on their part, adding the example of espionage visits by folks from Japan to Hawaii during our land and sea maneuvers and concluded that they, of course, "had no foxy schemes" but really "just wanted to be sociable." Furthermore, he cited the example of the opposite situation, when Japan would in theory be our obliging host during a tactical or strategic exercise of her armed forces. He observed that American visitors could not get close to such military exercises in the vicinity of Japan. In fact, he noted our own ignorance of such operations until well after they had concluded. Frederick added: "We're the greatest advertisers in this old world!" At the same time, he supported Secretary of State Kellogg's pointed advice to be alert to enemy propaganda. [43]

France

One of Frederick's strongest critiques concerning relations with Europe focused upon the failure of certain of our World War I allies to re-pay a considerable amount of money loaned by Washington in support of England and France in their efforts to rebuild after the war. While England did manage, after some years, to meet these obligations, France proved derelict, and Frederick took note. "Common honesty!" Frederick declared was a simple requirement for France to display with regard to its monetary obligations to America, and a good example resides in "the kind of common honesty England has shown" in retiring its debt to us. [44]

Persian Gulf

American oil holdings in the region of the Persian Gulf were growing because gas-guzzling Model T Fords were beginning to be produced in large numbers. Accordingly, Frederick expected that private American companies would be looking closely to protect their investments, perhaps by American diplomatic and military pressure. Before the century would end, the Gulf War nearly 70 years later would validate his concern about the military consequences of Iraq's invasion of Kuwait as a threat to American access to Persian Gulf oil. Frederick deplored the behavior of the "oil anarchists," who placed their foremost concerns in the welfare of their overseas investments. They had no right, he believed, in pressing the United States to counter threats to their concessions by sending military forces in behalf of so-called "American interests."

The World Court

Frederick dismissed the effort by World Court advocates to arrange for the United States to join the League of Nations by way of its judicial arm. He pondered the question of why Americans should give up their enviable life by yielding its governing authority to "those who owe us, who hate us, who laugh at us!" He concluded that the enthusiastic advocates of world government should go ahead to Europe and "let the people of the United States alone." [45]

1926

A letter written by Kenesaw to his sister in New York expressed a concern that seemed to crystallize the underlying tensions believed to have existed between Arthur Brisbane and Frederick in their respective editorial roles at *The New York American*.[46] One might conclude that an additional factor might have been at play that could have ruffled William Randolph Hearst's public image. The exceeding candor of Frederick's columns brought policies of the US Government into focus, poked holes in the pretence of foreign royalty, and scrutinized cultural problems such as New York City crime, widespread divorce, religious bickering, corruption of officials, delinquency of "American allies," the threat from Japan, and activities of the Ku Klux Klan. It seems likely that Frederick and *The New York*

American, after two years of co-existence, may well have arrived at a mutually-agreeable separation.

During mid-year of 1926, Frederick, perhaps with the political arena in mind, relished the idea of raising his large family in the atmosphere of a small-town, when he returned to Indiana to become editor of the Logansport *Pharos Tribune*. The paper introduced Frederick to its readers as one with "incisive mind and insight into public matters" and "a command of picturesque language that brings back memories of the late Theodore Roosevelt." [47] The account went on to state: "He is fearless and just, and his writing has attracted the attention and praise of the greatest literary men and editorial writers of the nation, and he was recently described by humorist George Ade as America's greatest after-dinner speaker."

Frederick commenced writing columns called "Reason," appearing several times each week from 1926 to 1933 in the Logansport *Pharos Tribune* and a number of regional newspapers. Brother Kenesaw kept close tabs on Frederick's career steps, realizing that his journalistic efforts from Indiana to New York City and back did not provide steady remuneration for a family of six children. This concern was probably at the root of young Kenesaw II's remarks to his uncle Kenesaw that Frederick: "likes the *Pharos Tribune* work and is pretty satisfied." Young Ken also noted his father's speech-making activities were promising in the new medium of radio, adding: "If these go across we will be all set." [48] Excerpts of selected "Reason" columns are found below.

The Nation

Frederick determined that the political off-year of 1926, when the presidency was not at stake, was a boring affair during which the national parties showed little zest for partisan differences. He poked fun at the candidate who emphasized oratorical skills devoid of consistent content: "The spellbinder, going over the land, carries a campaign map, showing prevailing political winds in different localities, and thus determines, before each speech, just where he stands until train time."

Frederick paid appropriate homage to efforts of the nation's principal relief organization to reduce disease: "The Red Cross stamp is with us again. For nineteen years this little soldier has been fighting tuberculosis . . . In the midst of increased mortality from automobiles, murders and poison liquor, it is a sensation to find some agency at work to keep people away from the cemetery."

The matter of appropriate government spending priorities came to the fore when President Coolidge chose to override the work of Congress by not implementing legislation enacted into law. The area of defense was among the most important to Frederick, who commented: "In his message, the President said it was nobler to rival other nations in the building of the most beautiful capital than to rival them in warlike preparations. If we ever do make Washington the most beautiful capital in the world, we will have to guard her night and day or some other power may carry the torch to her as the British did in the war of 1812."

With an eye toward war against England, Frederick recalled the victories of the *USS. Constitution* and supported the idea of turning "the most heroic battleship in our history" into a museum, hoping to save the ship from the scrap heap: "Congress should pass in a hurry an appropriation to save "Old Ironsides."

Frederick, a respecter of old institutions like the barber shop, one of man's few remaining bastions, became nearly poetic in the face of the woman's arrival on the scene, changing it into a beauty parlor: "It is no more the forum of the Republic . . . this old shampooer loved his art; he grew ecstatic, his bosom heaved, his breath came in billows, his shoulders lifted, he jammed you, he crammed you, he clutched you, he crashed you, he inundated you with impunity, his nostrils dilated and his eyes rolled, as, rising in grand crescendo, he hoisted you out of your hide! But, Alas, he has gone!"

Frederick's made a brief summary of the life of a commendable figure in our political history, Speaker of the US House of Representatives, the late Joe Cannon of North Carolina: "Mr. Cannon was the last of 'the old school' of American politics. He was for many years the most picturesque figure in our national life, because he was perfectly natural." [49]

Morality

The final year of Frederick's New York venture in journalism was at hand. While many of his daily commentaries were of a critical nature, on one occasion, he was inclined to celebrate a happy event, the sixteenth birthday of the Boy Scouts of America. He wrote a special editorial for *The New York American*, summing up the essence of scouting for the youth of the Nation. He praised the Boy Scouts for moving past "this artificial day" back to "the rugged habits of the old frontier." Frederick placed great stock in learning right from wrong and the scouting organization that, by instilling self-respect, "reaches the pinnacle of good sense." [50]

The rapidly changing times of the 1920's, especially with the wide popularity of the new broadcasting medium of radio, presented Frederick with fodder for editorials, many of a contentious sort. One subject of the day would endure for many generations -- the matter of smut being delivered to living rooms by the entertainment industry. Frederick had a strong prescription to take care of this problem, very similar to his recently-stated thoughts on the ills of the American stage: "Somebody should deodorize it, sterilize it, disinfect it, fumigate it, quick-lime it, cremate it -- and forget it!" [51]

As author of a book that became a successful Broadway play, Frederick wrote as "an insider" who saw a negative influence in the theater. His sharp critique of growing immorality on the New York stage evoked strong words in one editorial: "The Mayor of New York has at last discovered that most of Broadway's shows are a disgrace to civilization. The average New York producer is not an artist. He is just a garbage merchant." [52] In retrospect, such a judgement appearing in the featured pages of *The New York American* would surely test the sensitivities of corporate management that paid Frederick's salary.

Politics

Frederick paid attention to President Coolidge who "told the American Legion at Philadelphia that our government cannot remain representative unless people go to the polls and vote" and took the White House deeper into the topic by writing: "We wish the President had told them also that our government cannot remain representative if candidates for the United States Senate can spend millions for their nominations and get away with it." Frederick seemed to be laying out the purpose of "campaign finance reform" that would gain popular attention three-quarters of a century later.

Religion

Frederick was skeptical about the religious instincts and thought processes of a segment of the population that inhabit the heartland of the USA. He lost patience with folks who showed a peculiar bent: "After a man fails at everything else, he can let his hair grow long, wrap himself in a horse blanket, boycott the bath tub, sleep in swamps, eat roots and herbs, mumble strange sounds, lean an un-manicured ear against the Milky Way, receive a command to found a new cult -- and the multitudes will leave their happy homes and follow him!" [53]

Frederick looked to Thanksgiving Day as the national holiday with utmost significance, while acknowledging a state of indifference that existed in the populace-at-large. In the back of his mind were his Mennonite ancestors who sought and found religious freedom in William Penn's province in 1749: "The Pilgrims were willing to cross the ocean to gain freedom of worship, but many in this time are not willing to cross the street to obtain the same privilege. The Creator has done more for this fair land than any other in the history of mankind and, if there is one day the American should celebrate, that day is Thanksgiving." [54]

Judicial system

One of the features of the criminal justice system that drew Frederick's ire was a tool in the hands of state governors to pardon lawbreakers. On this subject, he wrote: "Pardoning power is too wide. Aside from youthful offenders, pardons should be few and far between, except where new evidence creates a reasonable doubt of guilt . . . We have wept our way to asinine supremacy. America leads the world in crime!" [55]

The landmark trial of Teapot Dome concluded with a finding that altogether displeased Frederick, and he summed up his reaction in the following paragraphs, speaking of the defendants, the former Secretary of Interior and the oil executive: "How strange that the only twelve men in America who knew that Fall and Doheny were not guilty should happen to get together in that jury box in Washington!"

Other "Reason" editorials noted that the United States did not always convey a model of society for others to follow. The matter of autonomy for the Philippines continued to be a subject in American political circles, and Frederick wrote that its people would have an opportunity to observe our country in deciding about governing themselves: "When the Filipinos read of the alliance between crime and government in Chicago and of this last gun battle resulting from it, they may find it somewhat harder to understand our point of view the next time we inform them that they are incapable of self-government."

Foreign policy

Frederick criticized the US decision to send Marines into Nicaragua as a tactic to influence the election of a president in that country. It should not be difficult, he considered, to understand why "anti-American demonstrations" might occur there and went on to acknowledge a lack of moral justification in our nation's foreign policy: "There are two factions down in Nicaragua fighting for control of the government and our bankers are going to loan six million dollars to the faction now in power. This means that our government will stand by the crowd that borrows the money. The flag follows the loan."

European royalty

Frederick rarely portrayed foreign royalty in a favorable light, but in the case of a visit by Roumanian Queen Marie to the United States, his optimism broke through: "After days wasted in flat formalities, she met real life in the northwest; she met farmers, their wives and children and the Sioux Indians . . . The Queen will doubtless recall Dakota and Montana as the high spots on her American visit." [56]

World affairs

Despite his persisting criticism about troublesome aspects of daily life in the United States, Frederick proved to be a great defender of our system of representative government. Although he knew about the frailties of self-government, he had a measure of confidence in mankind's ability to solve many problems of society. As a bottom line, he could rejoice at signs that our nation excelled in the world community:

"Lucky America!" England has industrial unrest. France has debts and fears. Germany owes everybody. Italy has Mussolini. Spain has a dictator. Turkey has a tyrant. Chili and Peru have hatred. Mexico has revolution. China has pyorrhea. Russia has a political zoological garden. Greece has continuous revolt. The Balkans have continuous vaudeville. Japan has earthquakes. Poland has fits. Denmark fears a Coup-d'Etat -- whatever that is. And Uncle Sam has peace.

Frederick's grasp of international relations enabled him to point out how countries such as Japan and England had taken advantage of China in commercial relationships. With this in mind, and his negative view of the international organization born of World War I, Frederick took the side of the Chinese to suggest a wiser diplomatic stance than to continue to show fealty to such countries: "The most grotesque and pathetic thing in this world is China's statement that she will pay her dues as a member of the League of Nations if foreign nations will let her increase her tariff laws enough to get the necessary money. The only thing that could possibly be more grotesque and pathetic is China's willingness to belong to a League with all of her oppressors."

1927

This year brought wide attention to Frederick as a public speaker and as a talented person in the field of drama. He was invited to deliver his "Cornfield Philosophy on Current Events" to the Executive Club of Chicago, an address slated for broadcast on the Chicago Daily News radio station WMAQ. [57] A few weeks after the performance of his play *Look Who's Here* in Logansport's Luna Theatre, *The Copperhead* appeared there. Finally, The Los Angeles Playhouse also featured *The Copperhead*, and Lionel Barrymore expressed satisfaction at its success there, some nine years after its successful run on Broadway. [58]

The Nation

Frederick was impressed by the harmonious make-up of our diverse society and supported equal treatment for all. At the same time, he found humor in the challenge to spelling and pronunciation of the English language represented by the need to assimilate family names reaching our shores from eastern Europe: "There was an explosion in Chicago the other day, and the following gentlemen were injured: Peter Wietszak, John Korchinsky, Sigmung Mietszywogski, Michael Ezchar, John Buhalko and Peter Longvitz. Now everybody sing the 'Star Spangled Banner!'"

Greatness

Abraham Lincoln's birthday was always an occasion to be noted in Frederick's writings through the years, but in 1927 he chose to honor the women who helped to mould Mr. Lincoln's character: "Nancy Hanks brought him into the world, and Sarah Bush saved his life. Together they mothered him and together we should honor them. [59]

Frederick marked the dramatic moment of Charles Lindbergh's pioneering flight over the Atlantic Ocean as well as its likely boost to prospects for our military aviation readiness. On this momentous occasion, Frederick continued to write while Lindbergh was in the air: "The gallant Lindbergh goes roaring above the lonely blackness of the midnight sea, and, as the rain beats against our window, we pray that God will send kindlier weather down the pathway of this boy . . . P.S. He's there!" [60] Frederick added that this landmark flight "should rustle the cobwebs that encompass the development of the Nation's wings."

Culture

The Eighteenth Amendment, enacted to curtail the role of alcohol in our national life, was a serious effort in Frederick's mind, but he allowed a touch of humor to work its way: "Prohibition appears to have robbed Kansas of her old time ruggedness. Two of her state legislators had a very savage battle, the climax of it being reached when one of them threw a sponge at the other."

Farmers

Frederick's support for the Nation's agricultural sector was rooted in the welfare of the people who tilled the soil, but he also addressed the practical importance of keeping those folks in a positive frame of mind. Thus, he was quick to point out that Washington should pursue fair negotiations with them, concluding: "We have had many strikes in this Country, but we would have a real one, if the farmers were to strike."

Workers

Frederick cited a prediction that workers' wages would exceed $10,000 by the year 2000. He also took into account the likely impact of a failure to solve the problem of growing industrial discord in the nation. Writing of the phenomenal projection in wages, he wrote a caveat: "This looks good on the surface, but if you figure on the seventy-three coal strikes between now and then and the seventy-three resultant boosts in prices, you'll see that our great grandchildren will not have much left over for riotous living."

Religion

Frederick deplored the arrival of jazz music in America, finding it to be harmful in its effect upon American culture such as our strong religious values. Yet, he admitted that virtues embodied in Scripture would survive this new threat to organized religion: "The Bible has marvelous vitality. 'The Old Book' rides serenely on, regardless of all human tides." He also had reason for optimism and strong praise for the leading evangelist of the day: "Billy Sunday has rebuilt many wrecked lives, and they have stayed rebuilt."

Women

Frederick noted the advancement of women into jury duty and politics and strongly supported their concern about military readiness: "Woman has shown that she is as free from sickly sentimentality in government as she is in the jury box. The three women in the House of Representatives are not Pacifists; they are for a navy big enough to keep the Declaration of Independence hanging on the wall of the national household."

Children

When Frederick commented upon an item about the House of Windsor, he could not have known that the royal pair he criticized for "child neglect" would, in ten years, become the English King and Queen, and the baby girl to whom he referred would later become the monarch in a reign exceeding half a century. Referring to George V, he wrote: "The King of England sent a wireless, informing the Duke of York and his wife, on their way to Australia, that their little girl in England had cut her first tooth. This Duke and his wife, who put the ocean between themselves and their little girl may have blue blood, but they haven't any RED blood."

Politics

Frederick had misgivings about President Coolidge's tendency to support military readiness, [61] but he took an objective view of whether the President should run for a third term: "If foreign war or domestic discord should threaten the nation, and the majority of the American people wish to place their destiny in the hands of their president, they should and would elect him for the 3rd term." (Frederick's reasoning would appear to bear fruit with the advent of World War II, when Franklin D. Roosevelt was elected to a third term in 1940 and, with the war still underway, for a fourth term in 1944.)

Judicial system

For Frederick, a rare moment of pleasure and satisfaction resulted from a Teapot Dome ruling by the senior judicial body in the Nation: "Three cheers for the Supreme Court of the United States! Its unanimous cancellation of the Doheny oil leases, on the ground that they were fraudulently obtained through former Secretary Fall, is the finest thing this tribunal has done in fifty years!"

Law enforcement

Good news came to Frederick who was concerned about how to solve the problem of rising crime in America -- in at least one case, deterrence appeared to work: "One Chicago gangster was shot on the morning of election, and all the rest were good all day. Here is an object lesson for the gentleman who insists that punishment does not deter crime!" On the subject of crime, Frederick's criticism of weak law enforcement spawned a hard-hitting article that succeeded in getting the attention of one "big city" newspaper when it was reprinted on the editorial page of *The Chicago Tribune* under the heading of "Read It and Weep." [62]

Frederick's writings and speeches maintained that celebrity criminals tended to get easier treatment in courts of law than ordinary citizens, and he rarely failed to speak out about this unfairness. If the case involved an oil executive, Frederick observed closely and detected one such example of courtroom procedure: "That Judge in the Harry Sinclair case at Washington deferred passing sentence for one month. It was the Judge's own idea. It's a perfectly horrible experience for an American judge to have to send 'one of the nice people' to jail."

Often, Frederick would place himself in judgment of judicial processes that appeared to promote law-breaking rather than to deter misguided men from performing nefarious acts. In one case, he came down on the side of strong medicine for those who used gimmickry to gloss over evidence of evil deeds: "The attorney for defendant Croarkin, who murdered a little boy in Chicago, is trying to get him out as a defective, because he played with dolls when he was fourteen. They ought to hang this devil at least once, even if he believed in Santa Claus when he was thirty!"

National Defense

Frederick was critical of the President's national defense policies, in particular, with regard to navy development because the White House expected other countries to negotiate in a mutually-agreeable spirit. He felt that this notion was wishful thinking: "If President Coolidge could really get the nations to limit their naval building to his figures, he would go down in history as emancipator of the world. If they come to Mr. Coolidge's conference at all, they will bring more jokers than were manufactured by all the playing card companies in the United States last year." [63]

Frederick commented upon the statement of Secretary of the Treasury Andrew Mellon that World War I had cost 35 billion dollars, explaining that money spent in a timely manner for a just cause could perhaps avert costly military hostilities. With regard to America's entry into that conflict as an example, he stated: "One billion dollars added to our naval force in 1914 would have given Germany such a respect for our shipping that those submarine atrocities which plunged us into the fray would not have occurred. Safety is always cheap!"

Foreign policy

By weighing developments in Russian policy in the 1920's, Frederick found a remarkable disparity between Communist bluster and Communist action: "Soviet Russia calls the United States bad names, but when she has a real job to do, she comes straight to headquarters. She has just retained Col. Hugh Cooper, Chief Engineer of the Muscle Shoals power project to build a seventy-million-dollar dam across the Dneiper." Meanwhile, learning about Russia's legalization of the sale of vodka for the first time since the 1917 Revolution, Frederick noted that the Bolsheviks took a page from the Czar's notebook "for the same reason the Czars retained it -- it is easy to subdue a country that is drunk."

175

Combining his perspective on a foreign territory and an American city with unbridled corruption, Frederick agreed with a presidential action and explained why he did so: "President Coolidge was right to veto the act of the Philippine Legislature, calling for a popular vote on the question of independence. As a matter of fact, the people of the Philippines are no more capable of self government than the people of Chicago."

Prevention of war through international efforts seemed to Frederick to be a fruitless task, quite beyond the scope of recent international efforts to achieve general agreement on disarmament: "Unless our so-called civilization can be made safe from war, the human race should stop propagating and turn this world over to the beetles."

World affairs

Frederick's analysis of Mussolini, the swash-buckling "grand leader" of Italy, concluded that mutual agreement on arms limitation with that country would be a futile undertaking: "Much of Mussolini's power rests on his appeal to the long dormant imperialistic ambitions of Italy. He wishes eagles to perch upon his shoulder, not doves!"

A touch of history in the making appeared in Frederick's comment about the once-powerful Austro-Hungarian Empire, dismantled after World War I. As an example, he discussed the conclusion of a meaningless diplomatic pact: "Sweden and Austria have signed a treaty not to go to war against each other. There's no particular reason why this should give the Swedes a sense of increased security, for Austria is a poor, old, battered derelict, with nothing but a past."

Writing of other countries that do not have traditions akin to our own, Frederick moved his telescope to focus upon Europe, apparently still clinging to labor unrest that marked the post-war period: "Austria has been cut to pieces, and Vienna is now little more that the capital of a memory, but she holds on to her old time dignity. A postal employee refused to tip his hat to the postmaster and was reprimanded, whereupon there was a general strike."

Frederick developed sympathy for China as a victim of plundering by European countries and Japan and again displayed his dislike for the nations long preeminent in commercial rivalry in the world: "The British, French and Japanese Consuls in Shanghai snubbed the American Consul the other day, calling on the Cantonese commander without saying anything to our representative about it. It is perfectly natural for Great Britain, France and Japan to have no respect for the United States, since we have never robbed China."

International problems should be dealt a healthy dose of pragmatism, according to Frederick's prescription for keeping American out of foreign wars. One element in his thinking was to welcome permanent warfare between the major players on the world stage, excluding American participation. His formula looked like it might solve big problems in this regard if the United States could just draw up a seat, out of range, and watch the war dogs go at it: "How sweet it would be if Russia were to get into a war with China or Japan, or with both of them. For years she has been sticking her long, warty nose into the affairs of every other nation in the world. Her expectations of widespread revolution have been fantastic, and the fears of our own statesmen have been grotesque, but Russia's efforts have been an endless offense to the world."

Finally, an item from Japan suggested important cultural differences between our two nations. The gist of such differences marked a Japanese state occasion, from which Frederick was able to draw both "good and bad news." According to his own interpretation of results, he concluded: "The funeral of the late Emperor of Japan was a great success, more than seven hundred people being crushed in the jam."

1928

This year proved to be an engaging one for Frederick because, after just two years back in Indiana from his New York jounalistic venture, he decided to re-enter politics as a candidate for Governor. Speaking to voters in terms of differences within his own party, he reasoned: "The people have a right to know this year whether a candidate belongs to the Abraham Lincoln wing or the Jeff Davis wing of the Republican Party of the state of Indiana. . . I belong to the Abraham Lincoln wing." (This is a good indication, one would suppose, that Frederick's "Bull Moose" tendencies remained strong in 1928.)

Frederick's efforts failed when party regulars, thinking back to his involvement in Teddy Roosevelt's Progressive Party in 1912, maneuvered to deny success to a candidate avowedly set upon its reform. Meanwhile, the indominatable Progressive continued to write "Reason" in the Logansport *Pharos-Tribune* and did a stint writing a series of cartoons featuring "Old Judge Pepper." [64]

Frederick's banquet appearances were illustrated by an address to the annual dinner of the Indiana Society of Chicago, held at the Palmer House hotel in December. In a non-deprecating moment, he recalled his appearance at the Society in 1920 when he made "one of the greatest speeches I have ever heard." For this corporate-minded audience, he told of dropping out of high school in order to get into business: "I met the study of Latin, resolved that a dead language should rest in peace, and plunged into the world of the 'Red Front Drug Store' at Logansport." [65]

The Nation

In the 1920's, it was becoming clear that young people were leaving farms and finding livelihood in population centers of the nation. Frederick believed that voting trends would work to the disadvantage of the nation because country people "do have a little something to say about their government, but in the cities government is a machine-made product, pure and simple."

The matter of the income tax, established by the 16th Amendment to the Constitution in 1913, was, in Frederick's view, a natural, built-in cause for controversy: "The action of the United States Senate meets with the same old reception . . . All who have incomes are against it, and all who have none are for it."

A light touch with dreadful consequences fitted into Frederick's style in commenting upon the leading professional sport in his home state: "The late speedway races at Indianapolis, were a total failure. There was a great crowd and wonderful weather, but nobody was killed."

To illustrate a theorem that progress frequently comes by surprise, affecting the nation's future growth and prosperity, Frederick cited early American history: "When Thomas Jefferson bought Louisiana from Napoleon, violent opponents ridiculed the idea of purchasing a vast area so remote from the eastern seaboard that nobody would ever visit it."

The reputation of New York "as timid" in military security matters was belied, Frederick concluded, by the lessons of history: "When the Spanish War came and again when the World War came,

New York rushed to Washington and implored Uncle Sam to send the whole navy over to protect it."

Shifting suddenly to the Civil War era, Frederick found remarkable that, according to one biographer, General Ulysses S. Grant used no profanity throughout the conflict, even "when the jealous military politicians had him arrested for taking the war seriously and pursuing the enemy without permission from the bureaucrats."

Culture

The field of genealogy, Frederick pointed out, could be hazardous in terms of what mischief our troops might pursue in foreign lands: "Our soldiers in Nicaragua have found a settlement of fair-skinned descendants of English pirates. All of us can find a pirate or two in the family tree, if we climb high enough."

Frederick's reminder of the ills of alcohol focused upon the widow of brewer Adolphus Busch, whose estate exceeded five million dollars, observing: "Not many of the widows of the gents who lapped up the product of the late Mr. Busch left anything like that much."

The possibility that frivolity on the part of people should crowd out sober contemplation of important trends in society, and government caused Frederick to call to task two negative hallmarks of the 1920's: "No matter where you tune in on the radio, they're dancing -- dancing from Cape Horn to Greenland and from Australia to Spitzbergen . . . If some genius like Edison could only harness the wasted horse power of our dancers and our gum chewers, it would do all the work of the world!"

There seemed to be little public interest in high-level negotiations going on in Europe to bring about general agreement as to substituting the idea of peace for the notion of war: "It now looks as if the world's interest in the Paris conference to outlaw war would be utterly eclipsed by the visit of England's supreme golf authority to the United States to bring about the adoption of a larger and lighter golf ball."

Colleges and universities are institutions that hold a certain promise for the future of the Republic, and Frederick had little patience for young folks who trivialized the opportunity to gain such education. He had these words for students at the University of Michigan who scalded their fellow students: "they should be sent to feeble-minded homes."

Religion

"Old time religion" was one of Frederick's preferred topics, and he was taken aback when a member of the Methodist Episcopal board of education observed that "religion is no longer taught in the home." Frederick countered by writing: "And the fact that it is not . . . is responsible for nine-tenths of all the troubles this age is heir to."

One of Frederick's highly-regarded citizens, Thomas A. Edison, was criticized by British novelist Arthur Conan Doyle "for doubting the existence of a future life." Frederick made his own conclusion: "Edison doesn't know any more about it than anybody else, but we do know that if the human race had not always had an unconscious faith in immortality, it would have jumped into the river ages ago."

Criticism was not Frederick's only implement for bettering society by addressing the divisions between denominations of Christianity. On one occasion, for example, he found reason for optimism: "In the midst of all this religious furor, ladies and gentlemen, take your hats off to the Salvation Army. It attends strictly to its own business; it fights nobody but the devil!"

Although Frederick was not at odds with the purposes of the Anti-Saloon League, he criticized their practice of distributing pro-Hoover literature in churches: "We need religion in the building of American character more than everything else, but the mixing of politics with religion kills its appeal."

Government

This commentary has again addressed the highest level of government. Although the Vice President would be ready to take over the Presidency in an emergency, his real importance under normal conditions, Fred believed, was negligible. This judgement was not to underestimate the long-windedness of aspirants for the job: "The Vice President is only a spare tire, but it may be difficult to have V.P. candidates stop making acceptance speeches for the simple reason that it is hard to keep air in a spare tire."

Frederick set his sights on government corruption in any form to include the tradition of sending free mail to constituents by members of Congress, with taxpayers picking up the tab: "Our statesmen are now dumping five tons of political buncomb into the mails every day, all of which is for the purpose of re-electing our statesmen to their present positions . . . If they want to send out their speeches, let them pay the price." [66]

Women

Having been a steady supporter of women in their struggle to gain suffrage, Frederick also recognized their persistence in holding onto their gains under the 19th Amendment to the US Constitution: "After a lady makes the front page you can't shove her back among the want ads any more than you can make a Bengal tiger's mouth water for spinach after he has once tasted blood."

Frederick's interest in women's rights was well-documented, but less known was his appreciation of the French expression "Vive la difference!" Thus, he discussed a fashion item that was causing "the wholesale destruction of rattlesnakes in Texas" in order to accommodate the ladies' "demand for snakeskin shoes." He suggested their motivation in seeking such exotic footwear to be clear: "The fair sex is getting even for that serpent that tempted Eve." Another ladies' fashion item caught his attention -- the scanty sportswear of large numbers of young American women during the "Roaring Twenties." His appreciation of this development was expressed as a matter of national pride when he observed: "the average American girl could show Europeans some scenery that would make them forget all about the Alps."

Farmers

Frederick's support of farmers became clear in his opposition to President Coolidge's veto of legislation that would have benefited the agricultural sector of the US economy: "We give tariff protection to great industries . . . we fix public service charges . . .we have given empires of land to corporations for building railroads . . . Let's help the farmer, or go out of the aid business entirely!" [67]

Frederick supported presidential-candidate Herbert Hoover's campaign pledge to grant relief to the agricultural sector and advised farmers to exercise patience, writing: "it took the same government twenty-five years to give the Wright brothers the Distinguished Flying Cross, and only one of them lived to get it."

Politics

Frederick continued to criticize public officials such as the governors of Indiana and Illinois, who were in trouble with the law. He also believed that judicial loopholes frequently enabled prominent figures to evade appropriate punishment. As a result, he conceived a solution when he learned about a citizen who planned to take a rocket trip to the moon. Frederick's thought was that "if the gentleman had room for two passengers, the people of Indiana and Illinois should take up a collection and send their governors along."

Frederick followed with interest the current campaign for the Presidency between Republican Herbert Hoover and Democrat Al Smith, expressing his view about the Democratic candidate's recent appearance in sporting attire: "Seeing Al Smith in his bathing suit reminds one of what Bismarck said: 'I've seen three kings without their clothes on, and none of them were very beautiful.'" Continuing on the subject of politics, Frederick speculated about the future of radio as a campaign tool. Going further in the technological revolution, he made a prediction 20 years before the fact . . . "when television becomes an everyday matter, one and the same campaign speech can be made for everybody."

Foreign policy

Immigration policy was an issue that began to receive public attention in the late 1920's, particularly as it applied to human traffic entering the United States from Mexico. The ups and downs of American relations with that country seemed to be an additional irritant affecting public opinion. Frederick decided that it was time to take action: "Far be it from us to throw any sand in the gear box of our relations with Mexico, but Uncle Sam should put Mexican immigration under the quota system which is now applied to European countries. More than 78,000 came to us across the Rio Grande last year."

National Defense

Military training remained a major interest of Frederick as it related directly to the readiness of our armed forces. When the National Association of State Universities proposed that civilians instead of military personnel would be in charge of Reserve Officers Training Corps, Frederick demurred: "Better still have the officers drill with fairy wands instead of guns, and let them study Mother Goose instead of army tactics."

The matter of seeking international agreement to prohibit future wars did not support American interests, according to Frederick's summary. The attack on Pearl Harbor in just over a dozen years would bear out his warning: "Secretary Kellogg's outlawry of war program marches gaily on, the Japanese being the last to indicate their support of it. The net result of it will be that the United States, lulled into false security by this international lullaby, will go to sleep and let our national defense go to seed, while other nations will wink the other eye and keep their powder dry."

Frederick's concern for national security ranged from tactics and strategy to materiel procurement and intelligence practices. He deplored an American penchant for spilling secret information through the news media: "England is building in secret a mystery airplane which may make her first in aviation from a military standpoint. America's weakness is that she can't do anything of a military nature in secret. As soon as the effort is big enough to have its picture taken, we broadcast it, even down to the smallest detail."

Europe

Readers of Frederick's columns were exposed to his attention to nuances in governmental practices, as in the case of England, where the Crown enjoys only symbolic standing with regard to politics: "The statement that King George has approved Secretary Kellogg's treaty, outlawing war, means that the British premier has approved it and told the king 'Sign here!' The king is the drum major of the British procession, but the premier decides where the procession is going." Furthermore, upon learning that Austria's president was likely to be reelected, Frederick proceeded to bring international affairs down to the household level when he observed: "this isn't such a great honor, for there's nothing left of Austria, except Vienna and nobody thinks of Vienna any more, except when they go to the bakery."

Russia

Displaying a fundamental understanding of Russia's experiment in communism, Frederick pointed to the hypocrisy of Bolshevism, by which the upstart regime proclaimed one thing and sought the opposite. At the same time he finds a Scriptural basis for his critique: "The Apostle Paul announced that the love of money is the root of all evil, but Russia has learned that an abiding respect for money is the root of all material progress. Since the Soviet opened its red doors for business in 1917, it has hammered capitalism, but now it humbly begs its pardon and offers vast concessions to all foreigners who will enter and invest."

Royalty

Home-grown philosophy found its way into Frederick's essays such as the one that spoke of the great value he assigned to a capacity for individual initiative. Upon learning that the Duke of Baden had given Sweden's Queen Victoria an island in Lake Constance, he mused: "We've always wanted an island, not caring so much where it was or what it was, just so it was an island."

1929

Being a parent was a responsibility, he felt keenly, and perhaps in a special way on the occasion of his eldest son's graduation from Columbia College a few days after his 19th birthday. Among thought-provoking impressions he acquired in visiting the campus on this occasion was the greeting the son received from college friends, "something like 'Slats'." In thinking about "how his mother and you ransacked the world for a name that would combine dignity and power -- and now they call him 'Slats'."

The Nation

After the national election and the changeover in the White House from Coolidge to Hoover, Frederick's perspective noted a cardinal difference between heads of state of the American republic and of nations adhering to royal traditions: "Monarchs, clinging to their thrones and ex-monarchs, trying to get them back must be bewildered to see Mr. Coolidge turn with a smile from the greatest office in the world, glad to get back to private life where he can walk without being guarded and fish without being photographed."

On a sober note, Decoration Day at the Soldiers' Home in Marion, Indiana impressed Frederick deeply. His thoughts were about the physical beauty of the institution that had been built for survivors of the Civil War and converted to a rehabilitation center for the wounded of the more recent World War. His description was of "a beautiful place with its trees, flowers, and winding walks," but Frederick completed the sentence with "but over all hangs the dark cloud of disaster." He viewed the rows of white crosses but paid more attention to something else that impressed him: "the sight of the living wrecks, those with sick minds in strong bodies. While many will come back, more of them are beyond recall." His reverent impressions then turned to bitter thoughts: "As we contemplated their sacrifice, we thought of the unworthy and the ungrateful . . . We thought of motion picture actors, living in golden frivolity, refusing to pay their income taxes; of crooked politicians profaning the temple these heroes had preserved, of human swine, trampling the laws of the country which protects them, in pile still higher their pyramids of greed."

Frederick had heavy criticism for the "deplorable" action of the Grand Army of the Republic "when it declined the invitation of the Confederate Veterans to hold a Blue and Gray reunion next year." He went into persuasive detail to express his condemnation of such behavior. [68]

Culture

Another example of Frederick's capacity for a consistent attitude regarding civic crimes of public officials related to the visit of the Justice Minister of Denmark to Sing Sing Prison in New York. Frederick was moved by the opportunity this afforded the distinguished guest, who "will feel more at home as one by one he meets statesmen, temporarily behind the bars."

A serious development in the arts was addressed by Frederick who noted a large number of Broadway actors and actresses were being enticed to Hollywood's talking motion pictures because of pay "ten times as much as New York producers" could offer. Frederick lamented Fox Film's success in signing up "two hundred stars and near-stars for the talkies."

Religion

Examples of religious bigotry and hatred pricked Frederick's conscience and sent him into a critical mood against the purveyors of such attitudes. In a reminder of disturbing violence in the Middle East, he was highly critical: "These ghastly massacres in Palestine should warn all decent people to stop playing with fire for political purposes, for there have been days when what is now occurring in the Holy Land could have occurred very easily in the United States." He added : "In the presence of religious hatred, men are barbarians, and civilization is only lipstick."

Albania's king created public interest when he abandoned his Muslim faith in order to marry a wealthy Italian Christian lady, with the "result that the Mohammedans and Christians are shooting at each other." This example occurred to Frederick as just one example of many that give religion a bad name: "The world's candidates for Heaven make the devil laugh 'til his sides are sore."

Finally, the House of David denomination broke into print with the news that King Ben Purnell took about a million dollars to his grave. Frederick offered a pragmatic interpretation of the widow's theology, namely that the King's successor Queen Mary "needless to say, believes in the resurrection of the body."

Politics

Mindful of the state that had been the spawning ground of political Progressives such as the LaFollettes within the framework of the Republican Party, Frederick noted that efforts to locate a tame elephant as a prop in marking the Party was ill-conceived, that in fact "a wild elephant would be more typical of Wisconsin's Republicanism."

On the occasion of the birthday of Civil War hero US Grant, "a chivalric victor and as unassuming as a private soldier," Frederick recalled that, regrettably the great general "permitted himself to be drawn into politics for which he had no taste and no ability."

Having grown up in a small town where he learned first-hand about working a small family farm, Frederick could identify parallels between rural life and the world of politics. He noted the account that "a gentleman in Maryland has invented a machine that milks four cows simultaneously." Working on that proposition, Frederick realized that "this is little to brag about in view of the fact that we have political machines capable of milking millions of taxpayers at one and the same time."

Government

Nearly 75 years ago, Frederick was delivering the same argument being used in later years concerning the issue of gun control. Opponents of this political proposition have continued to paraphrase Frederick's argument: "The trouble with a law against the sale of firearms is that the thugs have theirs, and the law would operate only to keep the law abiding citizen from getting the necessary implements for defensive purposes."

Frederick's concern for national defense showed plainly in his writings about the activities of pacifists who appeared in organized fashion in Washington, DC to lobby against measures to bolster the military establishment. [69]

Criticism of the Nation's Capital remained one of Frederick's favorite topics as he outlined a comprehensive exchange of social niceties that mark the Federal bureaucracy. Not one to support the practice of sponsoring luncheons and dinners when there is work to be done, he offered a synopsis of this wasteful and non-productive practice: "The eating season is now in full blast at Washington . . . the Senators feeding the Cabinet, the Cabinet the Diplomats, the Diplomats the Judges . . . During the day they pass the buck and during the evening they pass the prunes. Statesmanship at Washington does not demand brains of high order, but it does call for marvelous digestion."

The Presidency

Demonstrating the ill-gratitude of political processes, Frederick addressed the issue of naming the record-breaking dam built in the Southwest after extensive advocacy by one Senator Hiram Johnson of California. By all rights, the technological marvel ought to have carried the name of its persistent partisan, but instead, "the Senate proposes to name the dam after Hoover," the President of the United States, Johnson's "ancient enemy." To Frederick, "Here's the most bitter dose in modern times."

Women

Concern for the dignity of the fair sex, Frederick was a dedicated critic of those aspects of society that denigrated women on the beaches and swimming pools. In his judgement, a feeling of shame and embarrassment for skimpy female attire reached even beyond the confines of this sphere in space: "The recent eclipse of the sun was perfectly natural, for it's enough to make the old boy hide his face to look down on the 1929 bathing suits."

187

The circumstances of the robbery of "two gentlemen of Topeka, Kansas of $14,000 by a 'dashing brunette,'" Frederick theorized, probably caused the victims to "join the large majority who are said to prefer blonds."

Once in a while, Frederick would set aside thoughts about the Ku Klux Klan, World War debts owed by Europe to the United States, crooked governors in a number of states, the dead-end career of professional pugilism, the Civil War, the Founding Fathers, Abraham Lincoln, and Theodore Roosevelt and turn to the American woman, whom he dearly loved. On this occasion, he thought deeply when "the other night we saw a pretty girl, dressed in the fashion of thirty years ago. . . She led you back to the days when man respected woman . . . We wish we might call back to the United States that great respect of other years . . . But only the women of America can call it back." [70]

Farmers

A lament that Congress had tended to slight the interests of farmers through the years found Frederick to be pessimistic of any change among current legislators. He concluded: "Nothing could be more appropriate than for these United States senators to put on their marvelous acrobatic performance on the farm relief bill just as the circus season is opening."

Negroes

Frederick showed great respect for the man who, under highly-unfavorable social conditions, made the most of his life and was inclined to help his fellow man through a sense of generosity. He contrasted the well-to-do southern "slave-holding planter" who "sat on his pillared portico, sipping mint julep and discussing *The Constitution*" with a gentleman "born in slavery" who donated much more than the planter possessed, a sum of $100,000 to Fisk University of Nashville, Tennessee.

Frederick pointed to the regrettable custom in America to shortchange Negroes who have made distinct achievements. While he saw considerable merit in a piece of legislation now before Congress by which an aged Negro, Matthew Henson, who had been with Admiral Peary on his expedition to the North Pole, would be granted a pension, Frederick also felt that "but for his color, Mr. Henson would have been decorated and pensioned long ago."

Child labor

President Hoover called a conference to study the problem of child labor which, from Frederick's vantage point, placed the United States in a poor position, using a powerful comparison: "While savages rarely abuse their children, our so-called civilization exploits them horribly in city sweat shops and in eastern and southern cotton mills."

Celebrities

Sympathy for American heroes who find themselves in desperate financial situations in their latter years was evident in Frederick's view when he cited the sad case of George Rogers Clark, "the intrepid conqueror of the West." He concluded that Clark would gladly have traded the rich adulation he received "a thousand times" for some assistance in his "bare and bitter old age."

Criticism of Charles Lindbergh that appeared in a New York daily newspaper was not a matter that Frederick and most Americans would tolerate. One charge was that, in landing his plane where people were assembled to greet him, his wheels splashed mud on some of them when he landed. Another problem seemed to be that he had later gone on his honeymoon without filing a story about it with the paper. Frederick noted his support of the idea that "Lindbergh regarded his wedding as a matter of personal interest, rather than a thing of world-wide concern." Frederick then quipped: "there are times when even a newspaper should mind its own business."

His experience in politics built in Frederick an ability to distinguish between successful people and those who sought fame. Learning that an academic in Georgia looked forward to the day when high medical achievements and first-rate education would combine to "produce a race of mental giants," Frederick believed, however, that "it's a lot simpler to be just an ordinary man and hire a good publicity agent."

Marriage

Visiting the topic of marriage, Frederick took notice of a happening in Eastern Europe that "inspired him greatly," causing him to remark: "If it were not so far, we would send a bunch of violets to those women of Hungary who mobbed the long-haired, unlaundered poet who started to read the verses he had written, extolling trial marriage."

Supposing that President Hoover was in need of hiring "an experienced disbursement officer," Frederick was prepared to suggest the name of one Gordon V. Thorne of Chicago, a man of "rare qualifications" because "he is now paying alimony to three former wives and living with a fourth."

Corporate matters

Criticism of "big business" remained prominent in Frederick's writings when he likened that activity to unfeeling corporations that gouged consumers with higher prices. He contrasted that notion, however, with his own observation about New York surgeons who "did much bigger business when they performed an operation and enabled a girl to walk after seventeen years of helplessness, due to infantile paralysis."

Corruption in whatever form was an easy target for Frederick's ire, and book publishers were now no exception. He noted that "Kentucky's governor was to testify "about the attempt of the school book trust to plunder the people." Frederick made a comparison, in which publishers came out looking bad, saying: "We grow excited if a bandit ties a bandana over his countenance and sticks up a gas station, but he is a small retailer. We should display a much greater contempt for the publishers and the politicians who through the years have pillaged millions of fathers and mothers" by producing new textbooks in order to make huge profits.

Law enforcement

When US missionaries would run into difficult times in foreign countries where they were seeking to convert native people, Frederick expressed mixed feelings about the obligation of the United States to hasten to their protection. Oddly, missionaries came to his mind again when reading of the county board's action in Chicago "to install electric light bulbs which lock into sockets after it was estimated that $25,000 worth of them are stolen every year." Frederick shook his head at this situation, writing: "And yet we send missionaries to China."

190

Judicial system

The workings of our justice system, according to Frederick, were illustrated appropriately in the following instance: "A burglar in Utah walked on his hands to keep the authorities from tracking him, but his acrobatic performance isn't in it with that which Justice gives to every criminal case when She jumps through hoops and skins the cat at the command of the technical criminal lawyer."

Although Frederick usually showed little consideration for those who earned their way into prison, he found some level of understanding of their plight in his observation about convicts in Texas who prayed for their ailing warden "and then presented him with a loving cup." It seemed to be a surprising reversal when he acknowledged that a number of those fellows incarcerated may have richly been deserving of parole: "If the world had treated them as well as the warden did, some of them would not have gone behind the bars."

The Supreme Court's decision to give jail time to oil-magnate Harry Sinclair brought forth favorable comment from Frederick's pen: "Our prayers as citizens should be for more of such decisions, for the common man asks only that his government be honest . . . that the Goddess of Justice be chaste!"

The inequality of judicial sentences was illustrated in a Pennsylvania court, when a seventeen-year-old received twenty-five days in jail "because he went fishing on Sunday," while the state "fails to prosecute Senator-elect Vare, charged with spending millions to buy voters on the hoof."

Frederick's thoughts concerned the death of three schoolboys in Chicago as a result of an automobile accident by a drunken driver. Justice in this case would mean, in his judgment, that the offender "should receive at least one electric chair."

In the late 1920's, Frederick thought of a process, positive in tone and featuring a practical effect upon society by solving congestion problems. Instead of enlarging prisons, as was being seriously considered, he wrote: "A better way to relieve congestion is to take prisoners out of doors and let them build roads. They like it so well they make few efforts to escape . . . there are enough roads to build to keep everybody busy." In so saying, Frederick was beating the next president, Franklin D. Roosevelt, to the punch in subsidizing public construction during the Great Depression through the Civilian Conservation Corps. The C.C.C. focused, however, on the unemployed rather than prisoners.

Frederick had no problem with capital punishment, but when people took justice into their own hands for a man on death row, there could be "a horrible festival of barbarism," as in Texas. While the man was going to be executed anyway, he believed that the witnesses to the lynching "shoved their civilization backward several generations."

National Defense

Continuing his observations about the results of the Washington Naval Conference, Frederick concluded that the Uncle Sam, "in scrapping his fine fighting ships after the Conference, won the heavyweight jackass championship." Adding to America's difficulty in keeping up with other nations is that we find "the vision of world peace to be most intoxicating, but the trouble about it is that if we turn around to spit, we can't start again."

Frederick was skeptical of negotiations designed to limit "the use of poison gas in time of war." His prediction was that a nation "in a bloody corner" would indeed resort to the use of such weaponry "to save itself." He concluded, more than 70 years ago, that America might become vulnerable in a future time when "squadrons of air bombers drop their deadly gases upon American cities." Because of his belief in a continuing threat to America, he welcomed as "a fine business proposition" the US decision to equip the army and navy with a total of some 710 "fighting airplanes," the cost of which equaled the price tag of a single battleship.

Foreign affairs

Frederick held little hope that international negotiations just approved by the United States would have any positive effect upon prospects for global brotherhood. In fact, he viewed the Kellogg Treaty as "only a matter of international hat-tipping."

Europe

Frederick delivered a rebuke to the practice he had seen of the mediocre quality of our diplomatic representation in London when he saluted the selection of Charles G. Dawes to be US ambassador to Britain. In his view, "we have sent such an unbroken line of stuffed mattresses to the Court of St. James, we would like to observe the English reaction to a human being."

For once, Frederick had kind thoughts about a European nation, but these thoughts had to go back centuries to find an argument for financially prominent Americans like Ford and Rockefeller "and others who have profited" in America to display some gratitude. They now had an opportunity "to pass the hat and reimburse Spain" for the estimated $5,500 Christopher Columbus' voyage was said to have cost.

The demand by a prominent German movement to return that country's colonies lost after World War I found little support from Frederick who suggested that "the next step will probably be a demand that we apologize to the Kaiser and pay him a vast indemnity . . . The Allies need a guardian!" Frederick had a prescription for Germany on how to qualify for American loans, observing that it should stop "spending one billion dollars a year for booze." Instead, he recommended that the average German change his tastes: "If this bunch of foam-blowers would dip their tonsils in buttermilk for a while, they could pay their debts."

Ten years after the peace treaty at Versailles, Germany managed to pronounce its own interpretation as to the repayment of its debt following the World War. Many others may well have reacted the same way as Frederick did when he posed the question: "Who WON that war?" He proceeded to make a prediction that would suggest the emergence of an aggressive power in the center of Europe: "when the strategic time comes, Germany will demand the return of her colonies, and she will get them."

Relations among countries of Europe was an attractive topic for Frederick because the United States was not directly affected by issues that began and ended on that continent. It was with some satisfaction that he could judge Russia the bear to be "very foxy, if a bear can be foxy" in its efforts to gain a military advantage over its European neighbors. Frederick as self-appointed judge viewed Russia's seemingly one-sided proposal for disarmament not unlike that of the Europeans, who could be every bit as cunning: "Other European powers, long engaged in selling gold bricks to others, will not fall for a brick, so poorly gilded."

South of the border

Frederick's readers learned that "this Mexican revolution would be very serious, if it had as many privates as generals in its ranks." The turbulence of political rule in Mexico led him to produce a practical formula for bringing greater stability to the country. Upon hearing its authorities speak of the value of military indoctrination, Frederick concluded: "If Mexico is ever saved it will be by giving the people education and land, and ruling them with a club until the education has taken effect."

Regarding things further south of the border, Frederick pondered the words of President Gomez of Venezuela, who "informs the world that peace now reigns in Venezuela, but he appears to be utterly unable to account for it."

Asia

On a serious note in the international realm, Frederick liked what he heard from Dr. Li of China on a visit to Indiana. Valuing "more than all the conquered dividends of imperialism" was the declaration that: "America is the only nation that has consistently treated China with international decency." But, regardless of these kind words, Frederick's sentiments were influenced by a report that China claimed to have the capability to deploy an army of fifty million men. His conclusion? "It may be better for the rest of the world to let China continue to smoke opium."

Royalty

The Logansport vantage point occasionally differed sharply from the broader global scene. As an example, it was observed that "While the authorities to the East are looking for the $20,000 worth of pearls lost by the princess of Braganza in a Pullman car, we wish they would also look for the perfectly good razor we lost last week in lower twelve."

The 1930's

For three long years we've been so close to the Wolf that we could tell whenever he had been eating Onions. . . We are Not on our last legs. When I was only Five Minutes old I heard people saying we were "going to the dogs" and I've heard the same thing ever since. But I've been looking for those "dogs" a long, long time – and I've never seen them yet!

-- Frederick Landis, *The Hoosier Editor* [71]

How the country would have rocked with laughter if radio could have brought home the incident of the flies from the near-by stable that bit members of the Continental Congress through their silk stockings and caused them to hurry to a conclusion.

-- Frederick Landis, *Radio Guide* [72]

The Great Depression brought us into the 1930's when Frederick would briefly enter the race again for the Republican nomination for Governor in 1932. He became a regular commentator on radio and continued his "Reason" columns in the Logansport *Pharos Tribune* until 1933, when he began producing his home-grown monthly magazine of humor and satire, *The Hoosier Editor*. In 1934, he wrote a new, brief column about recollections of life, "Here at Home," in the *Logansport Press*, and published ten issues of *The Hoosier Editor* through October, completing 12 issues before his untimely death in November. The source of items cited in the following pages are from Frederick's column "Reason" unless otherwise indicated by footnote.

1930

Kicking off the new decade, Frederick showed that he was for all of society, from the workingman to those who handled a great deal of money. On January 23, he addressed the Illinois Bankers Association "Annual Mid-Winter Dinner" at the Palmer House Grand Ball Room in Chicago. Giving himself maximum leeway to address issues foreign and domestic, serious and comical, and of course the Great Depression now in full swing, he selected the catch-all approach with: "Things in General." [73]

The Nation

A hometown item from Evansville, Indiana caught Frederick's attention when it stated "the glad tidings that Helen Marie Krock, only six weeks old, has a lower front tooth." The occasion brought to mind the problem that can result in families, he wrote, when the original owner of a baby's first denture can become a matter of doubt and possible controversy . . . whether "the tooth belonged to Amos . . . Obediah . . . Cinderella . . . and Petunia." Leaving such complications aside for the time being, Frederick chose to congratulate the parents, the Krocks, baby Krock, "and to any other little Krocks that may be roaming about the premises."

A positive sign in the old game of North vs South appeared in a small ceremony in Maryville, Missouri, as Frederick noted. The occasion was the burial of a former Confederate bugler who died at the age of 92. The warming touch -- "a beautiful symbol of a reunited country" was the role of former Union bugler, Nat Sisson, who at 88, "sounded taps over the grave of his friend, H. P. Childress."

Shifting to our national immigration policy, Frederick longed for our adoption of a strict system like that of England instead of allowing "criminals by the thousands" who are "bootlegged into the United States." The matter of regulating the process of immigration into the United States came under review in the early 1930's because of the apparent diplomatic stance of some countries seeking to open up the flow of citizens wishing to depart their homelands for greater opportunity in the USA. Limitations on immigration, Frederick observed, should be determined only by the receiving nation, recognizing such a right is the same as that of an ordinary citizen who has the last word on "who shall come into his house and eat at his table."

The changing times were underscored by Frederick's deep respect for the pilots of the early 1930's, who risked their lives alongside Charles Lindbergh, working for the United States Postal Service. Again, he would have recalled that his eldest son young Kenesaw had flown around the state two years previously in behalf of Frederick's campaign for Governor. Although commercial flying would become routine in the aftermath of a "World War II," the true perspective in the early years of flight was expressed by Frederick in the following way: "As you lie in your warm beds these stormy nights, think of the dauntless flyers who dash through the skies, carrying Uncle Sam's air mail."

The report that the risk of fire would bring about destruction of the building in which Patrick Henry uttered his famous "Liberty or Death" speech, St. John's church in Richmond, Virginia, caused Frederick to pause in hopes that this important part of our history could be preserved. He observed that, prior to that patriot's address "he was an obscure country lawyer, but when he finished it, he was world famous."

Culture

"It was ghastly up against the saws and knives of the operating room," wrote Frederick the first time one of his children faced surgery in the local hospital. It's foolish, he believed, to think you could "jolly him" because "never get it into your head that kid of yours doesn't know you, for he has complete blueprints of you; he has been through you with a lantern from cellar to cupola."

The discovery of a new star, billions of miles away, impressed Frederick of a real miracle that "the marvelous thing of this life is the lifting of man from the cave to the stars, from the hairy beast, whose shallow brain was filled with lust, ignorance and superstition to the scientist able to send his audacious dreams on voyages to unseen worlds." Yet, he must conclude that the wife of an astronomer must bring a terrible jolt to him when she shifts his focus to the humdrum of family life and "sends him to the grocery for fifteen cents worth of clothes pins."

Frederick made no secret of his distaste for the jazz craze that he felt was exerting a bad influence upon our culture. In this vein, he called to task the well-known leader of classical music, Walter Damrosch, for praising the new technology of radio for its merit in delivering "good music." Frederick concluded: "Either Damrosch is a great humorist or he has a most unusual receiving set, or, if he will tune in on ours, he will get a barrel of jazz for every drop of civilized music."

Frederick's admiration for Abraham Lincoln appeared in his editorial that recalled the practice of the young railsplitter to read *The Life of the Father of our Country* by "flickering fireplace light," and then pointing out a report that one of his routine letters would now draw a higher auction price than one of General Washington's letters written during the winter of Valley Forge.

As an experienced public speaker, Frederick was able to form opinions about the "do's and don'ts" for this activity. One matter to take into account was the optimal length of an oration as on the occasion of the speech by a Chinese admiral who was interrupted by gunfire from the audience. Frederick's conclusion was simply that there was no justification for the shooting of a banquet speaker "unless he talks more than half an hour." Failing to meet that guideline, a speaker should expect "that the bombardment should become quite general."

Radio

The fall of 1930 was an occasion for Frederick to recall the role of radio broadcasting in his campaign for Governor in 1928, when his son Kenesaw II went to the airwaves and gave speeches for his ill father. This was the moment two years later when Frederick signed a contract as weekly commentator for radio station WLW of Cincinnati. His sponsor was The American Stationery Company for his delivery of "comments on the events of the day." His talks as "the Hoosier Editor" began on October 3, and took place each Friday evening at 8:30. [74] The year was also memorable for Frederick because *The Copperhead* was adapted for radio and presented by WLW Cincinnati radio as the Crosley Theater's "play of the week" December 28, December 31, 1930 and January 3, 1931. [75]

Marriage

On the domestic front, Frederick took note of the fact, reported by a reputable Indiana judge of divorce cases, that "much marital discord is due to excessive love-making during hot weather" and appealed with the suggestion "that gentlemen advance with caution during dog days."

With regard to Frederick's conclusion about "the decline of man," he noted an unfortunate occurrence in New York, in which a lady in pursuit of her husband knocked on the door of an apartment sheltering a poker game; what then transpired was that two other husbands, "thinking it was their Juliet," left by way of a window causing one to break his leg.

Celebrities

Sometimes it appeared that one's social position assumed premium importance, at least as Frederick's occasional observation would allow. He noted the case in which a gentleman on the faculty of Yale University failed in his application for citizenship because "he refused to swear to fight for the United States in time of war." One explanation for Professor Douglass Clyde McIntosh Dwight's response on this matter was his likely concern that "he might get part of his name shot off."

Newspaper clippings revealed the enthusiasm of crowds in the United States and Great Britain betraying hero worship for those who have attained prominence in government. Take, for example, the mad scrambles when the Prince of Wales tossed a match to the ground in England, and former president Coolidge threw a snipe in front of a throng in Los Angeles. Proof, Frederick wrote, that "there are just about as many nuts on one side of the Atlantic as the other."

Religion

Signs appeared that Great Britain might have to contend with an uprising in India that could threaten the integrity of the British Commonwealth. Frederick's conclusion was that "hundreds of millions of Hindoos are hopelessly and insanely divided in their allegiance to conflicting religions," meaning that "as the masses fight about the next world, John Bull will rule them in this one."

A news item from Mendota, Illinois led Frederick to limit his response to but a few words. The facts were that "the Rev. James A. Wilson shot two members of his congregation," yet his congregation of some 500 members "bitterly protested against his indictment." Frederick's conclusion: "We don't know where we're going, but we're on our way."

According to a published report, a legal fee of half-a-million dollars was charged by former Secretary of War Newton D. Baker for assistance in gaining an increase in a lady's payments from her late husband's estate. Frederick was taken aback and could only think of a passage of Scripture: "Blessed are the meek for they shall inherit the earth."

Spiritualism became popular after the slaughter of World War I, attracting many followers. In this connection, Frederick discussed the promise fostered by spiritualists like Arthur Conan Doyle, who had recently died. Although he had nothing to say about his own impressions on the subject, Frederick did conclude that the whole idea of spiritualism "is sufficiently interesting to fascinate the tenderfoot, and it is perfectly easy for the yarning soul to become a devout believer."

Politics

The need for "campaign finance reform" was evident to Frederick, even during the Great Depression because of the role of money in shaping congressional legislation. The problem lay, he believed, not only in financial contributions to political campaigns, but also in the inherent wealth of those who chose to become candidates for Congress. Frederick recalled the olden days when "the people of the country had goose flesh when it was announced that a millionaire had made his way into the United States Senate." He contrasted past years with the early 1930's, in which millionaires in that body "are exceeded in number only by the English sparrows," foreign birds he frequently chastized for invading our shores.

Frederick was fully supportive of the recent triumph of the popular will in replacing Party conventions with primary elections at state level. In fact, he had borne scars from the Indiana state convention when he ran for Governor in 1928 and suffered defeat by powerful off-stage maneuvering at the moment of his probable victory.

Government

Frederick was duly impressed upon learning about the policy of the Cuban President's policy to cut in half his own salary. Upon quick reflection, however, Frederick concluded that "it will not be necessary to vaccinate any of our statesmen to prevent the thing's becoming an epidemic in the United States."

Preparations for the upcoming World's Fair in Chicago in 1933 included action by the US Department of State to obtain exhibits from all interested countries. This seemed to open up particular opportunities for tropical countries, Frederick believed, as they were likely to respond single-mindedly "by sending pineapples."

Law enforcement

Gun control, a hot subject in Mexico, was a matter for discussion in Frederick's column. His bottom line was one familiar to this day about laws limiting the right to carry guns: "Even if it should work in Mexico, it wouldn't work in this country, for while decent people would turn in their guns, the crooks would hold on to theirs."

Faithful to his plan to keep citizens of Chicago aware of their shady law enforcement processes, Frederick took note that the country of Corsica, long known for its banditry, revealed that it stood above all other nations in respect for the law. His interpretation, however, was that "Corsica has shipped her bandits to Chicago."

Ever considerate of his fellow man's choices, Frederick lamented the consequences suggested by a medical opinion from the renowned Dr. Mayo that "the suppression of emotion injures the heart." According to Frederick, the condition then produced a corollary: "If you let your emotions run wild, you land in a penitentiary."

The lynching in Marion, Indiana in August 1930 was supported by many of the city's citizens, a sobering fact that, in Frederick's view, reflected something beyond the horror of that crime. It urged him to speak out again about the public malaise in most communities occasioned by a troubling record of weak law enforcement. He wrote that the residents of all cities had lost faith in their courts because of "many murders that have not been punished adequately and many that have not been punished at all."

Among the deficiencies of law enforcement, as seen by Frederick was a growing tendency to find psychological arguments for freeing defendants in cases involving abuse of the young. As he described the invidious process, "Experts are now getting ready to fondle the glands, climb the family trees and explore the environments of beasts who have committed horrible crimes against children." His recipe for dealing with the problem: "We would hang the whole crowd and investigate their mental condition afterward -- if at all."

Judicial system

The question arose about how much protection should be accorded to prisoners after they have completed their term of confinement. The Indiana Parole Board recognized the difficulty of getting useful employment if the candidate for a job must reveal the details of his residence behind bars. Frederick summed up the problem: "The board trial judge, the prosecuting attorney and other officials who recommend the parole" should follow through and "stand good for that man."

Frederick's typewriter went to work in criticism of the Indiana State Bar Association that opposed reform measures by the state Supreme and Appellate Courts in order to protect monetary opportunities available to lawyers. He believed that reform was needed to change a system wherein lawyers "still sit in the dim and musty cellar of antiquity, holding sweet communion with the bats of fiction and technicality."

Europe

Frederick proposed a solution to the situation in Europe where Italian dictator Mussolini, in the midst of his countrymen, "barks" at France, at a time when the French premier, while among fellow Frenchmen, "barks" at Italy. In order to save the lives of ordinary people, Frederick reasoned that the two national politicians should "fight it out" themselves.

The tinder box of Europe brought Frederick great satisfaction in the existence of the Atlantic Ocean as he summed up relations among various states on our eastern flank: "England does not trust France; France and Italy arm against each other; France and Germany snarl at each other; Germany and Poland hate each other; and so do Poland and Russia; Rumania builds a Black Sea fleet against Russia and Russia's hand is against everybody."

Russia

Frederick again found cause to deal with developments in communist Russia including the realization that the Soviet Union hid its secrets behind an alleged workers' paradise. He expressed his sentiments on this subject on the occasion of a visit by Americans, 450 in number, to that communist state: "they will observe all of the posies, but none of the weeds."

202

Frederick rejected the religious persecution going on with the harsh atheistic policies of the Soviet state and posed his own philosophy about the power of The Almighty in all of the World's cultures: "Persecution makes martyrs, not infidels; the history of all religions proves it. Young Russians, half a century from the cemetery, may shake their fists at the sky, but as years pass and, one by one, they bury those they love, they will change their minds." [76]

1931

In a moment of recollection of small-town life before the turn of the century, Frederick treasured the "old days" of his youth in Logansport when he and Kenesaw ushered at the local "Grand Old Opera House." In exchange they took the opportunity to "see every show and go behind the scenes and watch the stage hands make the sets and actually converse with the heroes of the mimic world!"

The average family's preparation for Christmas, Frederick believed, brought about a labor of love. His bottom line was "No matter what you have to do to make this Christmas a success for kids and old folks, do it." The down-side of this seasonal event, to him, was financial ruin as he declared: "And if you must fall, fall grandly. Fall as Rome fell. Fall with your face toward the cashier . . . then lie down in dreams of bankruptcy."

The Nation

Frederick spoke over WLW Cincinnati the evening of May 22 in behalf of the poppy sale. His "brilliant and forceful address" appeared in full in the *American Legion Auxiliary Bulletin*. In his speech, his theme included a bottom line: "If you should see one man without a poppy on his coat, ask him the question: "Are you an American?" [77]

When the United States Senate was looking into the case of an international banker who had lent money to Germany "for golden commissions," Frederick was concerned that such bankers "would pawn Uncle Sam's wardrobe, beaver hat and BVDs" for personal profit. He concluded that they had no right to expect the US Treasury to come to their aid if such loans were defaulted, adding: "The control of this country's interests should be moved from New York City to Washington."

The year brought Frederick's expression of regret that we will be handing "the babe of 1932" a most discouraging New Years gift. He was referring to troublesome conditions overseas as well as the continuing Great Depression that would likely result in drastic economic changes here at home. Thus, he reasoned that "Europe is in the greatest ferment since it caught fire in 1914, and on top of this, there may be an economic readjustment which will change human relationships more than anything else has done since the abolition of slavery."

Marriage

One newspaper item persuaded Frederick to comment about a most unusual occurrence that was inexplicable . . . A gentleman from Cincinnati was caught shoplifting a pair of shoes, and his explanation to the judge was that they were intended as a gift to his mother-in-law, leading Frederick to conclude: "It would have been wrong to put that man in a prison; they should have put him in a museum."

The topic of divorce was frequently a matter for Frederick's close attention as in the justification for divorce offered by two ladies from different states. One was awarded the decree "because her dearly beloved did not take a bath in four months," and the other became separated "because her mate bathed twice a day and she had to clean the tub." With some exasperation, Frederick concluded: "What's a fellow going to do!"

Politics

The pulse of the American people was measured by Frederick in connection with their taste for an appropriate Presidential candidate when Theodore Roosevelt Jr. addressed a convention of the American Legion. Frederick considered that "since Teddy's time we have had Taft, Wilson, Harding, Coolidge and Hoover -- five vegetarians." It seemed reasonable to conclude, he wrote: "No wonder that the people are beginning to want a little raw meat."

The subject of a sales tax that was under discussion caused Frederick to be concerned with the plight of people. Instead, he offered a solution that would spare them this added burden. In his view, such a tax "could be made to apply to all of the politicians in the United States who are sold on the hoof."

The subject of upcoming national political conventions brought to Frederick's mind the eventful sessions that had taken place in Chicago -- "hard fights" such as those that "nominated Lincoln in 1861, Garfield in 1880, Blaine in 1884, Harrison in 1888, and Harding in 1920." In addition, his own involvement in Theodore Roosevelt's Progressive {Bull Moose) Party in 1912 produced a memorable event in Chicago when Teddy's candidacy brought about a split in the Republican vote.

Government

Frederick's solution to the growing indebtedness of the Nation was straightforward. He drew from the example of the Russian Government that "has cut public expenses to the bone, firing an army of office holders who did nothing on earth but draw their breath and their salaries." This process suggested an opportunity to "cut the fat" in Washington: "As a mere starter we could cut out fifty per cent of the gentlemen now living off of us."

As the end of 1931 approached, Frederick took issue with President Hoover's Secretary of War who made the judgment "that the Filipinos were unfit for self-rule." He wrote that the President's declaration "will doubtless impress the Filipinos tremendously as they read of our unbroken crime wave, the carnival of graft among politicians in our great cities and our national deficit at Washington."

Judicial system

The failure of courts to mete out appropriate punishment in the case of the murder of a New York woman, Frederick wrote, was just another example of ineffective law enforcement throughout the United States at all levels of government. He concluded: "Our poor weather-beaten Goddess of Justice has been challenged so many times it would require the mathematical genius of an Einstein to count the total: she has been slapped in the face by triumphant crime until her countenance is as tough as the hide of a rhinoceros."

France

The subject of the poor record of the French to resolve their financial indebtedness to the United States following World War I came to the fore. With regard to the problem, Frederick recalled that France "whose bacon we saved in the World War . . . called us 'Uncle Shylock' although the goods sent to her had been greatly under-priced."

1932

Frederick again became a candidate for the Republican nomination for governor in 1932 but was defeated. The scenario was familiar, according to local newspaper coverage under a subtitle of "History Repeats." At the State Convention in Indianapolis on June 9, Frederick's solid showing was a trigger for the opposition to act. The Logansport paper's explanation follows: "It was then that the drive to stop Landis was started by the same group that fought him in 1928" when one candidate was selected "to do the trick" and it worked. Frederick withdrew his candidacy when the outcome became clear. [78]

In a time when the Great Depression continued to test the fiber of ordinary Americans, Frederick touched on a lighter theme in his editorial, a topic of a feline nature. He wrote about the kittens that had been born in an unlikely place like the pan of a basement furnace in the state of Washington. Applying his hometown wisdom, he noted that "in spite of their humble birth, they can be just as successful on a back yard fence at midnight as if they had been born in the lap of luxury."

The Nation

A positive note for the New Year was to be found in Frederick's report that Frederick Eberson of the University of California was able to discover the germ that "caused infantile paralysis," opening the way for prevention of the disease by developing "the vaccine to halt the progress of the germ."

Another encouraging item was brought to public attention in the form of masterful progress in saving the lives of the newborn, as Frederick wrote: "Thanks to medical science," we can overcome old nemeses such as: "diphtheria, scarlet fever, and small pox . . . that killed children wholesale" and so often had been reminders of "the white hearse always on the way to the cemetery."

Lest the reader limit Frederick's storehouse of knowledge and his wise perspective, there was his view about the unnecessary pulling of teeth in dental offices, which were enough "in this country in the last ten years to pave a highway from Chicago to Indianapolis." He went on to apply his critique to the dentists' professional brothers whose appetite for unnecessary diagnoses would address "lumbago, nearsightedness, floating kidney, ingrown toe-nails or just common, everyday heebie-jeebies," with the consequence that "they will subtract most of your dining room furniture, unless you are on your guard."

On the birthday of the noted Benjamin Franklin, Frederick drew a parallel between the humble beginnings of Abraham Lincoln and "Old Ben." Then he pointed to Franklin's success in achieving France's support of the American Revolution at a decisive time. In addition, he represented Pennsylvania and brought "his patriarchal presence and counsel" to bear in the Constitutional Convention."

In an unusual spate of unselfish collaboration, Frederick commended representatives of labor and industry in Chicago in efforts to "put a great and indispensable" railroad system "on its feet." He perceived a positive development in their deliberations as "co-workers" instead of "enemies."

A story justifying national pride, welcome during privations of the Great Depression now underway, appeared in Frederick's report about his visit to the fabled ship *The City of New York* that carried Admiral Byrd's expedition "to the frozen southern extremity of the world." He recalled the heroics involved in that bold voyage: "the commander and crew of that little craft fighting its way through the white fury of the land of mountainous icebergs" and the unmatched courage in their expressed interest in "wanting to do it all over again."

Culture

Having not had occasion to comment upon the Arts of our culture for some time during the rigors of the Great Depression, Frederick learned of, and wrote about, the large value ascribed to a certain Rembrandt painting. Pondering the great artist's last days of poverty, when "he made chalk sketches for anybody who would give him the price of a ham sandwich," Frederick concluded in a somewhat imaginative line of thought: "Artists ought to be allowed to respond to an encore a century after their demise in order to participate in the gravy."

207

Much has been written about the greatness of Lincoln's Gettysburg Address, whose brevity of two minutes seemed to many present on the stage to have been inadequate for the occasion, following the two-hour peroration by the renowned speaker Edward Everett. Frederick pointed out that "it was not until the newspapers of Great Britain hailed it as a masterpiece that Americans 'discovered' its excellence."

Frederick's arsenal of commentary had not entertained a fashion note for a lengthy period of time, but a development in Palm Beach, Florida that resulted in a city restriction "to stop men from going around with nothing on but trunks" saved the day. Frederick concluded with a deep appreciation of finer points: "This will not detract materially from the beauty of the landscape."

The Presidency

Frederick registered his objections to the Federal Government's waste of money by commissioning oil paintings to be made of US Cabinet members, only to be stored away in some attic long after such individuals have been forgotten. He advanced his feelings to include the Presidency in the case of Calvin Coolidge, whose artistic work was to cost the taxpayer some $2,500. If such a proposal were to be worthwhile, Frederick offered his own special concern: "If we are going to pay this much for his picture, we certainly hope Mr. Coolidge will try to look pleasant" for it would be a bad investment "to preserve his old expression."

One of the noteworthy measures taken by President Hoover was, in Frederick's view, his decision to reduce his governmental salary because none of his predecessors had mustered the good sense to consider such an act. This topic caused Frederick to recall the generosity of our first chief executive, who served two terms while refusing to accept any compensation. In fact, General Washington "had served through the American Revolution without pay." Frederick added the irony that some chose to accuse our distinguished leader, who used a platform at his first presidential reception, of the charge that he was seeking to appear as a royal personage of "the young republic."

Following the election victory of Franklin D. Roosevelt over President Hoover in November, Frederick took note of the possible consequences of Mr. Hoover's act in releasing pigeons during his speech supporting the sale of Christmas seals. As

Frederick surmised this situation, he concluded: "We wish he might with the same ease release all the lame ducks that will besiege him for appointments."

Politics

As a strong supporter of the existing Prohibition Amendment to *The Constitution*, Frederick could see the "handwriting on the wall" during the presidential campaign of the summer of 1932. He referred with regret to the fact that both Republicans and Democrats had decided to do away with the proscription against the manufacture and sale of liquor. As he expressed it, there was no spirit in the contest "when one party declares in favor of a Manhattan cocktail and the other declares in favor of a Bronx cocktail."

Frederick had been observing over a span of time that wealthy men were finding their way into the Congress, and he considered the trend to be detrimental to the goals of good government. One of the incentives, he believed, was the attraction of the Nation's Capital as a great social center, edging out the primacy of New York City in that regard. The crux of this setback for democracy was, in Frederick's words, that rich men "see things from the angle of their own selfish welfare to the detriment of the country as a whole."

Now that the national election was over, it was time for some levity, Frederick believed, leading him to hold up an event of some political note that occurred in Walla Walla Washington, where "a train struck a mule, derailing the train, but not hurting the mule whereupon it laughed at the engineer." Some political meaning appeared to underlay the animal's behavior, Frederick wrote, because: "since the last election the mules have been very chesty."

Government

The workings of our legal system became a worthy consideration as Frederick noted the sentence meted out to one John Zerfass of the State of Washington as a result of his having killed a man who kissed Zerfass' wife. This would seem to test the flawed rationale that had, in Frederick's view, become commonplace in government practice, that is: "In order to be consistent, the legislature of the state of Washington should now pass a law formally repealing the law of human nature."

In response to some forward-looking public thought about broadcasting debates in Congress, Frederick proposed that "it's a cinch that the Senate would have to put a gag on its orators." His reasoning was straightforward: "They run wild now, you know, with nothing to stop them except a stroke of apoplexy."

Immigration

One of the problems facing the United States in the new Millennium was a topic for Frederick's scrutiny much earlier -- the problem of undocumented aliens. In this instance, the area was not the border with Mexico but was the city of New York. The problem drew public notice when New York sought public funds in order to provide relief for its army of nearly one million unemployed. Frederick remarked: "If she would send back to Europe the foreigners who are not citizens and who do not intend to become citizens, she would find the problem greatly simplified."

Celebrities

Frederick responded to a newspaper item that covered a trip to Alaska by the socially-prominent Philadelphia lady, Mrs. Edward Biddle, who sought a change of scene in order to "rescue her nervous system from the ravages of our rushing civilization." His thought was that Mrs. Biddle was "playing the society racket" and instead "should have done her house work and taken care of her kids."

Judicial system

Frederick's sentiments about the criminal effects caused by excessive drinking, had a suggestion on strengthening the deterrent value of judicial punishment in such cases. Thus, a report in neighboring Rochester, Indiana that an intoxicated driver had injured two people by striking them with his automobile, led Frederick to propose: "We ought to have a law permitting every such victim to drive a truck over an offender."

Foreign policy

In criticizing Japan for not only absorbing neighboring Manchuria but also attacking the American consul, Frederick recalled that the United States probably made a mistake when it

210

"dragged Japan out of her antiquity and made her a modern power." This was accomplished, he noted by none other than Secretary of State Daniel Webster in the administration of President Fillmore, when he directed the US Navy to open the port of Tokyo, and Commodore Perry did the job. Frederick's conclusion: "If we had it to do over, we would let them sleep."

Europe

A proposal by the Italian dictator to cancel the remaining portion of the debt European countries owed the United States urged Frederick to examine "why Europe regards America as feeble-minded." First, it was clear that the United States had already shown diplomatic weakness by agreeing to a reduction of the European obligation for post-war loans by seventy percent. Second, "it is because so many silly Americans proceed to apologize for their own land the moment they set foot upon foreign soil . . . There seems to be a certain mental deficiency in the American that makes him incapable of national pride."

Japan

On the negative side of the New Year, he added the military conquest of Manchuria by the Japanese, at the same time suggesting that, while we can't be sure about the next step by Japan, one could speculate that "she could organize the greatest laundry the world ever saw."

1933

As the campaign heated up to decide on whether to repeal the Prohibition Amendment, with both political parties leaning in the direction of bringing back legal beer, Frederick was able to make his "dry views" known to the very last. He referred to "the persistent propaganda from Washington to the effect that beer is not intoxicating . . . if not, why are its champions not content with near-beer?" He recognized that the political sentiment was strong for repeal of Prohibition, but pleaded: "Let us not be made monkeys of this inspired chatter to the effect that what we are going to get is as modest as a violet, as charming as a daffodil."

Praise for the family canine was called for again in 1933, when the family dog would disappear for a number of days, only to return in his own chosen time. Frederick enumerated something of the animal's record, recalling that "we didn't want this dog in the first place, but for some reason he seemed determined to absorb our society." In fact, Frederick determined to remove him from the family circle by carting him out in the country and "dumping him" at a respectable distance from home. After driving about the area for a time, he recalled driving up to the house and sure enough: "there he was on the porch . . . he thought it was a game." Frederick finally admitted: "Now we wouldn't sell him for a million."

Frederick was capable of swinging widely in his commentaries . . . from a potential for world war to the life of a bird family in his back yard. Gazing out the window to watch his version of the "Chosen People," he reported on "the little thrush that for several years has established its bungalow in the hole of the rambo tree." In order to respect "this little fellow and his folks," Frederick concluded that it was prudent not to disturb this family that had found a home in the trunk of a dead tree.

As a regular CBS radio commentator with sharp views about controversial aspects of our culture and politics, Frederick appeared to be an authority on the subject of corporate control over the content of programs. Thus, he wrote about "political influence" that "extended its long, slippery arm into the radio stations of the country." (This remark brings to mind that a number of years earlier, his published editorials about national affairs such as "the Japanese threat" and "incompetence in American defense policy" may not have passed muster in the front office of Hearst's syndicated newspapers.)

The colors of nature became paramount in Frederick's thoughts as he viewed the green and gold of the corn crop during an automobile trip outside of town . . . "no more beautiful landscape in the world." Thinking back to his childhood and the labor involved in "hoeing fifteen acres of corn," he recalled how machinery had lightened the farmer's workload and speculated about the future . . .once the Great Depression becomes history, "it wont be long until the farmer has a radio on his cultivator with an awning top," permitting him to enjoy the fantasy of sitting in a major league ball park, watching his favorite team.

The "early thirties" were indeed a time of great change with advances in technology, now so evident with the automobile and the network of highways that would fall into place. For Frederick and, no doubt for many Americans, the mere thought in those years that trains and railroads might have an uncertain future brought a sense of dismay when he wrote: "no man ever privileged to ride beside the engineer can think of the decline of the old iron horse without a pang of regret." His fond memory of a thrilling ride in the engine recalled a glorious experience: "as she rocks from side to side and plunges on through the darkness, her arrow of electric light splitting the blackness of midnight, her open firebox painting lurid images on the inky way . . ."

From Frederick's perspective, there would have been no reason for the 1929 Stock Market crash and the ensuing period of hard times if the man-on-the-street had been "saving for a rainy day" when times were good just before World War I. In his judgement, the fault lay with "our great oracles" who declared: "Don't sell America short! . . . The law of gravity has been repealed!"

Outside the political arena for the time being, after his unsuccessful twin efforts to become Governor of Indiana, Frederick was beginning to turn to his favorite hobby and way of life, writing for popular consumption in the novel concept of a self-published, one-man monthly magazine to begin in November. This cottage-industry publication would engage his wife Bessie and four of their children, ages 16 to 11 -- Betsy, Frances Katharine, Charles and Lincoln. They would promote, produce, lick the envelopes, attach the postage, and mail 12 monthly issues to subscribers throughout the United States and in several foreign countries at "a dime a copy . . . dollar a year." Frederick chose, in the peak of the Great Depression, to give public notice of these intentions before the local Rotary Club, saying: "I will write it myself -- in the interest of the common man -- and I intend to have it plain, clean, readable. I wish to represent the attitude of old fashioned America -- the ideas of people interested in the home and church." [79]

The Nation

The early 1930's saw the automobile industry showing fancy designs, even "steamline bodies," rumble seats, running boards, chromium bumpers, whitewall tires and metal covers for spare tires resting in the front fenders. These stylistic changes met with Frederick's approval, but he found the need for deeper improvement: "What we really need is a mortgage with shock absorbers on it."

Even the administration of sports was fair game for Frederick's analysis, as in the case of the basketball team of Anderson, Indiana that was forbidden to compete in the vaunted state championships because of the presence on the roster of an ineligible player from another state. He credited the Athletic Association for halting "the shoddy custom," declaring "the time had come when somebody had to hit with a club the abuse of going out and importing players."

A Republican politician offering positive comment about the new Democratic Presidency was none other than Frederick, who chose to compliment "the First Lady of the Land -- and her originality and self-reliance." The source of his comment was Eleanor Roosevelt's "handling of her first reception at the White House" just a few days after the Inauguration festivities. His impression was that the President's wife "acted like an ordinary everyday American woman, instead of trying to perform like a cross between a queen and a museum freak."

Life in Logansport proceeded year-by-year measured through a series of high school graduation exercises, memorable occasions when one appreciated the progress of children and the continuance of that worthy institution -- our public school system. Commencement programs were usually happy occasions . . . "unless the speaker rambles on and on; everybody's interested in some boy or girl, sitting up there on the stage . . . you think of long-ago nights when you got up and gave them catnip tea and walked the floor with them."

Northern Indiana was plagued with heavy rains, causing rivers such as the Eel and Wabash rivers that merged in Logansport, bringing forth reports of drownings mostly of young men. In the early 1930's, it would have been unusual for girls to be risking their lives swimming in these rivers, when their recreational swimming would have been mostly in lakes of the region. These occurrences made Frederick's "hair stand on end," and his advice was: "Keep the kids at home; lock them up if necessary until the high water subsides."

Frederick reviewed the emergence of the modern physician whose physical appearance had seemed crucial to his professional success. In older days, the doctor "had to raise whiskers if he expected the community to take his pills with any degree of assurance." So it was that "a smooth-faced practitioner" was at a distinct disadvantage in comparison with "his hairy competitors." The emergence over a period of years of the modern physician meant that "doctors didn't come out into the open all at once." As a first step they "took one long step by husking the chin," choosing to "keep the upper lip concealed" and leading to various mustache styles such as "the Texas long-horn steer model."

The postal system always offered an indispensable feature of American life, centered in Frederick's recollection upon the simple postal card. The quaintness of life in towns and villages used to adorn the General Delivery of the post office as a vital center, where families would line up to receive their cards, sometimes written "from top to bottom" and turned around to provide "another layer sideways." The life of the community was quickened when word spread that a family had received a telegram, an event that was likely to produce the question up and down the street: "Who do you reckon's dead?"

The Great Depression brought about the suicide of a significant number of industrial and banking executives in the early 1930's. One example cited by Frederick was the president of the Studebaker Automotive Corporation, who, "sitting at a mahogany desk, raking in the mazuma" was not prepared to withstand the collapse of his vast holdings. In contrast, the common man, "knowing what it is to scratch week-by-week to keep a wife and a bunch of kids . . . has had enough whalebone in him to stand up under the buffeting of the waves." Frederick noted, as an example, the risk taken regularly by farmers who sow crops without knowing whether weather will reward him or bring him wholesale losses. Frederick did not concern himself with the fate of industrial giants . . . His sentiments lay with unheralded, hard-working folks: "the only really important people in the world."

A serious flooding season was upon Indiana and neighboring states, bringing forth an engineering solution from Frederick. His proposal was to do better than build levees; instead he suggested a series of reservoirs along the troublesome rivers. His point was: "Not only would such a system of reservoirs prevent floods; they would also prevent droughts in the rivers . . . when you can walk across most river beds without damaging your spats."

A prolonged dry spell brought a great deal of suffering in the Middle West before the arrival of a welcome rain. Frederick admired this favorable turn in the weather by referring to Mother Nature as "great old girl." He believed it was time to savor "cool velvet air to breathe, fleecy skies to gaze upon, and energy in abundance." To Frederick, the poet, "Rain was a God-send, a wonderful thing, a gentle missionary of loveliness, a sweet evangel of joy."

Frederick's memory of his early years was tapped when he read of the discovery in the river bed of an old pulley which had been part of an old grist mill. He regretted the disappearance of these small industries that were an important part of the local economies of a town, until people stopped buying grain from the local mill and factory in favor of the imported varieties. Thus was set in motion a trend that was troubling to him, when "our willingness for home industry to fail" became responsible for "the wave of industrial merging, with its efficiency, its mass production, its ability to send little competitors upon the rocks."

Culture

Ladies' clothing styles continued to be legitimate topics for Frederick's observation. The decade of the 1930's marked a major development in the trend to reveal more of the female body in public by the new popularity of "shorts." For Frederick, this trend was dismaying although he found the rare opportunity to praise the Illinois Appellate Court that ruled against tennis playing by Chicago girls in shorts because "otherwise it would have been a proposition of fig leaves next year."

An encouraging development to report resulted from a visit by the renowned Polish artist and political leader Ignace Paderewski to the campus of Stanford University as a guest of the student body. He demonstrated far more than his distinguished reputation, in Frederick's estimation, because of his generous response to an offer by students of Leland Stanford University to pay him $2,000 to appear on campus. As told by President Hoover who had once been a student there, the great pianist and composer (and first premier of Poland) accepted only a modest fee, a generous response indeed after learning that the students had failed to reach their fund-raising goal. Then, after Frederick noted that the maestro "proceeded to give his entire recital," he concluded: "That's a real man."

As the Prohibition Amendment was about to be repealed, Frederick expected that public hopes to ascend to a return of the "good old days . . . when one could purchase surcease from care at any emporium with swinging doors." He warned that the new beer, under the new regime beginning under the 21st Amendment, was not strong enough to meet expectations. So it had seemed that "half a dollar's worth of the joyful amber would enable the average Americano to lift sail and leave the shores of consciousness, forgetting creditor, income tax collector, rheumatism, insolvency -- even wife and child." Frederick suggested that, in truth, it would remain for "the barkeep to slip a little nitroglycerine into the beverage" to achieve desired results.

Mussolini called for Italian mothers to start producing more children, leading Frederick to comment that the Dictator would change his mind if he had to go through the process of child-bearing himself. In addition, Frederick, while acknowledging that parental responsibility was at fault in several legal cases, added: "we do not want any Mussolini to inform our folks what they shall do in the matter of raising families." His deep regret centered upon the damaging effects negligent and mentally-disturbed parents cause in society: "A lot of our crime, epilepsy, insanity, social delinquency starts with parents, unfitted to throw a life-line out through the years, a life-line that is unclean and which feeds alms-houses, asylums and penitentiaries . . . a ghastly tragedy."

The vulgarity of printed material circulating to family households should no longer be acceptable in the United States, Frederick reasoned, although he took to task the extreme practice of "the Hitler fellows" who were in the practice of burning books "on account of race prejudice." His focus on the American problem also fell upon "some stuff that's creeping into radio," adding: "The bird who sells filth represents the lowest order of animal life."

The planned suicide of the prominent multi-millionaire Joseph W. Harriman was prominently placed before the public through his letters of despair. This occurrence brought sharp reaction from Frederick who expressed "nothing but contempt . . . for when one has a family it is up to him to 'grin and bear it!'" He acknowledged that a man can become equally discouraged by career reverses, but his family is there to support him: "Life is not bereft of all joy, even if the whole world proscribe you, if in your home they are for you still!"

Frederick's critique of deficiencies in our culture was illustrated by the case in which a local child was killed when a truck ran over her. Writing of "this heedless, materialistic, machinery-calloused day of ours," he called attention to "the family whose fireside was darkened with the agonizing grief of death," while "the slaughter of this little child was but another entry in the long list which finds the surfeited reader decidedly indifferent." The excessive speed of the new automobile age was for him intolerable and pinpointed the urgency that our society "return to a civilized appraisal of rights and values."

Marriage

The scene of Logansport's prominent pundit shifted to the film-making capital of the world and the model of family accord that it presented to the nation. Arresting Frederick's attention was an item stating that "two motion picture actors who had been living together had separated again; while two had had been separated are once more in double harness." This situation sparked in him an initiative for Hollywood's home-building industry. He recommended "bungalows constructed with sliding center partitions, enabling the occupants to convert them into singles or doubles as circumstances demand."

Child labor

As he found himself uttering compliments about the presidency of Franklin D. Roosevelt, Frederick may have begun to believe that "the new regime" was a refreshing improvement in the Democratic Party. Not that this Progressive politician thought the Republican Party was beyond reproach! With respect to an age-old problem of our economy, that of child labor in the textile industry, Frederick was enthusiastic about the President's new code proscribing the practice. He wrote that, if FDR's action brings an end to "this infamy," it will prove to be "the thing longest remembered about his administration."

The Presidency

As a committed member of the Republican party, although one who drew suspicion from the hierarchy for "getting too many

Democratic votes," Frederick found, in the ascent of Franklin D. Roosevelt to the White House, the opportunity to write: "Everybody in the country wishes him the greatest degree of success, because that means the welfare of all of us." Noting that he happened to oppose the President's election, he acknowledged: "we are for him now and we shall be so long as he is the pilot of the ship." He pointed out the difference between the political system in the United States, where the majority rules, with "Central and South America where they grab their shooting irons whenever they lose an election."

The policy of President Roosevelt to select cabinet members by passing up his strongest political supporters was warmly welcomed in Frederick's commentary, who recalled President Abraham Lincoln's decisive action when he "bearded a whole bunch of lions in their den by naming his opponents for the nomination for cabinet positions." Frederick noted Mr. Lincoln's success in gaining and holding their support "by the most adroit diplomacy" while, at the same time, invoking a delicate Lincoln pleasantry when asked for a favor: "I have very little influence with this administration."

Continuing in a generous vein, this Indiana Republican gave great credit to the Nation's First Democrat who, despite his need for a wheelchair, demonstrated "vigor in taking hold of his new responsibility." He contrasted FDR's style with that of other men of means and physical limitations who might be more likely to be "going round the world, seeking the healing waters" and wrote "this man plunges into the most wrecking thing in the world, politics, and gives no quarter and asks none."

In President Roosevelt's first year in office, Frederick appraised the enormity of the task facing the White House. Acknowledging the distasteful prospect of the Nation's political leader running our industrial sector, which would be socialism, he realized: "there's a situation which backs all of us into a corner and asks us what we are going to do about the unemployment of millions." Frederick recognized the supreme power that FDR now was able by law to wield over our economy and concluded that, if his authority should be challenged in court, the President's position would be reaffirmed.

219

Staunch advocate and supporter of *The Constitution*, Frederick found that a "Rooseveltian revolution" suggested in FDR's recovery program was a sobering prospect for the American republic. Still, he recognized the seriousness of the Great Depression, with millions out of work, and acknowledged the President's need to act in authoritative fashion. Yet, he pointed to the gloomy prospect that "whatever changes are necessary in government to adjust human welfare to mechanical supremacy will be made without ceremony" and predicted that "in fifty years . . . everything except the process of digestion will be done by machinery." Frederick's pessimism rested upon the awesome power of the President of the United States in the existing circumstances of economic disorder, writing: "there is no power to lock the laboratory of the gentleman who is experimenting with our future;" yet he did not yet stake out an alternative course for curing the Nation's serious state of affairs.

Politics

Frederick made an appeal for greater selflessness among Americans appointed by an Administration to serve in important public capacities while turning down any remuneration. Unfortunately, he wrote, such appointees frequently do not recognize "the honor" involved in serving one's country and even take advantage of their position by enriching themselves at the expense of the taxpayer.

Government

The cause of veterans was clearly one to which Frederick laid claim, but he was not in favor of the "Bonus Army," organized and supported by a number of communities in its march on Washington to demand increased pensions. This "monkey business," in Frederick's view, would cause more harm to the cause of the worthy veterans, although he acknowledged the government's solid obligation to its old soldiers in contrast with its practice "of lending billions to banks and railroads."

A plan to provide a seven-million-dollar office building for members of the House of Representatives met with disdain on the part of Frederick, who noted that at the turn of the century, congressmen were obliged to live in apartments, a system that worked quite well. In those days, familiar enough to Frederick during his two terms, he recalled a Congressman's typical day: "he dictated his letters to his secretary every morning before starting out on his round of the departments to look after pension claims, try to land faithful supporters in soft positions, and attend to other things his constituents brought to his attention."

Frederick spoke of need for reform in our tax system in which "the rule of credits under the federal income tax system is rotten." As an example, he wrote that a millionaire such as John P. Morgan was able to profit by declaring stock market losses "because he had a foxy lawyer," adding: "but if a man's family is sick, and he is being crushed by the expense thereof, he can get no discount . . . Hardly square, is it?"

An investigation into the workings of the Morgan financial empire, Frederick predicted, "will not amount to a nickel's worth of horseradish" because of the unfortunate quality of government in which "money rules." Referring to the insurance scandal of 1905, when he had indicted that industry on the floor of the House of Representatives, Frederick wrote that "the real capital of this country is New York, where her conduct is determined -- and most of her wars declared."

"This new epoch," the technological age that was causing the loss of jobs by a large number of workers, was, Frederick believed, putting severe pressure upon Congress to take appropriate action. He urged legislators to take some remedial measure "in terms of social welfare, of economic justice, a thing few of them would have ever done of their own accord." He added that, without the emergence of this wretched state of affairs, the legislators would have returned to their standard practice . . . "The average officeholder reaches the end of his activity when he wins his office, and from that time on, he has devoted his time and attention to the one grand objective of getting it again."

Frederick read in the newspapers of word that descendants of the Astors and Vanderbilts would receive huge sums from the fortunes of those families. He found this news to be hard to take when ordinary families were quite short of the necessities of life. His position was that most folks wont have the opportunity "in 25 years" to think about leaving a will because of the government's growing tendency to control their wealth in the name of progress. His view was that "so far as we are concerned personally, we have no expectation of leaving any legacy for our posterity, except a liking for baked potatoes and sliced onions."

Law enforcement

Disconcerted in the extreme by the ease with which bank bandits roamed, committing murder in Indiana and neighboring states, Frederick called for stricter law enforcement and tough punishment for these crimes carried out by heavily-armed thugs in the otherwise-peaceful countryside. With this problem in mind, he observed that "mawkish sentimentalists would have us junk what little courthouse efficiency we have and regard crime as a disease instead of the result of common cussedness." His complaint was their tendency "to put hot water bottles to the feet of the murderer in the hope of converting him into a Little Lord Fauntleroy in the course of fifteen or twenty years." His judgement was that law enforcement remained "a farce, as it has been in this country for one hundred years."

On the matter of containing organized crime, Frederick found some possibilities in the example of the former president of Mexico, Mr. Diaz, who found a way to impede the crime traffic by hiring a number of the bandits operating in the mountain passes to be members of the police force. Frederick's point was that lessons learned would be effective in stamping out organized crime by persuading its leaders to accept high-paying jobs with the expectation that, as in Mexico, these ex-criminals would be in a position to capture and punish their former law-breaking associates.

A horrible accident on the highways when "a freight-bearing beast" that bore down on a mere passenger car in northern Indiana highlighted the danger of large trucks smashing into smaller vehicles on the state's highways. Frederick believed that trucks should not be free to use highways meant for automobiles and should not be "gigantic competitors of our railroads." He believed: "They should have their own highways."

Judicial system

Frederick's critique of the actions of many criminal lawyers was a frequent topic of his daily columns because he felt that officers seeking to enforce the law were placed at a disadvantage when faced with clever machinations of "shysters" with their clients. His description of such defense lawyers was "a greater nuisance than potato bugs, cut-worms, boll-weevil, corn-borers, Canadian thistle, rag weed, hay fever, corns and warts."

National Defense

Concern for the national defense was high on Frederick's list of favored topics to bring to the fore, as illustrated by the recent loss of the huge airship *Akron* and the question of how our military establishment should be configured. He pointed out that the dirigible was known to have had defects and concluded: "Let us hope that the big boys in charge of our army and navy know a little more about their specialties than those in charge of the late leviathan of the sky." On a related topic, Frederick wrote, as he had in the previous decade, that "aviation is as distinct and indispensable a branch of the national defense as the army or the navy, and it should at once be placed on a basis of equality in a newly created department with trained flyers to run it." (History shows that this reorganization would occur only following the new World War, to occur in eight more years.)

The safeguarding of sensitive national defense information was a serious concern to the Logansport sage, who regretted that all foreign powers maintained espionage forces charged with ferreting out information for possible use in active hostilities. He concluded that their task in targeting the United States was minimal: "We tell all our secrets, all about our army, navy and aviation, and all the outside world has to do is to subscribe to the newspapers."

The Swiss Government, famous for "cheese and the treaties that have holes in them," Frederick added, informed the United States and Europe that they could be effective in world disarmament by preventing war through the generous offering of their wealth to war-like nations. To Frederick, such a theory was ill-advised and the product of misguided optimists. His argument lay in the case often made that the first World War would have happened for other reasons, and a unified position by Western nations "would not have delayed Japan's more recent attack against China one hour."

Foreign policy

The appointment of inept ambassadors and their frequent approval by the United States Senate were, in Frederick's view, practices that ill-served the interest of our nation and its people, as demonstrated by one "flunkey," a Judge Bingham from Kentucky, who reportedly "made a violently anti-American speech" and "apologized for his country's attitude on several international questions." Frederick's editorial spoke of such errors "for the past forty years or so . . . by both parties" who chose diplomats "from among the fat and flabby aspirants for social distinction who have given fat campaign contributions in return for the privilege of wearing knee pants and a sword in some European town."

The London economic conference would become, for Frederick, a monstrous waste of time because "Uncle Sam" would appear as "Mary's Little Lamb in the midst of a pack of wolves." Our Secretary of State, Cordell Hull, Frederick advised, should end his participation because European diplomats "have cancelled Germany's reparation debts . . . and you and I, the taxpayers of America, are to pay for Germany's devastation; we are to pay for the war. Lovely, isn't it?"

One bit of satisfaction from the Great Depression seemed to Frederick to be that Americans "are not hearing every hour of the day or night about our duty to the world." He believed the United States was led down the wrong path of internationalism by President Woodrow Wilson and concluded that we should have "let the world take care of its own warts and bunions." Frederick was convinced that "the average foreign nation regards you as a nit-wit when you try to help it, and it then proceeds to give you the devil if you don't hand it something all the time."

Frederick noted the plan of "peace agencies" to hold a large get-together in Switzerland as a prelude to the scheduled international disarmament conference in Geneva. His lack of confidence in warlike nations summoning the wisdom to avoid a future conflict was matched by his sense that these well-intentioned groups would have little effect upon the major participants. Frederick suggested that, for example, "they will have about as much influence on Japan and France as the calling of a turtle dove to its mate."

Europe

A military display in Germany plus the growing strength of "the Hitler movement" brought Frederick to conclude that the United States, the nation that took a financial drubbing after World War I, would be prepared "to take her place in the show." He also predicted that one French leader's reference to Uncle Sam as "Uncle

Shylock" for seeking redress from its loans to European countries after the recent war would again look to America for funds to "open up the old slaughter house" again.

Germany

Even before Adolf Hitler had firmly entrenched himself as Dictator of the Third Reich, Frederick foresaw the inclination of Germany again to make war against her neighbors. Referring to the possibility that Russia, England and France might end up by becoming involved in the Chinese-Japanese war, Frederick wrote: "Germany gazes complacently at the discomfiture of her former foes and dreams of a setup which would permit her to sally forth and recover continental acres which she lost by the Treaty of Versailles."

The advent of stewing hostility in Europe between historic enemies France and Germany seemed to Frederick to be a natural progression from deadly patterns of the recent past. He referred to "Hitler's hot air" after only a few months as Chancellor that should be taken seriously. Having monitored the German leader's radical rise to power from his perch in Logansport, Frederick concluded: "When a fellow like Hitler is elected to leadership on a platform of defiance, the time comes when he must make good or get out, and politicians seldom want to get out."

Japan

As the decade slowly moved toward a dangerous world for the United States, Frederick continued to have sobering thoughts about a threat from Japan. Having written for some years about this, he now observed: "It's not conducive to peace of mind in the United States to hear that Japan now has the strongest navy in the world, for we have some property in the Pacific which Japan would not object to owning, and she has a habit of grabbing what she desires."

As in many earlier editorials, Frederick held that Japan, of all nations, should not be trusted by declarations of a willingness to enter into serious disarmament discussions with other nations. His conclusion was straightforward in his purposefully-understated words: "The gentleman who thinks that the Japanese character is to be changed from that of frigid, occult annihilator of every obstacle

225

in its pathway to that of a mild-eyed spring poet is slightly mistaken."

In the first issue of Frederick's monthly magazine *The Hoosier Editor*, he acknowledged a concern he would hold for a long time, the matter of President Roosevelt's extreme measures to get the unemployed millions of the nation back to work. While he stated clearly his opposition to excessive governmental direction of citizens' lives . . . he wouldn't "want Washington, for example, to regulate my liver," Frederick would remain satisfied "for Washington to run along and distribute its garden seeds -- and let me alone." He explained his understanding of the serious problem facing our nation in this Depression, that imaginative and unusual measures needed to be tried by the White House: "Of course, the whole proposition petrifies the Fathers of the Republic, sojourning on their distant star, but a crisis suspends a constitution . . . it is made for fair weather." [80]

Frederick concluded his commentary on 1933 by noting a familiar anomaly of the Great Depression . . . "We're in a terrible fix – there's no place to work, and there's no place to PARK!" [81] And, in a patriotic vein, he recalled, on the 15th anniversary of the Armistice of the first World War, America's generosity at the peace conference at Versailles:

> Here was the nation which had turned the tide of war, the nation which could demand any tribute -- he mightiest nation in the world -- and while others clutched for the spoils of war, this nation said: "I want no money; I want no land; I want -- nothing!"

He took the public pulse on the matter of the woeful state of the nation's joblessness: "Whether we like it or not, this new industrial world makes us our brother's keeper; we must keep him, not only for his sake, but our own." And Frederick unfailingly seasoned his cerebration with a mixture of humor and humanity: "The people of Hopkinsville, Kentucky, are indignant because a pet jackrabbit has been buried in their cemetery, but I'd rather stretch out for Eternity alongside a self-respecting jackrabbit than some people I know."

In the second issue of *The Hoosier Editor*, he billboarded his judgement of the state of "white-collar" crime: "We may not have the sculpture of ancient Greece, but we have many more CHISELERS!" Frederick went on to gently castigate a symptom of society's problems: "A lot of our trouble dates back to the time when Henry Ford first succeeded in making a nutmeg grater carry passengers!" Looking ahead, he suggested root differences between political systems that would fester for half a century through the Cold War: "I Would Not Care to Spend Christmas in Russia, Where They've Abolished Religion and Substituted Lenin for the Lord." His skepticism on a timely topic, the recent repeal of Prohibition, enlightened the reader about one prospect for a return of the old saloon days:

> It is interesting to contemplate the plans by which it is proposed to render the sale of booze not only harmless, but a positive benediction, one of the most profound ideas being that the customer shall take it Sitting, instead of standing . . . we should go one step further and have the absorber take it Lying Down.

In the Christmas spirit, Frederick closed his issue with a Union soldier's heroic tale, placing it in "a little pocket of wild beauty in an otherwise tranquil Indiana countryside . . ." [82]

1934

Frederick, having placed his youngest family members to work at home, gained momentum in publishing *The Hoosier Editor* magazine into the new year of 1934 through the final, October issue. At the same time, he jumped back into politics to wage a vigorous Republican campaign for Congress. His effort flew in the face of the Democratic Party's tidal wave of success during President Franklin D. Roosevelt's dynamic second year in office.

Having closed out his regular syndicated column "Reason" in the Logansport *Pharos-Tribune*, Frederick devoted his writing hours not only to his new monthly journal *The Hoosier Editor*, but also to a folksy editorial "Here at Home" in the *Logansport Press* during 1934, and selected excerpts appear in the following pages.

Recollections of boyhood

Frederick's early years frequently came into his thinking about the pleasures and rewards of life, as in his relationship with the Eel River for fishing and bathing purposes. He savored the memories of catching "Mississippi catfish . . . weighing all the way from twenty-five to one hundred pounds." He recalled this particular sea creature because: "any fish that had any sense of propriety reserved accommodations in the Blue Hole." And he recalled the basic qualities for a successful experience at that choice spot: "a strong line, an even temper, perfect technique and most of the afternoon."

Childhood as a farm boy brought back memories to Frederick who spent many hours with Kenesaw working on the "13 acres" across Eel River. The whistle that ended work at the spoke factory in town was a moment of delight because it meant a lunch time respite from chores for the boys who took advantage of the "chance to lie on the cool grass for a while." The old factory was a busy place with a hundred regular employees as well as ambitious young boys who "made a dollar now and then 'piling spokes.'"

By observing the antics of his older brother John, Frederick learned about the romantic potential of that fanciful stream, Eel River, and he wrote: "The girl of that time could dream she was gliding in a gondola through the velvet waters of Venice ...It took a good deal of imagination, but it was highly effective." His recollection of "that old New Year's reception" brought to mind that "it had an air about it: Slumbering graces came forth; flat lives discovered hills and valleys; there was laughter and the flash of wit, the talk of books and plays."

The Nation

Looking to the New Year, Frederick mustered an optimistic view of life under the Great Depression since 1929 while adding a worrisome thought for the future as he wrote: "For three years or more we have been parked at the wailing wall, one hundred and twenty million of us, yet we have lost nothing but some water we thought was wealth. In other words, we have lost something we never had!" Then Frederick brought the reader down to earth: "Every time I see a baby playing with a rattle box, I wonder how he's going to pay the debt we are handing him." [83]

228

"February can be As wild as she pleases—For she gave us WASHINGTON and LINCOLN!" was on the cover of the next month's issue, [84] bringing the following introductory remarks: "It might not be a bad idea to point out to our children that those two Immortals, who make February the aristocrat of the calendar, owe their glory to CHARACTER!" Speaking of Washington, he wrote: "His spirit is on guard tonight. It will walk the ramparts of this Republic forever!"

A fuller meaning of the Great Depression surfaced in Frederick's editorial listing local industries that disappeared in the now-familiar phenomenon of company mergers: "Knowlton & Dolan's foundry, the Torr and Shaffer stave factories, the Howe factory, King Drill Works, Ash & Hadley's furniture factory, Henderson's furniture factory, the Spoke Factory, Spiker and Harrison's buggy factory, the Woolen Mill, the Oil Mill, the Bliss slaughterhouse, the Uhl flour mill, the Logan Milling company, the Forest Mills, the Tannery, two brick plants, and the railroad shops of the Pennsylvania and Vandalia, Heppe's soap factory . . ."

Frederick's "Corn on the Cob" items in March found a lesson in history to relate to the 1930's gangster spree spreading across the United States: "Lincoln, Garfield and McKinley were each shot but once, and all of them died, but you can riddle an outlaw with lead, and he can recover and live to preside over old settlers' picnics!"

The question of self-government for the Philippines remained alive as its citizens asserted a desire for independence from the country that had liberated it from Spain in 1898. Frederick suggested that the United States was not ready to provide a response to their request, noting a problem endemic to Washington: "We are not fitted for the management of far-flung possessions; it calls for a nation that is hard-boiled, and we are not hard-boiled; we are only scrambled. We are not Caesars -- we are Pollyannas!"

The age of railroads had greatly changed the nation from the old covered-wagon days, as Frederick recalled. Nowadays, in the early 1930's, he noted the breakneck speed of a train that took but three hours from Logansport to Kansas. By contrast, Frederick remembered the early years when two local fellows, Clay and Nort Hand of Royal Centre headed for the same destination on "a slow, dusty, torrid and perilous journey of many weeks" by covered wagon, and "the Hand boys never came back."

Frederick continued to reflect his philosophy about the current dismal condition of the national economy, offering President Franklin Roosevelt's administration credit for trying to solve long-standing problems. He cautioned against people becoming discouraged: "Don't let anybody scare you by talking about revolution . . . Nothing could cause an upheaval in America except for the government to take away our flivvers and compel us to stay at home for a while . . . So, all in all, let us rejoice! [85]

At a time in our history when the condition of the nation was readily defined as economic turmoil, Frederick found another dimension of professional life that suggested a dismal future for the Republic. His reasoning was based upon a reliable report from the American Medical Association that the nation had too many doctors, and he added: "In addition to this, we have too many lawyers, preachers, writers, merchants, bankers, farmers, manufacturers, laborers, teachers, clerks, actors, traveling salesmen, printers, painters, singers and politicians. Otherwise we are all right."

To Frederick, who regularly delivered speeches on patriotic occasions, the arrival of Flag Day was special. He expanded beyond the simple remarks: "It was not made by woman over night -- this flag of ours -- but slowly woven in the loom of years . . . Justice is in it, idealism, achievement and opportunity for all." [86]

Still, in a reflective vein, Frederick observed the Fourth of July by recalling the "many misconceptions" that marked the original Day of Independence: "The truth is our ancestors were most reluctant to cut the tie which bound them to England, and even after Lexington, Concord and Bunker Hill, they hoped for an arrangement in which they might continue as British subjects, with a recognition of their rights." [87] He then noted the remarkable role of an Englishman, Thomas Paine, whose pamphlet *Common Sense* "crystallized the sentiment for independence" and recognized "the preeminent heroes of the Declaration of Independence; Thomas Jefferson wrote it and John Adams, with his eloquence, won its adoption."

Frederick wrote again in "Corn on the Cob" about one of his favorite topics, the automobile that continues to thrive in great numbers despite the persistent trappings of the Great Depression: "Henry Ford in his unguarded moments is a philosopher who states that what we need right now is the 'pioneer spirit.' But if we had

230

automobiles in pioneer days, the pioneer wouldn't have amounted to a tinker's dam." [88]

Culture

With the January issue, Frederick may have had in mind his maternal grandfather's missionary efforts in Sierra Leone during the mid-1800's, as he gave a brief lecture about a looming threat to American society: "We gave Africa our religion. She gave us her music and dances. We got the WORST OF IT!"

Describing Abraham Lincoln in February, Frederick at first referred to "God's Kings" of humankind – Alexander, Copernicus, Michelangelo, Shakespeare: "And then in a far-off land, across an ocean, over mountains, through a wilderness, out on a cold, bleak, lonely frontier in a cabin as rude as the manger of the Man of Bethlehem, he made at last a King of Justice -- and the Father of us all has made no improvement since He made Abraham Lincoln."

The rise to prominence on the stage and in Hollywood of Logansport's Richard Bennett and his family was a source of hometown pride to Frederick, who recalled how the elder Bennett began his acting career in Dolan's opera house. Starting out as a pants- maker, Bennett "worked hard and with native ability went to the top . . . contributing his own genius to the theatre" as well as that of his daughters Constance, Barbara and Joan, "all of them stars."

One of the stand-out cultural events of Indiana was high-school basketball, and Logansport with its 5,000-capacity Berry Bowl was at the center of this sport's activity. It was Frederick's role to make a "welcome home" speech there on the occasion of the Berries' return after a historic triumph at the State tournament in Indianapolis. In covering the subject in one editorial, he singled out the leadership of Logansport's masterful coach Cliff Wells: "the benefactor of all the boys who have played for him; he has told them never to quit -- and never to cheat!"

In domestic affairs, Frederick's commentary upon the gross imbalance in wages in the nation was deplorable, a condition that some might find still plaguing us in the 21st century: "Our alleged civilization is a hopeless hick, for it grudges pennies to its teachers, but showers gold upon its entertainers." [89] With a focus on Hollywood, he added a thought about cultural trends: "With the coming of warmer weather, the motion picture actresses are now exchanging their heavy husbands for lighter ones."

Frederick's next lament emerged over signs that the nation was finding itself in a revolution over male-female roles in society. As an example, barbershops were being destroyed as beauty shops were taking over. He sorely regretted the demise of the former, that "forum of the Republic, for woman's presence is salt upon the tail of free debate," noting: "The barber's chair was once our refuge. . . There one was safe from creditors; he who was lathered was immune; the constable pressed his hellish visage against the window in vain." And, finally, as he had recorded some eight years earlier, Frederick offered his ode to "the old shampooer." [90]

Religion

Upon the suggestion of one of his readers, Frederick chose to say a positive word about Jim Burwick, an unlikely preacher who came to be known as the "Railroad Evangelist." He noted the view of Mr. Burwick's associates on the railroad who knew him as "the drinking, swearing freight conductor who was converted at a revival at the Market Street Methodist Church." The bets seemed to be that "he would be an early backslider," but they appeared to be quite wrong, Frederick wrote, quitting his job on the railroad and becoming "an evangelist who did great and lasting good."

Women

Frederick appreciated the female of the species, placing them on a pedestal, but he also expected that they ought not to waver from their lofty perch. He lamented their growing temptation to smoke cigarettes and opposed the notion that nature's beauty should be enhanced by the application of paints, colors, and pencil marks that later came to be called "make-up." Eyebrow-plucking went beyond the pale. He applied scorn to such practices in his *Hoosier Editor* section "Corn on the Cob": "The cigarette output for 1933 was eight billion short. The only explanation is that the girls are now concentrating on painting their toe nails and have neglected the nicotine end of their careers."

As the Great Depression inched toward its end in the mid-1930's, another sign of a drooping society was a growing acceptance of the institution of divorce. Frederick noted one example: "A Chicago woman has issued cards announcing her divorce," and concluded, with deft sarcasm: "Divorce, once a scandal, has become one of our honored institutions, and it is entitled to all the martingales." Tongue-in-cheek, he suggested how the stodgy courtroom might yield to modish change. [91]

The Presidency

Frederick found occasion to be serious in "Corn on the Cob," comparing President Franklin Roosevelt's social demeanor with that of the previous century: "The President didn't put on any airs at the recent diplomatic reception, but it wasn't in it for simplicity with that day when Thomas Jefferson, in slippers and dressing gown, received the British minister."

Frederick's introduction to the April issue of *The Hoosier Editor* revealed a sense of frustration and futility about President Roosevelt's decisive measures to cure the economy: "The American Eagle is standing on his head; *The Constitution* is in moth-balls; the statues of our mighty are covered with goose flesh, but Spring is here -- and the Old Flag still waves. We'll come out all right; we'll save the country. We can't do otherwise for we have no other place to go."

Frederick drafted an open letter to President Roosevelt for financial aid in repairing the family home: "I see by the paper that you are going to arrange it so folks can get money to fix up their homes . . . a lot of things around our house ought to be fixed . . . up-to-date I haven't been able to get in on any of the easy money, but this opens the gate . . ."

In spite of Frederick's growing disdain for FDR's policies, he proved himself, after due reflection, to be flexible and reasonable and wish Mr. Roosevelt a "Happy Voyage," adding:

All of us hope the President will have a fine time on his trip to Hawaii

He has done more things in a short time than any other official in captivity.

With some of these things a lot of us do not agree, but he has done them patriotically and with unusual eloquence.

He has behind him the gamest bunch that ever did business under any flag -- the people of America.

Frederick had a high regard for FDR's success with his series of radio "fireside chats." In discussing whether this novel practice might have been such a successful tool if available in earlier Administrations, he concluded: "More than all our

233

Presidents from Washington to Franklin Roosevelt, Lincoln had in ample measure the values of the theater -- humor, mimicry, the art of story-telling, the delicate shading of expression, eloquence, passion, humanism."

Civil War ties

Frederick's commitment to the cause of war veterans appeared in an introductory passage to an early issue of *The Hoosier Editor*: "It was evening and rain was falling. An old veteran was sitting on the sidewalk and both of his legs were gone. He was selling pencils . . . I asked how things were going. 'Fine!' he replied. 'Things are getting better . . . I've taken in fifty cents today!' . . . Yes sir! -- This country's coming back! . . . Let's turn over a new leaf -- and have faith."

The genesis of a famous Union brigade had come to light in an account given by a person present at the time in Dolan's Opera House. During the intermission of a performance, the announcement was made about the firing on Fort Sumter, April 12, 1861. Frederick wrote that a man named Wilder "arose and left the theater, announcing that he was going home to southern Indiana and raise a regiment." That unit later became known as the historic "Wilder's Brigade of mounted riflemen."

Celebrities

A visit by General Grant to Logansport some years after the Civil War was cited by Frederick, who was eight years old at the time, to illustrate the near-disaster that local historians later recorded. After paying respects to the local Honor Guard, the "Old Commander" made his speech that was interrupted by the collapse of the platform from which he was addressing the crowd. Frederick wrote that General Grant, upon recovering from the dire situation, offered the explanation to one and all, "that the disaster was doubtless due to the fact that he, a Republican, and Mayor Jacobs, a Democrat, were speaking from the same platform."

"Corn on the Cob" in the summer of 1934 included Frederick's comment on some of the vagaries of Hollywood. One item catching his attention touched on the prudence of American ladies choosing American mates: "Ina Claire, the actress, is going to marry a German nobleman . . . all the empty-headed American gillies who pass up our homegrown Romeos for the foreign brand."

234

Politics

With the political bell ringing, Frederick began to travel away from his *Hoosier Editor* production shop to work for victory in the primary election campaign. He drove to Porter County, visiting the villages of Hebron, Kouts, Chesterton and Porter enroute to the main city of Valparaiso. Newspaper speculation noted that Frederick had been trying to decide which political race to enter this year: "Reports have it that Mr. Landis was drafted to make the congressional run by leading Republicans of the district while he was considering the prospects of declaring for the US Senate seat now held by Arthur R. Robinson,." [92]

Frederick continued his early campaign south to Flora in Carroll County, where brother Charles had published the *Delphi Journal* and had served as congressman for six terms at the turn of the century. Here Frederick addressed supporters and pledged that, if elected, "he would fight to the last ditch any movement threatening the integrity of *The Constitution* and the principles of Americanism." [93]

This summation appeared in a prominent Indiana newspaper: "Landis' tremendous lead was regarded as all the more remarkable as both his opponents had been rated as formidable contenders." The national representative of a pro-labor fraternal organization recommended that Frederick receive labor support in the general election. Normally in the Democratic Party column, labor organizations had learned that he was a friend of the workingman and had drawn a sizable number of Democratic votes because of his record. This labor lobbyist was most gratified "to know that victory perched on Frederick's banner." [94]

In Frederick's mind, the 1930's seemed to be producing many politicians with inflated ideas about their importance in the universe. In *The Hoosier Editor* of September, [95] he wrote: "This is the era of stupendous exaggeration. Swollen egos are snatching for the stars. Single-cylinder intellects are emitting cryptic profundities which would baffle Aristotle . . . ."

The youngest member of the Landis family Lincoln recalled that his father in this campaign of 1934 carried a gun on the floor of his automobile for protection against the Ku Klux Klan. (Our family held the notion that "Pop" had never fired a gun and probably couldn't hit anything if he tried.) He also frequently hired a "moon-lighting" state policeman to accompany him for distant speech-making trips at night for "protection."

Government

The *Chicago American* reported on selected portions of *The Hoosier Editor*. Frederick's analysis of President Roosevelt's plan for industrial reform was centered upon puffed cereal being blown one-at-a-time by individual workers. It illustrated the inefficiency of Washington bureaucrats now in charge of the national economy, referring to them as: "geese that would solve our problems by . . . stopping mass production, which has developed the highest wages ever paid, and going back to hand production, that used to pay a dollar a day, and couldn't afford to pay more now."[96]

Feeling the pressure of government demands on the average citizen to renew the financial fabric of the country, Frederick called out on his magazine cover: "It's about time for the taxpayers to hold another BOSTON TEA PARTY!" He continued a critique of Congress' legislation regarding agricultural reform, noting: "Before they cut the production of crops, our statesmen should have had a conference with old Mother Nature and learned her plans."

Frederick questioned the qualifications of one of President Roosevelt's cabinet members, Rexford G. Tugwell, secretary of agriculture: "Tugwell doesn't know a potato bug from a Lobster a la Newburg, but he's telling the farmers!" Frederick returned to this theme in his September issue, observing: "Tugwell once raised a prize-winning calf, and the calf grew up. It is the bull that he's been throwing down at Washington." Frederick closed out the August issue with an observation about the direction President Roosevelt's crusading Administration was taking: "This used to be a government of checks and balances, but we've issued so many checks we haven't any balance left."

Radio

Frederick's writing appeared in a new venue, *Radio Guide*, "America's Weekly Magazine for Radio Listeners," in three issues, June 9, June 16, and June 23. Its slogan was "Tells What's on the Air . . Any Time . . Day or Night." In the first issue, "Radio, The First Line of Defense," Frederick noted: "Radio did a great job during the recent Chicago fire, a fire which for a while threatened to equal, if not exceed, the conflagration which destroyed that city, back in the seventies (1870's)." Frederick wrote: "It had the fury of a demon; it wrapped block after block in the embrace of swift destruction; it leaped cross street after street, claiming new conquests for devastation, the brave firemen seeming but pygmies before its awful wrath. . ." [97]

Frederick speculated about how important radio would have been during the Colonials' efforts to gain freedom from England. As an example: "Before the adoption of the Declaration of Independence there was great indecision on the part of the members of the Continental Congress because they did not know how the people back home felt about the idea of severing all ties with England." Then he gave his assessment: "In our day, the radio would end all their doubts in a few minutes." [98]

Frederick turned his attention to the present day, describing the great value displayed by the invention of radio. He wrote about the role played by radio in covering the Great Parade of the Chicago World's Fair: "Led by the Unseen Marshal, Radio, that parade marched into millions of homes in city, town and out on the farm . . ." Then he wrote about the Marconi's of tomorrow, "youthful amateurs of radio with equipment which they have made with their own wits and hands, glad to send a radiogram back home for you -- absolutely free!" [99]

Law enforcement

The saga of gangster John Dillinger was the topic of Frederick's "Here at Home" coverage of events in and around Cass County and Logansport because the desperado appeared to make Indiana a laughing stock: "We couldn't catch him," and, when others turned him over to the State, "we couldn't hold him." Much of Frederick's comment related to "our lousy system of law enforcement," adding that, as a result of the disgust of the general populace, "many are tempted to sympathize with Dillinger, and now he has only to rob a bank and with the proceeds lift the mortgage on some widow's farm, in order to become a hero."

Frederick added some lore about the local region's earlier brushes with law enforcement, induced perhaps by John Dillinger's recent escape from the jail at Crown Point, north of Logansport. The Green brothers, Amer and Bill, charged with murder and dumping a body in Wild Cat Creek, met justice in different ways. As Frederick recalled: "Amer was taken from the jail at Delphi by a mob and lynched a few miles from Flora, while Bill took a change of venue to Miami county and was sentenced to life imprisonment."

Law enforcement in Cass County and Logansport was frequently in the hands of local authorities such as the justices of the peace. Frederick wrote of the case in which a distraught woman poured her tea pot of scalding water on a neighbor. In the course of the case presided over by one Henry Eidson, Frederick reported the justice's "habit of blending mercy, personal feelings and other ingredients with law enforcement." His editorial noted that after the evidence was presented, Mr. Eidson seemed to be impressed by the prosecution's work but went on to emphasize that the justice knew the defendant's grandfather and father, who happened to be his friends. As a result, the verdict was "Not Guilty."

In his "Here at Home" commentary on local affairs, Frederick called attention to a former Logansport policeman who gained experience in observing desperadoes John Dillinger and Harry Pierpont during his duty as a guard at Michigan City and Pendleton jails. This law enforcement officer had an interesting observation to make concerning these law-breakers. Frederick wrote: "Flynn believes that while Dillinger appears to have enjoyed the services of an expert press agent, Pierpont was the real leader of the band, excelling in brains and ruthlessness." He added that the latter's education ended in college, "when he started in the wrong direction."

Judicial system

Home-grown violence came to Frederick's mind after an altercation involving Logansport's Judge D. D. Dykeman, who was acting in the armed pursuit of a newspaperman. The case appears to have involved Frederick as "a local lawyer," although his precise role in it was not clear. What was evident, however, was that the journalist had made uncomplimentary remarks of the judge, even mentioning that the jurist had but one hand. The result was an honor for Judge Dykeman in the eyes of the citizenry, when, astride his horse, "he fired a volley at the offender," driving him out of town.

Having already staked out a position that the enforcement of criminal law in the nation suffered greatly, Frederick expressed concern in the final issue of *The Hoosier Editor* that in the recent Lindbergh kidnapping case, justice might not be served: "Let's

Hope Hauptmann's Lawyer Takes Care of Himself. We'd Hate to Lose Him!"

Foreign Policy
   In foreign affairs, Frederick took another look at his recent support of the idea of having established official ties with the Soviet Union in 1933: "If Russia's working her communistic racket here, we should end diplomatic relations and ship her representative to Moscow on the very first boat!"
   Frederick also wrote about one of his favorite fellow Hoosiers, General Lew Wallace, author of Ben Hur, upon the occasion of his assignment as American envoy to Turkey. Instead of a procedure by which "the new minister presents his papers and bows, after which the sovereign nods and bows, after which they back away from each other . . .

> The Sultan welcomed him most hospitably, and Wallace lingered for an hour of conversation, cigarettes and some coffee, without any cream in it.
> The Turks take it black, you know.
> This was the beginning of an intimate friendship, and as time passed along, the Sultan more and more counseled with the American minister about the affairs of Turkey, an honor rarely bestowed upon the representative of a foreign land.

And, after Wallace's term was finished, with a change in political rule back home, the Sultan "gave Wallace the highest possible proof of his friendship and admiration; he offered him the command of the Turkish army, an honor which he declined. So he returned to Crawfordsville, drew his broad-armed chair out under his beloved beeches, and wrote another novel."
   Frederick paid close attention to the troublesome world situation, seemingly with an impending dust-up between Japan and the Soviet Union. Showing no awe for the Emperor of Japan, he observed: "The Mikado says He's the Son of the Sun, but if He should go to War with Russia He'll find he isn't as hot as his Papa." (Japan's intentions, however, would soon focus in an easterly direction with the target of Pearl Harbor.)

Europe

Frederick continued to view the possibility of war involving our World War I allies, the very countries that had borrowed from the United States and failed to pay their debts. For him, current short-wave radio broadcasts to the United States had a special meaning for him: "It's easy to tell whether you have picked up Europe. Just listen and if they don't ask for something, then it is NOT Europe!"

He took time, however, to reassure his readers that indications of imminent hostilities across the Atlantic were no cause for concern: "Don't worry about this threatened war in Europe. I have two subscribers over there and with this vast influence I expect to be able to handle any emergency that may arise."

Japan

Frederick's "Corn on the Cob" in February's issue of *The Hoosier Editor* twitted the nation's conscience *in a remarkable warning, nearly eight years before the fact*, of the cynical attack on Pearl Harbor, cloaked in diplomatic chicanery: "It would be great to have a joint debate between this Japanese admiral, who says that Japan is getting ready to fight us, and this Japanese ambassador of good-will, who's coming over to tell us that Japan really yearns to press us to her wishbone."

Conclusion

With Frederick lying in the hospital on Election Day, his daughter Betsy reported in "Here at Home" an optimistic note about her father: "He is winning a battle up there in the hospital and before long will be back to take his place in this corner of the paper." She acknowledged that many candidates would be concerned about the final results of a hard-fought campaign and the realization that "half of them are to be disappointed." As for the Landis household, the meaning was also that today "means 24 hours closer to the time when our 'Pop' will be up and well again."

The day after the election results confirmed Frederick's victory, Betsy wrote from college: "You folks were very good. You gave a better tonic to the Hoosier Editor than we had yet been able to find. People from all over the District, from every one of the thirteen counties, came through loyally."

Frederick was elected to the US House of Representatives, the only Republican to prevail in congressional races in Indiana. Two days after election returns were reported in Indiana and across the nation, the local newspaper wrote: "While America went Democratic, even more so than in the 1932 election, Frederick Landis of Logansport, Republican candidate for congress in the second district, was swept into office by a majority unparalleled in local history." [100]

Another analytical article appeared on the front page of the Logansport newspaper in an article entitled: "A Man Runs Who Can Run." It summed up the importance of Frederick's victory: "Landis alone of all the twelve Republican contestants in the state achieved the triumph of whipping a militant, organized and packed-purse Democracy: if there is a vestige of vigor remnant in the moribund G.O.P., it rests with Landis over and above those who, until yesterday, were reckoned the rock of ages of the Republican party." The editorialist also concluded:

> The Second Indiana district catapults Landis into the national picture and Landis lists the Second District as the stockade from which Republicans repel Democratic attack even when it triumphs in its assault on Pennsylvania, the Verdun of Republicanism. [101]

The writer continued in the same vein, painting the effects of an election which swept many into oblivion . . . namely, that this election "had also cast upon the shore of national politics a new name, the name of a man who, it seems, can clip the whiskers off Santa Claus." He added:

> And that name is Frederick Landis--"Buckskin" Landis to the voters. And he did it lying down. If Buckskin can run a race like this one from a hospital bed, what will he do when he really spits on his hands, runs his hands through his hair, hitches his pants and really gets going.

Frederick died on November 15th, nine days after the election.

[Excerpts of Frederick's recollections his last year appear in Notes.]

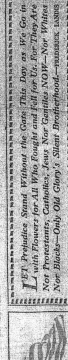

LET Prejudice Stand Without the Gate, This Day, as We Go in with Flowers for All Who Fought and Fell for Us. For They Are Nor Protestants, Catholics, Jews Nor Gentiles NOW—Nor Whites Nor Blacks—Only Old Glory's Silent Brotherhood.—FREDERICK LANDIS

OLD JUDGE PEPER
BY FREDERICK LANDIS

I FINE YOU FIVE DOLLARS FOR CONTEMPT. THE DIGNITY OF THIS COURT MUST BE MAINTAINED!

THAT EVENING —

Frederick offered commentaries in the 1920's as a radio commentator on CBS and above, as newspaper editor on Decoration Day and cartoonist.

SIX REASONS WHY HE SHOULD BE GOVERNOR

SON USES PLANE TO CAMPAIGN STATE FOR LANDIS, WHO IS ILL

Photo from Frederick's campaign brochure in his 1928 quest for the Republican nomination for Governor of Indiana; and newspaper item showing son Kenesaw [Bilo], age 17, who flew around the state making speeches for his father, sidelined by illness.

The Constitutional Amendment on Prohibition, that became effective in 1920, was greeted by Frederick's illustrated parody *Days Gone Dry*, published the previous year.

In 1933, he authored his first of 12 monthly issues of *The Hoosier Editor*, a magazine of humor and commentary produced at his home with the aid of his wife and children.

Put This VOTE-GETTER *at the Head*
of the Republican State Ticket

LANDIS *for* GOVERNOR

FREDERICK LANDIS

The people are for Frederick Landis. *He carried every county* where he made a Primary speech. He'll *speak in every county* between now and November. *You know* what that means to EVERY COUNTY TICKET, to the Congressional candidates and to Republicans everywhere. Landis meets the demands of the time.

He's the Man for the Job

Campaign literature for Frederick's 1928 run for Governor of Indiana.

7. Baseball, Wartime -- 1920's to 1940's

Baseball players have got to be more honest than preachers; and more honest than bankers. You see, it's this way -- one man in a bank goes wrong but the bank doesn't bust. One preacher backslides, but he does not bust the circuit. But one crooked baseball player can bust baseball.

-- Kenesaw, upon appointment as
baseball commissioner, 1920 [1]

I am hoping that your barracks are fit for the housing of human beings, which they were not 25 years ago in many cases . . .

-- Kenesaw to grandson, first family member
to join the Navy, 1942 [2]

Throughout his latter years, Kenesaw focused successfully upon freeing Baseball from the scourge of gambling; and, after Frederick's death, assumed a role during World War II of offering critique on the running of the war while supporting the morale of family members serving in the Armed Forces.

1920

Kenesaw's prominence as Federal Judge and, in particular, his position in the Federal League case in 1915 advanced his selection "to bring peace and order to Organized Baseball." [3] In the judicial realm, he attracted attention by criticizing President Woodrow Wilson for intervening in the case of a wealthy defendant who sold diseased cattle and misused the mails, declaring: "When the President of the United States paused in his great affairs to cut this sentence in two, I am forced to wonderment as to the frame of mind he must have been in to cut such a sentence." Kenesaw concluded that Mr. Wilson's real motive was to issue a presidential pardon. [4]

His judicial role brought him into cases involving the enforcement of the new 18th (Prohibition) Amendment of the *U. S. Constitution.* One such case was described in colorful detail by an unnamed citizen of Chicago. [5] On the political front, he was mentioned by Senator Kenyon of Iowa as a possible candidate for President. After the 1920 election, the Chicago trade press cited Kenesaw in its advice for President-elect Harding concerning his

Cabinet selections: "There are public men whose records are commendable, whose ability is par excellence and whose characters are above reproach, from whom to select. Mr. Harding should follow Lincoln in this respect and keep close to the plain people. What the country needs is officials who will enforce the laws, not violate them. A few more of the Landis type would not hurt." [6] For background, Reed offered a summary of his father's colorful record as Federal Judge. [7]

When rumors spread that the Judge might be offered the job of Baseball Commissioner, one of his old friends advised against the idea. William Jennings Bryan, President Wilson's first Secretary of State and three-time Democratic Presidential candidate weighed in: "I see they are trying to take you off the bench with an offer of 25,000 a year. Don't do it. I am sure big business is back of this offer. That is the way they do when they want to get rid of a judge whom they can not control. Don't give up the fight. We have only a few judges like you." [8]

In Baseball, news of a scandal, in which Chicago White Sox players were charged with conspiring "to throw" the 1919 World Series to the Cincinnati Reds, had shaken the sports world. A strong leader was needed to enable Baseball to regain credibility after the indictment of star players. One writer was supportive of Kenesaw, recallng his "no-nonsense style" on the Federal Bench . . . noting that Kenesaw would "purr like a kitten and coax like a summer's breeze but also whirl around on the bench and with eyes, blazing like a bobcat's, give a recalcitrant witness or scheming lawyer a verbal threshing that makes for truth and honesty in his court." [9]

In November, Kenesaw accepted a commitment to clean up Baseball, stating to the *Chicago Tribune*: "I have accepted the chairmanship of baseball on the invitation of the sixteen major league clubs . . . On the question of policy, all I have to say is this -- the only thing in anybody's mind is to make and keep baseball what the millions of fans throughout the United States want it to be." [10]

Another of Kenesaw's friends suggested the breadth of challenges facing the Judge: "When you have cleaned up Base Ball, Booze, Bankruptcy, Boodle, and other Bamboozling, why not take an afternoon off and fix up the Irish mess?" [11] *The New York Times* published two editorials describing Kenesaw,: "as arbitrator, a one-man court of last resort," and predicting: "peace will obtain in professional baseball for at least seven years, while the eminent jurist will also continue to strike terror into the hearts of criminals by retaining his position as a Federal Judge." [12] The article discussed his style as that of "a national figure for the important cases he has passed upon . . . and his wit, and sarcasm -- sometimes humorous and sometimes caustic, which he directs at prisoners and counsel from his bench, have made him famous." [13]

Kenesaw' selection was not based upon his baseball skills on a semi-pro team . . . He would "peg the ball around the town lot at Logansport, Indiana . . . was a pretty fair shortstop . . . but no big league scouts wasted any afternoons looking him over." Ken himself, speaking about his play as first baseman on Logansport's Goosetown team, recalled: "Our favorite enemy was the New Jerusalem team. It was an endless feud between us. However, we licked them no oftener than we were licked." [14] Nor did he assume a position because of the sophisticated, well-paid executive: "Appointed Baseball Leader . . . Judge Kenesaw Mountain Landis Now Has Supreme Control of Pastime at $42,500 a Year -- Talks With Reporter While Eating Lunch From Paper Bag." [15] Kenesaw's friend Mr.Bryan made one last shot to try to dissuade him from taking the job, writing: "I would like to see you on the Supreme Bench." [16]

Kenesaw agreed to become the first Commissioner of Baseball in the Chambers of his Chicago courtroom. The *Literary Digest* recorded the occasion: "Just as it began to look like a prosperous winter for the attorneys and others who profit through large legal wrangles, the great baseball war ended abruptly, and Judge Kenesaw Mountain Landis took his stand in the midst of the battlefield, monarch of all he surveyed." [17]

1921

Kenesaw's Baseball appointment became official in January. He insisted that his powers be absolute, but the owners sought to water them down through semantics in the contract. Kenesaw reminded the owners: "You have told the world that my powers are to be supreme . . . I wouldn't take this job for all the gold in the world unless I knew my hands were to be free." The text was quickly changed to its original meaning. [18]

In a frivolous aside, Ken was "honored" in the program of the Senatorial Record on the occasion of a meeting of the "Senate" of the spoof-oriented Indiana Society of Chicago, whose members were prominent in various professions. The "honor" was in keeping with the traditions of the organization as announced by the presiding officer of the "Senate of the Hoosier Republic": "The Chair rules that the Senate has no jurisdiction. All matters relating to war in either League -- even in the minors -- are under the jurisdiction of Judge Landis." [19]

One sports reporter posed a question about the new Commissioner: "What kind of a man is Judge Kenesaw Mountain Landis?" and offered this answer: "The consensus of opinion of those who have known Judge Landis for many years is that he is a genuine 'he-man;' one of determination and possessed of a reliable wallop. And this is well, for any other would fail in the task of regenerating baseball." [20]

As the National Game's first commissioner, Kenesaw faced the question of whether he could undertake baseball duties while keeping a Federal judgeship and decided that there was no problem. Still, certain others held a different view, and he became the target of congressional action. On February 21, 1921 Representative Benjamin Welty of Ohio presented his Statement "Conduct of Judge Kenesaw Mountain Landis" before the House Judiciary Committee. [21] An impeachment resolution charging Kenesaw with receiving pay for both his commissioner job and federal judgeship was introduced in the U. S. Senate in February by Senator Dial of North Carolina, who was angered by the Judge's leniency in the case of a low-salaried teenager charged with embezzlement. Kenesaw had concluded simply that the lad was woefully underpaid as a courier with bank funds, and, consequently, responsibility for his action lay with bank directors. [22]

One local newspaper in opposition to the Judge's decision charged Kenesaw with "grandstanding." The editorial, while acknowledging difficult circumstances faced the young teller, reasoned: "If the defendant could not make enough money at the bank to meet expenses, he should have looked for work elsewhere." [23] A prominent Negro preacher in Chicago, however, supported Kenesaw . . . Dr. H. M. Boynton, pastor of the Woodlawn Baptist Church, declared that Kenesaw should ignore the congressional action: "Landis is a big man, and the people want him and will have him . . . They have faith in his honesty and want to keep their faith in baseball, and they will fight Congress if it dares to remove from him his authority as federal judge." [24]

Another case that appeared in *The New York Times* confirmed Kenesaw's special consideration for defendants of modest means: "A Negro and a white youth, after pleading guilty to separate charges of stealing from the mails, received clemency today from Judge Landis, who deferred passing sentence, as he did in the case of the bank teller that brought attacks on the Judge in Congress." [25]

Representative Welty criticized, in his impeachment proposal in the House of Representatives, Kenesaw's decision to receive both the $42,500 baseball salary and the $7,500 congressional pay. A Negro newspaper supported Kenesaw in large print and made an appeal for Kenesaw's exoneration, disapproving of the Congressman who offered the impeachment proposal: *"The Chicago Advocate*, speaking for the entire race, wishes to extend to Judge Landis their appreciation for his fair and impartial justice handed out regardless of color or creed, paying no attention to such men as Senator Dial of North Carolina." [26]

John Heydler, President of the National League of Organized Baseball responded to criticism by Congressman Welty that, in receiving the top job in baseball, Kenesaw had been bribed by "the baseball magnates, involved in court difficulties . . ." To this charge, Mr. Heydler stated: "The men who put Judge Landis at the head of this work were determined that, whatever might happen to their investments, the game itself must be saved at all costs." [27] A small town newspaper in Oklahoma registered its view on the planned impeachment: "The charges are trivial and trumped up. It is an effort to pull down, piece by piece, one of the most striking and upright characters of the times." [28] A poem, whose origin is unclear, but perhaps the same newspaper described Judge Landis as a lion. [29]

Kenesaw took note of criticism he was receiving in Congress from Senator Dial and chose to reveal facts concerning the legislator's record on slave-labor in certain states: "I would like to know what he pays his little girl employees." [30] A week later, a major sports publication noted: "The eyes of the country are centered on Judge K. M. Landis of Chicago" and called attention to Kenesaw's tendency to treat defendants of modest means with special consideration. The article referred to "his many striking decisions where, to say the least, mercy tempered the law most boldly." [31]

Kenesaw's son Reed recalled several interesting actions by his father with regard to Capitol Hill. [32] First, Kenesaw "immediately sent a telegram to all Senators, urging them to vote for his impeachment in order to enable him to defend himself in the well of the Senate." Reed continued, stating: "None of the other congressmen wanted Father impeached but did want him to come down and defend himself because they knew what a performance it would be." Finally, the Southern legislator succeeded in killing the impeachment proposal "by some expert maneuvering and thus prohibit Father from coming down and defending himself."

Second, Reed noted his father's perception of a tie-in between efforts to impeach him and to examine his responsibility to enforce the Prohibition Amendment. In court cases, Reed noted: "He had to find bootleggers and moonshiners guilty, and in each case he would make some sort of statement from the Bench along with his verdict expressing his disapproval of the Prohibition Act and his disbelief that it would ever work." This led a Congressional committee to subpoenae the Judge as they deliberated to consider repeal of the Prohibition Amendment. Reed explained that his father came forward with unexpected ammunition to offer in his testimony that summoned the congressmen's close attention. Kenesaw spoke of his previous day's round of visits to government officials: "Gentlemen, there was not a single office in which I was not offered a drink from the bottom right-hand drawer of my friend. This shows the farcical character of this Prohibition Movement."

Third, in another related instance, the Judge had occasion to visit Canada after his visit to Capitol Hill, as Reed recalled:

> Well, on his return, across the border from Buffalo, the train was held for an hour and a half, while his stateroom was given the most thorough search that the railroad conductor said that he had ever seen. It was quite obvious to Father that the Prohibition enforcement people had decided that, having testified as he did the day before in Washington, he of course would bring back some Canadian liquor and try to smuggle it into the United States and that they wanted to catch him. He of course did not smuggle any liquor and was not caught.

One editorial, appearing at first to praise Kenesaw's judicial actions, concluded with a jocular critique that suggests that Judge Landis might have overstepped acceptable norms: "Dismissal of impeachment charges against Federal Judge Landis was forced by the fact that Landis is intensely human, that he enforces the spirit of the law and is not frightened by its letter. A man of less courage and initiative never would have been permitted to take $7,500 from the government with one hand and $42,500 from organized baseball with the other." [33]

Public speaking continued as a part of Kenesaw's career, and his favorite subject was patriotism. His current theme was to explain America's purpose in entering the recent World War as he addressed a gathering of thousands assembled in Indianapolis: "The plain God's truth about it was that we went into that war because we were driven to the wall and had to go in to maintain our standard as a sovereign power on this earth." He also took a swing at the country's current foreign policy, concluding: "the Irish mess . . . this everlasting row about the controversy between Ireland and England" should not concern the United States." [34]

The country was also concerned about the uncertain course of events in communist Russia, where Vladimir Lenin was beginning to seek American assistance in his "New Economic Policy" called NEP. In the meantime, communists and socialists were perceived to be engaging in revolutionary activity in the United States. The Central Executive Committee of the Communist Party of America declared "May Day" as Labor's International Holiday. Its program was spelled out in detail in the publication: "Proletarian Revolution or Wage Slavery," a document Kenesaw chose to keep in his personal file for possible future reference. [35]

Kenesaw's sudden involvement as supreme authority in Baseball led to speculation that politics might become another direction for him to follow. More press interest in the Judge centered around an item in a small-town Illinois newspaper that touted him as a bright political prospect. Kenesaw's reputation led this newspaper to call for his candidacy for Governor of Illinois, finding in him the qualities that would serve the State well: "Illinois is in dire need of a political Moses who can lead its people out of the wilderness of machine politics . . . Judge K.M. Landis is the sort of man to whom one day the people of this state may turn for guidance out of the unsavory taxation swamps and back to normal government. He is radical enough to place the people's interests before the interests of greedy politicians, and such men are rare nowadays." [36]

As official arbitrator of the National Game, Kenesaw reached the judgement that, the White Sox players, despite having been acquitted in court for gambling during the 1919 World Series, would be banned from Baseball for life. His declaration established a strong position to prevent a recurrence of such behavior by players and also demonstrated his strong authority to rule the game: "Regardless of the verdict of juries, no player that throws a ball game; no player that undertakes or promises to throw a ball game; no player that sits in a conference with a bunch of crooked players and gamblers where the ways and means of throwing games are planned and discussed and does not promptly tell his club about it, will ever play professional baseball." [37]

A colorful reaction favoring Kenesaw's decisive action appeared in a music score, reminiscent of the manner in which his landmark decision against Standard Oil in 1907 had been set to music in 1907. The "How Do You Do" theme, featuring performances by Jones and Hare, "the Happiness Boys," was published by the Ted Browne Music Company of Chicago. One verse included the following: "How do you do, Judge Landis . . . Every time that there's a scandal . . . You shine out just like a candle . . . There's no job that you can't handle . . . How do you do." [38]

In the weeks following the first radio broadcast of a major league baseball game by radio station KDKA in Pittsburgh, Kenesaw made news wearing his judicial robes. He settled a dispute involving the building trades of Chicago, as described by a *Chicago Tribune* commentary, which goes on to defend the Judge's decision to hold both positions, baseball commissioner and judge at the same time: "The greatest public service of the year has been rendered by Judge Landis. He has knocked down a pernicious and destructive system of operation which prevailed in the building trades and which kept the people from getting the homes they needed. He has practically obtained a settlement which removes an obstruction to industry and housing." [39]

Kenesaw received grassroots support from his "Uncle Jake" of Seven Mile, Ohio, who wrote from the area of Ken's early childhood. Elderly Jacob Kumler was referring to his "Neph's" bout with Senator Dial over child labor in South Carolina, with a harsh appraisal of senators in general: "Your note to me some time ago secured and I think you were correct in your statements . . .That Bunch have more Shisterrs in their Profession than any Profession Class I can think of fully half of them would not hesitate to rob Widows & Chrilden when they have opportunity Yet - we have to have them I guess. All in usual Health here and Send much Love and will remember you wi our Suplications and Preyers." [40] Two weeks later, a small-town Midwestern newspaper also echoed its support for Kenesaw in this case:

> Every once in a while some clown jumps into the spotlight by attacking Judge Landis and his baseball salary. The fact is Judge Landis is the most potential figure in Chicago today. During the war Judge Landis, single-handedly and alone, put the fear of God in the heart of the great crowd of German sympathizers in that city. Only recently he stepped in and brought clarity out of chaos in the Chicago building industry, an action national in its moral effect. [41]

The opening game of the 1921 World Series was a moment in history because radio brought the event into many homes for the first time. That game is particularly remembered because it was called for darkness in late afternoon, causing fans to become irate. Their tempers flared, according to one writer in later years, to the extent that they blamed the new Commissioner. This happened to be an auspicious moment when Grand Admiral of the British Fleet Lord Louis Mountbatten, who joined Kenesaw and his wife on the occasion, remarked: "My goodness, Judge, but they are giving you the bird." [42]

Sadness came to the Logansport Landises -- Frances, Charles, Kenesaw and Frederick with the passing of Kate November 23, 1921. A telegram to Frances from an uncle and aunt observed: "With the dear ones gone before . . . what a joyful time they are having . . . we send our love and sincere sympathy to you all." [43] That Kate's death was a shock to Kenesaw is suggested in his letter to August Herrmann, President of the Cincinnati Reds ball club, in which he stated his intention to attend the National Association Meeting in Buffalo, New York in December, while acknowledging: "Owing to a good deal of confusion, apparently I overlooked until today the last paragraph of your letter of November 8." [44]

On that occasion, he had in mind his landmark decision, banning the White Sox players a few months earlier when he offered remarks to the Minor League officials:

> Baseball, he told them at the annual dinner last night, must be better in its morality than any other business because it serves a great, overwhelming influence on public opinion and because "the ideals of fandom are the highest ideals." He warned against any undue optimism "over the return from the slough into which we were precipitated in the fall of 1920," adding that "baseball is still on trial in America and will continue on trial as long as baseball is played."

He also spoke earnestly about the need to bring back the draft system into the National Game, saying: "It cannot be a good thing for something calling itself sport that it is within the power of any individuals in that sport to place a stone wall in the path of advancement of a ballplayer." [45]

Toward the end of the year, a struggle erupted between the game's major celebrities of 1921 . . . Babe Ruth, the "home-run king" and Commissioner Landis. The case involved Ruth's participation in exhibition games following the 1921 World Series. This practice was against baseball's rules, and Kenesaw let it be known that he would not allow Ruth and two other New York Yankee players, Bob Meusel and Bill Piercy to be an exception.

After the players proceeded to "barnstorm," Kenesaw took action. In December, he ruled that all three would be punished, declaring: "This situation involves not merely a rule violation, but rather a mutinous defiance intended by the players to present the question: Which is the bigger, baseball, or any individual in baseball? There will be an order forfeiting their shares of the World's Series funds and suspending them until May 20, 1922, on which date and within ten days thereafter they will be eligible to apply for reinstatement." The *Chicago Tribune* followed with the comment: "it was not expected that Ruth would be asked to forfeit the entire amount of his share of the last World's Series." [46]

1922

After deliberating about his two positions for over a year to avoid the impression that he was being forced into a decision, the Judge resigned from the bench effective March 1. Meanwhile, the *Chicago Tribune* surveyed readers as to whether Kenesaw would serve well as mayor of the city, and the idea was forcefully supported. [47] Citing "public confidence" in Kenesaw's "honesty and Americanism and courage," a colonel from Texas sent him a telegram requesting a statement concerning recent activities of a subversive nature: "We are exceedingly anxious for your views on the Ku Klux Klan and kindred secret political organizations in regard to operations in our locality." [48] Ken replied: "I concluded it would not serve the purpose for me to get into that Ku Klux controversy. This conclusion was largely induced by the very definite opinions expressed to me after leaving Texas by several rather sensible public officials, who are going to the mat with the Klan." [49]

In the meantime, Kenesaw in Chicago and Frederick in Logansport received word of the unexpected passing of Charles in Ashville, North Carolina. Now there were just the two Landis boys and sister Frank surviving.

Shortly after the 1922 baseball season began, Kenesaw gave an interview about golf, in which he included comments about how the New York Yankees were playing without the skills of Babe Ruth and Bob Meusel: "It is not with Landis, judge or high priest of baseball, that we are concerned at this time, however . . . only in Landis the golfer. The surest way to learn about a man is to play golf with him. No hidden recess of his soul can hold its secret against this test. Whatever feeling of awe there may have been among his companions vanished when he topped a tee shot and said: 'You damned old fool, keep your head down.' That was enough to convince us that he had walked with kings of swat and Standard Oil companies without losing the common touch." [50]

A few weeks later, a lady who apparently had served on a Congressional staff and had known Charles contacted Kenesaw and recalled Charles' opposition to the seating of a polygamous Congressman-elect. Describing it as "the masterpiece of the Fifty Sixth Congress" followed by a moment when "the House and galleries went wild," she noted that "the speaker's gavel was powerless to restore order, and the people shouted themselves out. No other speech in Congress had evoked such enthusiasm since the days of the Civil War." [51] Kenesaw acknowledged her thoughtfulness, writing that her remarks confirmed his own impressions of "the constructive work" Charles had done on the Mormon question. [52]

Generous recollections of "the Landis boys," all of whom had worked for the hometown newspaper in earlier years, were expressed in an Indianapolis newspaper by a family member of the *Logansport Journal's* former owner. Interestingly, her appraisal accorded John "superior intellectuality" over his brothers. [53]

In May, the U. S. Supreme Court ruled that the Sherman Anti-Trust Law did not apply to Organized Baseball, a judgement certain to have delighted Kenesaw. There was little doubt that he would have seconded the sentiment of President John Heydler of the National League that this action would stabilize the structure of the Game and "insure protection for the owners and players as well as benefit the public." [54]

An invitation came from Dayton, Ohio for Kenesaw to be "distinguished guest and featured speaker" at the 58th annual reunion of his father's regiment, the 35th Ohio Volunteer Infantry on September 21. Unfortunately, the Judge found it necessary to decline because of the pressure of "duties in connection with baseball at this season of the year." If that were not the case, he wrote: "Nothing but a stone wall would be permitted to keep me away from this particular reunion." [55]

Kenesaw turned his attention to a letter he received from an elementary school pupil in California, who, in excellent handwriting, wrote of his teacher's opinion that the Judge "will help to make baseball a cleaner game. [56] Kenesaw responded, assuring the Second Grade: "The game is getting better each year." [57]

Haphazard play by the New York Yankees during the race for the American League pennant in the summer of 1922 attracted the attention of Kenesaw, who was prepared to deal with serious distractions such as gambling occurring in baseball games. The "inside story" of this occasion appeared in the Portsmouth, Virginia press, which explained the occurrence and the results of the Judge's actions: "Just before the players left the club house for the field to play the last game with the Red Sox on the 26th of June, they were informed that Judge Landis would speak to them -- meaning both the Red Sox and Yankee players. After the players were penalized, they pulled themselves together and played ball that ultimately won the American League flag . . . but going the way they were heading to disaster until Judge Landis brought them to their senses." [58]

Kenesaw's nephew Major John Landis looked to the interests of his fellow officers, appealing to his uncle for assistance. Kenesaw responded to John's request in behalf of one Major Cadwalader, who though highly qualified, was being discharged from the Army: "If I wanted to insure the killing of Major Cadwalader, I would attempt to get action in his behalf . . . Would you please tell me why in God's name a man of the qualifications of Major Cadwalader should so imperil his reputation for sanity so as to deliberately take an examination for permanent commission in the US Army?" [59]

1923

Operating in the rarified air of Chicago, Kenesaw chose to keep close ties with some of his Kumler relatives back in Ohio. Cousin Charlie Kumler, a fellow lawyer, proved agreeable with this notion and invited the Judge back to a familiar Ohio neighborhood: "A representative of the Y. M. C. A. of Dayton, asked me this morning to write you to ascertain if you could possibly address that body on some Monday evening the latter part of February. I shall be glad if you can accept so I can shake your paw and talk to you about bye-gone days." [60] Kenesaw planned to respond by joining forces with his cousin later on: "Of course it would be bully to come to Dayton on such an occasion as you mention, but I am trying to work out from under a mass of stuff that I have taken on . . . I am expecting, however, to get to Dayton for part of a day some time during the next eight or ten weeks, and of course you and I will have a reunion." [61]

Early in his third year on the job as commissioner, Kenesaw asserted his authority over the owners in the case of two-year-old charges against pitcher Rube Benton, recently purchased by the Cincinnati Reds from St. Paul of the American Association. The Judge ruled in favor of Benton playing for the Reds because of his recent "unimpeachable conduct" as a major league player, and due to the inaction of baseball's previous administration on charges that

Benton failed to report a tip he received during the first game of the 1913 World Series. [62]

During a visit to celebrate baseball in Waterbury, Connecticut, the Judge divulged some aspects of his personal life to a reporter who noted: "You must travel a fast pace if you want to keep up with the Commissioner – an early riser, a fast walker, and a devotee of healthy exercise." He also wrote about the Kenesaw's recent heavy load of work: "He is strong and wiry physically. The only occasion he ever was in poor physical condition was when he was both federal judge and baseball commissioner. Then he was working from 6 a.m. to 10 p.m. and even later, without a moment's rest. He finally became exhausted and had to take a complete rest. After a tour of the baseball training camps a year ago, he returned to his office completely recuperated." [63]

During the same day Kenesaw attended festivities at the Polo Grounds in New York where he appeared with Christy Mathewson of the Boston Braves and the Mayor of the city. He "presented the world championship rings to the Giants and helped John McGraw pull Old Glory to the staff head to open the home season of the New York Nationals." [64]

Kenesaw found that the Black Sox scandal of 1919 again reared its head in correspondence between Shoeless Joe Jackson and the Commissioner during the 1923 baseball season. Jackson's letters did not appear in the files of the Indiana State Library, but Judge Landis' replies were there. The first letter indicates confusion about the authenticity of a letter from "Joe Jackson," while the second gets right to the point:

> Baseball
> Kenesaw M.Landis,
> Commissioner
> June 20, 1923

> Registered Mail, deliver only to addressee.
> Mr. Joe Jackson
> Bastrop, La.
> Dear Sir:
> I have received a letter dated June 12, purporting to come from you and to bear your signature. In substance, it is an application for reinstatement.

The signature thereto does not appear to be yours; therefore, beyond this communication to you, no action will be taken thereon.

Very truly yours,

Kenesaw M. Landis

Continuing with "the Jackson affair," Kenesaw had an occasion to write again to "Shoeless Joe:"

July 16, 1923

Mr. Joe Jackson
Bastrop, La.

Dear Sir:

Your letter, which is dated 7-29, came here in my absence and, through an error in forwarding, was delayed in coming to my attention.

Before I can pass on your application for reinstatement, it will be necessary for you to forward me for consideration in that connection, a full statement in detail of your conduct and connection with the arrangement for the "throwing" of the World Series of 1919. I feel I should say to you that there will be no reinstatement of any player who had any connection therewith.

Very truly yours,

Kenesaw M. Landis [65]

Turning from baseball to politics, the Judge responded to Arthur H. Vandenberg, editor of the *Grand Rapids Herald* in Michigan with a note on the subject of the Baseball Commissioner's possible interest in getting into the political arena: "Acknowledging your note of the 31st with enclosure, while I have not the slightest interest in that governorship, nor in any other thing of a political candidacy nature, I must confess to you that I am human enough to like what you said. On this I am reminded of what Lincoln said about gingerbread, namely, that he reckoned nobody ever quite liked it as much as he, and got so little of it." [66]

At this time, Kenesaw, the commissioner, seemed to revert to his judicial days. He ventured into the international political arena, drawing comment of a major city newspaper during a speech-making appearance in Iowa: "It is deplorable that anyone in the

257

United States should suggest recognition of the Soviets," proclaimed Judge Landis. He went on with a scathing reference to a senator from Iowa before the Hawkeye audience of American Legionnaires: "It is lamentable that you have in this State a man of quite superior vocal accomplishments who is telling us all about the wonders of the Soviet government." [67]

Meanwhile, Kenesaw found a life-long friend in the cab of a passenger train, the *Seminole*, later the *Illinois Central Flier*, on one of his trips during his early years as baseball commissioner. When the train was in a stretch between Milan, Tennessee and Cairo, Illinois, the Judge "was tired of riding the cushions" and joined the engineer, one Colie Chandler, as he was directing the train northward. The incident was explained fifteen years later by Mr. Chandler as he headed for his reserved seat in the Commissioner's box to cheer for the Chicago Cubs in the 1938 World Series. Back in October 1923, the engineer recalled: "The Judge just wanted to stand up in the cab, but I made him take my seat. He was blowing the whistle all the way and was having the time of his life." Then Chandler added: "When we got to Cairo, the Judge crawled down out of the cab wrote my name on an old envelope. He said that I was to be his guest at the next World Series and I have been sitting with him ever since. Each year, I tell him good-by he slaps me on the back and says that I am to be his guest next year." [68]

The move from Logansport to make Frederick's career in New York City was thought by some in the family to have been a risky proposition. At least Frederick's nephew, Army Major John Landis, on active military duty, wrote a cautionary remark to Kenesaw: "Drop me a line and give me the lowdown as to how Fred is getting on in his eastern venture.. . . I hope that he will be able to make this go. It would be great if he could and hell if he doesn't." [69] Kenesaw responded, indicating some optimism about Frederick's likely success in the "big city:" "The last time I was in New York, which was at the Army-Navy game where he, young Ken and Fred were my guests, he seemed to be in good fettle and said that everything was in accordance with his liking." [70]

258

1924

Kenesaw was touted as a grassroots candidate for President in 1924 by a Middle Western journalist who placed an advertisement in newspapers, describing: "One Man the People Believe in -- Millions of People of Both Parties Would Ride on the Landis Presidential Train." [71] This writer also wrote an editorial citing his reasons for trying to start a presidential "boom" for the Commissioner of Baseball: "There is one man in the country who can restore confidence with our present form of government. Ohio has been the Mother of Presidents. The East has had its quota of Presidents. But the Middle West owes it to the people of this country to put up the ONE MAN who has the confidence of the voters of all political parties -- Judge Kenesaw Mountain Landis." [72] A newspaper from Butler County offered support in terms of a sports enthusiast: "Judge Landis is the apotheosis of umpiring, the monument of baseball magnates' determination to cease to do evil and learn to do well. Judge Landis is a character because he has character." [73]

As interest grew in the presidential race in 1924, Kenesaw's putative candidacy for Vice President appeared to be confirmed by the content of a telegram from the "American Tribunal" to the chairman of the Illinois delegation to the Republican National Convention of 1924: "Will you have placed in nomination name of Judge Landis for Vice President? Every Delegate, every Newspaper advised, Everybody, Everywhere, knows Landis' progressiveness, integrity, courage and they want Landis . . . The delegate who introduces the name of Landis to the Convention will make his name glorious in the pages of history." [74] Kenesaw quickly sent a telegram to the Delegation Chairman:

> I have just received what purports to be copy of telegram addressed to you and other delegates by a so-called quote Manager, Landis campaign for Vice President unquote last night. Not only was this done without my knowledge or authority, but in no conceivable circumstance would I have anything to do with that nomination. If the suggestion comes from any quarter, hit it hard. Please answer. [75]

Meanwhile, back in the world of sports, Kenesaw's daily regimen included baseball business in the form of a visit by two players of the New York Giants, Jimmy O'Connell and Cozy Dolan,

259

who sought their return to the game after the Commissioner had banned them for involvement in an attempted bribery case. The Judge, determined to keep the evil of gambling at bay, turned down their request for reinstatement. [76]

Writing to a former colleague many years previously when young Kenesaw was working at the *Logansport Journal* as a court reporter, the Judge had occasion to recall those days. After dropping out of the 10th grade in order to learn shorthand, he had applied his skill in jobs as court reporter before his chums graduated from high school. In response to a letter from a man who had served as a printer on the *Logansport Journal* and remembered young Ken in his work at the paper, Kenesaw wrote, with self-deprecation, about his young career in the 1880's: ". . . acting as a short-hand reporter (picking up sermons, speeches, lectures, etc.) That work (such as it was) was done by the undersigned. I may not have been much of a judge, nor baseball official, but I do pride myself on having been a real shorthand reporter." [77]

1925

In baseball matters, Kenesaw refused to rule on a disputed call during the World Series between the Washington Senators and Pittsburgh Pirates. It concerned whether centerfielder Sam Rice actually caught Earl Smith's eighth-inning drive, and the Commissioner told Pirate manager Bill McKechnie that the umpire's call could not be "changed off the field." [78]

Kenesaw kept in touch with the older generation of Kumlers residing in Ohio. He wrote to 87-year-old Uncle Jake, one of his favorites: "I am sending you a newspaper photograph that was taken during the first World Series game at the Pittsburgh ball park last fall. Tell your athletic grandson that the man standing in front of the railing at my left was Tris Speaker, manager of the Cleveland Ball Club." [79] Not a shy fellow himself, Uncle Jake responded, mixing some family pride with a possible touch of humor: "My Dear Neff . . .Your fine picture to hand Some days ago have been so busy Husking Corn could not find time to write Sooner - Mighty fine of you to send it to the Old Uncle think will have it Framed and Hung up be Side of Washington and Lincoln." [80]

1926

Kenesaw was concerned about Frederick's financial situation upon leaving his position with the *New York American* and returning to Logansport. [81] In addition, his concern may have been related to the circumstances of Fred's separation from the Hearst newspaper because of the possibility that Frederick's writings might have rankled New York City readers and upper-level officials of the Federal Government. Such may have been Ken's reason for writing to sister Frances (Frank): "That's a pretty tough break that family at Logansport is getting." [82] As noted in the previous chapter, Frederick's independence and candor on the editorial pages of William Randolph Hearst's *New York American* may well have proven unpalatable to corporate management of the newspaper.

Kenesaw attended one of the last annual reunions of his father's regiment in August 1926, when he paid homage to its strong reputation: "There was a brotherly, a family spirit present in that 35th Ohio Volunteers. Indeed that family spirit was responsible for the success of the regiment." [83] His judgement was a reminder of the positive tone exhibited by his father's appreciation of the Southern landscape and his congenial approach in discussions with Southerners during the 35th Ohio's "pilgrimage through the Confederacy." [84]

Included in Kenesaw's baseball responsibilities were certain mundane matters like distributing World Series tickets to the Game's managerial establishment on an equitable basis. In one instance, the President of the Cincinnati Reds requested an allotment of fifty tickets for 1926, believing that his team was a likely contender to meet the Yankees in the major event of the season. He obliged with "forty reserved-seat tickets, and I now think six box seat tickets" for Yankee Stadium. [85] As it turned out, however, the St. Louis Cardinals won the National League pennant for the first time and proceeded to beat the Yankees, also the Cards' first victory in World Series play.

The realm of baseball suffered a temporary setback in 1926 from indications of possible scandal after a charge that two of baseball's Greats, Tris Speaker and Ty Cobb, had been involved in "throwing" a game in 1919 between Cleveland and Detroit. The question of what action the Commissioner might take in response to these allegations gained wide attention among sportswriters.

1927

In January, Kenesaw made sports headlines when he downplayed the importance of the charge against Speaker and Cobb. His decision not to pursue the matter tended to defuse the matter, and the Judge's inaction in the case suggested that he was acting in "the best interest of the Game."

Kenesaw agreed to do a series of articles for the journal of the Izaak Walton League of America, *Outdoor America*. In his essay, "A Whole America," he referred to "Abe Lincoln, outdoorsman and patriot" . . . whose "every thought was influenced by the forces of nature." Kenesaw discussed the League's work for children across the United States and concluded: "Then may we say -- "we sportsmen, fishermen, hunters, outdoorsmen bequeath to you, our children, a country where hunting, fishing and all outdoor sports may be yours. We leave to you a country with an outdoors, a whole America." [86]

In the summer of 1927, as the date for the annual reunion of the 35th Ohio Volunteer Regiment again approached, Kenesaw received a family invitation from his cousin and good friend Charley (Gus) Kumler. He implored Kenesaw "to come to Seven Mile and eat chicken with us on the evening of Aug 25 after the reunion." [87] Ken planned to attend the reunion but regretted that he could not be present at the feast afterward because of another commitment. [88]

At the regimental reunion, one of the unit's last get-togethers, he praised the veterans for their courage, noting that for them "there was no preliminary training . . . a man was home on Thursday and on the following Sunday afternoon was under fire before the enemy." Then he proceeded to lament the fact that scarcely half of registered voters in the nation choose to exercise their right at the ballot box. adding: "It is difficult to say just what to do with the slothful citizen. I would not go to the slothful citizen with a prayer . . . I would make it a duty, and if he did not recognize it I'd make him pay the penalty." [89] Kenesaw promised to support the reunion through his own funds, and the Permanent Recording Secretary of the Regiment acknowledged receiving his check for $257.10, total cost of the affair. [90]

1928

Kenesaw found an opportunity to pay for his sister Frank's visit with her sister-in-law Cora, Charles' widow in Colorado. Then, while on a golfing vacation in Clearwater, Florida, he experienced a rare roadblock when he was challenged at the ticket booth of a local ball game. The matter was solved . . . "while the Commissioner was digging into his pockets, Secretary John Gorman of the local Robins ball club appeared on the scene and escorted him into the stands free of charge." [91]

Kenesaw informed his nephew and unofficial confidant Major John Landis of Frederick's decision to re-enter the political arena by running for the Republican nomination for Governor of Indiana. In a jocular aside, Ken affirmed his brother's zeal for the campaign: "I suppose you know Fred is willing to be fo'ced." [92]

Kenesaw received an invitation to attend the 64th reunion of the 35th Ohio Volunteers but was unable to make a commitment that he might not be able to fulfill. [93] After a few weeks, Kenesaw confirmed that he could not attend the affair -- likely to be the last get-together of survivors of his father's regiment: "Inescapable obligations will require me to be about one thousand miles away from Hamilton on the date of the reunion." [94]

After Frederick lost the gubernatorial nomination in June through last-minute maneuvering by Party strategists, an uncertain situation in the Logansport household surfaced in correspondence between Kenesaw and his namesake Bilo. In the words of the young college senior, "My last year at Columbia begins in ten days and family finances are not in a shape to send me back . . . I will have to make up the work I missed during the Indiana primary campaign, and because of that I don't think I will be able to do any work on the side. I am writing you with the hope that you may be able to loan me enough to finish up. I need a thousand dollars, either in the form of $500 now and $500 in January, or in monthly editions of $125 for eight months. If you are able to do this it will mean a lot to me." [95] "Uncle Squire" responded, characterizing the check as an outright gift: "It is not a loan. Herewith first installment." [96]

Young Kenesaw II, at 18, reported to his Uncle Squire about his participation in Columbia University's upcoming transatlantic debate: "We lock horns with Oxford next Monday evening in the 'greatest intellectual battle of the century'. If it is at all possible that you may be in this neighborhood on the night of the debate, let me know." [97] He enclosed a copy of his write-up as a member of the 1929 Columbia University debating team, scheduled to debate Oxford University on: "Resolved: That America Should Join the League of Nations." [98] Uncle Squire responded: "I congratulate you. I wish you all the luck in the world and hope you clean 'em up . . . Wish I might sit in on that debate." [99]

Kenesaw performed his self-assigned task of informing family members of accidents and deaths, in this case the news of a fatal automobile accident involving cousin Preston Kumler, who had served in the American occupation of Germany after the World War. Ken informed cousins Daniel and Jessie Kumler of Dayton, Ohio [100] and pledged "to ascertain the status of the case of the man who ran that Chevrolet into Preston." [101] The Judge's generosity for the year also extended to his brother John's widow, Daisy, in the form of a check that enabled her to pay for a new coat. [102]

1929

Kenesaw was late in sending the next installment of his "not a loan" support to Kenesaw II for his last year at Columbia College: "Very carelessly, I neglected to send you the enclosed before I went away from here on Thursday of last week. I am sorry this happened. It will not occur again, if reason does not totter from her throne. Luck." [103]

Back to Baseball, Kenesaw exercised his authority to the dismay of team owners in a forerunner of the now-familiar "free agency" procedure in the Game. The Judge found certain clubs responsible for "covering up" transactions that kept players under their control with fines for those clubs and the freeing of players from contracts. [104]

Kenesaw's bent for vaudeville, valued within the family although not evident to the public at large, was illustrated by names he used in correspondence with wife Winifred. In a telegram across town in Chicago, he chose not to overload his epistle with substance and to use a unique spelling style:

Dear George:

A fireman just came in and said he came here because Wrigley sent him. I said, what can I do for you, he says, you know, Judge, my daughter won the prize for pulchritood at Galveston (small town in Indiana near Logansport), I says, for what, he says, for pulchritood. I says I congratulate you and her, he says, fine. I says what can I do for you, he says, well, I want her introduced to the crowd before the first World Series game. I says, just introduced, he says, yes. George, don't it beat awl.

William Hemingway. [105]

Kenesaw's thoughtful financial assistance enabled Bilo to meet expenses through graduation from Columbia College. Now it became time for further tuition and subsistence to young Ken at Indiana University Law School as well as to younger brother Frederick Jr. for undergraduate courses. Kenesaw II managed to keep communications flowing from the college campus to his generous Uncle Squire, writing: "Pebo (young Frederick) and I are both settled here and like the school very much. The law school seems to be very good, and I am just beginning to get the hang of it . . . I am glad to have Pebo here with me this year, and I think he likes the idea also." [106]

The Judge's trusting way of handling finances with his namesake nephew was illustrated in this letter: "I am sending you herewith check signed in blank. I have forgotten what you wrote me would be the amount to be inserted in these monthly checks to meet the requirements of you and Pebo. You fill it in." [107]

1930

Kenesaw and Winifred's grandchildren, Nancy, Keehn, and Susanne Landis and Bill and Jodie Phillips recalled summers in the cottage at Burt Lake, Michigan, where Judge and Mrs. Landis enjoyed the company of their son Reed and daughter Susanne Phillips. Fishing and boating were favorite diversions there, while winters usually found Kenesaw pursuing the golf ball in Florida and Arizona. Fishing was popular in the north woods, and Kenesaw joined with other middle-aged gentlemen on frequent trips in the direction of the Canadian border. Kenesaw and Winifred enjoyed hotel living in the Chicago Beach and Ambassador East throughout the decade.

The next few years provided disappointments and deaths of family members as well as financial challenges that Kenesaw arranged to meet head-on. He started off the New Year by making arrangements for his namesake-nephew to undergo treatment for tuberculosis at an established facility in California. The Judge's generosity solved a financial squeeze for brother Frederick. His younger brother's main income was from editorial work at the local newspaper, and additional funds from radio and public appearances appeared insufficient to cover young Ken's medical expenses. Kenesaw wrote to Bilo, enclosing "something useful" and made plans to visit him shortly after his nephew's arrival in California. [108]

Bilo wrote to his uncle in November from California that the doctors had become quite optimistic about his improved healing during the summer in Logansport. Young Ken also informed the Judge that he was running short of money and hoped that he would not require further treatment in California the following year. [109] The Judge replied with a check for $500. [110]

In his next letter, Bilo reported that he had disappointed the American Legion, whose delegation had called upon him in California, thinking him to be the Judge. [111] He wrote again, having read that Uncle Squire had had a minor operation and then stated frankly: "I realize this is a bad time to tell you, but I am broke and the wolf is getting close to the door." [112]

1931

The Judge faithfully responded to Bilo's latest request for funds for subsistence at the posh Arrowhead Springs resort, sending him a check for $500. [113]

It was becoming apparent that the old Kumler clan of Ohio was dwindling in size, and in the latest telegram to the Judge, the news was about the death of his good friend, cousin Charlie Kumler of Dayton, Ohio, son of "Uncle Jake." [114]

The Judge continued to receive requests for money from Kenesaw II, the latest being three months since the last one, but containing promising news about young Ken's medical condition:

> Finances are again at rock-bottom, but otherwise everything is soaring. The X-rays indicated that there was no activity, and my lack of temperature and my general feeling of exuberance tend to bear that out. [115]

The Judge forwarded another check for $500 and reported that, upon his return from Florida, Jodie Phillips had a mild case of scarlet fever. [116]

Following the tradition that a promising lawyer could enter the practice of law without a law degree, young Kenesaw applied to the Bar Association in Logansport for admission to the Cass County Bar, and his application was approved. [117]

Keeping grandsons, Bill Phillips and Keehn Landis, up to date on their shared passion of fishing, Kenesaw wrote to Winifred with a message to deliver to them about his expedition to the North country via St. Paul, Minnesota: "I am going to fish in a new place where there is said to be a moose." [118]

The Judge learned from his cousin Gus Kumler that Uncle Jake at 93 had deteriorated mentally and was spending his latter years in a nursing home, leading the Judge to respond about "the God Almighty theory" that the earlier generation "endeavored to engraft upon you and me." [119] Thus, Kenesaw questioned the authenticity of the United Brethren Church and the short-sightedness of the Almighty. The Judge also learned that brother Frederick was in serious condition following an automobile accident that occurred enroute from Logansport to Cincinnati for his scheduled radio appearance on WLW. [120]

A letter from Bilo at Logansport told of his aspirations to resume study for a law degree in the fall, in the healthful atmosphere of the University of Southern California at Los Angeles, He also forwarded an estimate of costs for the academic year -- $1,600. Bilo reported that he "felt fine" and prepared to do the necessary study under these positive conditions, acknowledging his gratitude for the Judge's great assistance. He also reported that his father's condition was improving from injuries in the automobile accident but still experienced the "effect of the shock." [121] Uncle Squire responded with a check and with details about getting together for a Chicago visit enroute from Logansport to California at the Chicago Beach Hotel. [122]

Kenesaw was mindful of the financial contributions that he had been making for members of his extended family. Beyond the family's needs, however, he usually drew a line as in the case of "the Volunteer Gospel Crusaders" in behalf of "the Chicago Infants Free Milk Depot," which sought support from his wife. The basis for his demurral was the organization's lack of endorsement by the Chicago Association of Commerce. [123]

In another instance, Kenesaw received word of a minor traffic violation charged to his wife. Instead of phoning her, as some husbands might choose to do, saying: "Honey, you got a ticket, but I don't think you should pay it," he composed and mailed the following from his Chicago office to his Chicago hotel:

> Dear Madam:
>
> Referring to recent correspondence on the subject of taillights, we beg to transmit herewith communication this date received from Mr. W. W. Fairbairn, of Alanson, Michigan, the same bearing date September 23rd and relating to an activity which has lately had consideration at your hands. May we beg of you, madam, that you will observe Mr. Fairbairn's memorandum, communicated to his epistle by means of a red lead pencil? With reference thereto, it is the earnest hope of the undersigned that you will "pay no money to Ransley."
>
> Assuring you, madam, that we are with you to the last ditch.
>
> Yours very truly, KML [124]

The Great Depression had just taken a toll on Bilo's plans to pay for Law School in Los Angeles because of the suicide of a Logansport bank president. The result was the collapse of the bank holding the money that the Judge had recently forwarded for college expenses. Bilo also reported "feeling fine and liking the work" at Law School. [125] Continuing his correspondence with the Judge about the positive outcome of the deposit in the bank now in receivership, Bilo also felt that his progress in the law course seemed to be going well. [126] The Judge replied, helping to solve the problem of Bilo's funds being temporarily tied up in the bank disaster and advising young Ken in decisive terms to be sure to eat proper food as required for his health. [127] Then he hurriedly mailed a note to Bilo with monthly funds, again, advising Bilo to "get the right kind of food." [128]

1932

Kenesaw exchanged letters with Kumler cousins Daniel and Jessie of Dayton, Ohio and considered a Chicago visit to feast upon "fried mush, stewed chicken, ham and eggs and puddins." The inspiration was Kenesaw's who offered a challenging thought -- "What more -- in God's name, man -- can anyone want?" [129]

One of the few occasions in which Kenesaw chose not to send financial help to members of his extended family occurred in this case of brother John's widow, Daisy, saying: "God knows you could have that money if I had it or could get it, but I can't." [130]

Working in his office in Chicago at 333 N. Michigan Avenue, Kenesaw stayed in close touch with Winifred who was relaxing at Burt Lake Michigan by sharing "the good and the bad" with her, writing about eating and golf -- that he had "done a good job devouring chicken and vegetables at home" and adding: "but it took me 110 strokes to play Skokie in the afternoon, which was not so good." [131] In another letter, he commented on a misfortune of Reed's, suspecting in jest that the future might find him "breaking another leg in some way . . . or fracturing his skull." He then suggested that Winifred "tell him for Christ's sake to avoid it if he can." [132]

As Bilo wound up his academic year at the University of Southern California Law School, the Judge planned on his nephew's stopover in Chicago for a visit enroute back to Logansport. [133] By this point, he had already spent a great deal of emotional energy and monetary resources in behalf of young Ken's education at Columbia University a few years ago and young Frederick's first year at Indiana University and more recently Ken's health treatment and residence in California. Now he extended his thoughtfulness on a personal level to Fred's boys Charles and Lincoln, inviting them to join him at Wrigley Field for the third game of the World Series between the Chicago Cubs and New York Yankees. [134] A memorable occasion it happened to be . . . Babe Ruth's "called shot game." Little did we realize at the time that Charles' and my only exposure to Major League Baseball would provide us the unique experience of having witnessed a historic event in terms of the sport.

1933

Kenesaw learned of the sudden death March 12 of his niece Mary Holden, the only child of his late brother John and of Daisy Landis at Cincinnati, following a blood transfusion and an operation, and he sought details from sister Frank. [135] Later in the year, Daisy's beloved housekeeper Minnie also died, and Kenesaw wrote to her on the occasion of her second tragedy in 10 months: "Minnie has been emancipated . . . When such a character shoves off on that big trip (whatever it is), it is those in the disrupted situation left behind that are out of luck. And when they are grown-ups, they've just got to take it on the chin. Seems to me that's what we put in all our time doing. Love." [136]

Kenesaw continued to receive updates from Bilo on his health condition. Now in a sanitarium in Rockville, Indiana, young Ken reported the doctors' view that he had been improving since last fall. [137]

1934

The coming year would deliver a heavy blow in the loss of Kenesaw's younger brother. Events started off, however, with guarded optimism regarding the Logansport branch of the family. Kenesaw's hopes that Frederick would finally gain political success after two defeats in gubernatorial races in 1928 and 1932 and, of course, the financial stability that should go with victory. The issue now rested upon Fred's ability to win a congressional seat in the difficult climate of FDR's vast, nationwide popularity. Humorist and playwright George Ade wrote Kenesaw that he was ready for a session "to discuss our plans for putting Buckskin (Frederick) back in Congress." [138] They were somewhat reassured by early prospects as Frederick took his campaign on the road in the Second Congressional District. Results of the primary showed a strong win for Frederick against formidable opposition. Now, the true test would reside in the fall election.

One of the memorable baseball events of the year was the Judge's decision to eject star St. Louis Cardinal outfielder Ducky Medwick from the last game of the World Series with the Detroit Tigers. His action was in response to the fans' bombardment of Medwick with fruit from the stands. While not a popular decision, it reflected the unquestioned authority Kenesaw exercised over the National Game.

Although delighted with Frederick's primary election win, Kenesaw became concerned about Frederick's health as the campaign went on. With the stress of speechmaking and extensive travel, Frederick was stricken with pneumonia during the last days before the election. It was a serious problem as reflected in a letter of concern to Kenesaw from sister-in-law Daisy, brother John's widow, who had learned that the Judge "was very worried about Fred." [139] As it turned out, in a matter of a few days, Frederick had achieved a decisive victory, the only Republican congressional candidate to win in Indiana, despite a heavy Democratic victory in the nation, but he died nine days after his election. Kenesaw's written reaction to close friends and relatives was "there wasn't a damned bit of sense to that thing . . ." [140]

1935

Kenesaw and Winifred continued to spend the fall and spring seasons in Chicago, living in the Ambassador East Hotel. They frequently visited their son Reed's family in the city, and enjoyed Sunday dinners in Glencoe with their daughter's family, the Richard Phillipses. In the summer, "the tribe" (consisting of son Reed's family and the Phillipses) regularly assembled with the Judge and his wife at their Burt Lake cottage in Michigan.

While the Commissioner was often able to screen his gentler nature from inquiring reporters, he showed great concern for his special people, particularly older relatives. Through personal visits to Logansport Landises and Ohio Kumlers, he enlivened family ties and boosted the spirits of those he had known in years past.

Like Charles and Frederick on the turn-of-the-century Chautauqua circuit, Kenesaw did not shrink from employing vaudevillian skills, even for culinary purposes . . . During one of his visits to Ohio, the Judge gained the attention of the clientele of a Cincinnati restaurant, where the cook had not mastered the art of frying corn meal. Kenesaw proceeded to entertain his relatives by going into the kitchen, rolling up his sleeves, and preparing the ingredients to the satisfaction and delight of all, including his host, cousin Clarke Marion. [141] The Judge's unconventional initiative

271

may have been prompted by recalling his childhood when his father Abraham once wrote in a letter to Charles . . . "the mere mention of mush and milk made my mouth water."

Kenesaw II, long stricken with tuberculosis, continued to require treatment, recently at a charitable institution in Denver, the National Jewish Hospital. He kept Uncle Squire informed about his pneumo-thorax treatment: "The treatment by collapsing my lungs continues without complication, and the doctors have every hope it will prove as successful as it usually does." [142] The Judge responded: "I think you have put up a great exhibition, including fortitude and patience, and that 50% of the same devotion to some occupation after you get back on your feet would bring great success." [143]

Young Ken, aware of the Judge's concern about the financial status of Frederick's family following his death, kept tabs on legislative developments in Congress where "the House Appropriations committee approved, 14 to 5, an amendment to the Deficiency Appropriation Bill providing a year's salary of $9,500 for my mother." He passed this information to Uncle Squire along with later word: "The salary item has passed both Houses and has been signed by the President." [144]

Meanwhile, The Judge's sister Frank, residing in Logansport, wrote to him describing how even the youngest child was "pitching in" to help Frederick's family cope with financial requirements. The tone of her letter did not resound well with Kenesaw at the time. Recalling his early years on the Logansport farm, he was not impressed. When she mentioned 12-year-old Lincoln's job of delivering newspapers as "a tragedy," he wrote: "Have you forgotten that before I was the age of Lincoln, I got a *Journal* route that got me up six mornings a week at 3:30; that, in addition to that, I did my share - and it was a substantial share - in taking care of the 13 acres, including hoeing 8 acres of corn and digging that ditch as my father's colleague in the enterprise of draining the swamp created by the construction of the railroad?" [145] His gruff talk revealed his knack of getting to the heart of an issue, whether in the courtroom or in family matters. He was no one's fool, yet his concern for relatives always led to a sympathetic hearing and ususally a generous response.

272

Kenesaw II wrote his uncle the usual, promising health report: "The doctors here believe that my lungs are steadily and gradually healing." [146] The Judge promptly sent a note, showing that he too was vulnerable to sickness that was making the rounds: "Certainly I'm pulling for you. I'm getting back on my feet . . . I did have one hell of a time, with flu in Arizona, something else after I got back to Chicago, followed by what the vet called "blood-pressure." [147]

As the Commissioner with a solid public image of fairness for the less forunate, Kenesaw received occasional mail seeking support for various social causes. It was his nature to be inquisitive about their relative merits, and, in some cases, he looked into their credentials. Thus, a formal solicitation "The Moro Educational Foundation," which the Judge had supported in previous years, no longer met his criteria. Consequently, although it bore the same signature as that of a president who had appointed him to the federal judiciary in 1905, his marginal notation was "put in pismire file." [148]

1936 to 1938

The Judge, anxious to take up golf after a brief illness, informed his physician: "It is my unpleasant duty to report that my waistband is getting tight due exclusively to the enlargement of my abdominal perifery; otherwise I am normal." [149] To another, who had recently prescribed iron tablets, he remarked: "If my head was as good as my body, what a great Baseball Commissioner I would make." [150]

The Judge received a letter from a Kumler cousin who had been associated with a former vice president of Standard Oil of New Jersey, a gentleman who expressed a positive opinion of Kenesaw's ruling against the company 30 years earlier. This man proved to be a convincing witness to the facts of the case because he stated that he "kept the rebate books himself." This was another instance that tended to confirm his company's guilt in accepting illegal rebates as ruled by Kenesaw in 1907. [151]

The Judge answered Bilo's invitation to come to Denver, where he had been practicing law, but the Judge allowed as to his probable need for relaxation following the upcoming World Series in New York, and that would hold him close to his home base. He took the occasion to herald the beauties of Northern Michigan . . .

"goddelmities's pet territory" and turned to prose: "The trees never had such color, and the ground was one great Oriental rug, the like of which the Armenians and the Arabs and the Turks and their predecessors have for endless centuries been trying to fabricate." [152]

In a continuing matter for the Commissioner's attention, Kenesaw struck a blow for players' rights, later known as "free agency." This decision led to the important release of 100 St. Louis Cardinal farm-team players. It was a statement against corporate greed in the pattern of family tradition, a reminder of the early 1900's when Frederick introduced legislation in Congress against the insurance industry, and Kenesaw pursued violations by Standard Oil.

1939:

After trying out his legal practice in Denver, Bilo determined that the city was "not a lawyer's town" and wrote to Uncle Squire suggesting that he might wish to try out the practice of law in the Judge's own backyard -- Chicago. For all of the generosity he showed to his nephew, the Judge responded "that he could offer no advice on the problem presented, that the matter was one that every man should decide for himself." [153] Possibly, the Judge's reaction was founded on a sense that one "Kenesaw Mountain Landis" was sufficient for Chicago at any given time.

The year 1939 proved significant in terms of baseball history -- Kenesaw was on hand to dedicate the National Baseball Museum and the Baseball Hall of Fame in Cooperstown, NY. After paying respect to the first players admitted to the Hall of Fame, he proceeded "to dedicate this museum to all America, to lovers of good sportsmanship, healthy bodies, clean minds." [154] Kenesaw's sister-in-law, Daisy, invited him to be her guest during the upcoming World Series in Cincinnati, but the Judge declined and changed the subject by adding a family update -- his late brother Charley's son John was a newly-assigned colonel slated to teach military affairs at Indiana University. [155]

Baseball matters remained in the sports pages with Kenesaw's opposition to the expanding "farm system" that he feared would increase control by the Major Leagues over the Minor League clubs. [156]

Kenesaw, at left of platform, was guest speaker at U.S. Grant Birthday Celebration in Galena, Illinois
April 27, 1919.
Photo from R. Phillips file.

Cartoon depicting Kenesaw's new responsibility as the first Commissioner of Baseball.   *Sporting News*, March 12, 1921.

The American Contractor
The Business Journal of Construction

| Volume XLII | SATURDAY, SEPTEMBER 10, 1921 | Number 37 |

HAS HE OPENED A NEW ERA IN LABOR AGREEMENTS?

Kenesaw attended to federal judicial responsibilities in 1921, after being named Baseball Commissioner, by arbitrating Labor's case against the Chicago Building Trades industry.

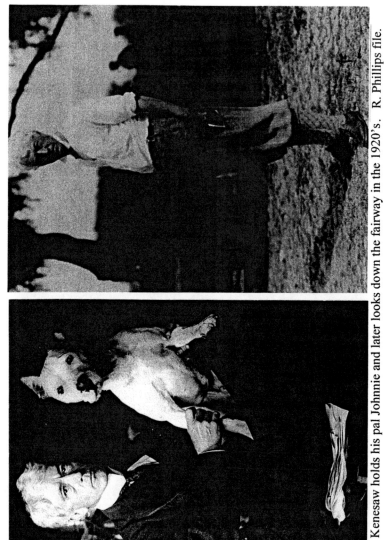

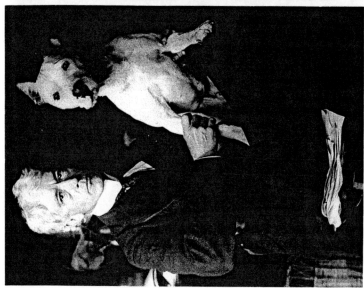

Kenesaw holds his pal Johnnie and later looks down the fairway in the 1920's.   R. Phillips file.

38

Kenesaw and Winifred at the Fountain of Youth, St. Augustine Florida, April 2, 1930.

Kenesaw and Winifred in their suite, the Ambassador East Hotel, Chicago, in 1939.   Photos from R. Phillips file.

Top row: "Uncle Squire" with Lincoln at "called shot" Game 3, 1932
World Series in Wrigley Field [TFL file]; Lincoln, Frederick ("Pop"), and
Charles, Culver Military Academy, 1934; Bottom row: Kenesaw and "his
catch" at Burt Lake, Michigan in 1940; and relaxing the same year with
daughter Susanne Phillips in their boat.   R. Phillips file.

1940

Kenesaw assisted in paying for funeral services in Butler County for his elderly cousin Katharine Landis, who had apparently never married and spent a career in Washington, DC. She lived alone and died without close relatives. [157]

The Judge continued to enjoy the diversion of golf, fishing and sailing. As he grew older, he made the transition from sailing to power-boating, frequently choosing to drive his small boat in the big waves, "watching old mother nature doing her stuff." Burt Lake was a favorite place for the Judge to relax with Winifred, their son Reed's and daughter Susanne's families, with grandsons Keehn and Bill and granddaughters Nancy, Joanne and Susanne. [158] Grandson Bill fondly recalled that he and the Judge "did a lot of fishing" and related that in 1939 he made his grandfather a complete diving suit, but the Judge chose not to wear the helmet.

Kenesaw's son Reed recalled his father's fishing days up in the area of Minneapolis-St. Paul, Minnesota in his last years. With a group of old friends on a large houseboat, "they would fish all day and play poker after dinner." The Judge liked to play golf in the winter in Arizona before changing to Clearwater, Florida, where he and his buddies played 36 holes until he was in his mid-70's. [159]

War clouds were beginning to get Kenesaw's attention because of his interest in national affairs, and he was followed closely the assigments and whereabouts of his nephew, Major John Landis of the Regular Army.

Meanwhile, Kenesaw would devote great energies to "go to bat" for his extended family that would soon become involved in war. Yet, baseball remained his primary concern, and although he acted against growing control by the Major Leagues over the Minor Leagues, he had no problem with recruiting at high school level. Perhaps thinking of his own youth, dropping out of high school to find work, Kenesaw denied an appeal from the Wisconsin Interstate Athletic Association seeking to prohibit Major League teams from recruiting high school athletes.

The Judge showed a continuing vigilance to possible gambling threats by focusing on a report that he brought to the attention of Connie Mack, President of the Philadelphia Athletics. Before listing a series of gambling activities observed in the right-field stands of Mr. Mack's ballpark on April 16, he stated: "I wish you would get to work on this thing, and let me have a report of

275

progress at the end of your series with Cleveland, May 2." Then he advised what to do with "these rats" when caught in the act during a ball game: "throw them out of the park on their heads every time they come inside the park." [160]

The Judge had started as Commissioner at age 55 during "the Roaring Twenties" and continued through the Great Depression into the recovery of the 1930's. Now in his 70's, he would look after Baseball's interests with the advent of World War II against Japan, Germany, and Italy. In baseball terms, Kenesaw had to steer the National Game through the thicket of military enlistment of star players. As a patriot, he followed avidly the progress of American forces, observing their successes at the Battle of Midway, the invasion of Normandy, and the rapid drive across France. Meanwhile, his personal agenda of corresponding with family members appeared in private letters, beginning before Pearl Harbor and continuing until his death in November 1944.

1941

In the year that marked the death of the fabled Lou Gehrig, the Judge averted the specter of possible gambling in Baseball by rejecting Bing Crosby's effort to buy the Boston Braves while the Crooner owned a racing enterprise. The year also witnessed the military enlistment of Detroit Tiger star Hank Greenberg, signaling that other prominent baseball players would be leaving the Diamond to enter military service. This caused the Judge to weigh the effects of such a development upon the National Game as the possibility of American involvement in the war grew stronger.

As war approached American shores in 1941, Kenesaw recharged his batteries by exchanging views on strategy with nephew Colonel John Landis. He also sensed that aging Landises and Kumlers of rural Ohio might need his insight on the ultimate disposal of Hitler, Mussolini, and Tojo.

In the run up to the Japanese attack and President Franklin D. Roosevelt's declaration of war, the Judge exchanged letters with Colonel Landis, reflecting concern about the growing threat of hostilities. The Judge displayed an affection for this friend and confidant of many years: "I agree with you absolutely in all that you say about Hitler, Mussolini and military activity. You're dead right." [161]

Kenesaw lamented the recent transfer of his nephew colonel to assume command of a replacement training center at Camp Croft, South Carolina – not "real troop duty" but better than an administrative job. As in World War I, Kenesaw understood John's wish to go where the action was. Meanwhile, the Judge found an opportunity to invite John to get together at a historic game "on the 28th of May, when the Washington Club will play their first game under the lights. If you could get loose, I would like to have you come up. I'll buy you a drink." [162]

Kenesaw received word from Colonel John that he was transferred from the training command to a purely administrative post, a major setback to this career officer who hankered for "a piece of the action." For the Judge, such a blow to his fellow-strategist was unwarranted and proof of the poverty of wisdom at the Army's leadership level: "My own inference would be that, if they found out you are useful at Camp Croft, they would want to get you some place where it will be impossible for you to render any real service. The more I see of this thing . . . the more I am impressed that the job (of running the military establishment) ought to be turned over to a bunch of hod carriers and shoemakers." [163]

As events of 1941 unfolded with ominous meaning for the United States, for its armed forces, and for Baseball itself, John's letters, suggesting that our capabilities on the battlefield were overstated, provided fodder for the Commissioner's thought processes. His natural skepticism about US military readiness seemed to mesh with his late brother Frederick's comments that had pinpointed such deficiencies in the 1920's. The Colonel observed that the balance of seapower in the Pacific had just shifted "from us to them" and that he hoped that Secretary of the Navy Frank Knox "will stop bellering about how ready the navy is." [164]

A few days later, the Commissioner, playfully "demoting" the Colonel, decided to send John a summary of his thoughts on the war situation: "Dear Lieutenant: Thanks for those two notes. We agree on strategy. I will say to you that when that stuff came in from Pearl Harbor it damn near blew this territory off the map. Yours, KML" [165]

Realizing his inability to influence the war situation, the Judge soon commenced writing letters to the growing number of family members in the Armed Forces, frequently reflecting his bitterness that they are needlessly placed in harm's way because of aggression by Hitler and Tojo. At the same time, his letter-campaign with those in uniform sought to bolster their morale with all the word power he could muster.

Adding fuel to Kenesaw's resentment that Pearl Harbor had drawn us into another World War was his conviction that, for the first such engagement in France, in World War I, "the world long owed a debt" to America's veterans. [166]

1942

In 1942, the national game was beginning to suffer from the loss of players to military service, causing the Commissioner to inquire of President Franklin D. Roosevelt whether, with the country at war, the continuance of Major League play would serve the nation well. The Commander-in-Chief gave the go-ahead, asserting his view of the positive role of baseball games as the nation assumed a wartime footing. In his letter, the President took into account the favorable influence the game would have on the home front, not mentioning the likely morale-boosting effects on servicemen overseas. F.D.R. replied, in effect, "Play ball!" [167] This historic "Green Light" letter paved the way for the Game to continue, although over time, many of its stars gradually moved from the diamond to the Armed Forces.

On the heels of the Green Light letter, the baseball season blossomed into a historic finish, with St. Louis Cardinals, overtaking the league-leading Brooklyn Dodgers, before defeating the highly-favored New York Yankees in the World Series.

Kenesaw's main pen pal during 1942 was 92-year-old country preacher Uncle Lute of Norwalk, Ohio had long been a favorite of the Judge and frequently hobnobbed with Kenesaw and Winifred during their Florida winters. Besides, he personified for Kenesaw an extraordinary symbol of the old United Brethren Church, in which young Ken had been raised. This family tie of mutual respect and affection stood as a reminder that, in spite of the Judge's discomfort with religious ceremony which he shared with his brothers, God was in charge of the universe.

During World War II, Judge Landis, known publicly as the uncompromising baseball czar, demonstrated among family members his strong suit as a humanitarian. The advent of this great conflict confronted him with a new challenge in his late seventies --

he wanted passionately to live at least until an Allied victory and to learn that his beloved "soldiers" had come home safely. Landis proceeded to fight the war with the only instrument available to him -- writing letters in his patented, provocative style . . . spiced with humor and occasional vitriol, but always with affection.

With the onset of America's involvement in the war, the Judge again expressed concern for the military services and, in particular, for his family's growing participation in it. He had long felt deeply about his father's role in the Civil War and his son Reed's record in World War I. Now, Reed joined the Army Air Corps with the rank of colonel.

As the war situation began to involve his relatives, the Judge expanded his horizons. In addition to keeping a firm hand on baseball's tiller, he started a systematic program of writing to grandsons, nephews, nieces, and grandnephews in uniform, to reach full-scale in 1943 and 1944. At the same time, he would became a one-man communications center to spread the latest word about those in uniform to others in service, Uncle Lute, and to all concerned nieces, cousins, and in-laws.

The Judge's consultation with Rev. Kumler remained a top priority in 1942 as the list of wartime family correspondents started to grow. The pioneer among those entering active duty was grandson Bill Phillips. At the same time, grandson Keehn Landis at Princeton University enlisted in the Army Air Corps Reserve. And the Judge's strategic cohort, nephew Colonel John Landis, finally managed to get assigned to the war zone.

The Logansport branch of Landises, children of Kenesaw's late brother Frederick, also suited up in 1942. Nephew Fred was accepted by naval intelligence for imminent active duty; nephew Charles at DePauw University, enlisted in the Navy for deck officer training; nieces Betsy and Frances Katharine entered Navy training for WAVE officers; and nephew Lincoln became a cadet at the US Military Academy. The Judge accorded his "cadet nephew" at West Point the same attention that he offered his kinfolk on active duty. Kenesaw II, sidelined by the effects of his extended bout with tuberculosis, remained on the home front.

Kenesaw found a great measure of pride in the enlistment of grandson Bill Phillips in the Navy, the first family member to sign up for military duty following Pearl Harbor. He applied his memory of a similar atmosphere involving his son Reed on the occasion of World War I when he wrote to Bill: "I am hoping that your barracks are fit for the housing of human beings, which they were not 25 years ago in many cases." [168]

The Commissioner, at 75, continued to plan a get-together with Uncle Lute, at 92, and mixed such diverse thoughts as the old religious tie through the United Brethren Church and tough retribution for German and Japanese leaders. This was a reminder of Kenesaw's description of the Kaiser's "malice and insanity" in his "dream for world empire." [169]

Mayor Kelly of Chicago invited Kenesaw to serve on the committee for President Roosevelt's "Total War Day" celebration, featuring a large parade and other activities in support of veterans on April 6. [170]

Correspondence between the septuagenarian Commissioner-nonagenarian United Brethren preacher accelerated when the younger proposed a high-profile family reunion on the occasion of a major-league event honoring Americans in uniform: "I want you to organize your outfit . . . for a cruise to Cleveland for the All-Star Game July 7 or 8." [171] He then got down to details about the servicemen's All-Star extravaganza in Cleveland.: "As I told you in a previous letter, I am eating and sleeping you and your outfit and transporting you and that outfit out to and into the ball park and back to the hotel." [172] Then he emphasized his feelings about the future: "I want to live long enough to have a reunion with you when we can discuss the death penalties that have been carried out against the fellows responsible for present-day conditions on this earth." [173]

As if to advance the patriotic spirit of the President's "Green Light" letter six months earlier, Kenesaw was instrumental in arranging a special attraction to follow the 1942 All-Star game between the American and National Leagues. The successful event featured the winning All-Star team in a contest with players selected from the Armed Services. From Kenesaw's and Lute's vantage point, the Cleveland All-Star game venture was a big success, resulting in a newspaper article featuring the reunion of uncle and nephew. [174]

Kenesaw acknowledged a newsy telegram from his namesake Kenesaw II in Logansport: "It was bully to hear that Fred had arrived (on assignment as U. S. Navy seaman in England in 1942). I also got Lincoln's wire (about his appointment to West

Point) and it puffed me up big. Your outfit is entitled to feel pretty big about your contribution to this present debate." [175]

Kenesaw, having already offered his nephew tips on how to weather the rigors of plebe life at the Military Academy, failed to provide the magic which would have allowed the cadet to accept Uncle Squire's invitation to the World Series. The Judge then philosophized about how family members were being affected by the war: "I am sorry you can't come to New York the first week of October for a day. However, you have gotten mixed up with a hard-boiled bunch . . . Why any of you ever should get mixed up with the damned thing is utterly beyond my comprehension." [176]

Thinking of brother Fred's other offspring, the Judge now initiated correspondence with his 25-year-old niece Betsy who had left her job as dean of girls at Logansport High School to join the United States Naval Reserve on active duty. His humor was clear in alleging that he was not making a gift to her, but merely re-paying a loan she made to him. In a few months, he found himself sending a similar greeting to niece Frances Katharine, who followed in her sister's footsteps into the Navy. At this point, Betsy had entered the first WAVE officer training class, which was held at Smith College, Northampton, Massachusetts: "I am sending you herewith a check for $37.50, being the amount of the loan I negotiated from you at the LaSalle Street Station the day you departed for the wars. You put this where it will some day be available to you in connection with something that will be of real interest or concern to you." [177]

The Judge, with his new emphasis upon writing to relatives in uniform, did not neglect his regular correspondence with Reverend Kumler. Here he mixed the mundane with an update on a nephew in the Navy: "I am enclosing letter just received from Fred's boy Fred, who went through here about two months ago on his way to serve in the Navy as a bluejacket. Please return it when you have read it." [178]

The World Series in 1940 was memorable indeed, with the St. Louis Cardinals triumphant over the favored New York Yankees by coming back from an initial loss to take four straight. The event enabled the Judge to write to the United Services Organization (USO) a handsome check.

The Judge penned a detailed message to Uncle Lute, offering a full account of the whereabouts of the Logansport Landises in the current war situation and concluded: "While Fred

281

(his younger brother who died in 1934) went out some years before this whole thing broke, his progeny is doing pretty well." Then he closed with an assessment of pluses and minuses regarding our conduct of the war: "I am scared stiff about the Solomon Islands thing. I have just got a feeling that one of these days we are going to get bad news. There is one thing in this whole situation that I want to get to you: Although we have been over a hard road, beginning with that unforgivable catastrophe at Pearl Harbor, the private, both doughboy and bluejacket, apparently has measured up to the highest standards. The trouble seems to have been bad luck in the selection of official personnel at the top." [179]

Joshing from his 76-year-old vantage point with his crony, Rev. Kumler at 93, was one of the highlights of his last years. From his sick bed, the Judge acknowledged Lute's message and offered tongue-in-cheek medical advice to his elder of 18 years: "Your telegram came to me at the Presbyterian Hospital, where they were once more plowing through my old prostate. If you have it in mind to have any such thing done to you don't put it off until you get along in years, but take the bull by the horns, and let the worst come at once." [180]

1943

A number of outstanding players had begun to leave their teams to join the Armed Forces, raising the question of whether Baseball would be seriously affected during the war period. Of course, the Game, lacking the lustre of such stars as Hank Greenberg, Ted Williams, Bob Feller, and Joe DiMaggio, continued to serve as a source of popular diversion from the country's heavy involvement in war-related activities. A modern-times baseball analyst noted the impact on the Game from military service and also the major contribution the Game was making for the war effort. [181]

In 1943, the Judge's agenda of boosting the morale of relatives in uniform and his advancing age did not deter him from giving full attention to baseball matters. In fact, the year proved memorable for decisive actions Landis took at its beginning and end, which, respectively, affected the travel of all ball clubs and reinforced the integrity of the Game. In January, the Judge convened an "emergency joint session" of the major leagues described at the time as "baseball's most important" since Kenesaw became commissioner following the 1919 Black Sox scandal. [182] The meeting produced limits on travel patterns of the major league teams, in particular, their regular winter training trips to Florida and California. The "Eastman-Landis line," based on Landis' earlier consultation in Washington with Joseph Eastman, Director of the Office of Defense Transportation, prescribed that such travel be kept east of the Mississippi River and north of the Ohio and Potomac Rivers.

If 1943 was a memorable year in baseball, it also gave new impetus to Landis' personal agenda of monitoring the actions of family members in the Armed Forces. Joining the ranks of those in active service were the two grandsons of Kenesaw's late, older brother Dr. John Landis, and the Judge corresponded with these grandnephews, Ira and John Holden. Ira, although dislectic, had become a pilot at age 16 and joined the Army Air Corps, training pilots at Bemidji, Minnesota. John enlisted at Cornell in Naval Reserve officers training and after graduation entered naval officers' training at Notre Dame.

A few weeks later, Kenesaw wrote to Lincoln while planning a trip to New York with granddaughters Susanne and Jodie, invited nephew Charles stationed at Norfolk to a get-together. His invitation was to attend a mini-reunion, apparently not realizing the constraints imposed upon plebes by the West Point system: "Your brother Charley will drop in to see your Aunt Winifred and your cousins Susanne and Jodie at the Roosevelt Hotel in New York on his way from West Point to Norfolk. It would be a great delight to us if you could, without calling off the war, drop in too." [183]

The Judge, thinking of his son Reed's record in the first World War, had special reason to support his grandson Keehn in flight training. To him, who would soon become a fighter pilot in Europe, the Baseball Commissioner offered several messages from the home front. In one such letter, he mentioned an event that had occurred during World War I, when Keehn's father Reed, now Chief of Staff at Stout Field, Chicago as a colonel, had been set to depart for Europe in World War I. On that occasion, there was a royal celebration in the social whirl of New York City, attending Reed's send-off to join a flying squadron in France. It seemed that following a proper dinner uptown, Reed brought "the whole damned Army with him" and then moved out "on the town," running up a sizeable expense in his trail for the Judge to pick up. [184]

Writing again to grandson Keehn, aviation cadet (A.C.) in Texas, the Judge offered a critique of military abbreviations: "What the hellitis that all those A's and C's mean -- that is, unless it is a military secret?" and went on to criticize the woeful turnout of one-third of registered voters in the Chicago elections: "Possibly this 600,000 deficit was for the purpose of inspiring the fellow out there in New Guinea crawling through the jungle to greater heights of heroism." [185]

Soon after Kenesaw's Regular Army nephew, Colonel John, was sent overseas, the Judge sent him reassuring words about the Colonel's family and a report about the latest kinfolk to wear the uniform, following his attendance at the recent wedding of his Navy niece. He went on to reflect skepticism that women in their early 20's were ready to be naval officers: "Your cousin Betsy Landis of the WAVES got married. Her little sister Katharine is also in the WAVES and they apparently are proud of it." (After the Judge's death, Lieutenant Katharine was the only WAVE officer to be recommended by the Chief of Naval Operations for the Bronze Star for "Communications intelligence duties in active war zones.") [186]

A follow-up letter to his Regular Army nephew, Colonel John, now overseas, touched upon military aspects of Baseball business and expressed an interest in the impending enlistment in the Army of the Colonel's son Charley (the Judge's great-nephew): "I just got in from the All-Star Game at Philadelphia. It was a very, very interesting affair, and out of it we got a little over $90,000 for balls and bats for service use, which doesn't give me any grief . . . I have been expecting to hear from your Charley. If I can't get him in here, I will go out to his headquarters." [187]

In two weeks, Uncle Lute acknowledged Kenesaw's gift of an Air Corps documentary "30 seconds over Tokio," and Kenesaw received a letter from his nephew Charley (Fred's boy), serving on the destroyer *Bristol*. [188] Then, he added: "I feel no account, with these little bits of fellows fighting my war." [189] The Judge took note of his nephew Ensign Charley's participation in the Sicilian campaign, in a letter to his namesake nephew, Bilo (Kenesaw II), adding: "Just reflect a bit, Charley in that thing and your other brothers and sisters where they have been and are -- don't it beat hell? [190]

To keep the information flowing from the war zone, the Judge did his bit by updating nephew Ensign Charles, on duty on a destroyer in the Mediterranean. He spoke of the upcoming World Series, outlined his plan to send Major League baseball teams overseas to bolster the troops' morale, and provided the latest news about Charles' immediate family. [191]

The Judge received a telegram from his namesake nephew that Ensign Charles' destroyer was sunk in the Mediterranean Sea, and information was not available as to casualties and possible survivors. This prompted Kenesaw to write to the Navy, requesting information about "what happened to the officers and crew" and adding: "If under Naval procedure you are not at liberty to do this, I will understand." [192]

And so it fell upon him, after the World Series, to send disturbing news about this nephew to 94-year-old Uncle Lute: "Fred's (late brother of the Judge) boy Kenesaw telephoned me yesterday from Logansport that the *USS. Bristol* had gone down in the Mediterranean, with no report as yet of what happened to the men on board. Fred's boy Charley was on that ship when last heard from in September. The Navy communiqué stated no report of casualties had been received. Of course we are hoping." [193]

At last, the Judge had good news to distribute to kinfolk about his nephew Ensign Charley's good fortune following the loss of his ship, in this case to niece Edith, wife of Colonel John: "I have a telegram this morning from Kenesaw (the Judge's nephew) at Logansport -- 'Have cable from Charles that he is all right.'" [194] The Judge promptly wrote his lucky nephew a brief letter: "I infer you are still to be addressed in care of the old *Bristol*. It is a grief to think of her fate, but a great, great joy to reflect upon your present status. I am, therefore, sending the enclosed to you as a sort of Christmas reminder." [195]

In November, a few weeks after the Judge was seeking details about the sinking of his nephew's destroyer, the *USS Bristol*, and keeping relatives informed, he took, in the words of one scribe, "the most drastic step aging (at 77) Kenesaw Mountain Landis had had to take in his 23 years as autocrat of baseball." Referring to his action barring Philadelphia Phillies' owner William D. Cox from baseball for life because of gambling, the sports writer concluded: "The lank-haired, obtrusively autocratic old Federal Judge had been put in his job to squash just that kind of thing." [196]

Closing out correspondence for the year, the Judge again wrote Reverend Kumler, acknowledging an early Christmas card, and saying again: "I wish you were my next-door neighbor." [197] Finally, he wrote a line to his grandson Keehn: "To you in this war and after it -- whatever there is worthwhile. That is what I wish for you." [198]

1944

John Holden, Kenesaw's great-nephew (brother John's grandson), became an ensign and was aboard a landing ship tank (LST) when General MacArthur landed at Lingayen Gulf in the Philippines. The Judge's attention to family members in the Services continued its momentum.

Writing to his grandson Keehn, apparently not keeping the Judge well informed while in pilot training before an assignment overseas: "I haven't heard a word from you since you took Tallahassee. I suppose you still got it, although as to this I am dependent entirely upon my blind faith in your ability not only to take it but to hold it." [199]

From Great Lakes Naval Training Center, the Judge's other grandson Bill Phillips reported to a US Navy air base. Kenesaw had some questions for his young fishing buddy, with whom he had exchanged naval fundamentals during Bill's teenage summers at Burt Lake, Michigan: "We had one heluva time trying to figure out what probably had become of you . . . Such was my virgin confidence in the veracity of the Navy, to say nothing of my reliance upon the integrity of my own flesh and blood, that you may imagine the shock it gave me when Tuesday, Wednesday and Thursday went by and 'nothing doing.' All I can figure out is that you must have run into a blond." [200] Bill's grandfather fired off another morale-booster a few days later: "Tonight we will have a big time -- a 4-rib roast of beef, with potatoes whole. The only fly in the ointment will be that you won't be there. However, my belief is you have got the best of it . . . Let me know if anything comes along in the way of intelligence. I sometimes have to move about and I would like definite dope on your whereabouts whenever I can get it." [201]

One of the early letters sent by the Judge to his great-nephew Charles, the son of Colonel John Landis, included a wrap-up of a visit by Charles' family to Chicago. Then he gently admonished the young infantryman about the importance of writing letters: "Will you please have somebody let me know whether it is a fact that it has been proposed that the Army teach corporals how to write? I make this inquiry because a lot of damned rumors get out, and it is just as well to choke them off. Luck to you." [202]

The Judge commented favorably after seeing a photo of his grandson Bill's assigned ship, and he took the opportunity to reminisce again about their old fishing days and even to look for a reunion in the near future: "I saw a picture of that boat. She is a peach. I would like to see her spin in obedience to my orders. If you and I had her on the inland route, what a performance she would put up. Maybe we would have to add a foot or two to the channel between Burt Lake and Indian River, but that would be a trivial thing if we only had her up there. Well, old hoss, I am saving the bottle "against the day" when you get back." [203]

The Judge succeeded in spurring his young great-nephew Charley, an infantryman, to do his part in maintaining communication with family members, namely, with the Commissioner of Baseball. In his dutiful way, the Judge quickly responded to a letter from his youngest serviceman: "Don't worry about thinking of anything to write about -- you get along without the slightest difficulty. When the spell moves you, put your old fanny down at the desk, and don't put a brake on the pen." Then Kenesaw wrote that he had expected a visit from Charley and had made appropriate plans: "I arranged for you to come to the Ambassador hotel from the airport, where I had fixed it up for you to have a bed to sleep in and some side pork and hen fruit for breakfast. Whenever you are to come this way, let me know in advance, so I can make arrangements to sleep you." He also added family news about young Charley's cousins: "My grandson, Bill Phillips, is on a Pacific carrier. My other grandson, Keehn Landis, is somewhere toward being headed for overseas. My brother's boy, Charley, who got that destroyer shot out from under him off the African coast, is finishing up some sort of training in the east somewhere and is headed for duty on the *Wisconsin*. The rest of them about where they have been." [204]

287

Kenesaw wrote to Charley, awaiting assignment to the battleship *USS Wisconsin*: "I got your note. It's a funny thing that a fellow has got to be putting his time in at the things you are working on, all because a bunch of lousy bastards elsewhere got into a fight. I am hoping to live long enough to have you fellows with me at a celebration after the damned thing's over. Sometimes I fear that is a vain hope, but I am living by it and for it just the same." [205]

Kenesaw kept track of grandson Bill Phillips, who had headed out on his carrier to the Pacific and again made a promise to meet him royally when the war will be over: "I am saving a bottle of Old Grandad to enable you and me to properly celebrate your arrival when you come back." [206]

Kenesaw invited one of his Navy niece-lieutenants to visit his and Winifred's recently-rented home in suburban Chicago: "Betsy Darling . . . Now, honey chile, when you get within my territory, just blow in here, climb up on my back and I will piggyback you out to Glencoe." [207]

Kenesaw penned his Navy grandson Bill at sea on the *Yorktown* aircraft carrier, an allegory about his difficulties with suburban farming. In a baseball setting, God appeared as the pitcher and the Judge was at the plate, having a tough time getting a hit. He also added good words about his loyal chauffer: "Dear Bill . . . I wish you were within reach . . . Leonard Edwards is doing full time duty. He often speaks of you, and one of these days you should drop him a note. He considers that he belongs to your outfit. When you write to him tell him to remember you to grandmother and me. You know he is no slacker -- he was in the first war, in the machine-gun outfit, and became a commissioned officer, although he went in as a draftee." [208]

With young great-nephew Charles in the infantry in France shortly after the Normandy invasion, Kenesaw looked forward to a happy reunion after victory is achieved. The major operation just past, Kenesaw wrote: "counts for a bigger and blacker stallion for you to ride down the avenue at the head of the parade, with me sitting on the curb giving you a salute when the war is over." [209]

The Judge, now 77, noted that Colonel a.k.a. "Lieutenant" John's wife Edith and their two daughters Mary and Lorna (great-nephew Charley's sisters) paid him a visit: "Three very beautiful women left here yesterday morning. If you should ever make up your mind you don't like them, or one or two of them, just give them a one-way ticket to my establishment. I will take them in." He added the latest on his grandsons' service and was worried about John's soldier son: "Not much new here, except that Susanne's boy, Bill, apparently has seen a little action in the Mariannas, which is all to the good. Reed's boy, Keehn, is over in England, as we make it out, about ready (if not already) to see some real service. I am wondering, with a great deal of anxiety, as to (great-nephew) Charley's destination. That is much in my mind." [210]

In a letter to Uncle Lute, his preacher-confidant, Kenesaw seemed to reduce his forebears' Christian belief to the Old Testament's "an eye for an eye" as far as dealing with warlords after the present conflict is over: "I think a little bit of pure and undefiled 'united brethren doctrine' applied to those birds Hitler and Togo would ease up all of us. When it's going to come I don't know, but I'm still living in the hope of that reunion at your house. And I believe we are going to get it, 'durned' if I don't." [211]

The Judge attended his last All-Star game when he went to Pittsburgh for the annual game July 11th. Noting a lack of press coverage, Uncle Lute showed some concern about the possibility that Kenesaw had not in fact attended this annual, spectacular game and that his letter-writing had dropped off. As usual, he remarked "We'd welcome family reunion any time. Lovingly," [212] He apparently did not receive the Judge's reply.

As a plebe at West Point, this author had relished the Commissioner's moral support and particularly his description of upper-class hazing as the work of "pismires." Now, on July 13th, with the final year just ahead, came the opportunity to visit "Uncle Squire" in Chicago. [213] Files show that the next day the Judge resumed his letter-writing to grandson Keehn, now a fighter pilot flying from England and filled him in on his cousins: "Lincoln (Fred's youngest boy) was in with us. He came up yesterday afternoon from Logansport, had dinner and went back on the 11:30 train last night. His brother, Charley, who, you will remember, had a destroyer shot out from under him in the Mediterranean area last winter, is at sea on a battle wagon. The address of your cousin Fred, of Logansport, is enclosed." The Judge added that he wanted Keehn to "find out where this bird is located in England" and added his hope that his grandson might meet up with Fred, pointing out: "The last I got from or about him was that he was hooked up with the amphibian outfit." [214]

On the same day, the Commissioner dashed off a letter to his (Lieutenant Charles) nephew aboard the battleship *Wisconsin* soon to leave for duty in the Pacific with nitty gritty news: "Lincoln goes back to West Point or some other place ordered by the Army, in five days. From what I inferred from his conversation, he is laying for his four brothers and sisters to lay claim that the Navy had something to do with winning this war. It will be good to get you in the neighborhood again. Meanwhile, all luck." [215]

As the infirmaties of age slowed him down, the Judge remained a self-appointed, aging watchman over the status of all his relatives in the service during World War II. At 77, he kept on spreading the word to keep home-front morale at a high level. A good example of this effort was his final letter to his favorite pen pal, a few weeks shy of 95:

> I have a note from my son Reed's boy, Keehn, which shows that he is in it in Lombardy, astride a fighter plane. My brother Fred's boy, Fred, is doing something connected with the amphibious forces. A letter from my grandson, Bill, from the carrier *Yorktown* out in the Pacific where things are going on, closing with these words: "This ship don't take any guff from anybody."
> Your great grandnephew Charley (Fred's boy) is aboard the *Wisconsin*, apparently on her way to the Pacific from the east Atlantic waters. In other words, the family is scattered all over the area, and I am expecting almost any day to see that they have cracked down on you. Hold everything! One of these days we will get together for a reunion -- if not a cursing bee.
> Always yours, KML [216]

In August, the Judge, as one of his last formal acts in Baseball, named distinguished officials and baseball writers to an "Old Timers' committee" to choose exceptional Baseball individuals to honor by adding them to the Hall of Fame at Cooperstown.

In the Judge's final months, he wrote to Charles, his "infantry grandnephew," who was seriously wounded after the invasion of Normandy. Back to his personal agenda -- disturbing news that his young infantryman grandnephew Charley had become the latest casualty shook the Judge and stirred him to boost some family morale: "Dear Corporal . . . Your father (Colonel John

Landis) sent me a copy of your letter to your mother, written from the hospital. It does beat hell! I wish I was close by so that as you progressed I could piggy-back you to wherever it is that a convalescent vet wants to be piggy-backed to. It would be good just to have a session with you.   Everything worth while. Yours, KML" [217]

Not knowing where grandson Bill Phillips flat-top, the *Yorktown*, was located in the Pacific, Kenesaw kept on writing with news from the home front, about his recent move from a hotel residence to the house near Bill's parents.   He expressed his frustration: "We are busy trying to figure out whatever the hellitis you call the place where a feller is at when you don't know where he is at . . ." [218]

The Judge received worrisome battlefield news from his nephew, Colonel John Landis, which he forwarded to his fighter-pilot grandson Keehn based in England: "His boy (great-nephew) Charley, your cousin, is in a hospital in England. He doesn't tell me where the hospital is located, but Charley's address is enclosed." Determining Corporal Charley's need for a prompt visit by family members, Kenesaw sought to arrange a reunion of overseas family servicemen at the bedside of his great-nephew by including in his letter some background information: "I have a letter from your cousin Fred Landis, of the Navy, who is in England somewhere, and who tells me he is looking you up and hopes to get you and Charley and himself into a conference. I am passing this on so that, among you, you can call off the war long enough to get together." He then followed with his own assessment of the over-all war situation: "Nothing new here except that Hitler must have lost three wheel-barrow loads of balls in the last 72 hours -- which is quite a batch of balls for even Hitler to lose."   Then, the Judge brought grandson Keehn up-to-date on two family warriors: "Your cousin, my brother Fred's boy, Charley, who was on a tin can that attracted a submarine six or eight months ago, is back at sea, aboard a warship.   Bill (KML's other grandson Bill Phillips) is back here for ten days' leave from the Pacific, where he has been with a flat-top."   Finally, he expressed his belief that there is undue emphasis upon censorship of correspondence: "These damned fellers that read these letters before you get a chance to look at them would raise hell with me if I told you the names of any of these boats, in spite of the fact that I think they are all cock-eyed in affecting a horror of that sort of thing being done, just plain cock-eyed. Luck." [219]

In a final letter to his fighter pilot, grandson Keehn, the Judge engaged in healthy introspection and longing for the end of the war. He added a note of weariness: "I have had great joy reading the accounts of what you fellows have been doing. The deadest place in the world is this territory, where the only thing I can find to do is to read and re-read, and listen and keep on listening to what is written and talked about your progress." Then, he added a joyful note: "I am about to put out my advertisement for that great big black stallion for you to ride at the head of the parade when the gang comes back after the job is done." [220]

One of the Judge's last efforts to boost a soldier's morale appeared in a letter he wrote shortly before entering the hospital for the last time. Writing to his "battleship nephew (Lieutenant Charles)," he showed growing impatience in arranging an overseas reunion for his "infantry-great-nephew". The Judge's final letter to his Lieutenant Charley showed his keen interest in at least five family members in uniform. It also reflected KML's impatience with what he probably felt was too little effort by his military folks to get to the bedside of Corporal Charley because he now upgraded his earlier "suggestion" for such a visit to a "directive": "I am writing this merely . . . to tell you that if you get within reach of England . . . I want you to contact with your cousin Keehn and your brother Fred. Do this without delay, even if it's necessary to call off the war. I want one of you fellows to get to the hospital where little Charley is, so you can write me just what happened to him and how he is." [221]

If at this late time in the Judge's life he was feeling unwell, he didn't show it in his wide-ranging summary of what many of "his boys and girls" are doing in the war. He diligently kept in touch, answering all letters promptly, even to his last weeks, showing great concern and affection for his family. His final letter to Uncle Lute summed up all family members fighting the war overseas and ended with: "I am still fighting the war here. I don't mind whispering into your ear that this is not much of a place for a grown-up man to be putting in his time in the year 1944, when everything is being torn to pieces." [222]

Kenesaw's health soon put him into the hospital the first week of October, causing him to miss his first World Series game since he had become Commissioner in January, 1921. Baseball's League officials met in mid-November and recommended extension of the Judge's tenure, which would run out in January 1946, to an additional seven-year term.

The Judge's illness prevented him from going to the polls on Election Day in November. One of the Judge's granddaughters (granddaughter Jodie Phillips) recalled witnessing a verbal agreement he made with Winifred that since he would not be voting, his wife, who held opposing political sentiments, would abstain from doing so. Thus, his inability to get out to vote for Republican presidential nominee Dewey wouldn't help Democrat Franklin Roosevelt, who was in the Kenesaw's doghouse. Yet, young Jodie Phillips came away with the impression that the Judge, even in his weak condition, remained unconvinced that Winifred would keep her side of the bargain on this vital matter.[223]

With his health taking a decisive downturn, Judge Landis wrote a final letter to his wounded infantry corporal grandnephew Charley: "Luck to you, ole hoss, in every department of activity. It does beat hell how long it takes a letter to get from me to you and from you to me. I should think the damned fellows could call off the war long enough to let our mail get through . . . Affection to you, ole hoss--much affection--and when you get back there is a bit of "Old Granddad" you and I will give serious consideration to." [224]

Kenesaw Mountain Landis, American czar, entered the hospital the following week and died in November 1944, five days into his 78th year. He had been a young State Department aide, a corporation attorney, federal judge, and baseball's first commissioner. He was also a nephew, an uncle, a grandfather, and a great-uncle [225] and his last action was to carry out a personal agenda as his great-nephew's friend.

To the Judge, this wounded soldier typified America's youth who went to war solely because of German and Japanese aggression, and he felt a sense of despair because of his own inability to control such fateful events. The aging "czar of baseball" was not in charge of this crisis and could only conclude, as at his brother Fred's death ten years earlier: "It makes no sense at all, not a damned bit." But he chose to adopt a positive spin on his relatives' role in the war, displaying deep affection and, in the case of Corporal Landis, offering to become young Charley's best pal.

Chapter 1 Notes

1. Savoyard, "The Brothers Landis", *Pittsburgh Times*, February 26, 1906.
2. *Deed L2 348*, March 16, 1795: *Joseph Showalter to Frederick Landis & 9 other trustees for place of worship and burial* and Richard S. MacNamee, "Pictures from Memory Wall," *Notes on Charlestown Township, Chester County*, 54; Chester County (PA) Historical Society, research by Susanna Marion Baum, 7th-generation descendant of progenitor, Frederick Landis.
3. Oscar Kuhns, *German and Swiss Settlements of Colonial Pennsylvania*, (Ann Arbor, MI: Gryphon Books, 1971), 172-173.
4. John A. Hostetler, *Hutterite Society,* (Baltimore: Johns Hopkins University Press, 1974), 7.
5. John Dillenberger and Claude Welch, *Protestant Christianity*, (New York: Charles Scribner's Sons, 1954), 63.
6. The author consulted Landis Family Reunion reports, Mennonite census reports, emigration reports, and Mennonite history publications, Landis Family Archives [LFA].
7. "Who are the Mennonites" brochure, Germantown (Philadelphia) Information Center, 1995.
8. "Brief Sketch of the Landeses," *Third Landis Family Reunion* August 18, 1913, (Collegeville, PA: Ursinus College, 1913), 1. Also H. Frank Eshleman, *Annals of the Pioneer Swiss and Palatine Mennonites of Lancaster County and Other Early Germans of Eastern Pennsylvania*, (Baltimore: Genealogical Publishing Co., 1969), 75-76.
9. *"Pennsylvania Dutch" and Other Essays* (Philadelphia: Lippincott and Co., 1882), 78.
10. In the judgement of Martin Luther, Ulrich Zwingli, and John Calvin, Anabaptism was "a revolt." Hostetler, 6-7.
11. "The Hirzel Chart," *Report of the 31st Reunion of the Landis-Landes Families* August 19, 1950, (Bethlehem, PA: Times Publishing Company, 1952), 25-27.
12. Sources included: Family reunion reports, letters from Henry Landis from Switzerland in 1913, Mennonite journals, and document from Mannheim, 1983, LFA.
13. D. H. Landis, "Landis Connection with Switzerland," *Bi-centennial of First Landis Settlement in Lancaster Co. and Seventh Annual Landis Family Reunion* August 4, 1917, (Lititz, PA: Executive Committee of the Landis Family Reunion, 1917), 5.
14. *"Swiss Exiles," "Pennsylvania Dutch" and Other Essays*, (Philadelphia: Lippincott and Co., 1882), 87.
15. Frank Diffendorfer, *German Immigration into Pennsylvania Through the Port of Philadelphia from 1700 to 1775*, (Baltimore: Genealogical Publishing Co., 1979), 17.

16. Interview with Susanna Marion Baum.
17. *"Pennsylvania Dutch" and Other Essays*, 89.
18. View of Susanna Marion Baum based on descriptive accounts in Timothy Rice, *Deep Run Mennonite Church East: A 250 Year Pilgrimage 1746-1996*, (Morgantown, PA: Masthof Press, 1996), 20.
19. Charles W. and Mary S. Landis, *Landis Family Genealogy*, Section 1, 1; also Hermann & Gertrud Guth & J. Lemar & Lois Ann Mast *Palatine Mennnonite Census Lists 1664-1793*, (Elverson, PA: Mennonite Family History, 1987), 39.
20. Rudolph Landes to Jacob Rupp, April 13, 1787, published in J.S. Hartzler and Daniel Kauffman, *Mennonite Church History*, (Scottdale, PA: Mennonite Book and Tract Society, 1905) 401-405; as cited in Don Yoder, editor, "Notes and Documents: Eighteenth-Century Letters from Germany," Don Yoder, editor, *Rhineland Emigrants Lists of German Settlers in Colonial America*,(Baltimore: Genealogical Publishing Co., 1981), 120-121.
21. The author traveled to Gau Heppenheim in July 2001, visited the old church and the home of the Henrich Landes family, and gained details of Landis genealogy from his "Cousin" Hermann Scholl of the Heppenheim Village Council.
22. "The German Palatinate," *Mennonite Encyclopedia*, (Scottdale, PA: Mennonite Publishing House, 1957) 1-10.
23. Charles W. and Mary S. Landis, Section 1, 1; also Werner Hacker, *Auswanderungen aus Rheinpfalz und Saarland im 18. Jahrhundert [Emigrants from Rhenish Palatinate and Saar Region in the 18th-Century,]* (Stuttgart: Theiss Verlag, 1988) 510. Bucks County (PA) Historical Society.
24. Israel D. Rupp, *Thirty Thousand Names of Immigrants*, (Baltimore: Genealogical Publishing Co., 1965), 212-213.
25. Henrich was reported to be in Blooming Glen (later Perkasie), just north of Philadelphia December 1, 1749. *Report of the 33rd Reunion of the Landis-Landes Families* August 16, 1952,, (Allentown, PA: H. Ray Haas and Co., 1954), 52.
26. Bucks County (PA) Courthouse Office of *Deeds, Book 10*, Doylestown, PA, 537-538; also *1790 Census of Bucks County*, Bucks County Historical Society; Thomas G. Myers, *A Record of the Descendants of David Kulp of Bedminster, Bucks County PA*, (Harleysville, PA: Mennonite Library and Archives, 1990), 1; and Timothy Rice, 5.
27. Timothy Rice, Appendix A, 2-3.
28. Kuhns, 172-173.
29. *Letter of Administration granted to Philip Landis*, February 1, 1803 from title search by Susanna Marion Baum at Chester County (PA) Historical Society; also Thomas G. Myers, *A Record of the*

Descendants of David Kulp of Bedminster, Bucks County PA, (Harleysville, PA: Mennonite Library and Archives, 1990), 1-3; Research and evaluation by Susanna Marion Baum.
30. *Deed V103*, Chester County archives, West Chester, PA courthouse. Research by Susanna Marion Baum.
31. Timothy Rice, 8.
32. Kuhns, 172-173.
33. Frederick Landis, *The Hoosier Editor*, July 1934. [LFA].
34. Timothy Rice, 8-9.
35. Ibid.
36. Chester County archives researched by Susanna Marion Baum.
37. Interview with Susanna Marion Baum.
38. Literature provided at "Waynesborough," acquisition by and interview with Susanna Marion Baum.
39. Abraham H. Landis, article in *Dayton Telegraph*, May, 1874.
40. J. S. Hartzler and Daniel Kauffman, 401-405.
41. Research made and photo taken by Susanna Marion Baum.
42. Names of the Mennonite settlers as mentioned in *Deed L2 348*, March 16, 1795 *Joseph Showalter to Frederick Landis & 9 other trustees for place of worship and burial*: Mathias Pennepacker, Jacob Johnson, Christian Whistler, Christian Clemens, George Clemens, Frederick Landis, Henry Fox, Abraham Whistler, and Abraham Holderman. Chester County (PA) Historical Society, research by Susanna Marion Baum.
43. General Wayne's name appears in many towns and counties. Research by Susanna Marion Baum.
44. A. H. Landis, Logansport, to son Charles at Wabash College, May 24, 1881, LFA.
45. Charles H. Kumler note forwarded October 23, 1937 to Kenesaw by Dayton friend, Albert Scharrer. LFA.
46. This manuscript encompasses the male lineage only of the Landis and Kumler ancestry.
47. Swiss Kumlers, descendants of French Huguenots, were members of the Swiss Reformed Church. N. D. Kumler, *Kumler Family Genealogy* and Charles and Mary Landis, *Landis Family Genealogy*.
48. Faust and Brumbaugh, *Lists of Swiss Emigrants in the Eighteenth Century to the American Colonies*, (Baltimore: Genealogical Publishing Co., 1972), 135-141. The author visited Maisprach in 2001 but was unable to find descendants of the Kumler family, nor a home, nor tombstones in the village cemetery that bore "a Kumler connection." These facts suggest that, unlike the Landises of Hirzel, the Swiss Kumlers of Maisprach were only "transient Swiss folk," whose stay in Switzerland began upon their exile from France in the

late 17th century and their departure to America some 50 years or so later. They apparently left no footprints in Maisprach.

49. Charles W. and Mary S. Landis, Section 2, 1.
50. Norman D. Kumler, *Kumler Family Genealogy.*
51. *Memoirs of the Miami Valley,* vol. 3, (Chicago: Robert O. Law Co., 1919), 402.
52. Ibid., 402-03.
53. Ibid., 403-04.
54. Daniel C. Kumler, *Memorandum Book, Going to Africa,* a daily diary, 1855 by Josiah D. Hatch. Bristol, Maine; in care of J. Perkins, NY, NY. LFA.
55. Author's note: "palaver" related to "witch palaver" conveys cruel acts of a secret society.
56. Charles H. Kumler note forwarded October 23, 1937 to Kenesaw.

Chapter 2 Notes

1. Reed Landis archives. Kennesaw or Kenesaw"? is a good question. As a term of geography, the former is accurate; Union Army of the Cumberland used the single "n;" hence Kenesaw Landis.
2. F.W. Keil, *Thirty-Fifth Ohio*, (Fort Wayne IN: Archer, Housh & Co., 1894) viii.
3. Whitelaw Reid, *Ohio in the War*, Vol. 2 (Cincinnati: Moore, Wilstach & Baldwin, 1868), 229.
4. Savoyard, "The Brothers Landis," *Pittsburgh Times*, circa 1905.
5. Daniel C. Kumler, *Memorandum Book, Going to Africa*, a diary, Landis Family Archives [LFA] included this passage:
    > Three and 1/2 million in otherwise happy America are slaves . . . belong to masters who can sell them when they will . . . God help me to labor until every yoke is removed.
6. Research indicates that Israel was a great-grandson of Abraham's Uncle Henry Landis, as cited in Charles and Mary Landis, *Landis Family Genealogy*, 11
7. The charge against Abraham's cousin Israel Landis read:
    > Donnell, Landis, and Richardson believe they are advancing the Cause of the Rebellion --they are professing Christians -- by remaining in jail among the Rebels we have had, none are more potent for evil than they. Brigadier General Ben Loan to General J. M. Schofield, March 18, 1862, *War of the Rebellion*, Series 2, vol. 1, (Washington: Government Printing Office, 1902), 272.
8. Keil, 3.
9. The regimental historian added:
    > We came not like northern men before us, to fawn upon the slave master, and weigh our words, lest we should give offense; but we were here with muskets in our hands to assert the freeman's rights. Keil, 4.
10. Ibid., 11.
11. Ibid., 102.
12. A.H. Landis, 12 miles East of Gallatin Tenn., to Daniel Kumler, Dec 3-4, 1862, LFA.
13. Keil, 103.
14. A.H. Landis to Daniel Kumler.
15. Ibid.
16. Keil, 103.
17. A.H. Landis to Daniel Kumler.
18. The historian wrote in some detail about the problem of assisting the citizenry during wartime:
    > We fed the families of Rebel soldiers, so that they could fight us with more assurance, knowing that their families were being taken

299

care of, while they were trying to shoot us. Keil, 80.
19. The early results of Civil War fighting, in the view of one writer, would prove decisive:
   The capture of Fort Donelson . . . by its moral and strategic results was one of the turning points of the war. Matthew Forney Steele, *American Campaigns* vol. 1, (Harrisburg, PA: The Telegraph Press, 1943), 167, 186.
20. Keil, 42-43.
21. Ibid., 42.
22. This was an example of successful Confederate trickery:
   One day some of our troops . . . met soldiers dressed in union blue having in their wagon two coffins . . . "union soldiers who had died in hospital" . . . a week later, we found the identical wagon . . . the fraud practiced was that the coffins contained revolvers. Keil, 44-45.
23. Unit respect for the Butler County colonel was assured because of an incident in which he refused orders to move wagons laden with stores without first unloading the supplies for his troops. Keil, 49-50.
24. Ibid., 103.
25. Ibid., 104.
26. This writer points out that much of the credit gained by Col. Morgan, as in these forays into Kentucky in December 1862, should be given to his sidekick, Lieutenant Basil Duke. Stuart Sanders, "Duke's reign of success with Morgan's raiders," *Washington Times,* July 24, 1999.
27. A.H. Landis to Daniel Kumler.
28. The historian of the 35th regiment reported this item, which was left out of official Union records:
   On the opposite side of the Cumberland River, a flock of sheep could be seen almost any day . . . It was planned to send parties across . . . The detail . . . proceeded to corral the sheep, belonging to a lady . . . she rushed into the field, flopping her dress, crying: 'Shoo shoo' . . . the sheep escaped through the intervals. Keil, 106-107.
29. Ibid., 107.
30. R. L. Mitchell, surgeon in charge, General Hospital #1, Gallatin (TN) Medical Report, April 25, 1863. LFA.
31. Certificate, General Hospital #1Gallatin (TN), May 2, 1863. LFA.
32. Keil, 107-108.
33. Robert Meiser, "Thomas shows he's no slacker in taking offensive," *Washington Times*, January 8, 2000, B3.
34. Keil, 108.
35. Ibid., 109.
36. Ibid.

37. Ibid., 110-111.
38. Ibid., 115.
39. Lack of interference by Rebel gunfire enabled the troops of the 35th to enjoy a bath while crossing. Keil, 116.
40. Ibid., 116-117.
41. A. H. Landis, Pigeon Valley, Georgia, to Mary Landis, September 14-15, 1863. LFA.
42. A. H. Landis' Report in "The Rebellion," *History of Butler County, Ohio.* (Cincinnati: Western Biographical Publishing Co., 1882), 221. LFA.
43. The 35th Regiment was directly affected by the uncertainty of supply delivery by rail. Keil, 118.
44. Keil, 118-121.
45. A. H. Landis' Report, 223.
46. F. H. Gross to Major General George H. Thomas, *War of the Rebellion*, October 11, 1863, Chattanooga, TN, Series 1, vol. 38, Part 1 Reports, (Washington: Government Printing Office, 1891), 259.
47. Keil, pp. 123-125.
48. Gross to Thomas, 260.
49. A.H. Landis to Mary Landis, September 14-15, 1863.
50. Ibid.
51. Ibid.
52. Ibid.
53. Ibid.
54. The historian described the serious lack of information available to lower levels of the Union Army. Keil, 126.
55. The author of the 35th noted: "there was no unity of purpose between Bragg and his lieutenants." Keil, 127-129.
56. Ibid., 130.
57. Meiser.
58. Keil, 131.
59. Reid, 221.
60. Lieutenant Colonel Henry V. Boynton, Report to Capt. J.R. Beatty, September 24, 1863, Chattanooga, TN, Series 1, vol. 38, Part 1 Reports, (Washington: Government Printing Office, 1891), 434-435.
61. *Civil War Veteran Tells How Landis' Father Aided Kin,* unidentified Cincinnati newspaper, circa 1924. LFA.
62. A. H. Landis' Report, 222-23.
63. Plaque at the site of "Hospitals, Left Wing, Union Army" at Chickamauga National Military Park. Photo taken by Donna B. Landis, June 1987, LFA.
64. Keil, 140.
65. Cozzens, Peter, *This Terrible Sound: The Battle of Chickamauga,* (Chicago: University of Illinois Press, 1992), 290.

66. Ibid.
67. Constantin Grebner, *We Were the Ninth: A History of the Ninth Regiment, Ohio Volunteer Infantry, April 17, 1861 to June 7, 1864, , ed.and trans. Frederic Trautmann.* Kent (OH): Ken State University Press, 1987; cited in Peter Cozzens, 150.
68. Gross to Thomas, 261.
69. Ibid.
70. Reid, 221.
71. Ibid., 221-222.
72. Boynton Report, 435.
73. *Civil War Atlas,* (West Point, NY: United States Military Academy, 1941), prepared to accompany Steele's *American Campaigns,* Map 95.
74. Gross to Thomas, 261.
75. A. H. Landis' Report, 222-223.
76. Ibid., 223.
77. Cozzens, 326, 341.
78. Furtive cooperation between "enemy soldiers" enriched the humane atmosphere:

> "Hello, Yank. Have you got any water?"
> "Yes, what's the matter with you, Johnny?"
> "I am wounded and waiting to die," answered the Rebel, who had been shot through the bowels.
> The Yank raked away the dry leaves so that the little fires that smouldered all around would not touch the Rebel, then gave him a drink. The column kept on, and the Yank was soon alone amid a score of wounded Confederates. He passed among them, giving each a drink until his canteen was empty, then started off through the brush to find his command. The dying soldier called the Yank back. He was going the wrong way; the Confederates were "thicker than hell just beyond those bushes." The Rebel pointed out the right direction, and the Yank was soon safely back with his regiment. Cozzens, 442.

79. A. H. Landis' Report, 223.
80. Cozzens, 442-443.
81. Boynton Report, 436.
82. Gross to Thomas, 263.
83. Ibid., 262.
84. Ibid.
85. Keil, 156.
86. Keil, 157-158.
87. Boynton Report, 436-437.
88. Plaque at Cloud farm hospital site, photo taken by Donna B. Landis, June 1987. LFA.
89. A. H. Landis' Report, 223.
90. Reed G. Landis' recollections of stories related by his father, Judge Kenesaw Mountain Landis. Reed Landis archives.

91. "The Battle of Chickamauga," *A Civil War Times Illustrated Special*, Cover, vol. 8, no. 2, Harrisburg, PA: Telegraph Press, May 1969, 43.

92. Plaque, "Hospitals, Left Wing; Union Army," located at the Chickamauga National Park, states:
> About 10:30 on the morning of September 20th this hospital became untenable due to the proximity of the enemy. Before its capture, as many of the wounded were evacuated via the Rossville Gap to Chattanooga by ambulance, wagon, or on foot.

93. *Memoirs of the Miami Valley*, vol. 3, (Chicago: Robert O. Law Co., 1919), 404.

94. Gross to Thomas, 263.

95. An officer of the 6th Indiana remarked:
> Things looked desperate, and I began to think of Libby {Prison}.

Cozzens, 255.

96. Abraham's after-action report provided the details of the battlefield three days after the fighting:
> Rebel dead were buried and ours unburied, and nearly all of them were stripped of their pants and shoes. Their appearance was most revolting . . . recognition was impossible . . . at least three hundred of our wounded, all suffering from the gnawings of hunger. Every last wounded Rebel had been removed. The question might be asked: why did we not have them removed to our hospital? We had no ambulance, no wagon, no vehicle of any kind, and the Rebels refused to furnish us any; in addition, our energies were taxed to their utmost. A. H. Landis' Report in "The Rebellion," 223.

97. Ibid.

98. Ibid., 224.

99. Keil, 158-160.

100. The medical mission may have continued as "of secondary importance" to the fighting mission.

101. One analysis published long after the Civil War posited the possibility:
> Had Bragg followed his victory aggressively and marched north -- Lincoln's task of saving the Union would have been made much more difficult, if not impossible. "The Battle of Chickamauga," *Civil War Times*, (Harrisburg: Telegraph Press, May 1969), 47.

102. A. H. Landis' Report, 222-224.

103. Ibid., 223.

104. Ibid.

105. Ibid., 224.

106. Ibid., 223.

107. Ibid., 224.

108. Ibid., 223-224.

109. Ibid., 224.

110. Ibid.

111. Ibid.

112. Ibid.
113. Ibid.
114. Ibid.
115. Ibid.
116 Reid, 221.
117. "The Battle of Chickamauga," 43.
118. Keil, 159-160. The regimental historian offers evidence that the pledges by Confederate generals after the battle, in Dr. Landis' words, "were not realized:"

> On the 16th of December a detachment was sent from our brigade to that battlefield to look after the bodies of comrades that fell in the engagement . . . The dead lay unburied, or partly uncovered. Nearly all bodies found were recognized by marks on clothing, or by pins with names inscribed, fastened on the blouses, or most frequently from letters found in blouse pocket. The ground on which the regiment was engaged on the 19th, was simply a stony ridge on which there was scarcely soil enough to cover the bodies of the dead . . . The rains with the decay of the bodies removed the soil and left the skeleton exposed. The blue garments showed at once the union soldier.

119. Writing to Uncle Jake Kumler, Abraham explained the challenge of obtaining a suitable box for the bodies of Sgt. Stokes and Simon Kumler:

> If I had not taken the matter in hand myself, there is no telling when those bodies would have got home . . . The undertaker told me I might go to the Capt and I prevailed upon him to give transportation . . . we concluded to put one of the bodies in the case, and the other in the box.

A.H. Landis letter, Chattanooga, to Uncle Jake Kumler, Seven Mile, Ohio, January 7, 1864, LFA.
120. Reed G. Landis' recollections of stories related by his father, Judge Kenesaw Mountain Landis, Reed Landis archives.
121. General Grant related his unintended visit to Confederate troops near Lookout Mountain:

> The sentinel on their post called out: "Turn out the guard for the commanding general," and, I believe, added, "General Grant." Their line front-faced to the north, facing me, and gave a salute, which I returned.

The Personal Memoirs of Ulyssees S. Grant, (Old Saybrook, CT: Konecky and Konecky, 1992), 362, Timothy F. Landis file.
122. General Grant wrote of the meaning of the war and its results:

> There was no time during the Rebellion when I did not think, and often say, that the South was more to be benefited than the North . . . The system of labor would have soon exhausted the soil and left the people poor. The non-slaveholders would have left the country, and the small slaveholder must have sold out to his more fortunate neighbor. Soon the slaves would have outnumbered the masters, and, not being in sympathy with them, would have risen in their might and exterminated them. The war was expensive to the South as well as to the North, both in blood and treasure, but it was worth all it cost. Ibid., 360-61.

123. A. H. Landis, elected Companion of the First Class of the Military Order of the Loyal Legion of the United States, forwarded August 1, 1889 by order of Maj. Gen. Lew Wallace,commander, LFA.

124. Keil, 158-159.

125. Col. Newell Gleason, Report near Atlanta, Georgia, Headquarters, 2nd Brigade, 3rd Division, 14th Army Corps, August 16, 1864, *War of the Rebellion*, (Government Printing Office, Washington D.C., 1891), 789.

126. Reid, 228.

127. Gleason, 789.

128. The regimental historian painted a picture of a tactical situation seemingly made-to-order for Abraham as a prime target of Rebel cannon batteries:

> The undergrowth in front of our lines was removed which exposed our works to the view of the Rebel artillery . . . The colors were in full view of the Rebel batteries on the mountain; and without notice or warning, "zip" came a shell, and struck the bank of fresh earth within four feet of the colors. The shell did not explode, and thus no one was hurt; but we got into the trench without loosing (sic) time; and for an hour or so they sent in a hot compliment of shot and shell. Keil, 193.

129. The cannonball resides in the Cass County Historical Society Museum, Logansport, Indiana.

130. Gleason, 789.

131. According to its published history, the 35th Regiment, shifted to the right, drawing Confederate fire; during this action, the regimental commander testified that Abraham Landis was severely wounded while standing at his tent in the regimental breastworks. Keil, 193-194; also sworn statement by Major Budd.

132. Details of events leading to Abraham's cannonball wound, as related by his grandson Reed:

> Dr. Landis during this battle set up his field hospital, consisting of a kitchen table and 4 or 5 strong soldiers to hold the patient while he operated, practically at the base of this hill and during the battle, the regimental colonel called out to grandfather, "Look out, Landis! Here comes a spent minie ball." The story goes on that grandfather looked up and saw that this cannonball was loping along the ground like a badly-thrown bowling ball and that it was going to miss him, so he continued his operation. Reed G. Landis' recollections of stories related by his father.

133. Testimony delivered after the war by Abraham's regimental commander in response to Dr. Landis' application for a disability pension follows:

> Before me   the undersigned authority, in and for said County, personally came Joseph L. Budd . . . was personally well acquainted with Dr. Abraham H. Landis who was Assistant Surgeon of said Regiment. That on the 22nd day of June 1864, near Kenesaw Mountain in the State

305

of Georgia the Said Dr. A.H. Landis was wounded in the following manner. The Rebels were engaged in shelling the Breastworks at the time. Affiant was about twenty feet from the Said Landis at the time of said Casualty and saw the same. Affidavit, December 5, 1865, US National Archives, Washington, D.C.

134. According to its commander, the 3rd Brigade moved from its tactical position after the Confederates withdrew, and, the following day, the brigade was ordered to Marietta to garrison the city. Gleason, 790.

135. The house in Marietta, with columns "said to be the largest residence columns in America," was the Howell home, subsequently the Sessions or Owenby home; it had been designated as "1850 Masterpiece of Southern Architecture," *Atlanta Constitution*, Gravure Pictorial Section, unknown date, 1924, courtesy of RoseMary King, Landis family descendant.

136. Keil, 196-197.

137. Ibid., 196.

138. Ibid.

139. Charles and Mary Landis, *Landis Family Genealogy.*

140. Daniel Kumler persisted in overcoming "a paper-trail" in his determination to find Abraham in the atmosphere of continuous fighting in the war zone of Tennessee:

Letter of introduction: Head-Quarters, Cincinnati, Ohio, Aug 17, 64.

To: Lt. Col. Fairleigh, Comdg, Louisville, Ky.
Colonel: *I have the honor to introduce to you D. C. Kumler Esqr. a citizen with whom I am personally acquainted and know him to be thoroughly (sic) He wishes to go to Chattanooga to bring away his son-in-law Surgeon Landis, 35th Inft. Ohio Vols, dangerously wounded. Please give him the necessary facilities.*
Very Respectfully,
Your Obt. Servt.
(signed) Fred C. Kemper Capt. A.A.G.
1st Endorsement: Head-Quarters, Louisville, Ky. Aug 18, 64
To: Capt. Kemper A.A.G., Cincinnati, Ohio
Friend Capt: *Gen. Sherman ordered that no person should go beyond Nashville and could not give the pass as you requested..*
Very Respectfully,
Your Obdt Servt.
(signed) John Enoch Capt. A.D.C.
2nd Endorsement: Head-Quarters, Louisville, Ky. Aug 19, 64;
I know Kemper and his preacher is proof.
(signed) Thos. B. Fairleigh, Lt. Col., Cmdg

3rd Endorsement: Head-Quarters Military Command, Nashville, Tenn.
Pass to Chattanooga to care for severely wounded son
(signed) R. M. Launer A.A.G.

Union papers dated August 17,18, and 19, 1864 found in Butler County Ohio Landis Family archive.

141. Gen. Thomas once more is cited for recommending against the costly frontal action by Sherman against the heavy Confederate entrenchment's on Kennesaw Mountain. Meiser.

142. Reid, 230.

143. Reed G. Landis' recollections of stories related by his father.

Chapter 3 Notes

1. Charles, Wabash College, to Kenesaw, age 16, Logansport, May 28, 1883, Landis Family Archives. [LFA].
2. It is no surprise that, to the present day, all archival material relating to the Landis boys at the Butler County Historical Society in Hamilton, Ohio is stored in "the Kumler file." Uncles and aunts of the Kumler branch predominated over Landises, 8 to 4. In the family circle of cousins, nieces, nephews and in-laws, Landis and Kumler relatives remained a vital part of the Logansport Landises.
3. Savoyard, "The Brothers Landis," syndicated column, early 1900's. LFA.
4. Editorial, *Chicago Evening American*, February 14, 1908, Chicago Historical Society. [CHS].
5. F. W. Keil , *Thirty-Fifth Ohio*, vi.
6. Reed Landis archives.
7. Abraham's selection of Logansport as a future domicile brought forth the following account:
   > Many years later, Abraham visited his lawyer son Kenesaw in order to look over the old site that he had considered buying back in the 1870's. The particular locale had, in the early 1890's, blossomed near the LaSalle Street train station in the prominent center of Chicago. This prompted Kenesaw to remark: "Sir, if it hadn't been for your bad judgment, I would now be one of those young blades driving down Michigan Avenue in a carriage, instead of spending my youth cooped up in a law office." Interview of K.M. Landis II appearing in J. G. Taylor Spink, *Judge Landis and Twenty-Five Years of Baseball*, (New York: Thomas Y. Crowell Co., 1947); 8-9.
8. A.H. Landis, visiting Logansport, to Frank, Seven Mile, November 3, 1871.
9. A. H. Landis wrote "Dear Uncle" to Jake Kumler from Chattanooga Jan 7, 1864, that he was sending home the body of Simon, LFA.
10. Interview with Susanna Marion Baum, April 21, 1999.
11. Norman Kumler's *Kumler Family Genealogy*.
12. A.H. Landis, Washington, D.C., to Charles, Wabash College, March 17, 1874, LFA.
13. Ibid.
14. Senator Sumner is still remembered as the victim of a beating by Rep. Preston Brooks of South Carolina for describing Stephen Douglas of Illinois to his face as a "noisome, squat, and nameless animal . . . not a proper model for an American senator." Richard H. Baker, "An historical minute: The caning of a senator," *The Hill*, private

newspaper in Washington, D.C., May 28, 1997; 11.
15. Abraham was referring to Vice President Henry Wilson under President US Grant. A.H. Landis to Charles, March 17, 1874, LFA.
16. Reed Landis archives.
17. Ibid.
18. As told by Ken to Alfred Henry Lewis, "Judge Landis," *Human Life* (Boston) October, 1907, 5, CHS.
19. Ben Ezra Kendall, "Landis, 50 Today, Drops Stern Judge Role in Home Affairs" *Chicago Daily Tribune,* November 20, 1916, 1; CHS.
20. Editorial, *Chicago Evening American*, February 14, 1908, CHS.
21. Kenesaw, Chicago, to Frank, Logansport, August 8, 1935, CHS.
22. Mary, Logansport, to Charles, Wabash College, September 15, 1879, LFA.
23. Dr. Landis apparently considered Sam Tilden to be presidential timber in 1879 for the election scheduled for 1880. A. H. Landis, Logansport, to Charles, Wabash College, December 8, 1879, LFA.
24. Mary, Logansport, to Charles, Wabash College, December 8, 1879, LFA.
25. Kate, Logansport, to Charles, Wabash College, December 8, 1879 LFA.
26. Reverend Luther Kumler, Logansport, to nephew Charles, Wabash College, December 8, 1879, LFA.
27. Reed Landis archives.
28. Ibid.
29. Ibid.
30. John, Logansport, to Charles, Wabash College, April 29, 1880, LFA.
31. Young lady, Rockford, Illinois, to Charles, Wabash College, January 16, 1881, LFA.
32. Charles appears to have been moved by verses of *The Bible* in the *New Testament* including several chapters of the *Book of Mark* that speak of the "hardness of the heart," LFA.
33. Charles B. Landis' notepad entries while at college, March 20-22, 1881, LFA.
34. Mary's letter, covering several points, consistently came back to a concern about money and Charles' planned "tramping" to Indianapolis:

> Dear Carl . . . I still grunt round each day bringing some new ache or pain Pa says I must take some medicine I suppose I ought not complain a woman canot expect to go through what I have and still be young at 49 years of age . . . while Pa was gone to Ohio I had to help Ken a good deal with wattering and feeding and it was so cold, I have not been quite well since . . . carl I have been so worried about the tramp you talk of taking it looks to me like the worst kind of an undertaking . . . Frank is

310

still at home   will go to Layfaett in about two weeks and she
would like to help . . . She just rec 5.00 for a book   I will
enclose it to you   . . . this thing of stealing rides is rather
dangerous and not at all respectable.   many a poor fellow has
got his death in that way and I would never see an easy moment
while you was gone . . . you did not send any socks   read this
over 3 times and burn it   ta ta   ma
    Sister Frank enclosed a note:
       You watch out Carl,   Wait till your running for Congress. Just
you do as I expect you will and we will all feel glad and rejoice
for shortcomings. The money matters now.   Wish I was rich.
Enjoyed   your   piece   in   the   *Sunday   Journal.*   Mary,
Logansport, to Charles, Wabash College, March 8, 1881
with note from Frank, LFA.
35. Portions of Frances' separate letter to Charles follow:
       Dear Carl . . . I'm good as new again & am getting ready to
go to LaFayette to do up the town . . . I want to do something
while there to make my wallet "bug out."   If you have any sug
to give send 'em up & I will act accordingly if they are good
ones. Wish you would go along, I'd give you all you could
make & the benefit of my society besides I will let you know
when I go & if I make lots of money, will remember you in my
will.   Frank, Logansport, to Charles, Wabash College,
March 8, 1881, LFA.
36. Additional comments in Mary's letter follow:
       we are all well   we are going down town to shop some and will send
you a draft for 95 dollars which of course you will be glad to get and will
undoubtadly put to the best possible . . . Carl my last terible headache
was Sabbath a week and was brought on by eating 2 spoonfuls of sliced
onions for supper Sat night . . . Carl we aint going to fret if you don't get
to "say your piece" but I do think it will be so mean if they rule you out
just because you are crooked in your course. now good by acknowlege
this by a card if nothing more Carl be careful and keep your hand on
your pocket book by by love Ma.   Mary, Logansport, to Charles,
Wabash College, April 12, 1881, LFA.
37. Additional portions of Frank's letter appear below:
       Fred came in last night to know whether he was any body's
uncle. Squire is studying the Pitman system.   You ought to
take the same.   Walt is at it too.   Frank, Logansport, to
Charles, Wabash College, April 12, 1881, LFA.
38. E. E. Worstell, Ft. Lauderdale, FL, to Kenesaw's widow, Chicago,
December, 1944, CHS.

39. On the Sabbath, May 5, 1881, Charles referred to *Psalm 90*, verse 12 and in his notebook and commented:
> Surely all is vanity. How flexible the human mind is. There is nothing, beyond the conception of God, but yet how limited is even our conception of him.

40. Abraham's letter to Charles is excerpted below:
> Since I saw you I had a nice visit to Ohio, was at Arcanum, Dayton, Hamilton, 7 Mile and old Millville, spent just 3 weeks and had a grand old time. I saw the old cabins where I went to school 52 years ago last winter. It is an old fashioned round log cabin and if could see it, about the last thing you would think of would be that it was once a school house. What do you think of the unpleasantness between Garfield and Conckling? It is unfortunate and I trust will not result in a permanent rupture in the Rep. ranks. I must confess I am neither politician nor Statesman enough to decide which is in the wrong. I would like very much to go to Crawfordsville and see and hear you knock that debater but will have to deny myself. Abraham, Logansport, to Charles, Wabash College, May 24, 1881, LFA.

41. Kenesaw, some 30 years later, November 23, 1912, commented to George Primrose and Lew Dockstader, following their performance in Logansport's American Music Hall that he had seen them when he was working at the theater as an usher at the age of 16. Thomas Arthington, "Theatres and Acting," *A History of Logansport and Cass County*, Logansport: self-published, 1987, Juanita Hunter file.

42. Kendall.

43. Ken's ambition was too great as a teenager to be successful in a brakeman's position, as noted by his son Reed:
> It was very disappointing to him that he was kept in the office ... and, in checking up on the history of the various presidents of railroads in the United States, he discovered that they all had originated in the operating end of the railroad. So he asked the boss, the division superintendent, to let him be a freight brakeman.
>
> This man liked Dad apparently and told him that he wasn't going to have him running around on top of freight cars ...
> Reed Landis archives.

44. Kate, in a private note, sent a letter to keep in touch with her college brother:
> God bless your dear little soul. I've hardly heard from you since your return to school. Pa left here yesterday to make you a short visit. Ma gave him some lay down collars & you will have to watch him or he will get them on up side down or hind side foremost. Button him up & have lots of fun. If you have any dirty duds you can send them home with him. Dont send any collars or cuffs ... We all went crashing Monday eve & Ma rode down the hill just as gay as a lark. She could get into position just as quick as I or any of the girls.

Kate, Logansport, to Charles, Wabash College, February 15, 1882, LFA.

45. John's tongue-in-cheek advice was thorough and pragmatic:
Dont throw your Arms around like the sails of a windmill. It may create some enthusiasm but hardly enough to take you by the slack of your pants, and the coat collar, and throw you out through the transom . . . Dont weep. Tears are a good thing in their place but they are not one of the essentials of an oratorical contest. Do not go with the expectation of getting a ride on the shoulders of the crowd. Carried away by your magic words, and thrilling periods, the populace, mad with enthusiasm and lager, may unconsciously tote you home on the splinters edge of a hicory rode . . . Last and not least. Give them Hell God Bless you, and give you the palm. Hoping to clink lager, and munch switzer with you soon.   John to Charles at college, March 14, 1882, LFA.

46. Letter from Fred Munson, Logansport, to Charles, Wabash College, April 7, 1882, LFA.

47. "Dear bro" John continued:
I expect to join a surveying party of the Atchinson, Topeka & Santa Fe. When do you have the commencement dance? Answer soon. Will have to close.   John, Logansport, to Charles, Wabash College, June 16, 1882, LFA.

48. The letter was forwarded to Charles by a young lady "of Logansport," when she was in a married state. Emma, Maple Grove, MN, May 28, 1882, LFA.

49. Charles, Wabash College, to friend Emma, October 19, 1882, LFA.

50. Young Ken continued to cajole his college brother to help him get his first job out of Logansport:
Now Gussie put in your best licks to him and do your best.
Put it to him right away and write me immediately as the question needs attention. Remember you must see that it passes that part of the house and when you come to Indianapolis I will make it dusty for you.
I got your infernal old valentine . . . As you will observe this infernal short hand has ruined my long hand but I will bring that up soon. You must commence studying pretty soon now. Well I must close.
P.S. Be sure and talk pa up on the Indianapolis question.
Kenesaw, Logansport, to Charles, Wabash College, February 16, 1883, LFA.

51. Mary continued her newsy letter to Charles with excerpts below:
Pa gone   you gone   Ken gone   Walt, Fred, Katie, and I for dinner   Walt and Fred expect to go about the 15 of March dear me I get blue over it   wish we could all go to some good town together where you could all get work and have a home with us   send your clothes home with Pa when you want

313

washed   the boots the boys have worn some   John could not
have got to the Office without them severel mornings   dont
give them away for they are very useful   now good by from
your mother.   Mary, Logansport, to Charles,
Wabash College, February 20, 1883, LFA.

52. Walter, Logansport, to Charles, Wabash College, March 14, 1883,
LFA.

53. Charles continued his "pep-talk" to persuade Ken to get educated in
college:

> I will be home three weeks before starting out on my
> summer work and if in that time and the succeeding 5 or 6
> months you can make me a clod hopper of a short hand writer
> You could come here and work away the whole business if you
> would watch your corners and profit by a little of my
> experience -- which I would give you free of charge . . . Rec'd
> a long letter from Gresh yesterday (Otto Gresham). Come over
> Friday and I will try and give you an idea of the life I have led
> for the last four years. Success to you.   Charles, Wabash
> College, to Ken, Logansport, May 28, 1883, LFA.

54. Reed Landis archives.

55. Walter elaborated his thoughts to Charles on his Mexican
expedition in a conversational tone:

> Your long and very interesting letter came to hand several
> days ago, and its contents were like bread to the hungry or
> water to the thirsty traveler . . . The party was made up of five .
> . . If we dont hear from the rest of the gang we will probably
> go out by ourselves. If we do so we will buy a broncho apiece
> and a pack mule & take supplies for two months.

Brother Walt went on to invite Charles to visit him in Mexico
after graduation and "in the future:"

> Would give a good deal if you could put in your summer
> vacations with us. You would probably not have the luxury nor
> rub up against as much erudition as you will in camp on the
> Ohio, north of Louisville, but you would have more fun, see
> more and learn much of the manners, customs and language of
> the Aztecs . . .
>
> I propose to see something of foreign countries sometime, but
> will accumulate first and then travel like a gentleman and a
> christian . . .
>
> Well presume this will reach you shortly before the great
> event of your life -- the completion of your college education. I
> regret that such a stretch of plain, hill, valley and mountain
> forbids my presence to witness your honors, and to
> congratulate you hand to hand and face to face . . .Walter,
> Chihuahua, Mexico, to Charles, Wabash College, May
> 31, 1883, LFA.

62. Mary's letter to Charles continued in her typically newsy, all-disclosing fashion:
the arrangement at present is that I go to see you graduate   I am resigned to this decree so if nothing happens I will go tuesday morning   Katie thinks we cant both leave and she insists that I go . . . I will send you 50 and when I come will get some more   now you must stretch this as far as possible   I want to get my buggy done up and some other things   Do you see how tis Ken had a splendid visit with you   He cant get done talking about it.   Mary, Logansport, to Charles, Wabash College, June 8, 1883, LFA.

57. Kate, Logansport, to Charles, Wabash College, June 8, 1883, LFA.

58. Mary, Logansport, to Charles, Jeffersonville, Indiana, July 9, 1883, LFA.

59. Frank, Logansport, to Charles, Jeffersonville, Indiana, July 9, 1883, LFA.

60. Fred, Logansport, to Charles, Utica, Indiana, August 24, 1883, LFA.

61. Mary, Logansport, to Charles, New Albany, Indiana, August 31, 1883, LFA.

62. Reed Landis archives.

63. Ibid.

64. Ibid.

65. Numerous references have mistakenly asserted that Gresham had served as Dr. Landis' commanding officer, citing "a wartime bond" between the two men which allegedly had led to Gresham's selection of Ken to be his secretary in Washington. According to Van Horne's History of the Army of the Cumberland, however, Gresham and Landis served in different armies; hasty research may have confused similar-sounding names:
Gresham was assigned to Gen. *Blair's* 17th Corps, Army of the Tennessee and Landis belonged to a regiment of Gen. *Baird's* 3rd Division, 14th Corps, Army of the Cumberland.

66. Judge Walter Q. Gresham, Chicago, to Abraham H. Landis, Logansport, June 14, 1888, CHS.

67. Reed Landis archives.

Chapter 4 Notes

1. Caption of photo of the five Landis boys "twenty years ago,"*Washington Times*, 1902, date unknown, John H. Landis archives.
2. Ben Ezra Kendall, "Landis, 50 Today, Drops Stern Judge Role in Home Affairs," *Chicago Tribune*, November 20, 1916, p. 1 Chicago Historical Society [CHS].
3. Undated editorial commentary, *Cincinnati Journal*, enclosed in letter from Fred G. Stephenson, Cincinnati, to Kenesaw, Chicago, December 10, 1922, CHS.
4. Reed Landis archives.
5. One writer of the period describes Charles' accomplishment as a journalist after graduating from Wabash College:

    While yet a very young man, and after some excellent work on the *Logansport Journal*, of which he was city editor, he purchased the *Delphi Journal*. He soon gave the paper a distinctive personality. He was audacious – the Democrats called it impudence – pragmatic, dogmatic, partisan, stalwart. But he was always brilliant, and even Democrats read him, generally with the result that, like Mistress Tam o'Shanter, they "nursed their wrath to keep it warm." It was about the best country paper in the State, excellent as a local newspaper and popular for its saucy and brilliant comments on political affairs.

    Syndicated writer Savoyard, "The Brothers Landis," undetermined Philadelphia newspaper and others, circa 1906,.Landis Family Archives [LFA].
6. Mathew F. Steele, *American Campaigns*, War Department Document No. 324, Office of Chief of Staff; vol. 1 (Washington, D.C.: United States Infantry Association, 1943), 536, 665, 667.
7. Thomas B. Van Horne, *History of the Army of the Cumberland*, vol. 2, 46.
8. Walter Q. Gresham, Chicago, to Abraham Landis, Logansport, June 14, 1888, CHS.
9. Reed Landis archives provide the following information about Judge Gresham:

    Gresham was quite a citizen and one who had a great deal of national prominence and in the early days of Father's legal career, his practice before Judge Gresham, he made quite an impression upon the old man apparently . . . President Cleveland was reelected to a second term. Mr. Cleveland at that time foresaw some difficulties in the future, and he appointed what was then known as a bipartisan cabinet, making this very prominent Republican, Judge Gresham, his secretary of state. Judge Gresham took Dad down to Washington with him as his secretary.

10. Robert Donnell, "Five Very Interesting Men Named Landis; A Unique Quintet In an American Family." *Havana Post*, July 30, 1907, CHS.
11. Document signed by Judge Walter Q. Gresham, March 15, 1893, CHS.
12. Albert J. Beveridge to Kenesaw, Washington, April 11, 1893, CHS.
13. Mary,Logansport, to Kenesaw, Washington, April 11,1893, CHS.
14. Mary continued her writing streak to keep young Kenesaw bonded to the household:
    > My dear
    > . . . I have a clip I wanted to send tis a picture of Ott Gresham binding grain He has a big hat on and looks like a cowboy I wonder if He ever saw a wheat field . . . Say don't those pants need pressing tell Grover that only one can do it like Ma do you suppose Mrs. Cleveland irons Grovers nees out when they bag or do they give them to the poor when they get out of shape they would clothe a whole Family woulden they . . . I expect if Walt knew when you would be here he would come let me know so I have time to get the feathers off said Hen . . . any child could read your writing tis plain and beautiful Lovingly yours, Mother Mary, Logansport, to Kenesaw, Washington, April 17, 1893, CHS.
15. Kate had fun with her slap-dash remarks aimed at her "little brother:"
    > Dear Squire.
    > I entertain my P. E. Club tomorrow night & would be so glad if you was here to spend the eve with us. We are all well. Now that you are dining out a good deal, dont overdo, as you might have a spell like the one you had after being at Col Kreutzbugus, and we women would not be there to tuck you in your little bed . . . Let us know when you'l arrive & we will meet you . . . It seems such a long time since we pressed your pants & they surely need it by this time . . . Write us. Thine, Kat Kate, Logansport, to Kenesaw, Washington, April 17, 1893, CHS.
16. Setting a record for the most letters written in a given period of time, Mary persisted to keep Squire in the loop:
    > My Dear Ken
    > . . .we are all well but a goodeal disapointed because you are not coming home but we will save the Hen untill your coming write and tell me about your trip to New York I see that Grover bumped his head who pressed your pants . . . thought we might go to Chicago to day . . . Mary, Logansport, to Kenesaw, Washington, April 23, 1893, CHS.

17. Kate and Mary teamed up to keep Landis-type humor alive, this being Kate's recent effort in Kenesaw's direction;

We have been banking on your coming for a month. Now our hopes are knocked into smithereens. "White man is mightily uncertain" (Her reference to "white man" in the 1890's in Indiana was a humorous distinction from the American Indian.) . . . Did you see anything of Walter at the reunion? . . . Honestly Squire its awful lonesome here. Write us all about this trip. I thot of you the night of the ball & in my imagination saw you whirling . . . Tell Grover to put Iodoferm on his wound and it will be well in a few days. We've been afraid he'd get erysipilas in it. This is honest - no joking. Write us soon.

Kate, Logansport, to Kenesaw, Washington, April 23, 1893, CHS.

18. John kept in touch with his younger brother at the Nation's Capital:

My Dear Ken:

.I will go to the Delphian Baths over next Sunday if there's no probability of your coming. I shouldn't want you to miss me so let me know please. I saw Mrs. Charles recently (Your S.S. Friend) She asked much of you & said to tell you she meant to give you a good shaking when she saw you. Guess she's forgotten how big you are . . .

Walter hasn't been here since you were here -- You best let him know when you are coming.

P.S. No new cute things.

John, Logansport to Kenesaw, April 23, 1893, CHS.

19. Frederick Landis' treatise "Logansport:"

It was with a graceful gesture that the Creator wrought the Wabash Valley, fitting it for the maintenance, comfort and happiness of the thousands later to thrive upon its hillsides and in its meadows . . .

Were some haughty warrior, who died before the decline of aboriginal predominance, to have his eyes opened for but one gaze at the Wabash Valley he would behold it so far removed from what it once had been that attempted explanation would be folly. The sight would be confusing and wearisome. Where are my legions of daring braves? Alas! they, too, have been assimilated unto earth, and my mighty nations are now represented by thin bands, quartered in the reservations so far apart that there is no communication; Their liberties abridged, their spirit gone. My people have faded from the earth and the only memory there is that lives is kindled when the plow uncovers the moulded arrowhead in the cornfield. The echo of the war dance comes back to me in my misery and wails a requiem at my mound.

Give me eternal night, life is as useless as the weapons buried with my bones.

No better inland cities are to be found between the oceans than those which
prosper in the lap of the Wabash Valley, and the natural beauty which surrounds
them would justify the presumption that the founder of these cities had arranged the
hills and rivers at his pleasure. A more attractive object than the surrounding of
Logansport cannot be found in all the vast galleries of Nature's beauties . . .
Longwell and Cummings Directory, 1892-1893, ISL.

20. "Touchdowns," an unidentified publication in Detroit about 1910, CHS.

21. The correspondent continued in detail his description of Kenesaw's treatment of State Department bureaucrats:
With clothes in disarray, and the general color-scheme of his makeup like unto a breach of the peace, Mr. Landis roved hither and yon, leaving a wake of taste-desolation among the delicate deskites. They looked upon him as a barbarian; the ironical Fates had given them into his sinister power, and they must be mute . . .
Another favorite subject of Kenesaw's attack on what he perceived as hypocrisy was the British ambassador, and, as in other matters, he did not hesitate to share his philosophical bent with the Secretary of State on this prominent envoy:

Speaking of Sir Julian Pauncefote, neither Secretary Gresham nor Mr. Landis had any mighty confidence in that ambassador from Albion . . .
Gresham made an appointment for "next Thursday at three o'clock." Sir Julian called a follower, half secretary, half lackey.
"Put that down," said Sir Julian to the lackey secretary; "I'm quite sure I shan't remember it."
The transaction irritated Mr. Landis, who was present, and who hated airs and affectations.
It was the next day; Sir Julian was again at the State Department. As he was about to depart, he paused a moment in Mr. Landis' room.
"Let me see," he said; "I've an appointment with the Secretary for Thursday at three, haven't I?"
"I'm quite sure I can't remember," returned the implacable Mr. Landis, surveying Sir Julian with an agate eye. "You might better ask your secretary."   A.H. Lewis, "Judge Landis," *Human Life*, (Boston: October 1907;
p. 6; CHS.

22. "The Man Who Imposed a Fine on Standard Oil," *New York Times*,

August 11, 1907, CHS.
23. "Touchdowns."
24. Reed Landis archives.
25. Ibid.
26. "Landis the Man! He is the Most Talked of Person in America! Landis the Judge, " *Chicago Sunday Examiner*, August 11, 1907, CHS.
27. "A Group of Brothers," *Indianapolis News*, May 5, 1900, p. 2, LFA.
28. Reed Landis archives.
29. Alfred Henry Lewis.
30. Reed Landis archives.
31. John, Cincinnati, to Kenesaw, Chicago, January 2, 1896, CHS.
32. *Lafayette* (IN) *Journal*, March, 1896, LFA.
33. "Charles B. Landis Nominated on the First Ballot for Congressional Honors," *Crawfordsville* (IN) *Journal*, March 1896, pp. 16-17, LFA.
34. Editorial comment in *Crescent*, March 1896; an unidentified Democratic newspaper of the 9th Indiana congressional district, LFA.
35. "Charles B. Landis Nominated on the First Ballot . . ."
36. "The Convention and its Work," *Crawfordsville* (IN) *Journal*, March, 1896, 10, LFA.
37. Chicago Bar Association certificate, Sep. 21, 1896, CHS.
38. Albert J.Beveridge, Indianapolis, to Kenesaw, Chicago, September 14, 1896, CHS.
39. Editorial, *Chicago American*, February 14, 1908, CHS.
40. John, Cincinnati, to Kenesaw, Chicago, October 25, 1896, CHS.
41. Rev. George Funkhouser, Union Biblical Seminary, Dayton, Ohio to his nephew Kenesaw, December 14, 1896, CHS.
42. Kenesaw's son continued with his description of his father's legal career in Chicago:

> when he was addressing a jury, with his final address to the jury, the bar association would turn out pretty strongly to listen to his presentation . . .   Reed Landis archives.

43. Landis family lore.
44. Charles continued his examination of the central worth of political parties:

> I believe in the Republican party first, and after that -- in the Democratic party . . . the Democratic party we had before its name was captured and appropriated by the tambourine players and serpentine dancers who went crazy over the cross of gold and crown of thorns at the Chicago convention. "Landis Makes a Hit," *North Vernon* (IN) *Republican*, January 5, 1898, LFA.

45. "Landis Makes a Speech," *Indianapolis News*, January 6, 1898, LFA.
46. Charles explained that his intentions were for genuine reform of the Civil Service System:

> just as Mr. Cleveland did abuse the law on leaving the presidential chair by ousting 1,800 Republicans from the

government printing office and substituting the same number of Democrats and then placed them in the civil service category. "Editorial comment," *Warsaw* (IN) *Times*, January 6, 1898, LFA.

47. "Editorial comment," *Terre Haute* (IN) *Mail*, January 6, 1898, LFA.

48. The *Washington Post* editorialized on Charles' speech on Civil Service Reform:

> Mr. Landis has sprung into distinction at a single bound by the sensible and courageous manner in which he attacks the shams and humbugs generated under the shadow of civil service reform, and he promises to be a potent champion of reason and wholesomeness in legislation. "It Struck the Right Chord: Public Comments on the Speech of Representative Landis," *Indianapolis Journal*, January 6, 1898, LFA.

49. Chicago's major newspaper went on to describe Charles' maiden speech:

> Congressmen on the floor and spectators in the galleries did not require calling to order by Speaker Reed, for they did not want to lose a word uttered by the smooth-faced, heavily-built Indianian who was posing for the first time in the national arena of debate and winning golden opinions from his audience regardless of political affiliations . . . "Landis Makes a Big Hit," *Chicago Tribune*, January 7, 1898, LFA.

50. Charles appeared to gain the attention of one and all in his first appearance on the floor of the House:

> Representative Landis of Indiana had his time extended three times, and the thirty minute granted him at the start were strung out to an hour and forty five minutes . . . It is with irrepressible joy that Mr. Reed witnesses the birth of a new House attraction, and he recognized in Mr. Landis a character to his liking. "Landis, Indiana Orator Who Made a Hit in Congress," *Dayton* (OH) *News*, January 7, 1898, LFA.

51. "Mr. Baker's Book: Congressman Landis of Indiana, Famous in One Speech," *Pittsburgh Leader*, January 11, 1898, LFA.

52. Charles placed the spotlight upon the Cleveland Administration, criticizing its performance:

> They have bulldozed and cowed national conventions; they have demoralized and stampeded senators and representatives; they have hypnotized presidents of the United States. "Touched by Landis," *St.Paul* (MN) *Dispatch*, January 11, 1898, LFA.

53. Charles received generally favorable commentary from a newspaper that did not find sympathy with his expressed position on Civil Service reform:

> Though he has taken a superficial view of the civil service question, he is devoted to ideas rather than to isms. If he does not get side-tracked he is going to become a conspicuous figure

in Congress. "Gossip from Washington: Leader in Civil Service Fight Should Find Better Occupation," *Philadelphia Telegraph*, February 5, 1898,. LFA.

54. "Political Gold Brick: Congressman Landis Defines a Democratic Speech," *Washington Post*, February 13, 1898,. LFA.

55. "Enthusiastic for Grand Old Party Hundreds of Republicans are in Kokomo to Nominate a Congressman," *Kokomo News*, March 20, 1898, Indiana State Library [ISL].

56. "Feared a Record Vote: Representative C.B. Landis' Amendment Supported by the House," *Washington Post*, May 20, 1898, LFA.

57. Mary, Logansport, to Walter and Kenesaw, attending the 1898 reunion of the 35th Ohio in Butler County, Ohio; CHS.

58. "Enthusiastic: Eloquent Address Delivered by Congressman Charles B. Landis," *Muncie* (IN) *News*, September 18, 1898, LFA.

59. Walter wrote Ken shortly after his arrival to assume his duties as Postmaster of Puerto Rico:

> The boat goes to New York this afternoon and as there will not be another for a week will send you a line. Got in here two days ago . . . Have met Consul Hanna and he said he remembered you through correspondence with the State Department.   Walter, Puerto Rico, to Kenesaw, Chicago, October 6, 1898, CHS.

60. *Chesterton* (IN) *Tribune*, November 20, 1898, LFA.

61. *Certificate*, Chicago Club, Jan. 20th, 1899, CHS.

62. Charles continued criticism of a colleague and affirmed his support of US foreign policy:

> Liberty begs that we remain, because she sees the greedy nations looking on . . . She knows that should we sail away, other nations would land their soldiers, and that their mighty guns would frown budding hope to death. [Applause] . . . In the sacred name of liberty I contend it is our duty to remain in the Philippines." [Loud applause on the Republican side.]

"Landis Again!" *Indianapolis Journal*, January 31, 1899, LFA.

63. "A Beautiful Roast!: Given Henry Johnson by Our Eloquent Congressman, Charles B. Landis " *Covington* (IN) *Republican*, January 31, 1899, LFA.

64. Another editorial discussed Charles' critique of his fellow Republican:

> He said Mr. Johnson complained of ill health, but . . . had always been strong enough to malign the President, who was the head of the party to which he belonged and whose motives no member of the opposite party had ever presumed to assail.

"Hon. Charles B. Landis," *Terre Haute* (IN) *Express*, January 31, 1899, LFA.

65. This regional newspaper elaborated upon Charles' negative remarks about his colleague:

Mr. Johnson does not represent the people of Indiana . . . They know also that Johnson is prejudiced against the president because the latter refused to appoint one of the former's favorites to office. "Landis Flays Johnson," *Marion* (IN) *Chronicle*, February 1, 1899, LFA.

66. Another commentary discussed Charles' final initiative in his debate with Mr. Johnson:

To be certain that he was not doing Mr. Johnson any injustice, he telegraphed the editors of the Republican newspapers of the Sixth district, and received replies from all but one (that being Mr. Johnson's personal appointee for postmaster) repudiating the Johnsonian sentiments of hostility to the administration policy of expansion. These telegrams he proceeded to read, to the intense enjoyment of the great audience in the chamber and galleries. "Flayed Again: Henry U. Johnson Mercilessly Lashed by C. B. Landis," *Richmond Palladium*, February 25, 1899, LFA

67. "Landis Floors Henry U. Johnson," *Madison* (IN) *Courier*, February 25, 1899, LFA.

68. Walter, Puerto Rico, to Kenesaw, Chicago, March 3, 1899, CHS.

69. "Not Out for Governor: Mr. Landis will be a Candidate for Renomination," *Indianapolis Journal*, May 20, 1899, LFA.

70. "Terrific Blows Are Delivered by Congressman Landis," *Indianapolis Sun*, May 20, 1899, LFA.

71. "Good for Landis," *Indianapolis Sun*, May 20, 1899, LFA.

72. Walter explained the suspect measures he seemed to take to sending Puerto Rican cigars to Kenesaw:

I handed them to Capt. Hodgkins of the steamer Blake which is engaged in the coast and geodetic survey service. These people can get stuff in without complications with the custom house officials.

Walter, Puerto Rico, to Kenesaw, Chicago, June 22, 1899, CHS.

73. "Civil Service Reform and the Politicians,"*Indianapolis News*, August 2, 1899, LFA.

74. The favorable local editorial about Frederick's early journalistic efforts stated:

"The passing of Maine" was cleverly done in Sunday's Journal by Frederick Landis, the young attorney, brother of Charles Landis, the congressman. It is always a pleasure to us to recognize brains and genius wherever found. Fred has no superiors in the younger generations of this city.

Editorial, *Logansport Journal*, November 17, 1899, Frederick Landis collection, ISL.

75. Mary, Logansport, to Kenesaw, Chicago, December 9, 1899, CHS.

76. Walter, Puerto Rico, to Kenesaw, Chicago, December 14, 1899, CHS.

Chapter 5 Notes

1. "A Group of Brothers: They Have Attained Distinction in Various May 5, 1900, 1, Landis Family Archives [LFA].
2. Charles, Washington, D.C., to Kenesaw, Chicago, January 2, 1900, Chicago Historical Society [CHS].
3. "Landis Settles the Roberts Controversy," *Madison Courier*, January 8, 1900, LFA.
4. "The Utah Whirlwind," *New York Sun*, January 25, 1900, LFA.
5. The commentary on Charles' interchange with Congressman Littlefield continued following Mr. Littlefield's assertion that Mr. Roberts had the legal right to be seated in the House of Representatives:

   > Landis responded: "Let us write over the arch of yonder door: 'No polygamist shall ever enter the American Congress.'" . . . Both Members scored a triumph. The lawyer won the intellect of Congress; the layman won the heart.

   "Conspicuous in the Roberts Debate," *Detroit Free Press*, Jan 29, 1900,. LFA
6. "The News and Congressman Landis, *St. Louis Tribune*, January 31, 1900, LFA.
7. "Editorial Comment," *Cincinnati Christian Standard*, January 1900, LFA.
8. "A Group of Brothers . . ."
9. This criticism of Charles' position against the seating of the polygamist in the House of Representatives went on to challenge the Republican party on the question of corporate favoritism:

   > The Republican platforms, both state and national, need to be tornado-proof in 1900. No fake planks will weather the storm.

   "Hedging for 1900," *Indianapolis Sentinel*, February 21, 1900, LFA.
10. Charles declared unequivocally that the lack of action by the Grover Cleveland Administration against the excesses of corporations would be changed under Republican leadership:

    > The Republican party will handle the trust question as it has handled all other questions and the people have confidence along this line. "Young Man not Afraid of His Country," Muncie News, February 24, 1900, LFA.
11. "Political Gossip," *Washington Post*, September 17, 1900, LFA.
12. Frederick called William Jennings Bryan to task for having the nerve to label the US presence in the Philippines "imperialism," when he had advocated such a foreign deployment of US troops under provisions of the Treaty of Paris:

    > And having done this, with the ghastly calmness of a public executioner, this same wandering autocrat of the trembling remnants of a plundered party now rallies the delusions of the

far-off foe, gives aid and comfort to the enemies of is country in time of war . . . this man stabs matchless valor in the back and in the stillness and the darkness sprinkles tears o'er the dimpled faces of sleeping babes and cast the weeds of mourning beside the cottage door! "Landis Speaks," *Anderson Herald*, precise date not listed, 1900, Indiana State Library [ISL].

12. The fact that this relative's letter remained in Kenesaw's files without an accompanying reply suggests that Kenesaw chose to save it as a piece of unsolicited gall . . . A number of efforts by family members seem to have reinforced his resolve to resist efforts by others to curry favor. This letter continued:

"Confidential" Have you any parties in mind that could float a good enterprise? It would require three hundred and fifty thousand ($350,000.00) dollars in cash, and as I could show you, it is a great winner.

Please take this matter up. Ohio relative to Kenesaw, Chicago, September 22, 1900, CHS.

13. Mary continued in detail to communicate in her own grammatical style to her son Ken:

There was a great fuss made of an Auto accident in which Fred was one of the figures there was not much to it . . . I suppose of course you have seen of Delight Sweetzer Prentice committing suicide by drinking Carbolic acid, her father and mother in Europe, poor girl tis to sad she seemed so full of life and Certainly had every thing money Could give her but she must have been unhappy poor girl . . . dear what a home coming for her parents to find their only Child dead by her own hand now my Dear when are you coming to make us a visit . . . Walt is having his "farm" planted in Orange trees

Mary, Logansport, to Kenesaw, Chicago in 1900, CHS.

14. Charles left no doubt about his belief in the critical role played by the newspapers in small towns, like his own *Delphi Journal*, in the neighborhood of Logansport:

Great movements either succeed or fail in proportion as they are advocated or opposed by the people who live in small towns and on farms, because the evenings of such people are devoted to reading and reflection, or to old-fashioned visiting . . . In molding these views, the country editor is the chief instrument; and, after they are molded, he is their chief exponent, and thus verdicts for history are made.

Charles B. Landis, "The Evolution of the Country Editor," *Success*, (New York:: McGraw-Marden Company) April 1900, Timothy Landis Family files.

15. Robert Donnell, "Five Very Interesting Men Named Landis; A Unique Quintet In an American Family," *Havana Daily Post*, July 30, 1907, CHS.

17. John, Cincinnati, to Kenesaw, undated turn-of-the-century, CHS.
18. Additional text of Frederick's essay on "The Black Man" and "Return of the Flags" follows:

> I. The Black Man.
> We are not just toward the Negro and therefore not just toward ourselves. It matters not why. It is enough that we are wrong. It is enough for us to know that during the midnight of the Nineteenth century, the demon of racial hatred crossed the Ohio river! . . .
> II. The Confederate Flags.
> a huge vestige of Mason & Dixon's line," has been found in the War Department at Washington in the form of many battle flags captured from the late Confederacy . . . Let us send these emblems home . . . They benefit no one where they are. The sole issue is "Shall the soldiers have them or shall the moth have them?" Frederick Landis, "The Black Man and the Return of the Confederate Flags," *The Illustrated Indiana Weekly*, January 12, 1901, 11, ISL.

19. The balance of Walter's letter, rambles about how Ken could benefit by leaving his work in Chicago:

> Since the American occupancy these collections amount to somewhere in the neighborhood of a million dollars . . . Probably an arrangement could be made for their collection on a contingent fee, say ranging from 50 per cent for the smaller claims to 25 per cent for a thousand dollar claim. Walter, Puerto Rico, to Kenesaw, March 3, 1901, CHS.

20. Mary's letter to Ken with the hometown perspective continued:

> what I most wanted to say is that C B (Charles) and I are expecting to start on our trip next Wed morning he was up monday and says we will see Niagara falls While we are going I am expecting a rare trial as I have never seen New York or the falls . . . we have been so short of gass this winter we could not safely invite any one to come, but with the more moderate weather we will be all right and before another winter we will have to make some other arrangements . . . a letter from Walt yes he is all OK. Mary, Logansport, to Kenesaw, Chicago, April 18, 1901, CHS.

21. Charles spoke his favorite theme of bringing together the North and the South:

> an eloquent description of the burial at the National cemetery at Alexandria of the dead soldiers brought home from the Philippines typifying in the burial side-by-side of boys in blue from north and south, the burial forever of the sectional hatred which for years endangered the very life of the American nation. "Landis on Optimism: Patriotic and Uplifting Address by Indiana Congressman," *Dunkirk* (NY) *Observer*, June 15, 1901, LFA.

22. Charles completed his address with the following:

> Why in Washington today a member of the senate or house finds it impossible to be placed on any important committee if

he is a known drunkard or gambler. I have been in Congress four years and during this time have seen only one drunk man on the floor of the house.

"The Glorious Day," *Ottawa* (KS) *Journal*, July 5, 1901, LFA.

23. "Landis is Optimistic: Says the Next House of Congress Will be Republican," *Muscatine* (IA) *Journal*, August 14, 1901, LFA.

24. *Program*, Marquette Club of Chicago, October 9, 1901, Timothy F. Landis file; and "Landis On McKinley," *Delphi* (IN) *Journal*, October 10, 1901, ISL.

25. "Landis, The Orator, Charms His Hearers," *Zanesville* (OH) *Times Recorder*, October 28, 1901, LFA.

26. Elements of Frederick's address in the Republican "love feast" follow:

We drink to Lincoln, the cabin born, into whose hands as a ragged child an outraged God placed emancipation-to Lincoln, who broke the chains of bondage, but ne'er a vow with country or with heaven . . . We drink to Grant-to Grant, the Chesterfield of war; to Grant, who was embarrassed most in the hour of matchless triumph; to Grant, who with the sword of victory knighted the kneeling foe and bade him rise . . . We drink to McKinley . . . He came in obscurity, in his cradle society cast no scepter-chance no crown, but ere he fell he was the Ben Hur in the race of nations.

"A Glowing Tribute, Paid by Frederick Landis to Republican Idols," *Logansport Journal*, January 2, 1902, Frederick Landis collection, ISL.

27. "Not All Smooth Sailing at the Ninth's Convention," *Indianapolis News*, March 20, 1902, ISL.

28. The editorial posed the possibility for Charles of his attainment of the position of US Senator, Governor of Indiana, and Vice President, and "the ultimate office:"

Indeed should the greatest nomination of all, that for the presidency, come to this district, we are modest enough to predict that Mr. Landis could attend to the requirements of the office and lend as much brilliancy to the distinguished position as any of the present available timber.

"The Man from Delphi," *Kokomo* (IN) *News*, March 20, 1902, LFA.

29. "The Landis Family Furnishes, out of a bunch of five boys, One Sixth of Indiana's Congressmen," *St. Louis Post Dispatch*, June 8, 1902, CHS.

30. "Favored Primary Two Years Ago," *Wabash Plain Dealer*, February 7, 1902, Indiana State Library.

31. "100 Years Ago," *Logansport Pharos-Tribune*, May, 2002, Juanita Hunter's Landis Family files.

32. Excitement in Logansport about sending a "Landis train" to the convention was high:

> The proposition to send a special train has aroused great enthusiasm and Logansport will be practically deserted on the day of the convention . . . The Journal is arranging for a special wire in the convention tent in order to bulletin the results every half hour so that those, who do not go will be informed of the progress of the proceedings from the time the convention meets until it adjourns . . .

"Fred Landis for Congress," *Logansport Journal*, May 15, 1902, Frederick Landis collection, Cass County Historical Society.

33. Robert Donnell.

34. The local newspaper proceeded to explain the crowded conditions for Landis delegates to the Congressional convention and the money-making efforts of the hotel proprietor:

> He puts seventeen men in each room and seven times seventeen on cots in each hallway and smacketh his lips and chortles with glee as he fareth forth to buy up the steel trust with the profits of a single night.

"Cass County's Congressional Candidate Confident of Success in Today's Battle," *Logansport Morning Journal*, May 21, 1902, ISL.

35. "Tribute Paid to Frederick Landis," *Logansport Morning Journal*, May 22, 1902, ISL; and Stewart T. McConnell's handwritten notes, Frederick Landis collection, Cass County Historical Society. Excerpts of the complete text follows:

> Gentlemen of the Convention:
>
> The young man is the coming power in all the great affairs of men in this Country whether in private or public affairs; whether in legislative enactment, in judicial decisions, or in executive councils . . . It is the voice of the people, which, we are told is the voice of God.
>
> Again, Gentlemen of the convention, Cass County nominates Frederick Landis.

36. "Over Nine Hundred Ballots Are Taken Without Result at Wabash," *Logansport Morning Journal*, May 22, 1902, ISL.

37. Two Indianapolis newspapers presented the details of the convention results and the enthusiastic Logansport reception for the young hometown nominee:

> Thousands of people, men and boys women and girls, gathered at the Wabash station long before the train pulled in and the platform and grounds about the depot were black with the crowd.
>
> the bands played "Marching Through Georgia" and "Hot Time" with a vigor that was never surpassed by them.
>
> No sooner had the ladies bestowed their compliments than he was escorted to the north side of the station where Earl Stewart

was in waiting with his handsome "Buckskin" colored horse, which Landis mounted.

All along the line of march redfire illuminated the streets and fireworks were furnished the marchers and bystanders as the crowd moved along. . .

When Landis appeared he was greeted with a deafening hurrah . . .

"Landis Wins Out, Defeating Steele on 1010th Ballot: Incidents of the Most Remarkable Convention Ever Held in Indiana," *Indianapolis Star*, May 22, 1902; and "Fred K. Landis Is Nominated," *Indianapolis News*, May 22, 1902, ISL.

38. "Fred Landis, Nominee, Returns in Triumph to Cass County Home -- Deadlock is Broken When Good and Cowgill Throw Their Vote to Landis," *Logansport Morning Journal*, May 23, 1902, ISL.

39. "Whole City Turns Out to do Honor to the Nominee for Congress and His Path Is Lighted With Tributes of His Loving Friends," *Logansport Morning Journal*, May 23, 1902, ISL.

40. "Lifted on Shoulders of Friends, He Makes a Speech of Acceptance," *Logansport Morning Journal*, May 23, 1902, ISL.

41. "Editorial," *Logansport Morning Journal*, May 23, 1902, ISL.

42. "Fred Landis; His Career," *Logansport Morning Journal*, May 23, 1902, ISL.

43. The local press produced a philosophical summary of the nomination of Fred Landis:

One of the most remarkable conventions ever held in Indiana has passed into history and a Cass County boy with a clean record is the nominee . . .

It was a contest of young blood versus skilled politicians and young blood by that essential ingredient of its competitive stick-to-it-ive-ness won out . . .

It was due entirely to the determination of Cass County to stick by Landis to the end that the convention closed in a manner so satisfactory.

"Landis is Nominated," *Logansport Journal*, May 23, 1902, LFA.

44. Frederick's acceptance speech moved quickly into the realm of heroism in the nation's history:

Our mission is as lofty as it was unavoidable and there is not a boy today who sleeps his long, long sleep beneath alien palms, but whose mystic forms the angels of future gratitude shall gently bear across the distant seas and place to rest upon the slopes of Bunker Hill.

"Landis' Acceptance," *Logansport Journal*, May 23, 1902, Frederick Landis archives.

45. Another small-town newspaper portrayed a favorable impression of the successful candidate:

Mr. Landis held the crowd for fully two hours, and perhaps such a thing was never better done than on that occasion.
"Fred Landis the Nominee," *Warsaw Times*, May 24, 1902, ISL.
46. The newspaper that favored Mr. Cowgill over Frederick Landis gave their support to Landis showing virile partisanship:

> The convention, in our humble judgement has acted wisely, and for the best interests of the republican party, and the only course for eleventh district republicans to pursue, is to drop all differences, forget the past, and make common cause against the arch political foe, degenerate democracy [Democratic party].

"Work of the Convention," *Wabash Plain Dealer*, May 24, 1902, ISL.
47. The local newspaper played upon the theme of Frederick Landis' youth:

> After he has reached an age of reasonable maturity the young man is to be trusted more than the old one. His perception is keener, his mind more subtle, his faculties brighter, his judgment better.

"The Crime of Being Young," *Logansport Journal*, May 29, 1902, ISL.
48. A Chicago newspaper summed up Frederick's victory and offered a description of his family:

> The nomination of Frederick Landis for Congress by the Republicans of the eleventh district adds one more triumph to the long list already achieved by the remarkable family of which the nominee is a member.

"The Five Landis boys," *Chicago Record-Herald*, re-printed in *Logansport Journal*, May 29, 1902, ISL.
49. An editorial of the Logansport paper presented a light-hearted iview of Frederick's his recent success:

> Under Fred's chrysanthemumic locks there is a level head and a whip-cracker tongue that will in due time make themselves felt in the halls of congress and in the country at large . . .

"The Chatterer," *Logansport Journal*, May 29, 1902, Frederick Landis collection, ISL.
50. Charles and Mary *Landis Family Genealogy*.
51. "Landis Aids in Search for Consul Staff," *Logansport Journal*, June 6, 1902; "Walter Landis Tells of Expedition's Work on Doomed Island of Martinique," *Logansport Journal*, June 8, 1902; and "Ashes of Pelee Fall on Landis," *Logansport Journal*, June 10, 1902; Juanita Hunter's Landis family file.
52. "They Are Running Yet: The Democratic Policy of Scuttle Aptly Described by Mr. Landis,"*Chicago Tribune*, June 25, 1902, LFA.

53. "Landis and Williams: Rival Orators Charm House with Their Eloquence," *Washington Post*, June 25, 1902, LFA.
54. "Landis Stirs House," *Indianapolis Journal*, June 25, 1902, LFA.
55. "Landis Smashed Clark," *Chicago Journal*, June 25, 1902, LFA.
56. "Got What They Deserved," *Pittsburg Chronicle Telegraph*, June 25, 1902,. LFA.
57. The syndicated journalist went into some detail as he analyzed the two congressmen:
    > Each side was delighted with its champion, and both displayed brilliant parts. Williams spoke like the doctrinaire and Landis was the man who never doubts and ever hopes.
    Savoyard, "A Hoosier and A Southerner," *Terre Haute* (IN) *Mail*, June 25, 1902, LFA.
58. "Landis' Great Speech," *Kokomo* (IN) *News*, June 26, 1902, LFA.
59. "Farmer's Life Good Enough for Congressman Landis: 1,000 acres in the Wabash Valley His Ideal Kingdom," *Logansport Journal*, July 8, 1902, from Juanita Hunter's Landis family file.
60. "Logansport Entertains President Roosevelt," *Logansport Pharos-Tribune*, September 23, 1902, Juanita Hunter's Landis Family file
61. "It Rained But They Listened," *Logansport Journal*, September 26, 1902, ISL.
62. "Landis in Roann," *Roann Clarion*, October 10, 1902, LFA, ISL.
63. "Frederick Landis," *Peru* (IN) *Republican*, October 31, 1902, ISL.
64. "Landis Closes His Speaking Campaign," *Logansport Journal*, November 1, 1902, ISL.
65. "Landis Victor by 4,877 Votes," *Logansport Journal*, November 2, 1902, ISL.
66. Joseph Cannon, Washington, to Kenesaw, Chicago, November 29, 1902, CHS.
67. "Landis goes to Washington," *Logansport Journal*, Nov 30, 1902, ISL.
68. Editorial comment, *Indianapolis Journal*, December 2, 1902,
69. "Fred Landis in Town," *Indianapolis News*, December 17, 1902, ISL.
70. In the years of Charles and Frederick in Congress early in the 1900's, offices were assigned according to a representative's committee assignment; their staffs were a few aides, and their residences were usually rentals in Washington hotels.
71. Editorial, *Denver* (IN) *Tribune*, June 4, 1903, ISL.
72. W. B. G., "Memorial Services in Cass County, Indiana," Unidentified newspaper, Louisville, KY, June 9, 1903, ISL.
73. "Landis to Speak at the Camp Fire," *Logansport Journal*, July 7, 1903, from Juanita Hunter's Landis family file.

74. "Burned at the Stake in Mississippi," and "400 Men Guard Jail; Quiet in Evansville,"*Logansport Journal*, July 8, 1903; from Juanita Hunter's Landis family file.

75. "Race War at Lafayette," *Logansport Journal*, July 9, 1903; from Juanita Hunter's Landis family file.

76. "Congressman Frederick Landis 'Says People Judge Negro Unjustly; Hopes to See End of Race Prejudice'," *Logansport Journal*, July 9, 1903; speech on the race problem delivered to Indiana Sons of Union Veterans in Peru Indiana, July 8, 1903, from Juanita Hunter's Landis family file.

77. "To an Outsider," *North Manchester* (IN) *Journal*, July 16, 1903, ISL.

78. Reed Landis archives.

79. "Ex-Congressman Eddy Says Landis Will Be The Man," *Olympia* (WA) *Daily Recorder*, March 18, 1903, LFA.

80. Senator Mark Hanna , Washington, to Charles, Delphi, September 2, 1903, LFA.

81. Charles' efforts to clean up drinking of alcoholic beverages in the House of Representatives resulted from a successful legislative scheme, only to be countered by the pro-saloon contingent:

    Toward the close of the last session of Congress he offered an amendment to the immigration bill providing that liquor should no longer be sold at the capitol. The House adopted the amendment with a whirl, as it had often done with similar amendments, relying on the Senate to follow its usual course and strike the provision out of the bill . . . A way had always been found to circumvent previous inhibitions of this character, the favorite plan being to serve the liquor in teacups under the name of "cold tea." Not a single solon of bibulous inclination thought for a moment that, when he returned this fall to look after the affairs of the nation, the sacred privilege of stepping into the House saloon and taking a nip whenever he felt like it would be denied him.

    The writer noted that in the end, legislators quickly managed to bypass their own anti-Saloon law:

    Owing to the closing down of the House saloon, liquor was smuggled today into many of the committee rooms at that wing of the Capitol.

    "Liquor Barred From the Capitol," *Indianapolis Star*, November 9, 1903, LFA.

82. Louis Ludlow, "Indiana Men Prominent in Extra Session: Landis Brothers are Cheered on The Floor,"*Indianapolis Star*, November 9, 1903, LFA.

83. Charles' speech, on his favorite subject of "Optimism," reached lofty
    proportions:
      His audience he had so thoroughly at one with him that his
      mood became theirs and they left the hall unconditionally
      committed to optimism. [83]
    "An Optimist's Message," *Randolph* (VT) *Herald and News*,
    December 10, 1903, LFA.
84. "Stayed and Were Rewarded with an Exceptionally Witty and
    Eloquent Address," *Rockford* (IL) *Register-Gazette*, December 14,
    1903, LFA.
85. "People Pleased by C. B. Landis, Tells of Beauties of Optimism and
    Says All Americans Should Have it in Liberal Quantities," *Rockford*
    (IL) *Morning Star*, December 15, 1903, LFA.
86. Mary, Logansport, to Kenesaw and family, Chicago, Dec 26, 1903,
    CHS.
87. "Hot Debate in House: C. B. Landis of Indiana in a Clash with
    Democrats," *Washington Post*, January 28, 1904, LFA.
88. C. B. Landis Shakes a Red Rag in the House and Angers Democrats,"
    Indianapolis Journal, January 28, 1904, LFA.
89. *Marion News-Tribune* cited in *North Manchester Journal* and
    recounted in "Only Noise," *Fair Play Journal*, March 21, 1904, ISL.
90. *Peru Journal* recounted in "A Word to Old Soldiers," *Fair Play
    Journal*, March 21, 1904, ISL.
91. *Hartford City Gazette* recounted in "Pull vs. Pride," *Fair Play
    Journal*, March 21, 1904, ISL.
92. Louis Ludlow, cited in "Another One Nailed," *Fair Play Journal*,
    March 21, 1904, ISL.
93. "Not Born With a Silver Spoon," *Fair Play Journal*, March 21, 1904,
    ISL.
94. "For Roosevelt," *Fair Play Journal*, March 21, 1904, ISL.
95. "Young Man," *Huntingdon Herald*, recounted in *Fair Play Journal*,
    March 21, 1904, ISL.
96. "Political Points," *Fair Play Journal*, March 21, 1904, ISL.
97. "Myers Extinguished by Roosevelt, *Fair Play Journal*, March 21,
    1904, ISL.
98. "Crowds Present at Peru," *Logansport Journal*, March 29, 1904, ISL.
99. "Ovation is Given Landis," *Logansport Journal*, March 29, 1904, ISL.
100. "Landis Sure of Nomination," *Logansport Journal*, March 29, 1904,
    ISL.
101. "Cass County's Son Cheered by Many," *Logansport Journal*, March
    29, 1904, ISL.
102. "Winner of Great Congressional Contest," *Hartford City Gazette*,
    March 30, 1904, ISL.
103. Editorial Comment, *Marion* (IN) *Chronicle*, May 1, 1904, LFA.

104. "It Gives Every Man a Chance," *Zanesville*, (OH) *Times Recorder*, August 10, 1904, LFA.
105. Charles, Washington, D.C., to daughter Mary, Paris, February 9, 1905, LFA.
106. Reed Landis archives.
107. Mary Lincoln Landis to her niece Lorna Landis, unknown date in the 1930's,. LFA.
108. Vice President Fairbanks indicated his own indirect support of Kenesaw for elevation to the Federal Judiciary in his letter to Ken's brother, noting:
     Soon as the election was over, I surrendered my claim to all patronage in Indiana and elsewhere.
     Vice President Charles Fairbanks, Washington, to Kenesaw, Chicago, March 16, 1905, CHS.
109. *Washington Post*, March 1905, CHS.
110. Kate, Logansport, to Kenesaw, Chicago, March 21, 1905, CHS.
111. Editorial, *Chicago Evening American*, February 14, 1908, CHS.
112. William Hard, "Kenesaw Mountain Landis and His Altitudinous Fine," *Saturday Evening Post*, September 14, 1907, CHS.
113. Editorial, *Chicago Evening American*, February 14, 1908, CHS
114. "Landis Lifts Up Voice For First Time; Is Cheered," *Indianapolis Journal*, May 1, 1905, ISL.
115. John, Cincinnati, to Kenesaw, Chicago, June 28, 1905, LFA.
116. Mary, Logansport, to Kenesaw, Chicago, and enclosed note from Kate to Ken, July 29, 1905, CHS.
117. F. D. Owens, "Indiana Offers a Remedy," Cartoon, *Indianapolis News*, December 13, 1905, LFA.
118. Speech of Hon. Frederick Landis, of Indiana, in the House of Representatives, Monday, December 18, 1905; *Congressional Record*, 59th Congress, First Session, CHS.
119. "New Plan of President to Control Insurance," *New York Times*, December 18, 1905, LFA.
120. "Landis Talks on Insurance," *Fall River Herald*, December 19, 1905, LFA.
121. "Landis Flays Big Companies," *Kalamazoo Gazette*, December 18, 1905, LFA.
122. Mary, Logansport, to Kenesaw, Chicago, December 25, 1905, CHS.
123. Ohio cousin to Kenesaw, Chicago, January 11, 1906, CHS.
124. John, Cincinnati, to Kenesaw, Chicago, February 5, 1906, CHS.
125. Savoyard, "The Brothers Landis," *Pittsburgh Times*, February 26, 1906, ISL.
126. W. H. Blodgett, "Fred Landis Busy in the Eleventh," *Indianapolis News*, February 27, 1906, ISL.

127. Blodgett, "Fred Landis Meets Dundee's Fair Maid,"
    Indianapolis News, March 1, 1906, ISL.
128. "Big Crowd Hears Frederick Landis," *Hartford City* (IN) *Gazette*,
    March 2, 1906, ISL.
129. Blodgett, "Fred Landis in a Lively Oil Town," *Indianapolis
    News*, March 2, 1906, ISL.
130. "Landis' Speech," *Hartford City* (IN) *Gazette*, March 3, 1906, ISL.
131. W. W. Moody, U. S. Attorney General, to Charles, Washington,
    March 3, 1906; Theodore Roosevelt, The White House, to Charles,
    Washington, March 3, 1906; and Charles, Washington, to Kenesaw,
    Chicago, CHS.
132. In the 1920's, Kenesaw's son Reed found the occasion to appreciate
    his father's legal work as federal judge in 1906 . . . his ruling in the
    Union Station Company case supported a "burden theory," developed
    by Reed and his colleagues of the Air Law Institute of
    Northwestern University. It became "the basis for federal regulation
    and control of airports throughout the United States."
    Reed Landis archives.
133. *Rochester* (IN) *Sentinel*, March 23, 1906, Timothy F. Landis file.
134. "Landis Again Named," *Wabash* (IN) *Plain Dealer*, March 29, 1906,
    ISL.
135. Theodore Roosevelt, The White House, to Charles, Washington, April
    16, 1906, CHS.
136. "Landis Makes a Great Speech," *Logansport Journal*, April 30, 1906,
    ISL.
137. Mary, Logansport, to Kenesaw, Chicago, May 26, 1906, CHS.
138. Ibid., June 6, 1906.
139. John, Cincinnati, to Kenesaw, Chicago, June 14, 1906, CHS.
140. "Landis Esteemed," *Huntington* (IN) *Herald*, June 28, 1906, ISL.
141. "Pays Compliment to Fred Landis," *Huntington* (IN) *Herald*, August
    11, 1906, ISL.
142. "Congressman Landis Much Commended," *Huntington Herald*,
    August 25, 1906, ISL.
143. Frederick's success in winning his nomination for a third term
    unopposed seemed reassuring, according to one journalist:
    > The moral of a modern political fable is that a few frogs can
    > do a mighty sight of hollerin' . . . The air is full of anti-Landis
    > frog music, but diligent inquiry reveals the fact that there are
    > only a few frogs as compared with the entire voting population.
    Louis Ludlow, "Men Against Landis Are Few But Noisy,"
    Indianapolis Star, October 19, 1906, ISL.
144. Frederick, writing perhaps with a touch of envy about "Colonel"
    William Jennings Bryan critiques the former Democratic presidential
    candidate:

If the Republic should disappear and a monarchy succeed, the colonel, still serving as the private secretary of his own voice, would continue to follow up and down the land, reappearing periodically with the seasons. Louis Ludlow, "Louis Ludlow Writes About the Old Eleventh District," *Marion* (IN) *Chronicle*, October 22, 1906, ISL.

145. "Vice-President Fairbanks Coming to Peru," *Peru* (IN) *Republican*, October 26, 1906, ISL.
146. "Editorial comment," *Cincinnati Times-Star*, October 24, 1906, LFA.
147. "'The Royal Family' of Indiana," *Cincinnati Enquirer*, October 26, 1906, ISL.
148. "Anti-Landis Club Issues a Letter to Voters of This District," *Marion* (IN) *Leader*, October 31, 1906, ISL.
149. "Ladies to Sing in Landis Meeting," *Warsaw Plain Dealer*, October 30, 1906, ISL.
150. "Great Speech of Frederick Landis," *Wabash Plain Dealer*, November 1, 1906, ISL.
151. "Congressman Landis' Speech," *Logansport Journal*, November 2, 1906, ISL.
152. "Effort to Involve Unions in Politics Condemned Today," *Marion* (IN) *Chronicle*, November 5, 1906, ISL.
153. "Eleventh District Develops a Landslide Against Frederick Landis for Congress," *Marion* (IN) *News* Tribune, November 7, 1906, ISL.
154. "Landis Beaten by More Than Three Thousand," *Marion* (IN) *Chronicle*, November 7, 1906, ISL.
155. "The Defeat of Landis, *Hartford City* (IN) *Times-Gazette*, November 9, 1906, ISL.
156. Frederick's defeat brought editorial criticism of the "anti-Landis club:"
   What the eleventh district needs is a dozen first-class funerals to thin the ranks of her pseudo-leaders.
   Editorial comment, *Hartford City* (IN) *Times-Gazette*, November 13, 1906, citing Ft.Wayne (IN) News, ISL.
157. *Chicago Evening American*; February 14, 1908, ISL.
158. Mary, Logansport, to Kenesaw, Chicago, November 12, 1906, CHS.
159. Ibid., November 18, 1906, CHS.
160. Kenesaw's son recalled visits to Wrigley Field in the early 1900's:
   . . . after I had become old enough to go to baseball games, Father used to take me to see the White Sox and the Cubs when they played in Chicago . . . Many times they would come out and lean on the edge of the box and visit with Dad, and I had the privilege of shaking hands with many of the ball players of those days.   Reed Landis archives.

161. Ibid.
162. Mary, Logansport, to Kenesaw, Chicago, May 1907, CHS.
163. Ibid., June 4, 1907, CHS.
164. "John D. Rockefeller's Answers to Judge Landis' Questions in the Spectacular Inquiry into Standard Oil Secrets," *Chicago Tribune*, July 7, 1907, CHS.
165. Robert Donnell, "Five Very Interesting Men Named Landis; A Unique Quintet in an American Family," *Havana Daily Post*, July 30,1907, CHS.
166. Reed Landis archives.
167. "Judge Landis As the Dark Horse President: Intrepid Chicago Man, Friend of the Masses and Believer in Rooseveltian Policies, is Put Forth as the Logical Candidate," *Zanesville* (OH) *News*, July 7, 1907, CHS.
168. "Here is Man Who Used John D. to set Precedent," *Chicago Examiner*, July 8, 1907, CHS.
169. Reed Landis archives.
170. L. G. Edwardson, "Judge Landis Seen as a Real Human Being," *New York Herald*, February 27, 1921, CHS.
171. "Judge Landis Fines Standard The Limit," *Logansport Daily Reporter*, August 4, 1907, Cass County Historical Society.
172. "Standard's Retort, Vice President Archbold Uses Abuse For Argument," *East Hampton* (NY) *Star*, August 9, 1907, ISL; the same issue included "The Remarkable Landis Family."
173. "Standard Oil's Spies Are Here," *Logansport Daily Reporter*, August 10, 1907, Cass County Historical Society.
174. "From the Directors of the Standard Oil Company to its Employees and Stockholders,"corporate literature critiquing Judge Landis' ruling against the company, August, 1907, Timothy F. Landis file.
175. "Federal Court Ruling is Handed Down Here," *Logansport Daily Reporter*, August 10,1907, Cass County Historical Society.
176. "The Man Who Imposed A Fine: Career of Kenesaw Mountain Landis, Tamer of Standard Oil Octopus, is Not Lacking in Originality," *New York Times*, August 11, 1907, CHS.
177. "Landis the Man! He is the Most Talked of Person in America! Landis the Judge," *Chicago Sunday Examiner*, August 11, 1907, CHS.
178. "Federal Judge Kenesaw M. Landis Says That The Standard Oil Fine will stand," *Logansport Daily Reporter*, August 12, 1907, Cass County Historical Society.
179. Chicago Examiner, August 18, 1907, Cass County Historical Society.
180. Donnell.
181. "New Tales of Lincoln," *Chicago Daily News*, September 11, 1907, CHS.

182. William Hard, "Kenesaw Mountain Landis and His Altitudinous Fine," *Saturday Evening Post,.*September 14, 1907, CHS.

183. Verses of the program for voice and piano were published after Kenesaw's Standard Oil decision:

> Says he to them "Old Standard Oil," The peoples' money you took, Rail Roads you like, but rob poor toil, I will give you now the "hook."

George H. Littlefield, "Can't You See The Coming Day," (New York: North American Music Company, 1907), Timothy Landis File.

184. "Judge K. M. Landis Chief Speaker at Reunion of 35th Regiment of Which His Father Was Surgeon," *Hamilton* (OH) *Republican-News*, September 19, 1907, CHS.

185. "Gallant 35th O.V.I. Holds Its Annual Reunion Today," *Camden* (OH) *Democrat-Sun*, September 19, 1907; and Program of Forty-Third Annual Reunion of the 35th O.V.I. Association, Camden, OH, September 19, 1907, CHS.

186. "Judge Landis Visits Scenes of Boyhood," *Dayton* (OH) *Daily News*, September 18, 1907, CHS.

187. The journalist, A. H. Lewis, also adds the following in his discussion of Kenesaw:

> Above and beyond all else, the Americanism of Judge Landis is of that "of-the-people, for-the-people, by-the-people" kind, which -- while rare and growing rarer, in proportion as Yorktown takes on the form of tradition and the outlines of Bunker Hill are lost in the mists and fogs of time.

Alfred Henry Lewis, "Judge Landis," *Human Life* (Boston) October 1907; 5, 33; CHS.

188. Theodore Roosevelt, The White House, to Charles, US House of Representatives, February 5, 1908, Timothy Landis file.

189. Theodore Roosevelt, The White House, to William Rossiter, Census Bureau, February 5, 1908, Timothy Landis file.

190. Theodore Roosevelt, The White House, to W. B. Allison, United States Senate, May 20, 1908, Timothy Landis file.

191. Editorial, Chicago Evening American, February 14, 1908, CHS.

192. "US Appellate Court Rebukes Judge Landis Who Assessed $29,240,000 Fine, *Logansport Journal*, July 23, 1908, Cass County Historical Society.

193. unsigned, undated letter in Kenesaw's family file at the CHS.

194. Reed Landis archives.

195. Ibid.

196. Luther Kumler Funkhouser, Dayton, OH, to Kenesaw, Chicago, May 24, 1937, CHS.

197. Mary, Logansport, to Kenesaw, Chicago, October 2, 1908, CHS.

198. Ibid., December 26, 1908, CHS.

199. "Landis, The $29,000,000 Oil Fine Judge," *Denver Times*, March 5, Timothy Landis file.
200. Unidentified clipping with annotation of the year 1909, believed to be from a Chicago newspaper, CHS.
201. Pamphlet, *La Crosse Chautauqua*, Redpath-Vawter, June 28-July 4, 1909, Timothy Landis file.
202. Mary, Logansport, to Kenesaw, Chicago, March 29, probably 1909, CHS.
203. Speech of Hon. Frederick Landis, Report of Progressive State Convention, Indianapolis, August 1, 1912, LFA.
204. Mary, Logansport, to Kenesaw, Chicago, June 14, 1910, CHS.
205. Frederick Landis, "The Angel of Lonesome Hill," *Scribner's Magazine*, March 1910, 302-311, Timothy Landis file.
206. Theodore Roosevelt, New York, to Frederick, Logansport, June 28, 1910, LFA.
207. Theodore Roosevelt, New York, to Kenesaw, Chicago, July 22, 1910, CHS.
208. "Sentiment in West Favors Landis for Supreme Bench," *Terre Haute Post*, December 9, 1910, CHS.
209. The unsigned note recalled an earlier event that indicated President Taft thought favorably of Kenesaw's actions on the bench:

    Note: There are some who remember being in the White House that August afternoon when that decision was announced it was remarked by one Theo Roosevelt that "that is the reason why I appointed Landis -- I knew that the Standard Oil gang did not own him."

    What did Taft say about Landis, then?

    Why, it is reported in the daily press bulletins from Sagamore Hill, August 4, 1907, that every member of Roosevelt's Cabinet, save that tired trusty Root (of all evil for him), gave the most hearty and loud approval of "this triumph of the Administration over the Octopus!"

    Oh, mores, Oh tempora!

    "Taft Once Called Judge Landis "Obscure Demagogue," *Detroit Times*, January 28, 1910, CHS.
210. *Cincinnati Enquirer*, August 24, 1918, John Landis archives.
211. Mary, Logansport, to Kenesaw, Chicago, February 21, 1911, with note from Kate, CHS.
212. Ibid., March 6, 1911, CHS.
213. Thomas Arthington, "Theatres and Acting," *A History of Logansport and Cass County, Logansport*: self-published, 1987, Juanita Hunter file.
214. Letter from Mary Lincoln Landis to her niece Lorna Landis; undated in the 1930's, LFA.

215. Speech of Hon. Frederick Landis, Progressive State Convention, Indianapolis, August 1, 1912, LFA.
216. "Progressives Open Fire on 'Bosses' in Indiana," and "Landis, in Harsh Arraignment of Old Party Methods, Denounces G.O.P. State Leaders as Convention-Stealing 'Bandits,'" *Indianapolis Star,* August 2, 1912, ISL.
217. Lest We Forget, Progressive Headquarters, 307 Majestic Building, Indianapolis, IN, 1912, LFA.
218. Correspondence, taken together, depicted Walter's vulnerable position in San Juan at a time when the Bull Moose movement was in full swing in 1912. Walter predicted Taft's loss in the election:

> What the people will do to the fat dub in the White House next November will be somewhat on the line of what he is doing to the Roosevelt fellows, only more so.

Letter, Walter, San Juan, to Kenesaw Chicago, August 3, 1912, CHS.

Walter enclosed an ominous official cable he had received the previous day from Washington, D.C.:

> The President has instructed the Department to notify you that he desires your immediate resignation as Postmaster on the ground that during your present term you have failed to devote the required amount of time to your duties.

Cable, US Post Office, Washington, D.C., to Walter, San Juan, August 2, 1912, CHS.

Walter replied by cable, August 3, 1912, to "Honorable First Assistant Postmaster General, Washington, D.C. that his full response was in the mail this date. His enclosed letter follows:

> I have the honor to acknowledge the receipt of your cable, stating that the President has instructed the Department that he desires my immediate resignation on the ground that during my present term I have failed to devote the required amount of time to my duties.
>
> In reply I have to state that the charge that I have not devoted the required amount of time to my official duties is not true. The reason alleged for asking for my resignation is a pretext which seeks to cast a reflection upon my record and reputation as an official to which I will not submit without this protest.
>
> If the political exigencies of the situation demand my resignation, or if some of the members of my family have been too active in support of the candidacy of Col. Roosevelt, and the President will base his request upon these grounds, which are the real ones, then I will resign. Otherwise I will not. I prefer to be removed.

Walter, San Juan, to US Post Office, Washington, D.C., August 3, 1912, CHS.

On the same day, Walter wrote a letter to "Bill," either a family member or trusted friend, enclosing a copy of the above cable and letter exchange with Washington, D.C., stating:

> The enclosed correspondence will perhaps be of interest to you. Of course, I will get the ax by cable as soon as my letter gets to Washington. I don't care much. I will be out to the farm for a time, and have enough money put aside until the crops come in next year.

Hand-written note added:

> I do not know what will be given out at Washington, but if the circumstances warrant, give this correspondence to the press.

CHS.

219. Charles and Mary Landis, *Landis Family Genealogy*, Indianapolis, 1954, unpublished, LFA.

220. "The Progressive Party Ticket," *Fairmount News*, October 1, 1912, ISL.

221. The gist of the Bull Moose campaign and Teddy Roosevelt's role in it were described by Reed who enjoyed a front-row seat. He was impressed by the sound relationship that his father enjoyed with TR during their lives:

> I can remember, during that Presidential campaign when Mr. Roosevelt and Mr. Taft were opposed for the Republican nomination to run against Woodrow Wilson. I went to the convention in Chicago and was lucky enough to get a seat down in the press gallery right below the stands and saw that hour and a half long demonstration and a genuine, real demonstration it was, for Mr. Roosevelt. Of course, he was not nominated, and he would split off into what was known as the Bull Moose Party. It was my privilege, as a young boy, to go with Father to the Roosevelt headquarters in the Congress Hotel when Mr. Roosevelt asked Father to run on the Bull Moose ticket with him as Vice President. Father did not accept that invitation and explained why to Mr. Roosevelt in such a manner that it did not disturb their relationship at all, and Mr. Hiram Johnson, senator from California, ran as vice president as I remember it. Of course, Mr. Roosevelt's campaign split off enough Republican votes from Mr. Taft's campaign to permit Mr. Wilson to be elected. It was during that campaign that Mr. Roosevelt went to Milwaukee to make a speech and was shot. The injury was not a major one, but he was brought down from Milwaukee to Chicago to St. Luke's Hospital for further treatment and while there, Dad took me down with him when he went to make a call on the ex-President. I was able to sit there in the bedroom with Dad and Mr. Roosevelt while they conversed about various aspects of the campaign and of the problems of the country and of the world. I remember very distinctly Father in attempting to leave Mr. Roosevelt in a more optimistic state of mind than he had found him, pointed out

what tremendous crowds Mr. Roosevelt was meeting as he went around the country and how enthusiastic had been his reception everyplace he spoke, and the ex-President spoke and said: "Yes, they turn out and they yell for me, but they aren't going to vote for me." He knew what was coming because he could sense the situation that the 3rd party movement just wasn't the American way apparently of doing the job, and this has been confirmed in later political activities.
Reed Landis archives.

222. "Mrs. Mary Landis Passes Away at Family Home Saturday After a Lingering Illness," *Logansport Times*, November 1, 1912, ISL.
223. "Federal Court in Logansport," *Logansport Times*, November 6, 1912, ISL.
224. Charles and Mary Landis.
225. "Inspiring Memory, A Great Address by Hon. Frederick Landis," *Union City Eagle*, May 29, 1913, ISL.
226. Hugh S. Fullerton, "Pastmaster, Thirty-3rd Degree Baseball Fan, to Sit as the Judge in Famous Federal Jumping Cases," *Saginaw* (MI) *Daily News*, April 21, 1914, Timothy F. Landis File.
227. "Face Trust Issue at Last," *The Sporting Life*, Philadelphia, PA, January 16, 1915, ISL.
228. "Trust Case in Judge's Hands," *The Sporting Life*, Philadelphia, January 30, 1915, ISL.
229. "Awaiting the Judicial Verdict," *The Sporting Life*, Philadelphia, PA, January 30, 1915, ISL.
230. "The Irony of Fate," *New York Tribune*, April 3, 1915, ISL.
231. "The Landis Trust Suit Decision," *The Sporting Life*, Philadelphia, PA, July 3, 1915, ISL.
232. "Some Idols Have Fallen," *Philadelphia Inquirer*, July 17, 1915, ISL.
233. Gerald Astor, *The Baseball Hall of Fame 50th Anniversary Book* (New York: Prentice Hall Press, 1988); 107-110.
234. J. G. Taylor Spink, *Judge Landis and Twenty-Five Years of Baseball*, (New York: Thomas Y. Crowell Company, 1947), 29, 39.
235. Reed Landis archives.
236. Frederick Landis file, Cass County Historical Society.
237. The essence of Vice President Fairbank's alleged erroreous or unwise remark appeared in Charles' letter to Kenesaw:
>You will see by the enclosed that they have already started their campaign of falsehood and vituperation against Fairbanks . . . Of course Fairbanks never said it - that "the Nation must look to its future." It's a dirty lie manufactured for campaign purposes . . .

Charles, Wilmington, Delaware to Kenesaw, June 14, 1916, CHS.
238. The enclosed unidentified newspaper clipping produced the heat and fire of Charles' strong critique:

Charles Warren Fairbanks, Republican nominee for Vice President, in an impromptu address at the alumni luncheon of Ohio Wesleyan University here today, said that some of the nation's flag might be imperiled and that the country must look to its future.

"Fairbanks Speaks in Ohio, Tells Wesleyan Alumni the Nation Must Look to its Future," unidentified newspaper, Delaware, Ohio, June 13, 1916, CHS.

239. "A Modern Soloman," *Kansas City Star*, August 14, 1916, CHS.

240. The case involving the city of Chicago brought Judge Landis into action at a municipal level:

In one of the most sensational periods which the United States District Court ever has witnessed, Judge Kenesaw Mountain Landis in the last two weeks has shaken Chicago to its very foundation. War on private bankers marked the beginning of the new activities of the Judge.

The handbook trust which for years been so deeply rooted that the city administration and the chief of police have been unwilling or unable to budge it or even to see its tentacles has been lifted bodily into the glaring light of day and laid open to the withering heat of public exposure.

"Landis Wakes Chicago: 'He Has No Equal,' Say Gamblers," *Chicago Evening Post*, October 7, 1916; and "Landis Ends Gambling Syndicate Quiz; Asks Police to Finish Job," *Chicago Evening Post*, October 5, 1916; CHS.

241. Ben Ezra Kendall, "Landis, 50 Today, Drops Stern Judge Role in Home Affairs," *Chicago Tribune*, November 20, 1916, CHS.

242. "Editorial Comment," *Seattle Post-Intelligencer*, December 20, 1916, LFA.

243. The *Chicago Tribune* offered a summary of Kenesaw's career and endorsed him:

When President Roosevelt appointed Kenesaw Mountain Landis to a federal judgeship in Chicago there were many people who doubted the wisdom of the selection. In the first place Kenesaw Mountain is a queer name and is more queer when the owner of it becomes a judge. In the second place it was reported that he was a dude and wore long hair. Then when Landis fined the Standard Oil Company $29,000,000 the people were sure that he was a crank playing for advertising, but Judge Landis went on with his work and he is going on with it yet. He never allows a lawyer to rob his client if he can help it. He prevents anybody from taking advantage of age and ignorance. When some lawyer gets on the good side of a feeble-minded client and gets an assignment of property Landis gets hold of him and straightens the angle out. He is doing this every day. He is fearless and we have not yet heard of an unworthy thing which he has done. Sometimes he assumes

duties which are not imposed upon him. He always does these things in the interest of the poor. We hope he may live to be a hundred years old or more. He got his military name because his father was a soldier.
This country is in need of more men like Kenesaw Mountain Landis.

"When a Feller Meets a Friend, Col. Theodore Roosevelt and Judge Kenesaw Mountain Landis," *Chicago Sunday Tribune,* April 29, 1917, CHS.

244. Reed's account of his father's efforts to enter flight training recalled:
Wilson swung his chair around and looked out the window over the White House lawn. It seemed to me that he looked out there for five minutes. We just sat absolutely still while the clock, great big clock, just ticked away. It probably wasn't over 15-20 seconds, and he swung around his chair and said, "Landis don't be a damned old fool. Don't think for a minute that I don't know just how you feel about this thing. Don't you suppose that I have feelings of the same sort, sitting here, ordering these tens of thousands, and, perhaps, millions of men into combat?". . . Wilson finally also added, "Now, I don't want you trying to go to Canada or anyplace else to get around this order of mine because if you do, I'll have you brought back and prosecuted for trying to hold two jobs at one time, which, as you know, sir, is against federal law."
Reed Landis archives.

245. President Wilson, Washington, to Judge Kenesaw M. Landis, United States District Court, Chicago, May 11, 1917, CHS.

246. R. A. Stephens, Danville [IL] to Frederick, Logansport, June 14, 1917, LFA.

247. "Great Crowd Gathers to Honor Departing Soldiers," *Wabash Daily Times,* September 5, 1917, ISL.

248. Reed Landis archives.

249. *Records,* Cass County (IN) Court, November 23, 1917.

250. One historical review noted the leading role played by Lionel Barrymore in *The Copperhead*:
Milt Shanks lays on the altar of his country's need the right even to his wife's love and to his son's respect.
Arthur Hobson Quinn, *A History of the American Drama* (New York: Appleton-Century-Crofts, Inc., 1927) vol. 1, pp. 258, 263-264; vol 2, pp. 395-398.
The Opening Night cast included: Evelyn Archer, Lionel Barrymore, Gladys Burgette, Thomas Carrigan, Raymond Hackett, Harry Hadfield, Ethelgert Hales, Chester Morris, William Norton, Albert Phillips, Doris Rankin, Grace Reals, Hayden Stevenson, and Eugenie Woodward. (Timothy F. Landis file)

251. "The Copperhead," *New York Daily News,* February 19, 1918, LFA.

252. "'The Copperhead,' Adapted From Book by Frederick Landis, Makes Good Melodrama," *Indianapolis News*, February 23, 1918, LFA.

253. The Optimist, "Copperhead is Drama's Very Best," Unidentified Chicago newspaper, December 3, 1918, LFA; and *Variety*, November 29, 1918, cited in: Margot Peters, *The House of Barrymore* (New York: Simon and Schuster, 1990), 563.

254. A Barrymore family biography offers several lines of description of the plot of Frederick's Novel *The Glory of His Country*, as carried forward in Augustus Thomas' play *The Copperhead*:

> The tragedy of Milt Shanks is that both his wife and soldier son die believing him a traitor to the North. Shanks's vindication finally comes when to save his granddaughter's happiness, he decides to reveal his true role in the Civil War . . . Gradually Milt Shanks unfolds his story: the midnight meeting with Lincoln in the Executive Mansion . . .the clock ticking on the mantel . . . Lincoln pulling a small flag from his pocket, laying Shanks's hand on the stars and covering the hand with his own. "I need you, Milt" says the president, mustering Shanks into the nation's service. "Your country needs you." . . . In the final scene, his most bitter enemy helps Milt Shanks into the blue coat of a Grand Army colonel . . . As the curtain falls Lionel stands alone on the stage, Lincoln's small flag in his hand, his face lit uncannily with joy . . . Dead silence. Then suddenly the audience were on their feet as applause burst from orchestra, balcony, and gallery. Up and down the curtain went while the demonstration grew louder.
>
> *The Copperhead* settled in as a solid hit . . . The stirring patriotism of *The Copperhead* spoke strongly to a nation at war; houses continued packed . . . *The Copperhead* was Lionel Barrymore pure and simple.

Margot Peters, 172-175, 183.

255. "Big Crowd Hears Plain Talk And Lively Music," *Logansport Tribune*, April 19,1918, LFA.

256. Captain John F. Landis, Fort Logan, Colorado, to Kenesaw, Chicago, May 7, 1918, CHS.

257. Reed, battlefield in France, to his family, Chicago, August 13, 1918, CHS.

258. Ibid., August 19, 1918, CHS.

259. Dr. Landis Taken by Death," *Cincinnati Post*, August 23, 1918, CHS.

260. "Landis Loses in Brave Fight, Noted Health Officer Forced to Yield to Grim Reaper; Reforms Introduced By Official Makes Cincinnati Department Conspicuous Throughout Country;" *Cincinnati Enquirer*, August 24, 1918, LFA.

261. Daniel Blum, *A Pictorial History of the American Theater*, (New York: Grosset and Dunlap, 1950), 120, 122, LFA.

262. Blum, *Great Stars of the American Stage*, (New York: Grosset and Dunlap, 1952), 55, LFA.
263. Royal Air Force official document of award for gallantry to Reed, battlefield in France, October 5, 1918, CHS.
264. Newton D. Baker, Washington, to Kenesaw, October 14, 1918, CHS.
265. Telegram, E.S. Beck to Judge Landis, US Court, Rockford, Illinois, November 12, 1918, CHS.
266. Reed, American Expeditionary Forces, France, to Judge Landis, Chicago, December 21, 1918, CHS.
267. Captain Preston Kumler, American Expeditionary Forces, Germany, to Kenesaw, Chicago, December 23, 1918, CHS.
268. "Editorial Comment," *Toledo Times*, December 1918, LFA.
269. "Landis Promises Wounded Yanks Hospital Reform," *Chicago Herald and Examiner*, January 20, 1919, CHS.
270. "A Chip of the Old Block," *New York Herald*, February 15, 1919, LFA.
271. "Bomb Plot to Kill 22 Leaders of Nation: Bomb Sent to Judge Landis; Found in Desk," *Chicago Herald and Examiner*, May 1, 1919, CHS.
272. "Letters to US Officials Bare Terrorist Plan," *Chicago Daily Tribune*, May 2, 1919, CHS.
273. Margot Peters, 189-190.
274. J. H. Kumler, Seven Mile, Ohio, to Kenesaw, Chicago, September 10, 1919, CHS.
275. Reed Landis archives.
276. Frederick Landis, *Days Gone Dry*, Illustrated by Gaar Williams, (Indianapolis: The Bobbs-Merrill Company, 1919).

Chapter 6 Notes

1. Frederick Landis, "Hoosiergrams," *Indianapolis Star*, July 11, 1923, Indiana State Library, [ISL].
2. Frederick Landis, "Reason," *Logansport Pharos Tribune*, August 18, 1928; Chicago Historical Society [CHS].
3. "Hon. Frederick Landis of Indiana," *Pamphlet* (Chicago: Management of The Chautauqua Managers Association, 1921), Landis Family Archives [LFA].
4. *South Charleston* (OH) *Daily*, cited in "Frederick Landis, Speaker and Writer," *Pamphlet*, LFA.
5. Frederick H. Gillett, Speaker of the US House of Representatives, letter to Frederick, Logansport, March 10, 1920, LFA.
6. Bainbridge Colby, US Secretary of State, quoted in "Frederick Landis, Speaker and Writer," *Chautauqua Pamphlet*, LFA.
7. "Hoosier Senate, Extraordinary Session," *Senatorial Record, Indiana Society of Chicago*, January 15, 1921, LFA.
8. "Inaugural Address of Mr. Fred Landis," *Senatorial Record, Indiana Society of Chicago*, January 15, 1921, LFA.
9. "Landis Lecture Proves Pleasant Surprise Sunday," *Brazil Daily Times*, August 21, 1922, ISL.
10. Frederick Landis, "Hoosiergrams," *Indianapolis Star*, June 14, 1923, ISL.
11. Ibid., July 4, 1923, ISL.
12. Ibid., July 9, 1923, ISL.
13. Frederick's recognition of the worth of the late President Harding steered him into the issue presently called "term limits." Also, Frederick saw in Harding's premature death a risk in changing the presidential term from four to six years. His conclusion:
     > It is not the people's government, if they can not elect the man they want as often as they want him. And in an emergency, they might want him greatly!

     Ibid., August 11, 1923, ISL.
14. Prohibition remained Frederick's commitment, and he described its place in American law:
     > "Fanatics" did not put the eighteenth amendment into the constitution; the brewers did that . . . State sovereignty has now been invoked in behalf of slavery, polygamy, yellow fever, child labor and booze.

     Ibid., June 6, 1923, ISL.
15. The beauty of the church steeple, the reassuring symbol of people of faith, was, in Frederick's view, the rallying point for Believers:
     > The pulpit forgave all who believed, but the bell forgave all those who heard.

It appealed to universal hope in the universal language
of music.
Ibid., May 23, 1923, ISL.
16. James W. Lowry, *Hans Landis -- Swiss Anabaptist Martyr in Seventeenth Century Documents* (Millersburg OH: Ohio Amish Library, 2003)
17. Knowing that Robert G. Ingersoll was widely-known for his non-belief in God, Frederick found this occasion an appropriate one to make a reference to the great orator:
Ingersoll assailed the Bible, but he had the decency to
stand outside the church when he did it.
Ibid., August 30, 1923, ISL.
18. International relations can, at times, be reduced to simple terms, and Frederick has done that in estimating the basic motivations of communist officials who turnedout in force in Russia for an American reception:
They were visibly depressed by the reported shortage of
labor in American harvest fields.
They may be flighty about some things, but these
Russians certainly can be relied upon at meal time. They
can hear a dinner bell in a boiler shop.
Ibid., June 30, 1923, ISL.
19. Author's note:
The impression held by Landis family members has been that Arthur Brisbane, nationally-known editorial writer of the *New York American* expected that Frederick would be his "ghost-writer." Family members also have believed that certain in-house pressures may have persisted during Frederick's tenure in New York as a result of his signature, hard-hitting style that may have drawn some luster away from Mr. Brisbane's more traditional editorials.
20. Frederick Landis, Americanisms, "Government Regulation of Prices," *New York American*, August 22, 1924, ISL.
21. Editor, *Evening Journal*; Editorial page, *New York Evening Journal*, August 22, 1924, ISL.
22. Arthur Brisbane, "Today," *Indianapolis Star*, June 1924, ISL.
23. Frederick Landis, "Time for America to Demand Its Rights in Naval Power," *New York American*, May 19, 1924, ISL.
24. Frederick Landis, "The March of Events," *New York American*, January 2, 1925, ISL.
25. There could be no reasonable argument for continuing to delay the national honor to Monticello:
The fact that Jefferson's home was not made a shrine long
ago is an indication of nationwide sleeping sickness.
Frederick Landis, "Jefferson's Home Should Be a Shrine," *New York American*, March 24, 1925, ISL.

26. Frederick Landis, "Britannia, Mistress of the Seas," *New York American*, June 12, 1925, ISL.

27. Frederick Landis, "The Druggist Fills a Public Need," *New York American*, June 12, 1925, ISL.

28. Frederick Landis, "Grade Crossing Evil Dies Hard," *New York American*, March 25, 1925, ISL.

29. Frederick Landis, "Public Is for Prompt Action to Avert Great Coal Strike," *New York American*, July 21, 1925, ISL.

30. Frederick Landis, "Hylan's Subway Finance Plan Means Cheaper and Better Homes for Everybody," *New York American*, June 6, 1925, ISL.

31. Frederick Landis, Masthead, *New York American, San Francisco Examiner* and other Hearst newspapers, May 30, 1925, LFA.

32. Frederick Landis, "Pershing All Right as He Is," *New York American*, March 25, 1925, ISL.

33. Frederick Landis, "Managers Must Clean the Stage," *New York American*, February 25, 1925, ISL.

34. It was Frederick's concern that such crimes as emerged from the Teapot Dome affair were not only clearly punishable themselves, but potentially could encourage greater lawlessness if not thoroughly prosecuted:

> No fraud, oh no! Nothing but peaches and cream and lily white innocence!..
>
> After reading this Teapot Dome decision one is forced to conclude that it is not right to let little lambs like Sinclair and Fall and Doheny run around alone in a wicked world without a chaperon.
>
> They have been abused and accused of grabbing things off, but this judge's decision proves once more that "Virtue is its own reward!"

Frederick Landis, "Americanisms," *New York American*, June 23, 1925, ISL.

35. Frederick's fuller discussion of the Scopes Monkey Trial follows:

> The poor old Goddess of Justice has had a lot of things done to her in the United States, but this is the first time that she has been compelled to give a sideshow and perform as a mermaid, sword-swallower and Wild Australian Girl.

Ibid., July 11, 1925, ISL.

36. Frederick Landis, "Anti-Evolution Amendment, Absurd as It Is, Has Backers," *New York American*, July 18, 1925, ISL.

37. Frederick Landis, "Wilbur's Change of View on Navy," *New York American*, February 4, 1925, ISL.

38. There seemed to be no time to waste, in Frederick's judgement for the establishment of a Department of Defense:

> We are familiar with the petty hates that divide little men in common life, the hates that make men proscribe those who differ from them, but to find such a Ku Klux temper in the

councils of the nation's defenders, such petty, bitter jealousies between different branches of a common public service is a most appalling commentary on the willingness of the bureaucrat to exalt his little zone of power without regard to the havoc which it may visit upon his country! . . .
Let us tear down the little departmental shacks in which these envious branches of our safety now snipe upon each other and over each other's heads upon the American people.
Frederick Landis, "A Single Great Department Needed to Assure the Nation's Defense," *New York American*, March 2, 1925, ISL.

39. Frederick Landis, "Keep Our Liners in American Hands," *New York American*, April 7, 1925, ISL.
40. Frederick Landis, "Rate Favoritism on American Ships," *New York American*, April 8, 1925, ISL.
41. Frederick Landis, "Turn Light on Aircraft Fiasco," *New York American*, January 14, 1925, ISL.
42. Frederick Landis, "Secretary of War Weeks Should Be Asked to Resign, " *New York American*, February 21, 1925, ISL.
43. Frederick Landis, "Timely Warning on Alien Propaganda," *New York American*, June 12, 1925; and "True American Spirit Shown in National Defense Rally," *New York American*, July 10, 1925, ISL.
44. The problem of France's disregard of its obligation to pay back its loan from the United States, Frederick viewed as inexcusable:
Can the mutual respect which is the basis of international co-operation--can this mutual respect exist among nations where common honesty is thus replaced by barefaced repudiation? Only a conference of bankrupts and confiscators would say so.
Frederick Landis, "France, Evading Honest Debt, Imperils Her Own Credit," *New York American*, January 27, 1925; and "France Intends to Pay Us, But --," *New York American*, April 22, 1925,ISL.
45. Frederick Landis, "Why These Renewed Attempts to Drag US Into League Court?" *NewYork American*, July 17, 1925, ISL.
46. Kenesaw's observation: "That's a pretty tough break that family at Logansport is getting" suggests that their brother Frederick would face financial challenges in re-settling his family of a wife and six children back in small-town Indiana, in pursuit of a journalistic or political career. Kenesaw, Chicago, to Frances, New York, May 11, 1926, CHS.
47. "Frederick Landis Comes to the Pharos-Tribune," *Logansport Pharos-Tribune*, about October 1, 1926, ISL. ISL.
48. Kenesaw II, New York City, to Kenesaw, Chicago, December 4, 1926, CHS.
49. This eulogy of Speaker Cannon came from Frederick's heart:
He won what no other American ever did--twenty-five nominations for congress from the same congressional district.

352

He was partisan to the core; he was for his party, right or
wrong . . .

To see this old warrior bring a national appropriation bill
upon the floor of the House of Representatives and fight it
through, was a thing of great delight . . .

He gave his country service of priceless value.

He had the respect and the affection of Democrats, as well
as Republicans.

Frederick Landis, "Reason," *Logansport Pharos Tribune*,
November 15, 1926, ISL.

50. Frederick Landis, "Boy Scout Movement Teaches the Law of the
Square Deal," *New York American*, February 8, 1926, ISL.

51. Frederick showed little patience with problems associated with the
early years of radio:

We have too many channels now for the distribution of
slime, without prostituting the radio. We have putrid plays and
printed pestilence until people must wear gas masks. The
merchant of filth should not be permitted to make the sky his
sewer--to throw his cans of garbage at the stars. If he has a
radio license, take it from him! Keep all such vermin off the
air. The American eagle should chase the buzzards!

Frederick Landis, "Reason," November 3, 1926, ISL.

52. Ibid., December 30, 1926, ISL.

53. Frederick offered little consideration of cult leaders and their naïve
followers:

"King" Benjamin Purnell, Ruler of the House of David, up in
Michigan, now greets his faithful followers through the bars of
the Berrien County jail . . .

Ibid., November 18, 1926, ISL.

54. The people of the United States get what they deserve in the quality of
government, according to Frederick, who continued:

The government is ours; it belongs to the people -- and
there is nobody in this Country but people.

We get what we want!

The swiftness of our pace springs from our over-
abundance and the decline of that religious spirit which
marked the days of the Pilgrims.

Ibid., November 24, 1926, ISL.

55. Ibid., November 4, 1926, ISL.

56. Ibid., November 5, 1926, ISL.

57. The Club newsletter quoted novelist Booth Tarkington's remarks about
Frederick'qualifications:

"I would walk ten miles through the snow to hear Frederick Landis make
a speech and I don't like walking or snow."

Frederick Landis, "Cornfield Philosophy on Current Events," *The
Executives' Club News*, Chicago, May 27, 1927, LFA.

353

58. Lionel Barrymore was gratified with *The Copperhead's* reception in Los Angeles, noting it:

> "inspired cheers, rave reviews, and seventeen curtain calls."

Brother-actor John Barrymore added that he:

> "longed for the kind of ovations that had greeted Lionel's Los Angeles *Copperhead* performances."

Margot Peters, 294, 297, 329.

59. Frederick Landis, "Reason," February 12, 1927, ISL.

60. Frederick Landis, "Reason: The American Eagle Proud of His Son, Lindbergh!" *Logansport Pharos-Tribune*, May 22, 1927, LFA.

61. Frederick's opinion about President Coolidge's stand on the strength of the US Navy follows:

> Mr. Coolidge wants to run again and he remembers that his economy program made him strong in days gone by and he may have thought that still greater economy at the cost of safety would make him powerful now. But he is mistaken!

Frederick Landis, "Reason," January 6, 1927, ISL.

62. A portion of the *Chicago Tribune*'s publication of Frederick's critique of Chicago appears below:

> Last Sunday's *Chicago Tribune* carried an editorial bitterly abusing Indiana for her shortcomings, but Illinois cannot high hat us.
>
> Chicago, with more murders than England, Scotland, and Wales combined!
>
> There's this difference between these neighbor states-- when Indiana indicts her governor she convicts him, but when Illinois indicts her governor SHE RE-ELECTS HIM!

"Read It And Weep," *Chicago Tribune*, April 11, 1927, LFA.

63. On the matter of national defense, Frederick was determined that the United States should ready her arsenal, regardless of the intentions of other powers:

> These nations will never cut out their navies until they decide that the airplane has taken the place of the fighting ship.
>
> And when it shifts from sea power to sky power, there can be no disarmament, for the sky will be black with commercial aviation and you can change an airplane from a dove of peace to an eagle of war, simply by changing cargoes.

Frederick Landis, "Reason," February 16, 1927, ISL.

64. Frederick's cartoons featured a series of seven illustrations of "Old Judge Pepper:"

65. Frederick's concluded his address to the Indiana Society of Chicago with the following:

> The old-fashioned Father and Mother gave to America the men and women who have made her the marvel of mankind . . .
>
> Their's was the biggest business ever known -- the building of a people, whose achievements would confuse the prophets of

old and the works of whose genius surpass the miracles of the scriptures.

A people, great in mind, but greater still in soul -- a people whose sense of justice shall some day lift the Flag we love so high, its stars shall mingle with the stars of Heaven.

(Great applause, the entire audience rising and cheering.)

"Address by Frederick Landis," *Souvenir of the Twenty-Fourth Annual Dinner*, Indiana Society of Chicago, December 1, 1928, LFA.

66. Frederick's serious concern about the "franking privilege" in Congress led him to cite specifics:

> The franking privilege should be limited to letters written by congressmen in the line of their public duty and to the distribution of documents which the government publishes for the public benefit.

Frederick Landis, "Reason," August 7, 1928, ISL.

67. On the heels of Frederick's defeat for the gubernatorial nomination by regular forces of the Republican Party, he maintained his practice of speaking out for "the little guy," such as thef armer:

> The President's strong language in vetoing the Farm Relief bill might be justified, if this country had never given charity balls for the benefit of private interests.

Ibid., May 28, 1928, ISL.

68. Frederick's essay on the ill-advised G.A.R. exclusion of the Confederate Veterans follows:

> The national convention of the G. A.R made a mistake when it declined the invitation of the Confederate Veterans to hold a Blue and Gray reunion next year.
>
> It was deplorable and it is regretted by the great majority of G.A.R. veterans and everybody else in the north . . .
>
> We hope the time will never come when any Americans, after they have bled and starved for a cause.
>
> The Grand Army of the Republic was misrepresented by its national convention in Maine, for the thin line of Blue harbors in its heart no resentment against the few survivors of the Lost Cause.
>
> Rather do members of the G.A.R. regard them as brothers from whom they were once estranged, but with whom they are now united in a better country.

Ibid., September 17, 1929, ISL.

69. Frederick devoted his entire column to this question of inordinate influence by private organizations opposed to military preparedness lobbying in the Nation's Capital:

> The amalgamated Olive Branch Wavers, consisting of anarchists, dreamers, international free-lovers and pious frauds, propose that we lapse into utter defenselessness to prove our faith in the Kellogg treaty

and lead the whole world to the altar of peace, notwithstanding the fact that the other parties to the Kellogg treaty constantly arm themselves . . . Frederick Landis, "We Should Drive All the Lobbyists Out of Washington;" Ibid., January 5, 1929, ISL.

70. Frederick's essay on the American woman follows:
The other night we saw a pretty girl, dressed in the fashion of thirty years ago.

She was not broadcasting: she was covered up.

She looked more like a queen than anybody we've laid eyes on in a long, long time.

We wish we might call back to the United States that great respect of other years.

But only the women of America can call it back.

They can call it back only by putting on some clothes, throwing their cigarettes away and letting the gentlemen drink the high-balls.

With man's respect for woman gone, civilization is only a varnished paganism, only a gilded lie! . . .

The dress that girl wore carried us back to the days when legs were the private property of those to whom they were attached .
. .

If any young bird had gone to a dance in those days, reeking of rotten hooch, we would have thrown his carcass out of the first window.

If any young bird had offered a girl a flask we would have broken his neck.

And if any girl had tossed her countenance to the ceiling and drunk like a long-shoreman, we would have had heart failure! Ibid., October 23, 1929, ISL.

71. Frederick Landis, *The Hoosier Editor*, November, 1933, LFA.

72. Frederick Landis, "Our Poor Forefathers," *Radio Guide*, June 16, 1934, ISL.

73. *Pamphlet, Illinois Bankers Association Annual Mid-Winter Dinner,* January 23, 1930, LFA.

74. "Frederick Landis To Appear Every Friday At WLW," *Crosley Radio News*, September 20, 1930, LFA.

75. Frederick Landis, "The Glory of His Country," *Play of the week,* December 28, 1930, December 31, 1930, and January 3, 1931; "The Crosley Theater," *WLW The Nation's Station*, Cincinnati, Ohio; LFA.

76. Frederick's editorial on the problem of religion in Russia and the problem of regarding religion continues in the following excerpts:
These Russians should have taken the Bible, perverted by their czars, and by its pages proved those czars to have been imposters.

They should have revealed the Christ as the friend of the poor and the oppressed and made the hope they cannot kill, their ally, rather than their foe . . .

For testimony, we need go only to the French agnostic, Voltaire, who said: If there were no God, it would be necessary to invent one!

Frederick Landis, "Reason," March 3, 1930, ISL.

77. The conclusion of Frederick's text on the revered poppy follows:

TOMORROW is not just another day. It is a sacred day, a day of gratitude.

It gives us the opportunity to remember those whom we owe a debt we can never pay, those whose lives were shattered while fighting for the flag . . .

Come with me; let us walk among these shattered men . . .

Let us help them while we may, for their days are numbered.

More than seventy of them answer the last roll call every day; more than twenty-five thousand of them every year . . .

And if you should see one man without a poppy on his coat, ask him the question: "Are you an American?"

"Hope in the Midst of Despair," *The American Legion Auxiliary Bulletin*, June 1931, LFA.

78. "Frederick Landis Dies," *Logansport Pharos-Tribune*, November 15, 1934, ISL.

79. Frederick elaborated on his intentions at entrepreneurship with *The Hoosier Editor*:

I am convinced conditions are on the upgrade and I take off my hat to the president with his great and audacious program, devoted to the welfare of the country . . . Regarding this modest enterprise of mine I have faith that things will be better . . . I will go into 34 states on the first issue . . . I am starting on a shoe string. I have had several financial offers but I don't want to have to call a meeting in the town hall when I get ready to express my own views. Neither will I accept any advertising which will influence what I have to say in any way. All my life I have wanted something of this kind. It will be a small magazine.

"Landis Is Confident Of Business Upturn; Plans For Magazine," *Logansport Press*, August 1, 1933, ISL.

80. "'Bon Mots' Flow From Frederick Landis Pen," *Indianapolis News*, November 6, 1933, ISL.

81. Frederick set the scene to welcome readers of his new publication:

On Thanksgiving day I shall think of all of you who have made this publication possible. Through the months we shall sit in the grand stand together and watch the jamboree of people and events, not so presumptuous as to think we can change it in the least, but counting ourselves extremely fortunate if we may be able to determine the nature of the

357

function, whether it be a cakewalk, a Halloween party or a wake.
The Hoosier Editor, November 1933. LFA.
82. Frederick's description of the Indiana countryside continued:
>   . . . a gem of cliffs, ferns, canyons, soaring trees, mirrored waters, spectral shadows, gliding fancies, whispering yesterdays, twilight patience, silent majesty, and far above, up a shimmering ladder of sunlight, the fleecy clouds; a rugged cathedral of Time, with a congregation of ages and a gospel of never-ending peace.
>   Ibid., December 1933. LFA.
83. Ibid., January 1934. LFA.
84. Ibid., February 1934. LFA.
85. Ibid., May 1934. LFA.
86. Frederick's description of the origin of our Flag continued:
>   It was not made by women over night—this flag of ours—but slowly woven in the loom of years.
>   Justice is in it, idealism, achievement and opportunity for all.
>   Yes, woven of threads, more strange than ever entered into flag before.
>   It is the flag of exiles—of old philosophers who made this sky the home of conscience, and of continental fighters who gave their rags a finer dignity than kingly robes.
>   It is the flag of Lincoln and prisoners of Andersonville who found starvation sweeter than disloyalty.
>   It is the flag of legions who only yesterday spent their lives to buy the safety of a world.
>   Liberty is in it—and the pioneer—the daring of men and the fine heroism of women—the character which crowned the old wilderness with glory—and the vision which saw unborn cities.
>   In it is sublime aspiration and patient burden-bearing—the genius of a Century's great and the fidelity of a Century's obscure.
>   No—it was not made by woman over night—this flag we love—but slowly blended of the best of all races, colors, creeds—the Rainbow Division of American progress.
>   Ibid., June 1934. LFA.
87. Ibid., July 1934. LFA.
88. Ibid., August 1934. LFA.
89. Ibid., April 1934. LFA.
90. In his final issue of *The Hoosier Editor*, Frederick recalled the demise of the beloved barbershop:
>   The old boy was a rhapsody of assault and battery. He reminded you of Sheridan's ride to Winchester.
>   This old boy rubbed it out, but the new one perfumes it in.
>   The old boy scoured you for a quarter, but the new one "cleans" you for a dollar.

You used to leap from the chair like Napoleon returning from Elba, but now you ooze out of it like a counterfeiter.

Oh, for the old Shampooer!

Ibid., October 1934. LFA.

91. Divorce, modern style, Frederick suggested, might take on new ideas to accompany legal procedures:

One thing is perfectly clear, and it is that the cold, bare ceremonies of the court room will do no longer.

We must envelop divorce in the dignified and reverential atmosphere to which its basic values entitle it . . .

And if the divorce be the climax of an elopement, as happens now and then, a little dash of romance could be injected by having the complaining Juliet swing down from the courthouse clock.

Let's honor divorce.

Let's do it right.

Ibid., LFA.

92. "Frederick Landis Speaks At Court House Tonight; All Republicans Invited," *Valparaiso Vedette-Messenger*, April 11, 1934, ISL.

93. "Frederick Landis Meeting Here On Friday Attracted An Enthusiastic Gathering," *Carroll County Press*, April 13, 1934, ISL.

94. "Landis Polls More Votes Than Both Opponents," *Indianapolis News*, May 9, 1934; "Landis Wins by Big Majority," *Logansport Press*, May 10,1934; and letter, Arthur J. Lovell, Washington, D.C., to A. E. Gordon, Indianapolis, May 14, 1934, ISL.

95. *The Hoosier Editor*, September 1934. LFA.

96. "Useful Satire," *Chicago American*, January 16, 1934, ISL.

97. Frederick Landis, "Radio, The First Line of Defense," *Radio Guide*, June 9, 1934, ISL.

98. Frederick Landis, "Our Poor Forefathers," *Radio Guide*, June 16, 1934, ISL.

99. Frederick Landis, "The World's Parade," *Radio Guide*, June 23, 1934 ISL.

100. "Landis Sweeps District," *Logansport Press*, November 8, 1934, ISL.

101. "A Man Runs Who Can Run," *Logansport Press*, November 8, 1934; "Frederick Landis, Congressman-Elect, Dies," *Indianapolis News*, November 15, 1934; "Frederick Landis Dies," *Logansport Pharos-Tribune*, November 15, 1934; and "Frederick Landis, Editor, Dead at 62," The *New York Times*, November 16, 1934, ISL.

* * *

Excerpts of Frederick's recollections written during his last year in *The Hoosier Editor* and "Here at Home" LFA.

Memories of January

In an early "Here at Home" column, he recalled local history associated with an old mansion in town, the Biddle House, where in the early days "it was a palace of the old frontier, when all around it were Indians and trees and silence and the river, when pioneers sat before its wide fire places and discussed the issues of the day."

One of the memorable local occasions, in Frederick's thinking, was the moment when passengers on trains stopping at Logansport would pay close attention to a human fixture of the old railroad depot, "perhaps the town's most widely-observed son . . . an unobtrusive old colored man who had been a slave." "Uncle Allen" operated a popular fruit stand there and was a "picturesque piece of life, touching times 'before the Civil War.'"

"A gorge and waterfall in Indiana?" One might suggest that only Frederick could find such a spectacular phenomenon in the flatness of the northern part of the State. Fitch's Glen is the place, and the prominent Logansport scribe uncovered a possibility that this scenic twist of nature should become a satisfying travel stop for the weary traveler of highway 29. As a park, this vantage point offers "the view of the Wabash River from the hill-tip which suggests the Hudson."

A love of Indiana was not far from the surface when Frederick settled in to do a bit of writing about small-town events. His admiration for the youthful vigor of an elderly friend, one Cale Banta, led him to conclude that "Ponce de Leon fell down in his effort to locate the Fountain of Eternal Youth because he hunted for it in Florida." The Spanish explorer's problem, Frederick believed, was that he failed to look where Cale found it: "somewhere near the banks of Crooked Creek." Cale was a challenge for Father Time because "the old man with the scythe and hour glass turns his horse and rides off in the opposite direction."

Memories of February

The last vestiges of the era of Chief Logan and the Indians along the Wabash River at Logansport were made real to Frederick when he wrote of Charles McPherson, "Indian Charley." He was "the last of the red men who lingered in the midst of the pale faces" in town. He gained respect as "one of the few of his people able to fit into the white man's picture, and he became an expert cabinet maker." Charley's association with "firewater" led to "nocturnal performances" that tended to unnerve Logansport's citizenry.

The history of Logansport's College Hill brought back memories of a noteworthy feature of the community, Smithson College, that, in Frederick's view, "was an outstanding institution of higher learning in early Indiana." Unfortunately, it was abandoned, and, when an opportunity arose to establish a "normal" or "teachers" college on the site, there was a lack of initiative on the part of the town's citizenry, according to Frederick. He went on to point out that Logansport's loss was Valparaiso's gain because that teachers college "grew to be the largest private, normal college in the United States."

In the early years of the town, the Barnett House served as a welcome gathering point "when travel was slow and distances were real," Frederick wrote.

This tavern featured "a double-deck portico" and "was a thing of beauty." Sundays were a special time for travelers at "the old Barnett," for they knew of the reputation of this Logansport attraction as its fame "went up and down the old canal."

Memories of March

Frederick's *Hoosier Editor* introduction for March offered reassurance to citizens, consumed in efforts to conquer the effects of the Great Depression:

You and I are lucky. Things are not exactly ideal, but we should thank the Lord that we live under the Stars and Stripes.

Unlike the fathers and mothers of Europe, we can step into the bedroom at night and look at the kids, when they are asleep, without wondering whether they will be shot in the Balkans, gassed in Flanders or bayoneted in Austria.

The month of March urged Frederick also to recall the homespun joys of the "great old days" in Logansport, noting that, not so many years ago, cows wandered around much as they pleased: "Cows used to go everywhere in our town. They were our honored guests; they had the freedom of the city!"

Memories of April

Frederick had a lot to say about the wanton slaughter of trees— "vandalism pure and simple." Then he had kind words . . . "New England protects her trees—and they glorify her," adding:

Take that old elm that used to stand in Cambridge, Massachusetts, the elm under which Washington assumed command of the Continental Army. It was honored throughout its long life, and there it stood in its last days, with limbs supported, like an old Revolutionary soldier on his crutches!

Reminiscing about the olden days that were being changed by the technology of the automobile, Frederick recalled the key role of the livery stable as a focal point of discussion of issues of the day. He cited those local equine establishments, "before the gasoline-drinking quadruped put the horse out of business." Frederick listed "such seats of profound disputations" prospering in Logansport: Earl Stewart's on Fourth street, Jim O'Donnell's on 3rd street, Morris' on lower Market street, and Sellers' on Twelfth street," but he called special attention to "the greatest of them all . . . Emmanuel Clem's Eighth street livery stable between Market and Broadway." Frederick viewed the latter as "the neighborhood club . . . night after night."

Labor difficulties in the 1890's reached down from the main offices in Chicago to workers in Logansport, and Frederick, a young aspiring lawyer, recalled the memorable appearance by the city's mayor, who demonstrated timely leadership. For a period of time, the risk of a strike with unknown consequences was believed likely when the mayor, B. C. D. Reed settled the issue when he "made the most adroit and convincing speech this community ever heard . . . and the men did not strike."

361

Memories of May

Ideas of "the old swimmin' hole" inspired Frederick to recall his youth, when he swam above the Davis Bridge over Eel River, not far from the family farm on the north side of the river. When opportunity presented itself, Frederick and probably Kenesaw swam there, but he also recalled "Flat Rock" "at the end of 17th Street. Speaking of the "downtown kids," Frederick was familiar with the place near the water-works dam, where they "peeled off their scenery" and dived at "the sportiest place of all: 'The Tumbles.'"

The name of Albert J. Beveridge Jr. appeared in the Logansport newspaper in an account of his nomination for the state legislature. Upon reading this item, Frederick recalled the days when he was serving his first term as Congressman, and the candidate's father, Indiana's Senator Albert J. Beveridge arrived on the occasion of a planned visit by President Theodore Roosevelt. Frederick showed his hospitable streak by offering the Senator a "pot luck" breakfast, because the makeshift host "was batching it." Finding nothing more appropriate in the pantry, Frederick recalled, he delivered to his guest a serving of ham and bananas "which he disposed of in short order." The following morning, Frederick offered the Senator a choice . . . the same thing or a change and, responding to Mr. Beveridge's request for a change, proceeded to deliver a breakfast of "bananas and ham."

One of Logansport's mayors of olden times was a character, Frederick wrote, referring to Charles B. LaSalle, who "made his way about the streets, dressed in Prince Albert suit and plug hat, smoking a long clay pipe." The mayor also had been Circuit Court judge and probate commissioner and lived at the courthouse" surrounded by a world of relics of pioneer days," that Frederick appeared to appreciate. A final recollection was Judge LaSalle's penchant for "a nip of 'corn,' but always insisted that it was just an 'appetizer.'"

Memories of June

Drawing from his own fireside, Frederick turned the spotlight on the plight of the ordinary variety of house dog, calling for reasonable treatment by the younger generation of their best friend:

During the hot weather the papers reported that children all over the country were bitten by dogs, which may or may not mean that the dogs are dangerous.

Why should we expect a poor dog, without a single college degree, to submit in hot weather to have the kids pull his ears, nose, tail and other outstanding characteristics, and smile gratefully for the torture.

Tell the children to let their panting friend alone in his misery, lest in profound musings over his discomfort, he forget for the moment that he is expected to have better manners than anybody else about the house. Let's give the dog a break.

Frederick called attention to the unveiling back in 1886, when he was a young teenager, of the tall Soldiers' Monument, that had attracted "multitudes from all over Indiana." On numerous celebrations of Decoration Day and Independence Day in later years, Frederick became the featured speaker. During that dedication,

Frederick recalled: "General William Gibson, one of the greatest inspirational orators who ever lived," delivered an address that he graciously brought to an end during a heavy rainstorm.

Some long time ago, Logansport used to have some town characters, but no one seemed to match "King Stewart," according to Frederick. He wrote that this fellow was "a tree trimmer who was a familiar sight in the garb of a sack "that came to his knees," and this "tall, slim colored man" was usually "pushing a cart." The man claimed to be regal, "an African king, and he was about the nearest approach to royalty Logansport ever had."

Frederick spoke like a man who ought to know when he wrote about Logansport's "Lovers' Lane" that extended in the country on the east side of town between High street and George street. In order to get a place on this "beautifully-shaded piece of road . . . a fellow had to save his spare change for a while to get enough to rent an equipage." When he had done this, he could transfer "his fair lady" to the place where "the trees on both sides formed an arch above it." Sounding like the voice of experience back in the 1890's, he recalled: "There the Romeos parked with their Juliets until it was hard to get through from one end to the other."

Memories of July

The July issue of the *Hoosier Editor* was a challenge for Frederick, and what does a frank author do in such a case but admit it. This problem is what his introduction is all about:

> *This number has been born amid great tribulation.*
> *It's been harder to bring into the world than those quintuplets up in Canada.*
> *Nobody should try to write when it's this hot.*
> *You can't make the Muse do the hoochee-koochee when it's hot enough to fry eggs on the cellar door.*
> *So he who does the best he can when the thermometer is playing leapfrog is entitled to the thanks of Congress, and should receive the Purple Heart—or something.*

Back when Frederick was eight years old, the shooting of a President made a lasting impression on him. He wrote in his editorial about a recent visit to Tick Creek, an area where people had been harvesting crops in the 1880's, and his recollection over many years of the reaction of men, mostly old soldiers, who were working there, when word of the sordid deed reached them. Frederick recalled "the expression of horror and wrath by those who had fought with Garfield in the Union Army."

Although the early 1930's found Logansport far from any kind of military action in the world, there was a reminder of our nation's security commitment when Bob Surendorf returned from a tour in the United States Navy. Frederick spent some time listening to the endless tales stemming from "an inexhaustible supply of strange experiences" related by "a Gob in this and foreign lands." For a native of Logansport, Surendorf exhibited, in Frederick's judgement "a fine line of sailor slang," gained while "on the deck of an American fighting ship."

Memories of August

With Frederick's campaign for Congress in full swing, he delivered as promised with the August issue of the *Hoosier Editor*, bringing the focus of his introduction to activities going on at his homestead in Logansport, one in which my brother Charles and I proved to be lucky gardeners:

> *Last spring our kids put out a garden, watering it, tending it and measuring the plants every day.*
>
> *Then they went away to camp and today two red, round tomatoes arrived in the back yard, so we're wrapping them up and sending them to the boys.*

I mention it just to let you know that something of real importance is going on in the country.

As the reader has learned well, Frederick tirelessly wrote about the great mistake of America getting involved in foreign wars, often referring to George Washington's solid, but largely ignored, advice. In his latest reasoning found in the August issue of the *Hoosier Editor*, he wrote, calling into serious question the national gullibility:

> *Who would have thought back in 1914 that we would ever so far lose our minds and so far forget our traditions as to lunge into that continental slaughter house?*
>
> *And that was the result of propaganda.*
>
> *It was the biggest gold brick ever sold to any nation . . .*
>
> *Let Germany tell us to keep within certain ocean lanes when we crossed the Atlantic?*
>
> *Never!*
>
> *Few of us expected to cross the Atlantic; in fact, few of us ever expected to cross Possum Creek, but we would perish before we would let the kaiser fence off the ocean.*
>
> *And so the propagandists kept on feeding us the mustard until finally we sailed in and fought for the birds who later gave us the laugh, but have steadfastly refused to give us anything else.*
>
> *And remember—that was put over on us merely by the papers and the prima donnas—but now we have an agency, which for purposes of propaganda, is so powerful it almost staggers the imagination—the radio!*

A momentous event took place in one Logansport household during the month of August in the year 1934: the silver wedding anniversary of Frederick Landis and Bessie Baker. The reader may wonder if the recent "Here at Home" article on the city's Lovers' Lane might have been inspired by the approach of this landmark occurrence. Frederick saw fit, in any case, to explain that President Roosevelt's austerity proposition to control silver discouraged him from finding an appropriate gift, but he noted his receipt of congratulations from the following personages: "Mahatma Ghandi, the Sultan of Zulu, the Mikado of Japan, Mussolini, Hitler, Stalin, Pilsudski and the Prince of Wales," adding, however, "All of these foreign messages were sent collect."

A challenge to the readers from the editor: "How many of you old timers remember the old court- house pump?" Without waiting for a written reply or a phone call, Frederick, who recalled this welcomed source of water when he was 12 years old, proceeded to remind the reader that folks used to get a drink from the attached cups and talk about "the weather or the state of the Union." The pump was a community fixture that afforded a clean water supply for the downtown neighborhood until progress in the form of redoing "the temple of justice in 1884."

Memories of September

With great joy, Frederick recalled his family's spring wagon visit to the County Fair when he and his older brothers tried to enter their western pony in a mule race. Although "Buck" fell far short of resembling a mule, "a dun pony with a stripe down his back and his upholstery was long and thick and his ears were promisingly long," the boys nearly convinced the judges that he was the real thing. Unfortunately, after winning the race, "Buck kicked one of the judges through a picket fence." They ruled against him, while acknowledging that he "looked something like a mule, something like a camel and a little like a mountain goat."

Well along in his campaign for Congress, Frederick was able to appreciate a break in the routine of travelling around the Second District by repairing to a local resort of national reputation, the Izaak Walton League. He also took time out to express his gratitude to those who labored there to make swimming and relaxation a pleasure for the multitudes that came to visit. Frederick wrote as if he had seen the facility take its place in the community, transforming "an abandoned farm into a public benefaction . . . blessed with water and hills and trees."

A fan of big league baseball, Frederick still showed a preference for the sandlot variety that took place across the street from the family home. He lamented the fact that residential growth had taken away these open spaces that permitted young boys to spend hours at their favorite sport. In comparison with the major leagues, these games were continuous, and "you could hear it for three blocks, and there was more action in a single game than in a whole world series." Frederick's conclusion that "the game the kids play" far outshone the performance of the professional baseball players.

Taking the kids to the country for some good fruit-picking was Frederick's fond memory as a young boy and remained a favored choice as a father. Also, he wrote, the autumn season is the one time when sentiment was strong for quiet, meditative relaxation. His aspirations for this activity targeted "elderberries, wild grapes, walnuts and hickory nuts," and he recalled the joy felt in school when the teacher called for the students to raise their hands -- "from picking and hulling walnuts, our hands were black as ebony."

Memories of October

The dissatisfaction of a journalistic occupation "in the big city" was the subject of "Here at Home," bringing to mind Frederick's own short-lived experience on the staff of the *New York American* in the mid-1920's. He wrote that a Washington correspondent expressed an interest in switching to a newspaper in the country, and this query brought forth Frederick's thoughts: "Strange as it may seem to some, this is the secret ambition of many a celebrated metropolitan journalist who has grown weary of the ceaseless grind and tumult of the big center." No doubt, Frederick was now enjoying greater freedom in Logansport -- "the tall timber."

With wistful thought, Frederick harkened back to his days as a sport-loving youth in Logansport, when fighting among the local baseball players was a standard occurrence. In fact, as he described the activity, it seemed to be more fun than playing the outfield. He recalled: "We were tough . . . there was more fighting on the baseball grounds by the old ice house on the banks of Eel River than there's been in the Balkans in a hundred years!"

As Frederick was hospitalized with "the grippe," "Here at Home" took on an ominous tone: "The writer of this paragraph is not with us today but 'the show must go on.'" The unsigned piece was authored by elder daughter Betsy, a student at Indiana University, who in subsequent issues owned up to her self-assigned responsibility. This particular item spoke of one of Frederick's favorite pastimes -- driving the family down town to get ice cream cones and added the memorable moment when on a short trip, the family dog was allowed to ride on the car's roof. As for the dog's feelings, the writer concluded: "He wouldn't have traded places with Mussolini."

Chapter 7 Notes

1. "Meet Landis, Fans' Hope," Interview, *Cincinnati Post*, November 21, 1920; CHS.
2. Kenesaw letter, February 20, 1942, to grandson Bill Phillips, the first family member to sign up for military duty after Pearl Harbor.
3. "Called Man of the Hour -- Judge Kenesaw Mountain Landis," *Sporting News*, January 15,1920, Chicago Historical Society [CHS].
4. "Wilson Arouses Landis' Anger," *Chicago Examiner*, July 1920, CHS.
5. A resident of Chicago penned the following account, describing a Prohibition violation and Judge Landis' decisive settlement of the case:
   > Imagine the scene. A spacious room, high ceiling, appropriately furnished for the expression of the majesty of the law. On one wall an impressive fresco of Moses descending the mountain bearing the tables of the law. On another, a knight in full armor setting out on a noble quest. A bust of Lincoln on a pedestal near the platform, a golden September sun illumining his wistful face. But the centre of all the life here is Judge Kenesaw Mountain Landis . . .
   > The judge said from the bench "I am having a perfectly bully time." The wistful smile seemed to deepen on the face of Lincoln. Moses tramped on down the mountain with the tables of the law, and I recalled that the wicked shall call for the mountain to fall on them, and lo, it did.

   Elmer Lynn Williams, "When the Mountain Fell on the Wicked," a citizen's unpublished essay, 4536 N. Hermitage Ave., Chicago, CHS.
6. "The Landis Type Needed," *Manufacturers' News*, Chicago, November 4, 1920, CHS.
7. Kenesaw's son provided this account of his father's law career:
   > The whole history of Father's legal practice was very successful, and it was true that when he was addressing a jury, with his final address to the jury, that the bar association would turn out pretty strongly to listen to his presentation. It was an ability to talk in an interesting, forceful and direct manner that continued throughout his whole life . . .
   > He was always a very much sought-after speaker for events of all sorts of character, and it was in his later years that he decided that he would stop this type of activity so far as possible because he just felt that there was no sense in his being a "free entertainer" as he called it when there were so many people who made their living in this manner. But he did make a splendid talk, and he was a great and firm believer in what he said . . .

   Reed Landis archives.
8. William Jennings Bryan to Kenesaw, November 6, 1920, CHS.
9. After Kenesaw assumed the position of Baseball Commissioner, a

writer offered these "personal glimpses" of Kenesaw in the courtroom:

> Prosecutors and lawyers for the defence sit down and keep silent when Judge Landis takes a witness in hand . . . He may inquire about the ancestry of the witness, his place of residence and his list of friends, to find out if the court might not know some of them; his hour for rising, how he slept last night and the state of his appetite. When he has made the witness feel "sorter homelike," the Judge resumes his questions . . . If he believes there is perjury on the stand or conspiracy among lawyers he will quit the bench without a word, leave the court room and remain in his chambers for ten or fifteen minutes. When he returns the truth usually comes out or the conspiracy is defeated.

L. G. Edwardson, "Judge Landis Seen as a Real Human Being," *New York Herald*, February 27, 1921; cited in "Personal Glimpses: Judge Landis Under Fire," *Literary Digest*, March 12, 1921, Indiana State Library [ISL].

10. "Judge Landis Signs As Baseball's Chief," *Chicago Tribune*, November 13, 1920, CHS.

11. J. M. Sheean to Kenesaw, November 13, 1920, CHS.

12. "Baseball Peace Declared; Landis Named Dictator," *New York Times*, November 13, 1920, re-printed in Gene Brown, *The Complete Book of Baseball* (New York: Bobbs-Merrill,1980).

13. "Landis a National Figure," *New York Times*, November 13, 1920, re-printed in Gene Brown.

14. "Meet Landis, Fans' Hope," *Cincinnati Post*, November 21, 1920, CHS.

15. James L. Kilgallen, "Appointed Baseball Leader Former Mediocre Player -- Judge Kenesaw Mountain Landis Now Has Supreme Control of Pastime at $42,500 a Year -- Talks With Reporter While Eating Lunch From Paper Bag," unidentified Chicago newspaper, November 13, 1920, CHS.

16. William Jennings Bryan to Kenesaw, November 29, 1920, CHS.

Kenesaw's agreement to become Baseball Commissioner resulted in a *Detroit News* dispatch from Chicago, which reported:

> Judge Landis was hearing a case in which a $15,000 bribery in connection with an income tax was charged when a committee of eight club-owners called on him . . .
> When informed of their mission he had them escorted to his chambers, where they were kept in waiting for forty-five minutes before the Judge would listen to the offer which added $42,500 to his annual income of $7,500 as judge.

17. "Personal Glimpses: Judge Landis, The New Czar of Baseballdom," *Literary Digest*, December 4, 1920, Timothy Landis File.

18. "Owners Break Bread and Bury Baseball Hatchet; Talk Turkey, Says Landis," *Boston Herald*, January 13, 1921, courtesy *Boston Herald*

American; JD Jordan A. Deutsch, Richard M. Cohen, Roland T. Johnson and David S. Neft, *The Scrapbook History of Baseball* (New York: BobbsMerrill, 1975; 110.

19. "Hoosier Senate, Extraordinary Session," *Senatorial Record, Indiana Society of Chicago*, January 15, 1921, Landis Family Archives [LFA].

20. Edwin A. Goewey, "Judge Landis, The Moses of Baseball, *Sisler's Weekly*, January 22, 1921, CHS.

21. *Hearings*, Committee on the Judiciary, House of Representatives, 66th Congress, 3rd Session; (Washington: Government Printing Office, 1921), CHS.

22. untitled report from Washington, D.C., *Shreveport* (LA) *Times*, February 13, 1921, CHS.

23. "Another Grand-Stand Play," *Lancaster* (PA) *Examiner*, February 14, 1921, CHS.

24. "Pastor Lauds Judge Landis – Chicago Preacher Says Whole Country Will Stand by Jurist's Acts," *Shreveport* (LA) *Times*, February 13, 1921, CHS.

25. "Landis Again Shows Leniency, Deferring Sentences of 2 Men," *New York Times*, February 18, 1921, CHS.

26. The editor continued his critique of the North Carolina senator and followed with a positive endorsement of Kenesaw's record as a judge:
    We, the Negroes of this portion of the country are thoroughly satisfied with the decision of Judge Landis, and have no fault whatever to find with them. All of the Negroes ever convicted by him have been proven guilty beyond all reasonable doubts.
    "Praises for Judge Landis from Negroes of Chicago," *Chicago Advocate*, February 19, 1921, ISL.

27. Mr. Heydler maintained that Kenesaw did not short-change his duties as a judge:
    There never was a more serious situation than that confronting the sport during the November conferences at Chicago.
    "Baseball Does Not Bribe Judge Landis," *New York Herald*, February 23, 1921, ISL.

28. "Judge Landis and His Critics," Maud, Oklahoma *Monitor*, March 3, 1921, CHS.

29. The unidentified editorial in poetry, entitled "Landis," apparently refers to efforts to impeach Kenesaw, and continues:
    Leonine, he stands at bay, defiant, Of the Feists that yelp and whine,
    Too sure of himself, reliant, On his spotless ermine;
    Grand old man of the bench, Just, and tried, and true,
    CHS.

30. "Personal Glimpses: Judge Landis Under Fire," *Literary Digest*, March 12, 1921, ISL.

31. "Judge Landis Seen as a Real Human Being," *The Sporting World*, March 19, 1921, CHS.
32. Reed Landis archives.
33. Frederick A. Stowe, *Political Periscope*, Peoria, Illinois, April 23, 1921, CHS.
34. "Thousands Hear Loyalty Appeal - Judge Landis in Patriotic Address Urges An Undivided Allegiance." *Indianapolis News*, April, 1921, CHS.
35. K. M. Landis file, May 1, 1921, CHS.
36. "Illinois Needs Landis in Governor's Chair," Lincoln, Illinois *Evening Courier*, July 30, 1921, CHS.
37. "Baseball Leaders won't Let White Sox Return to the Game," *New York Times*, August 4, 1921, reprinted in Gene Brown.
38. "How Do You Do," verses for music score (Chicago: Ted Browne Music Company, 1921), Timothy Landis File.
39. "Judge Landis," *Chicago Tribune*, September 3, 1921, ISL.
40. J. H. Kumler, Seven Mile, Ohio, to Kenesaw, Chicago, September 10, 1921, CHS.
41. Editorial comment, Charlotte, (MI) *Republican*, September 23, 1921, CHS.
42. Joe Durso, *Baseball and the American Dream*, 175.
43. Telegram, George and Susie Funkhouser, Dayton, Ohio, to Frances, Logansport, November 25, 1921, CHS.
44. Kenesaw, Chicago, to August Herrman, Cincinnati, November 27, 1921, CHS.
45. "Landis Urges Return of Draft System in Organized Baseball," *Portsmouth Star*, December 8, 1921, LFA.
46. Larry Woltz, "Landis Bars Ruth From Baseball Until May 20," *Chicago Tribune*, December, 1921, JD Jordan A. Deutsch, et al, 111.
47. "The Inquiring Reporter: Do you think Judge Landis would make a good mayor for Chicago?" *Chicago Tribune*, February 25, 1922, CHS.
48. Telegram, William G. Sterett, Dallas (TX), to Kenesaw, Vicksburg (MS), March 29, 1922, CHS.
49. Kenesaw, Chicago, to Colonel Sterrett, Dallas, Texas, April 6, 1922, CHS.
50. E.A.B., "Personal and Confidential," unidentified Detroit newspaper, May 1922, CHS.
51. Mary Iliff, Denver (CO), to Kenesaw, Chicago, May 22, 1922, CHS.
52. Kenesaw, Chicago, to Mary Iliff, Denver (CO), May 26, 1922, CHS.
53. The lady offered kind reminiscences of "the Landis boys of Logansport," John, in particular:

> Dr. Landis ranked high among Cincinnati physicians and held an important civic position in addition to his large private practice. Some of the friends of the family considered John to

have had the superior intellectuality, less showy, but thorough and painstaking.
Sarah S. Pratt, "Landis Brothers, Men of Integrity," a letter to the editor, *Indianapolis Star*, May 21, 1922, CHS.

54. "Court Decision for Baseball," *The Detroit News*, May 31, 1922, cited in Jordan A. Deutsch, et al.
55. Kenesaw, Chicago, to J. W. Myers, Dayton, Ohio, September 16, 1922, CHS.
56. Second Grade letter, Berkeley, California, to Kenesaw, Washington, D.C., September 28, 1922, CHS.
57. Kenesaw, Chicago, to Second Grade, Berkeley, California, October 14, 1922, CHS.
58. Robert Boyd, "Why Landis 'Called' Yankees," *Portsmouth* (VA) *Star*, October 20, 1922, LFA.
59. Kenesaw, Chicago, to Major John F. Landis, Camp Lewis, Washington, November 14, 1922, CHS.
60. Charles Kumler, Dayton (OH) to Kenesaw, Chicago, January 19, 1923, CHS.
61. Kenesaw, Chicago, to Charles Kumler, Dayton (OH), January 22, 1923, CHS.
62. "'Justice and Fair Play Violated,' Says Commissioner," *Pittsburgh Post*, March 9, 1923, cited in Jordan A. Deutsch, et al., 115.
63. "Hour by Hour With the High Ruler of Baseball," *Waterbury* (CT) *Evening Democrat*, April 27, 1923, CHS.
64. "They Shared the Cheers Before the Game," *New York Herald*, April 27, 1923, caption of photograph of Christy Mathewson, Major Hylan of New York City, Judge Landis, and John McGraw.
65. "The Landis Letters," the Commissioner, Chicago, to Joe Jackson, Bastrop, La., June 20, 1923 and July 16, 1923, ISL.
66. Kenesaw, Chicago, to Arthur Vandenberg, Grand Rapids, MI, August 2, 1923, CHS.
67. "Judge Landis in Action," *New York Evening Telegram*, August 18, 1923, CHS.
68. "Railroad Engineer Will be Guest of Landis at Series," *Associated Press* item, October 3, 1938, ISL.
69. Major John F. Landis, Fort Benning, Georgia, to Kenesaw, Chicago, December 12, 1923, CHS.
70. Kenesaw, Chicago, to Major John F. Landis, Fort Benning, Georgia, December 18, 1923, CHS.
71. The advertisement supporting the presidential candidacy of Kenesaw continued:

> Judge Landis would strike terror to the grafters and traitors. The situation is so serious; the people are going to lose faith unless something is done to convince them there is to be an

entire change . . .we must stem the tide by placing in power the ONE MAN who can restore confidence – Judge Kenesaw Mountain Landis . . . Millions of people would vote for him. "One Man the People Believe in – Millions of People of Both Parties Would Ride on the Landis Presidential Train," newspaper advertisement in 1924 by Roy W. H. Crabb, Battle Creek (MI), CHS.

72. Editorial, *Battle Creek* (MI) *Enquirer and News*, undated, May, 1924, CHS.

73. "Close-up On Landis the Czar," *Hamilton* (OH) *Herald*, May 6, 1924, CHS.

74. The telegram to the Chairman of the Illinois Delegation to the Republican National Convention continued:
> With Landis, Coolidge can carry the West and the Ticket becomes invincible . . . Landis today would be a more popular candidate for president than Coolidge himself. The delegate who introduces the name of Landis to the Convention will make his name glorious in the pages of history.

Attorney John Hugh Lally telegram, Chicago, to John G. Oglesby, Chairman, Illinois Delegation, Convention Hall, Cleveland, Ohio, June 10, 1924, CHS.

75. Telegram, Kenesaw, Chicago, to John G. Oglesby, Chairman, Illinois Delegation, Convention Hall, Cleveland, Ohio, June 11, 1924, CHS.

76. "Banished Giants Call On Landis" *Associated Press* item, October 7, 1924; cited in Jordan A. Deutsch, et al.

77. Kenesaw, Chicago, to E. S. Shaffer, Moline, Illinois, December 19, 1924, CHS.

78. "Protest of Rice's Catch Abandoned by Pirates," *Associated Press* item, *Washington Evening Star*, October 11, 1925, cited in Jordan A. Deutsch et al, 122.

79. Kenesaw, Chicago, to Jacob Kumler, Seven Mile, Ohio, November 21, 1925, CHS.

80. Jacob H. Kumler, Seven Mile, Ohio, to Kenesaw, Chicago, November 28, 1925, CHS.

81. A handwritten note was written on a letter from Kenesaw's nephew, John F. Landis, stated:
> A letter from Fred received yesterday states that he is returning to Logansport for permanent station.

Major John F. Landis, Ft. Benning, GA, to Kenesaw, Chicago, September 9, 1926, CHS.

82. Kenesaw, Chicago, to Frances, New York, May 11, 1926, CHS.

83. "Landis Invites 35th to be his Guests in 1927," *Hamilton* (OH) *Daily News*, August 27, 1926, CHS.

84. The 35th's "pilgrimage" was discussed fully in Chapter 2.

85. Kenesaw, Chicago, to Garry Herrman, President, Cincinnati Reds, September 23, 1926, ISL.
86. Kenesaw Mountain Landis, "A Whole America," *Outdoor America*, Izaak Walton League of America, May, 1927, Timothy Landis File.
87. Charles A. Kumler, Seven Mile, OH to Kenesaw, Chicago, August 15, 1927, CHS.
88. Telegram, Kenesaw, Chicago, to Gus Kumler, Seven Mile, OH, August 27, 1927, CHS.
89. "Glorious Reunion Held By Veterans," *Hamilton* (OH) *Daily News* Aug. 26, 1927, CHS.
90. J.W. Myers, Hamilton, Ohio, to Kenesaw, Chicago, September 1, 1927, CHS.
91. "Landis Almost Fails to Crash Gate," unidentified newspaper, March 17, 1928, ISL.
92. Kenesaw, Chicago, to Major John Landis, Fort Benning, Georgia, April 3, 1928, CHS.
93. Kenesaw, Chicago, to Captain J. W. Myers, Hamilton, Ohio, August 21, 1928, CHS.
94. Ibid., September 14, 1928, CHS.
95. Kenesaw II, Logansport, to Kenesaw, Chicago, September 13, 1928, CHS.
96. Kenesaw, Chicago, to Kenesaw II, Logansport, September 14, 1928, CHS.
97. Kenesaw, II, New York, to Kenesaw, Chicago, October 24, 1928, CHS.
98. The Columbia College Program for the upcoming debate with England's Oxford College included the following write-up on Kenesaw II:
    Kenesaw M. Landis, a Senior in Columbia College, sacrificed the greater part of his last college term in order to stump Indiana for his father.
    Program, Columbia University Debate Council: Debate, Oxford University versus Columbia University, McMillin Academic Theater, Monday, October 29, 1928, 8:15 p.m.; Subject: Resolved: That America Should Join the League of Nations; ISL.
99. Kenesaw, Chicago, to Kenesaw II, New York, October 29, 1928, CHS.
100. Telegram, Kenesaw, Chicago, to cousin, Mrs. Daniel Kumler, November 23, 1928, CHS.
101. Kenesaw, Chicago, to cousin, Mrs. Daniel Kumler, November 23, 1928, CHS.
102. Mrs. John H. Landis (Daisy), Cincinnati, to Kenesaw, Chicago, December 25, 1928. CHS.

103. Special Delivery, Kenesaw, Chicago, to Kenesaw II, New York, February 8, 1929, CHS.
104. "Bucco Owner Fined," *United Press* dispatch, March 16 1929, ISL.
105. Telegram, Kenesaw, Chicago, to Winifred, Chicago, September 26, 1929, CHS.
106. Kenesaw II, Bloomington IN, to Kenesaw, Chicago, September 28, 1929, CHS.
107. Kenesaw, Chicago, to Kenesaw II, Bloomington IN, October 1, 1929, CHS.
108. The Judge spelled out detail in his letter to his nephew:

> Dear Bilo:
> Doctor Post just telephoned to me that they were holding accommodations for you at Arrowhead Springs. I told the doctor to telegraph back that you would arrive next Tuesday. I have reserved for you Compartment I, Car 305, on the California Limited, Santa Fe, leaving Chicago 8:15 Saturday evening and arriving at San Bernardino 6:20 Tuesday morning, where you will be met by automobile from Arrowhead Springs which I will arrange for after I arrive at Los Angeles. I will get to Arrowhead some time Tuesday morning from Los Angeles, being unable to reach San Bernardino from Los Angeles when you arrive.
> Until Tuesday, luck and love to you. KML

   Kenesaw, Chicago, to Kenesaw II, Logansport, January 2, 1930, CHS.
109. Kenesaw II, Arrowhead Springs, CA, to Kenesaw, Chicago, April 6, 1930, CHS.
110. Kenesaw, Chicago, to Kenesaw II, Arrowhead Springs, CA, April 7, 1930, CHS.
111. Kenesaw II, Arrowhead Springs, CA, to Kenesaw, Chicago, December 10, 1930, CHS.
112. Ibid., December 31, 1930, CHS.
113. Kenesaw, Chicago, to Kenesaw II, Arrowhead Springs, CA, January 2, 1931, CHS.
114. Telegram, Leslie O'Connor, Chicago, to Kenesaw, Belleair Heights, Florida, January 26, 1931, CHS.
115. Kenesaw II, Arrowhead Springs, CA, to Kenesaw, Chicago, March 18, 1931, CHS.
116. Kenesaw, Chicago, to Kenesaw II, Arrowhead Springs, CA, March 23, 1931, CHS.
117. "Petition of Kenesaw Landis for Admission to the Bar", Cass County Bar Association Report Committee, *Report No. 22585*; April Term, 1931; June 17, 1931, LFA
118. Kenesaw, Chicago, to Winifred, Burt Lake, June 17, 1931, CHS.
119. Kenesaw, Chicago, to Gus Kumler, Seven Mile, July 1, 1931, CHS.

120. Kenesaw, Chicago to Frank, Logansport, July 17, 1931, CHS.
121. Kenesaw II, Logansport to Kenesaw, Chicago, September 15, 1931, CHS.
122. Kenesaw, Chicago, to Kenesaw II, Logansport, September 16, 1931, CHS.
123. Kenesaw, Chicago, to president of Chicago Infants Free Milk Depot, September 19, 1931, CHS.
124. Kenesaw, Chicago, to Winifred, Chicago, September 25, 1931, CHS.
125. Kenesaw II, Los Angeles, to Kenesaw, Chicago, October 6, 1931, CHS.
126. Ibid., October 24, 1931, CHS.
127. Kenesaw, Chicago, to Kenesaw II, Los Angeles, October 26, 1931, CHS.
128. Ibid., November 16, 1931, CHS.
129. Kenesaw, Chicago, to cousin Daniel Kumler, Dayton, April 7, 1932, CHS.
130. Kenesaw, Chicago, to Daisy (brother John's widow) Cincinnati, April 14, 1932, CHS.
131. Kenesaw, Chicago, to Winifred, Burt Lake, May 9, 1932, CHS.
132. Ibid., May 11, 1932, CHS.
133. Kenesaw, Chicago, to Bilo, Los Angeles, May 20, 1932, CHS.
134. As history would prove, this game became known as one of Baseball's great games, one in which Babe Ruth "called" his homerun by pointing to the spot in center field just before hitting it there.
135. Kenesaw, Chicago, to sister Frank, Logansport, April 14, 1933, CHS.
136. Kenesaw, Chicago, to Daisy, Cincinnati, December 7, 1933, CHS.
137. Kenesaw II, Rockville, Indiana, to Kenesaw, Chicago, June 8, 1933, CHS.
138. George Ade, Brook, IN, to Kenesaw, Chicago, May 30, 1934, CHS.
139. Mrs. John H. Landis (Daisy), Cincinnati, to Kenesaw, Chicago, November 4, 1934, CHS.
140. Kenesaw, Chicago, to Joseph Lloyd, Big Falls, MN, November 23, 1934, CHS.
141. Reminiscences of Kenesaw's cousin Clarke Marion, as related by his daughter Susanna Marion Baum, Landis family descendant..
142. Kenesaw II, Denver to Kenesaw, Chicago, March 19, 1935, CHS.
143. Kenesaw, Chicago, to Kenesaw II, Denver, April 11, 1935, CHS.
144. Kenesaw II, Denver, to Kenesaw, Chicago, April 11, 1935 CHS.
145. Kenesaw, Chicago, to sister Frank, Logansport, August 8, 1935, CHS.
146. Kenesaw II, Denver, to Kenesaw, Chicago, August 20. 1935, CHS.
147. Kenesaw, Chicago, to Kenesaw II, Denver, August 26, 1935, CHS.
148. Theodore Roosevelt, Jr., New York City, to Kenesaw, Chicago, December 13, 1935, CHS.
149. Kenesaw, Chicago, to physician, Chicago, March 2, 1936, CHS.

150. Ibid., March 8, 1936, CHS.
151. Kenesaw's cousin, Dayton OH, to Kenesaw, May 24, 1937, CHS.
152. Kenesaw, Chicago, to Kenesaw II, Denver, October 28, 1938, CHS.
153. A note typed upon a letter from Kenesaw II, Denver, to Kenesaw, Chicago, January 29,1939, CHS.
154. *The Sporting News*, Vol. 107, No. 18, June 15, 1939, CHS.
155. Kenesaw, Chicago, to Daisy, Cincinnati, September 23, 1939, CHS.
156. Edgar G. Brands, "Landis Dynamites Interlocking Farm System, Vetoes Expansion," *The Sporting News*, November 30, 1939, CHS.
157. Gus Kumler, Seven Mile, Ohio, to Kenesaw, Chicago, December 12, 1939, CHS.
158. Keehn Landis' recollections, LFA.
159. Reed Landis archives.
160. Kenesaw, Chicago, to Connie Mack, Philadelphia, April 27, 1940, CHS.
161. Kenesaw, Chicago, to John, Indiana University, Bloomington, IN, March 19, 1941, CHS.
162. Kenesaw, Chicago, to Colonel John Landis, Camp Croft, SC, May 2, 1941, CHS.
163. Ibid., July 21, 1941, CHS.
164. Colonel John Landis, Governor's Island, NY to Kenesaw, December 8, 1941, CHS.
165. Kenesaw, Chicago, to Colonel John Landis, Governor's Island, NY, December 12, 1941, CHS.
166. "Thousands Hear Loyalty Appeal -- Judge Landis in Patriotic Address Urges an Undivided Allegiance." *Indianapolis News*, April 1921, CHS.
167. President Franklin D. Roosevelt, Washington, D.C., to Kenesaw, Chicago, January 15, 1942, CHS.
168. Kenesaw, Chicago, to Bill Phillips, February 20, 1942, CHS.
169. "Thousands Hear Loyalty Appeal . . ." CHS.
170. Mayor Edward J. Kelly, Chicago, to Kenesaw, Chicago, March 28, 1942, CHS.
171. Kenesaw, Chicago, to Luther Kumler, Norwalk, OH, May 5, 1942, CHS.
172. Ibid., June 11, 1942, CHS.
173. Ibid., June 18, 1942, CHS.
174. Ibid., July 13, 1942, CHS.
175. Kenesaw, Chicago, to Kenesaw II, Logansport, July 16, 1942, CHS.
176. Kenesaw, Chicago, to Lincoln, West Point, August 24, 1942, CHS.
177. Kenesaw, Chicago, to Betsy, Smith College, September 9, 1942, CHS.
178. Kenesaw, Chicago, to Luther Kumler, Norwalk, OH, September 9, 1942, CHS.

179. Kenesaw's summation to Uncle Lute of his late brother Fred's family whereabouts during the war follows:

> Ensign Elizabeth A. Landis came up to Chicago some weeks ago with her younger sister Frances Katharine . . . having to do with the WAVES. Fred's Kenesaw is practicing a little law and contributing a column to the Chicago Sun three times a week. Frederick enlisted in the Navy and is now in London. Charley is getting into Naval Officer's Candidate School. Lincoln is at West Point. So that while Fred went out some years before this whole thing broke, his progeny is doing pretty well.
>
> Ibid., October 30, 1942, CHS.

180. Ibid., December 9, 1942, CHS.

181. Donald Honig, *Baseball: The Illustrated History of America's Game* (New York: Crown Publishers, Inc., 1990; 149-150.)

182. "Big League Teams To Train Near Home," *The New York Times*, January 6, 1943, CHS..

183. Kenesaw, Chicago, to Lincoln, West Point, February 3, 1943, CHS.

184. Kenesaw, Chicago, to A/C Keehn Landis, March 18, 1943, CHS.

185. Kenesaw, Chicago, to Keehn, training base in Texas, April 9, 1943, CHS.

186. Kenesaw, Chicago, to Colonel John Landis, APO Europe, June 5, 1943, CHS. Author's note:

> If the Judge had lived until after the War, he would have been gratified to learn that Betsy became an outstanding Navy WAVE recruiting officer and that, after the war, Katharine was recommended by the Chief of Naval Operations for the Bronze Star for performance of "Communications Intelligence duties in active war zones," the only WAVE officer to be so honored following the war. [CNO classified memorandum Serial 16620 23 Oct 1945]

187. Kenesaw, Chicago, to Colonel John Landis, APO Europe, July 16, 1943, CHS.

188. Ensign Charles Landis, *USS. Bristol* in the Mediterranean, to Kenesaw, Chicago, August 6, 1943, CHS.

189. Kenesaw, Chicago, to Luther Kumler, Norwalk, OH, August 24, 1943, CHS.

190. Kenesaw, Chicago, to Kenesaw II, Logansport, IN, August 24, 1943, CHS.

191. Kenesaw reported to nephew Charles about his visit with Charles sister while he was in Washington on baseball business:

> I saw Gid (Charles' sister Ensign Frances Katharine in the WAVES) in Washington last Wednesday, where I went to arrange with the War Department representatives about the overseas Major League series . . . Gid looks like an admiral, as did her little sister Betsy . . . I have written to your big brother at West Point to prepare himself for a session during these games. I am hoping to get him down to New York. Nothing

else new, except that the column in the Chicago Sun (written by Charles' brother Kenesaw II) is getting to be a pretty good column, according to the judgment of people other than myself. Kenesaw, Chicago, to Ensign Charley, in the Mediterranean, September 20, 1943, CHS.

192. Kenesaw, Chicago, to Commander Edward A. Hayes, Navy Department, Washington, D.C., October 14, 1943, CHS.

193. Kenesaw, Chicago, to Luther Kumler, Norwalk, OH, October 15, 1943, CH

194. Kenesaw, Chicago, to Edith, Colonel John's wife, October 26, 1943, CHS.

195. Kenesaw, Chicago, to Ensign Charley, in the Mediterranean, October 28, 1943, CHS.

196. "Sport: New Odds for the Phillies," *Time*, December 6, 1943, 79, LFA.

197. Kenesaw, Chicago, to Luther Kumler, Norwalk, OH, December 13, 1943, CHS.

198. Kenesaw, Chicago, to A/C Keehn Landis, in fighter training, December 22, 1943, CHS.

199. Kenesaw, Chicago, to Lieutenant Keehn Landis, in fighter training, February 17, 1944, CHS.

200. Kenesaw, Chicago, to grandson Bill Phillips, in Naval training, February 25, 1944, CHS.

201. Ibid., March 1, 1944, CHS.

202. Kenesaw, Chicago, to great-nephew Charles, March 1, 1944, CHS.

203. Kenesaw, Chicago, to grandson Bill Phillips, in Naval training, April 1, 1944, CHS.

204. Kenesaw, Chicago, to great-nephew Charles, April 8, 1944, CHS.

205. Kenesaw, Chicago, to Ensign Charley, Washington, D.C., April 18, 1944, CHS.

206. Kenesaw, Chicago, to grandson, Bill, Pacific area, April 19, 1944, CHS.

207. Kenesaw, Chicago, to Lieutenant Betsy, on naval assignment, May 20, 1944, CHS.

208. Kenesaw, Chicago, to grandson, Bill Phillips, the *Yorktown*, June 12, 1944, CHS.

209. Kenesaw, Chicago, to great-nephew Charles, APO, New York, June 21, 1944, CHS.

210. Kenesaw, Chicago, to nephew, Colonel John, on European assignment, June 30, 1944, CHS.

211. Kenesaw, Chicago, to Luther Kumler, Norwalk, OH, July 6, 1944, 1944, CHS.

212. Luther Kumler, Norwalk, OH, to Kenesaw, Chicago, July 13, 1944, CHS.

213. This author's visit to Uncle Squire during the plebe summer of 1944 was memorable and treasured because the Judge was about to enter his final illness:

On arriving in the hallway from the elevator at 333 N. Michigan Avenue, I was impressed by the simplicity and power spoken by the single word "BASEBALL" in large letters on the glass door of his office. It was a special occasion for me to be in the company of my late Dad's brother, my special uncle, bringing back warm childhood memories of his visits to Logansport and the cigar-smoking, politics-talking sessions with Pop on our front porch. Now, he appeared small and wiry, seated in a tall, elaborately-carved, straight-back chair when he arose and gave me a bear hug.

At 77, he had aged a lot since I had last seen him 10 years earlier at my father's funeral. Leading me in an energetic walk to his Studebaker Champion and an equally-energetic drive home belied his slight frame but seemed to confirm his reputation as a dangerous driver. He boasted about the merits of his economy car in the face of gasoline rationing during the war. While I also was partial to Studebaker as a worthy product of Indiana, I was impressed by Uncle Squire's major concession of giving up the "Cadillac seven-seater" because of wartime restrictions. I sorely missed Leonard, his chauffeur, who with his wife was a part of the family, and the limousine he drove to Logansport on memorable visits by Uncle Squire and Aunt Winifred in years past. Believe me, the image of such opulence in our small town bolstered my image among schoolmates.

After we arrived in Glencoe, I was soon convinced of his physical strength when he scampered through his large garden with onions, radishes and other vegetables. Man, was he happy with his plants! Yet, as I would learn later, his work since June to cultivate his "west 40" (acres), as he described the garden, was a probable cause of the over-exertion which would put him in the hospital in October. As expected, I continue to treasure my visit with him and Aunt Winifred and my cousins Susanne and Jodie. Uncle Squire was a vivid reminder of my father and a remarkable generation that Pop, Squire, and Aunt Frank personally represented for me.

214. Kenesaw, Chicago, to Lieutenant Keehn Landis, in fighter training, July 14, 1944, CHS.

215. Kenesaw, Chicago, to Lieutenant Charley, Washington, D.C., July 14, 1944, CHS.

216. Kenesaw, Chicago, to Luther Kumler, Norwalk, OH, July 26, 1944, 1944, CHS.

217. Kenesaw, Chicago, to great-nephew Corporal Charles, August 14, 1944, CHS.

218. Kenesaw, Chicago, to grandson Bill, the *Yorktown*, the Pacific, August 14, 1944, CHS.

219. Kenesaw, Chicago, to Lieutenant Keehn Landis, on flight duty in England, August 24, 1944, CHS.

220. Ibid., September 5, 1944,CHS.
221. Kenesaw, Chicago, to Lieutenant Charley, on the battleship *Wisconsin* in the Pacific, September 20, 1944, CHS
222. Kenesaw, Chicago, to Luther Kumler, Norwalk, OH, September 22, 1944, CHS.
223. Jody Phillips' reminiscences, LFA.
224. Kenesaw, Chicago, to great-nephew Corporal Charles, September 22, 1944, CHS.
225. Kenesaw's grandchildren recalled some of their moments with the Judge. His son Reed had three children: Nancy, Keehn and Susanne, while his daughter Susanne Phillips had two children: Bill, who was Richard Phillips Jr., and Jodie:

Nancy Landis Lucas noted that Kenesaw and Winifred spent Thanksgiving and Christmas with Nancy's father Reed, her mother and her brother Keehn. She recalled that he smoked cigars but didn't chew tobacco. Occasionally, they would have cocktails together before holiday dinners; the Judge drank only on such occasions.

She recalled: "He was always thin like my Aunt Susanne. He had a great sense of humor, and I had the opportunity to enjoy his company because I frequently traveled with him. We frequently spent summers with him at Burt Lake, splitting time with the Phillipses. Granddaddy spoke about how he carried Lincoln around during his father's funeral in 1934.

Keehn Landis recalled that the Judge and Winifred were closer with their daughter Susanne Phillips' children than with their son Reed's children. He noted: "Grandmother Winifred would address him by 'Squire;' he would call her 'Mad' (for Madame) -- this had no particular meaning other than normal way of speaking in the course of a day." Keehn frequently drove the boat at Burt Lake for the Judge and son-in-law Rick Phillips, getting up at 5:30 in the morning. The two of them ran a contest while fishing – betting on who got the biggest fish, smallest fish, most and least number of fish, kinds of fish and so forth.

The Judge was a real storyteller. He thought a great deal of Teddy Roosevelt, and that is where he got the term "Bully!" that he liked to use. "He was not a religious man – he and Winifred never went to church. The Judge told of one occasion when he attended the funeral of Jake Ruppert, owner of the New York Yankees, and referred to the acolytes as 'bat boys.' He went on to say that he expected Jesus Christ to come down during the service, open the casket, pick Ruppert up and take him skyward."

Keehn mentioned that when the Judge , accompanied by Reed, met with President Wilson, Reed believed that his father was "grandstanding . . . he wanted to show that he would just walk in on the President."

Susanne Landis Newland remembered the Judge's "great warmth and sense of humor that wouldn't quit . . . he told anecdotes, never about baseball . . . had a twinkle in his eye . . . a very human person . . . a man of his time." She recalled that he wasn't a good gardener and that "he trimmed an apple tree in the front yard at Burt Lake, and it died" . . . it was always a good joke around the house – "how he killed the apple tree."

The Judge enjoyed telling about how he competed in bicycle races as a young man, with the old-style bicycle with the large front wheel and small back wheel. He was a thin, little guy, and he would pin medals on his chest in order to intimidate the opposition before the start of a race.

The Judge had to cope with the old "party-line" telephone system at Burt Lake at times when he would have judicial business to discuss. So, he would listen to conversations, for example, of a couple of ladies for a while and, when he saw the opportunity in a lull in their conversation, he would say "Good bye." Then he had the line to himself. He had a cane that was heavily weighted, probably used for protection in case he would run into a hostile individual on his frequent walks through the woods at Burt Lake.

Bill Phillips thought the Judge always looked old to him through the years and never could see a change in the way he looked. Bill enjoyed fishing with him: "I think I was as close as anybody to the Judge. He and Grandmother Winifred came out most Sundays to our house from the hotel where they lived and had dinner with us. We fished a heck of a lot together. The Judge spent a lot of time insulting my technique of fishing, but we both had a good time. The general conversation was a kind a kid can have with a grandfather. I always looked forward to being with him. He was never short on comments about other people. He always appeared serious . . . never splitting his sides laughing."

Going around Devil's Elbow on Burt Lake, Bill recalled that the Judge collided with another boat . . . it was another judge, (a number of judges chose to live at Burt Lake). "They set up a court case and a trial to see who was at fault, and had a great time doing so." Bill also noted that the Judge was requested on several occasions to be officiator at funerals. He concluded that Jake Ruppert's funeral mentioned above was one such example.

"The chauffeur Leonard was a part of the family." Bill mentioned that once when Leonard drove the Judge to Arizona, "he got pinched by the police. They wanted to let him go when they realized the Judge was in the car, but the Judge insisted that they go to town and have a court case. The Judge acted as Leonard's attorney and steered Leonard's testimony to his World War I experience as a machine gunner." He noted that Leonard was a terrific cook, and that the Judge had him cook at any opportunity. "By the way, Leonard felt he was a member of our family because he didn't get along with his wife and had no other real family members . . . after the war I went to visit him in the hospital, where he had had his leg amputated, and when he saw me, he cried. He really was part of our family.

Jodie Phillips Garavanta recalled her relationship with the Judge: "I remember sitting on the porch at Burt Lake with my grandfather for an hour or so. Neither one of us would say a word, but we were still in good communication. On the one hand, he was a man of few words and only said what had to be said. When I was at college I would receive an occasional letter from him, consisting of a blank sheet of paper in an envelope. I knew he had been thinking of me. On the other hand, he was a wonderful storyteller. He enjoyed fishing, golf and 'Amos and Andy.' He never really learned how to drive. Mother tried to teach him and they used to laugh about how the police on Michigan Ave. would turn their backs when they saw him coming. He soon gave it up. When the dandelions were in bloom he always had one in his buttonhole. Of course it was dead most of the day. He never put a crease in his hat. When he bought a new one he would grab it, put it on and it stayed that way."

Landis Family Archives.

Bibliography

Books

Blum, Daniel. *Great Stars of the American Stage.* New York: Grosset & Dunlap, 1954.

Blum, Daniel. *A Pictorial History of the American Theater.* New York: Grosset & Dunlap, 1955.

Cozzens, Peter. *This Terrible Sound: The Battle of Chickamauga.* Chicago: University of Illinois Press, 1992.

Diffendorfer, Frank. *The German Immigration into Pennsylvania Through the Port of Philadelphia from 1700 to 1775.* Baltimore: Genealogical Publishing Company, 1979.

Eshleman, H. Frank. *Annals of the Pioneer Swiss and Palatine Mennonites of Lancaster County and Other Early Germans of Eastern Pennsylvania.* Baltimore: Genealogical Publishing Company, 1969.

Grant, Ulysses S. *The Personal Memoirs.* Old Saybrook, CT: Konecky & Konecky, 1885.

Hacker, Werner. *Emigration from the Rhineland and Saarland in the 18th Century (Auswanderungen aus Rheinfalz und Saarland im 18. Jahrhundert.)* Stuttgart, Germany: Konrad Theiss Verlag, 1988.

Hartzler, J. S. and Kauffman, Daniel. *Mennonite Church History.* Scottdale, PA: Mennonite Book and Tract Society, 1905.

Hostetler, John A. *Hutterite Society.* Baltimore: The Johns Hopkins University Press, 1974.

Keil, F.W. *Thirty-Fifth Ohio.* Ft. Wayne, IN: Archer, Housh Co., 1894.

Kuhns, Oscar. *The German and Swiss Settlements of Colonial Pennsylvania.* Ann Arbor, MI: Gryphon Books, 1971.

Kumler, Daniel C. *Memorandum Book, Going to Africa.* Bristol, Maine: privately published, 1855.

Lowry, James W. *Hans Landis, Swiss Anabaptist Martyr in Seventeeenth Century Documents.* Millersburg, OH: Ohio Amish Library, 2003.

McGuire, Thomas J. *Battle of Paoli.* Mechanicsburg, PA: Stackpole Books, 2000.

Peters, Margot. *The House of Barrymore.* New York: Simon &Schuster, 1990.

Quinn, Arthur Hobson. *A History of the American Drama.* New York: Appleton-Century-Crofts, Inc., 1936.

Rice, Timothy. *Deep Run Mennonite Church East -- A 250 Year Pilgrimage, 1746-1996.* Morgantown, PA: Masthof Press, 1996.

Reid, Whitelaw, *Ohio in the War,* Volume 2. New York: Moore, Wilstach & Baldwin, 1868.

Rupp, Israel D. *Thirty Thousand Names of Immigrants.* Baltimore: Genealogical Publishing Company,1965.

Steele, Matthew F. *American Campaigns.* Harrisburg, PA: Telegraph Press, 1943.

Yoder, Don. *Notes and Documents; Rhineland Emigrants, Lists of German Settlers in Colonial America.* Baltimore: Genealogical Publishing Company, 1981.

Documents

Boynton, Lieut. Col. Henry. *Report to Capt. J.R. Beatty, September 24, 1863*; cited in *War of the Rebellion,* Series 1, Vol. 38, Part 1. Washington, DC: Government Printing Office, 1891.

Budd, Major Joseph. *Affidavit,* December 5, 1865, Warren County, Ohio. Washington, DC: National Archives, 1865.

Civil War Atlas. West Point, NY: US Military Academy, 1941.

Deed L2 348, Charlestown Township, Chester County, Pennsylvania. West Chester, PA Court House.

Gleason, Col. Newell. *Report of Second Brigade, Third Division, 14th Army Corps, August 16, 1864*; cited in *War of the Rebellion,* Series 1, Vol. 38, Part 1. Washington, DC: Government Printing Office, 1891.

Gross, Surgeon F. H. *Report to Maj. Gen. George H. Thomas, October 11, 1863*; cited in *War of the Rebellion,* Series 1, Vol. 38, Part 1. Washington, DC: Government Printing Office, 1891.

Guth, Herman and Gertrud; Lemar J.; and Mast, Lois Ann. *Palatine Mennonite Census Lists 1664-1793.* Elverson, PA: Mennonite Family History, 1987.

History of Butler County, Ohio. Cincinnati: Western Biographical Publishing Co., 1882.

Landis, Charles W. and Mary S. *Landis Family Genealogy.* Indianapolis, IN: privately published, 1954.

Landis Family Reunion Report, Second Annual. Lititz, Lancaster County, PA: privately published, August 3, 1912.

Landis Family Reunion Report, Third Annual. Collegeville, PA: privately published, August 18, 1913.

Landis Family Reunion Report, Seventh Annual. Lititz, Lancaster Co. PA: privately published, August 4, 1917.

Landis-Landes Families Reunion Report, Thirty First Annual, August 19, 1950. Bethlehem, PA: Times Publishing Company, 1952.

Landis-Landes Families Reunion Report, Thirty Third Annual, August 16, 1952. Allentown, PA: H. Ray Haas & Co., 1954.

Loan, Brig. Gen.Ben. *Messages March 18 and 25, 1862 to General J. M. Schofield, War of the Rebellion:* Washington, D.C., Government Printing Office, 1902.

Memoirs of the Miami Valley, Vol. 3. Chicago: Robert O. Law Co., 1919.

Mitchell, Surgeon R. L. *Medical Report, April 15, 1863.* Washington, DC: National Archives.

"Pennsylvania Dutch" and Other Essays. Philadelphia: Lippincott & Company, 1882.

Pennsylvania German Society (Mennonite Immigration). Norristown, PA: Norristown Press, 1929.

Swiss Immigrants to the Kraichgau (Schweizer Einwanderer in den Kraichgau). Mannheim, Germany: privately published, 1983.

War of the Rebellion: A Compilation of the Official Records of the Union and Confederate Armies. Washington, DC: Government Printing Office, 1891.

War of the Rebellion: Official Records of the Union and Confederate Armies. Washington, DC: Government Printing Office, 1902.

Who Are the Mennonites? Philadelphia: Mennonite Information Center, 1997.

ABOUT THE AUTHOR

Lincoln Landis is a West Point graduate who served as a U.S. Military Liaison Officer to Soviet Forces in Germany during the Berlin Airlift in 1948 and the Berlin Wall crisis of 1961. As a White House consultant during détente in the mid-1970s, Dr. Landis evaluated U.S.-U.S.S.R. bilateral agreements. In the 1980s, he briefed U.S. Senators on the Soviet threat as a senior Defense analyst. In subsequent years, he has given lectures on Soviet affairs and written articles for a number of American and European journals, and his books include *Politics and Oil: Moscow in the Middle East*, 1973, and *Gorbachev's Hidden Agenda*, 1991. The author retired as a lieutenant colonel and resides in central Virginia.

From Pilgrimage to Promise: Civil War Heritage and the Landis Boys of Logansport, Indiana came about as the result of Dr. Landis' extensive research into family ancestry and his appreciation of the accomplishments of his father's generation.

LaVergne, TN USA
21 June 2010
186896LV00006B/107/P